Our Town Stepan (Ukraine)

Translation of
Ayaratenu Stepan

Original Book Edited by: Yitzchak Ganuz

Originally published in Tel Aviv, Stepan Society, 1977

JewishGen
מרכז עולמי לגנאלוגיה יהודית
The Global Home for Jewish Genealogy

A Publication of JewishGen
Edmond J. Safra Plaza, 36 Battery Place, New York, NY 10280
646.494.2972 | info@JewishGen.org | www.jewishgen.org

Our Town Stepan
Translation of *Ayaratenu Stepan*

Copyright © 2024 by JewishGen. All rights reserved.
First Printing: October 2024, Tishrei, 5785
Editor of Original Yizkor Book: Yitzchak Ganuz
Project Coordinator: Daniel G. Shimshak
Cover Design: Irv Osterer
Layout, formatting and indexing: Jonathan Wind

JewishGen Press is not responsible for inaccuracies or omissions in the original work and makes no representations regarding the accuracy of this translation. Digital images of the original book's contents can be seen online at the New York Public Library website or the Yiddish Book Center website.

Library of Congress Control Number (LCCN): 2024946699

ISBN: 978-1-962054-09-6 (hard cover: 328 pages, alk. paper)

About JewishGen.org

JewishGen, is a Genealogical Research Division of the Museum of Jewish Heritage - A Living Memorial to the Holocaust, serves as the global home for Jewish genealogy.

Featuring unparalleled access to 30+ million records, it offers unique search tools, along with opportunities for researchers to connect with others who share similar interests. Award winning resources such as the Family Finder, Discussion Groups, and ViewMate, are relied upon by thousands each day.

In addition, JewishGen's extensive informational, educational and historical offerings, such as the Jewish Communities Database, Yizkor Book translations, InfoFiles, Family Tree of the Jewish People, and KehilaLinks, provide critical insights, first-hand accounts, and context about Jewish communal and familial life throughout the world.

Offered as a free resource, JewishGen.org has facilitated thousands of family connections and success stories, and is currently engaged in an intensive expansion effort that will bring many more records, tools, and resources to its collections.

Please visit https://www.jewishgen.org/ to learn more.

Vice President for JewishGen: Avraham Groll

About the JewishGen Yizkor Book Project

Yizkor Books (Memorial Books) were traditionally written to memorialize the names of departed family and martyrs during holiday services in the synagogue (a practice that still exists in many synagogues today).

Over the centuries, as a result of countless persecutions and horrific atrocities committed against the Jews, Yizkor Books (Sefer Zikaron in Hebrew) were expanded to include more historical information, such as biographical sketches of famous personalities and descriptions of daily town life.

Following the Holocaust, the idea of remembrance and learning took on an urgent and crucial importance. Survivors of the Holocaust sought out other surviving residents of their former towns to memorialize and document the names and way of life of those who were ruthlessly murdered by the Nazis. These remembrances were documented in Yizkor Books, hundreds of which were published in the first decades after the Holocaust.

Most of these books were published privately, or through *Landsmanshaftn* (social organizations comprised of members originating from the same European town or region) that still existed, and were often distributed free of charge. The languages used to document these crucial histories and links to our past were mostly Yiddish and Hebrew. JewishGen has undertaken the sacred responsibility of translating these books into English so that the culture and way of life of these communities will be preserved and transmitted to future generations.

In 1986, a group of farsighted JewishGenners started a project to pool their efforts together in groups based upon their ancestors' towns and donate funds to translate the Yizkor books of their ancestral towns into English. As the translated material became available, it was made accessible for free at https://www.JewishGen.org/Yizkor . Hardcover copies can be purchased by visiting https://www.jewishgen.org/Yizkor/ybip.html (see below).

It is our hope that the translation of these books into English (and other languages) will assist the countless Jewish family researchers who are so desperately seeking to forge a connection with their heritage.

Director of JewishGen Yizkor Book Project: Lance Ackerfeld

About JewishGen Press

JewishGen Press (formerly the Yizkor Books-in-Print Project) is the publishing division of JewishGen.org, and provides a venue for the publication of non-fiction books pertaining to Jewish genealogy, history, culture, and heritage.

In addition to the Yizkor Book category, publications in the Other Non-Fiction category include Shoah memoirs and research, genealogical research, collections of genealogical and historical materials, biographies, diaries and letters, studies of Jewish experience and cultural life in the past, academic theses, and other books of interest to the Jewish community.

Please visit https://www.jewishgen.org/Yizkor/ybip.html to learn more.

Director of JewishGen Press: Joel Alpert
Managing Editor - Jessica Feinstein
Publications Manager - Susan Rosin

Notes to the Reader

The images in the original book were reproduced from photographs from the time of the first edition. These reproductions were already of poor quality, being pre-war and at least 30 or more years old. As a result, the images in the book are the best achievable.
A reader can view the original scans of the book on the websites listed below.

The original book can be seen online at the Yiddish Book Center website:

https://www.yiddishbookcenter.org/collections/yizkor-books/yzk-nybc314229/ganuz-yitshak-peri-j-ayaratenu-stepan

OR

at the New York Public Library Digital Collections website:

https://digitalcollections.nypl.org/items/380cca50-353b-0133-8001-00505686a51c

To obtain a list of Shoah victims from **Stepan (Stepan, Ukraine),** the reader should access the Yad Vashem web site listed below; one can also search for specific family names using family name option. These lists are continually updated by Yad Vashem, so it is worthwhile to periodically search them.

There is more valuable information (including the Pages of Testimony, etc.) available on this website: https://yvng.yadvashem.org/

A list of all books available from JewishGen Press along with prices is available at: https://www.jewishgen.org/Yizkor/ybip.html

For additional information, please visit: https://kehilalinks.jewishgen.org/stepan/stepan.html

Cover Photo Credits

Cover Design by: Irv Osterer

Front Cover:

The Synagogue's Aron Kodesh [Page 54]

Back Cover:

A Local Entertainment Group of Jewish Youth in Stepan, 1931 [Page 40]

Naftali Yaakov Gorinstein [Page 91]

The "Tarbut" School Teachers with their Students, 1934 [Page 26]

Rabbi Levi Yitzhak Kreizer — Shochet and Chazan [Page 127]

Sheinboim Family [Page 333]

Geopolitical Information

Map of Ukraine showing the location of **Stepan**

Stepan

Stepan, Ukraine is located at 51°08' N 26°18' E, 190 miles WNW of Kyyiv

	Town	District	Province	Country
Before WWI (c. 1900):	Stepan	Rovno	Volhynia	Russian Empire
Between the wars (c. 1930):	Stepań	Kostopol	Wołyń	Poland
After WWII (c. 1950):	Stepan'			Soviet Union
Today (c. 2000):	Stepan'			Ukraine

Alternate Names for the Town:
Stepan' [Rus, Ukr], Stepań [Pol], Stepyen [Yid], Stefan, Szczepan

Nearby Jewish Communities:

Krichil'sk 7 miles NNE

Horodets 10 miles N

Osova 15 miles WSW

Bol'shoy Zhëlutsk 15 miles NNW

Berestovets 18 miles S

Kostopil 18 miles SSE

Rafalivka 19 miles NW

Staryi Chortoryisk 19 miles WNW

Sarny 19 miles NE

Koloniya Olizarka 20 miles NW

Volodymyrets 21 miles NNW

Derazhne 21 miles SSW

Berezne 22 miles ESE

Berezhnytsia 22 miles NNE

Antonivka 25 miles SSE

Male Sedlishche 26 miles SE

Mochulki 27 miles SW

Ignatovka 27 miles SW

Kolky 28 miles W

Oleksandriya 28 miles S

Klevan 30 miles SSW

Zofyuvka 30 miles WSW

Introduction to *Our Town Stepan*

My father, William Shimshak, passed away when I was five years old and I really never knew him. I reached a certain point in my life when I desired to know more about my father. He was born in the town of Stepan and immigrated to the United States when he was 9 years old. I was overtaken by the idea that I could learn more about my father's life and family by learning about the town of Stepan.

From the wonderful genealogical resource book *Where Once We Walked* by Mokotoff and Amdur Sack I learned that a Yizkor Book for the town of Stepan existed and that the American Gathering/Federation of Jewish Holocaust Survivors had a number of Holocaust survivors from Stepan in their National Registry. So, I made two decisions. First, I wrote to the American Gathering/Federation of Jewish Holocaust Survivors asking that they send my contact information to the people from Stepan. Next, I went to the Widener Memorial Library at Harvard University and talked the librarian into lending me the Stepan Yizkor Book for one day (it was not their practice to lend books to people outside the Harvard community). I proceeded to go home and xerox all 364 pages of the book (I never questioned if that was legal or not).

After a short time, I heard back from three Holocaust survivors from Stepan. Together with the Yizkor Book in hand, though I really couldn't read it, and a few contacts from Stepan, I started on my quest to learn about the town. I have since spoken to and encountered tens of Holocaust survivors and/or their relatives. I heard and watched videos of so many stories. I had the privilege of meeting so many heroes.

In June 1993 I traveled to Stepan myself to experience the town in which my father and so many of my new acquaintances had lived. I have since posted pictures on JewishGen.com of my visit. I met with Yeshayahu Pery, one of the organizers of the Stepan Yizkor Book, in Israel before I departed for the Ukraine. Mr. Pery drew a map showing me the town of Stepan and the sites that I should be looking for, including the synagogue, cemetery, mikveh, and the street that contained the Shimshak family house. Subsequently I found that the synagogue was shut down by the Nazis and torn down years later, the stones in the Jewish cemetery were all toppled and broken, some being used as part of street curbing, the mikveh was boarded, and the Shimshak house no longer existed. There was still a special feeling walking the cobble-stoned streets alongside wandering animals and past houses that comprised the Jewish section of Stepan where my father had once lived.

Hearing about my planned trip, one of the Holocaust survivors put me in touch with her sister who lived in a town next to Stepan called Kostopol. Vera Woszczyna Shetincova grew up in Stepan, had married a non-Jew, and now lived in Kostopol with her two children. She was going to be making Aliyah to Israel soon. I was told that it was imperative that I see her. In the afternoon I traveled to Kostopol to meet with Ms. Shetincova. When I arrived, she immediately took me with her into a car driven by her son. He drove out into a forest like I had never before seen. It was dark and covered with trees. There seemed to be nothing else living in that forest. We just traveled deeper and deeper until we stopped by a large open area where a pit had been dug. It was here that thousands of Jews from Stepan were taken on the night of August 24th in 1942 and killed. In the middle of nowhere. You can read the stories for yourself in the Yizkor Book. Unbelievably, Ms. Shetincova had raised money and erected a memorial monument at this site in memory of the thousands. It was eerily quiet. I didn't know if anyone else might come to this G-d forsaken place in the future. Through the oppressive air my voice echoed as I said the Kaddish prayer for those who gave their lives. I was next driven to a forest in Stepan where another monument had been placed near the pit containing the remains of another 553 Stepan Jews. These Jews escaped the first slaughter by hiding in the synagogues and cemetery only to be rounded up a few days later. G-d bless Vera Shetincova for what she did to keep alive the memory of the thousands of Stepan victims of the Shoah. She has passed away and I wonder if anyone can still find these memorials.

I want to complete this introduction by giving credit to Yeshayahu Pery, who also passed away several years back. Anyone with an interest in Stepan owes a debt of gratitude to Mr. Pery. He was one of the persons to collect and organize the stories from the townspeople of Stepan in the Yizkor Book. He contributed some of the most informative stories in the book. But his work to keep the memory of Stepan alive did not end with the publication of *Our Town Stepan* in 1977. He made sure that Stepan had a memorial plaque in the Chamber of the Holocaust Museum on Mount Zion in Jerusalem along with more than 2.000 destroyed Jewish communities. He found a place in Beit Volyn of Yad Vashem (Center of the Jewish Volyn), 10 Corzin Street, Givatayim, Israel to have Stepan listed with other towns in the Volhynia section of the Ukraine that were liquidated in the Shoah. And Mr. Pery raised the funds to erect a memorial monument in the cemetery in Holon, Israel (Gush 11, Azor 7, Number 66) for Stepan alongside several hundred monuments for other towns wiped out during the Holocaust. On each side of this monument are stones containing the names of many of the people of Stepan who were murdered by the Nazis and Ukrainians (including 12 Shimshak relatives). On my trip to Stepan in 1993, I collected dirt from the two pits where the Jews of Stepan had been killed (one in Kostopol and one in Stepan) and broken stones from the Jewish cemetery in Stepan. These items were placed in a compartment inside the Stepan monument in the Holon cemetery. Every year, Mr. Pery would get Stepan survivors and their relatives to meet at the cemetery on the 12th of Elul, the day the Jewish community was liquidated, in order to say the Kaddish prayer. Unfortunately, that no longer occurs.

Before World War II, Stepan was a beautiful town filled with forests, farm fields and orchards. One Holocaust survivor wrote the following: My years of childhood and youth in Stepan were years of happiness. We lived in an atmosphere of selfless love and good heart. Despite the differences in education and wealth, no jealousy or hatred was felt. When one family had a happy occasion, all the town was happy; when someone was sick, the whole Jewish population worried; and when there was a tragedy, everyone hurt and cried. Sadly, the Holocaust put an end to that beautiful town of Stepan. But memories never die and I invite all the many people who have a connection to Stepan to use this English translation of *Our Town Stepan* to the fullest. We can all keep the memory of the town of Stepan alive.

Daniel Shimshak

Sharon, Massachusetts

Acknowledgments for *Our Town Stepan*

It took over 30 years to translate the Stepan Yizkor Book, *Ayaratenu Stepan (Our Town Stepan)*, into English. I started on this project very slowly in the 1990s. I translated several sections of the book myself. I sat at a desk with a stack of dictionaries and painstakingly attempted to translate. I chose what I thought were some of the more interesting sections at the beginning of the book. I was very proud of the work that I did though it took what seemed like forever. I knew I was in trouble and could never finish this work on my own. It seemed like a miracle. but two translators were found willing to take on this project and bring it to completion. Kol Hakavod to Yona Landau and Mira Eckhaus.

A special thanks to the JewishGen.org for posting the translations as part of their Yizkor Book Project. And a huge thanks to Lance Ackerfeld, the Yizkor Book Director, who pushed to complete the translations and provided the resources to make it happen. I hope that many people with connections to Stepan will find the English version of *Our Town Stepan* helpful in their genealogical pursuits.

Daniel Shimshak

Sharon, Massachusetts

Table of Contents

7   The Holocaust

8   The Ruins of My Town

9   In Memorium

10   Epilogue

11   Family Photographs

Our Town Stepan
(Ukraine)

51°08' / 26°18'

Translation of *Ayaratenu Stepan*

Edited by: Yitzchak Ganuz
Published in Tel Aviv, Stepan Society, 1977

Acknowledgments

Project Coordinator:

Daniel G. Shimshak

**Our sincere appreciation to Mr. Yeshayahu Pery, of the Stepan Society in Israel,
for permission to publish this material.**

This is a translation from: *Ayaratenu Stepan* (Our town Stepan),
Editors: Yitzchak Ganuz, Tel Aviv, Stepan Society, 1977 (H,E, 368 pages).

[Page 7]

Foreword to the book

Translated by Mira Eckhaus
Edited by Daniel Shimshak

This book was written and edited with overwhelmed emotions and great reverence - it serves as a monument to the vibrant Jewish life in our town of Stepan, which was cut short with diabolical cruelty by the German blood beast and its infamous Ukrainian accomplices.

We collected testimonies, fragments of memories and impressions. We have collected detail by detail from old scripts - and line by line, image after image, a picture of the Stepan community, a large and important city to its survivors and remnants, that no longer exists, is emerging before us.

Decades have passed since the community of Stepan was eliminated, and thousands of its sons and daughters, our parents and sisters, were sentenced to extermination amid torture and suffering, that the human mind cannot describe and bear. The pain is too great to be forgotten over time.

We considered our work both as a sacred work and as a duty. We spared no effort and trouble in order to restore what was and no longer exists and to erect a memorial monument for our town.

We were diligent and careful, to the best of our ability and in consultation with the people of the town, not to omit or distort any detail about the people of our town and especially with regards to those of whom there is no remnant left behind.

It is worth mentioning the esteemed contribution of the late Yitzchak Weismann, who, in the way of reconstructing and describing figures of the town's inhabitants, served as our guide for the completion of the entire project. To our great regret, the late Yitzchak Weismann was not privileged to see the completion of the commemorative project and passed away prematurely, in pain and sorrow for the loss of his son, Shai-Yeshayahu of blessed memory, who fell in defense of the homeland.

We would like to mention the great assistance of Israel Koifman with advice and guidance that contributed greatly to the content and form of the book.

We must also mention the extensive activity and perseverance in the enterprise of the book of Yeshayahu Pery (of the Prishkolnik family). Even while he was in the displaced persons camps in Germany, in 1946, and during his time in the Ma'apilim camps in Cyprus, he began recording memories of his father's house and the town in general as he remembered it since his childhood and until the German-Ukrainian infernal and madness period. Upon his immigration in Israel and the meeting of the town's survivors, during one of the first annual commemorations, - he began to initiate and act in the collection of material, recording memories from members, collecting photos of public importance, and also encouraged the townspeople to write their own articles.

[Page 8]

Yeshayahu Pery managed to convince and harness the committee's activists to this sacred mission. The financial means have been achieved, and the enterprise started.

Most of us, the townspeople of Stepan, are not professional writers, and we must thank the great responsiveness of members, who sent articles and also attached photos and certificates. The reconstruction of the families who lived in Stepan was also carried out by the members, who are: Leah Hashavia (from the Rudnik family), Batya Sheinboim (from the Becker family), Shlomo Sheinboim, Ze'ev Gorinstein, Mordechai Rassis and Yeshayahu Pery (Prishkolnik). A number of other members of the town assisted in this enterprise and we thank them for their work.

With all the great effort invested, we would like to point out that here and there, the reader will find linguistically and stylistically unpolished lists. We have brought similar facts from different sources and there are those who will see this as duplicity. But despite being aware of this, we have decided to allow anyone who wants and wishes to express what they know and remember from their personal point of view and from his past, and by doing so get a comprehensive and exhaustive picture, which will serve as an internal memorial candle and a monument of memory for generations and on which are engraved in letters of blood and fire the history of the life and the destruction of the town of Stepan.

The editorial staff:

Leah Hashavia (from the Rudnik family)
Batya Sheinboim (from the c family)
Shlomo Sheinboim
Yeshayahu Pery (Prishkolnik)

[Page 9]

The Generations of Stepan

The History of the Town and its Jewish Community

Yitzhak Ganoz and Yeshayahu Pery

Translated by Mira Eckhaus

Stepan - one of the oldest urban settlements in Volyn. The region where the town of Stepan is located is called Western Ukraine, and it is a part of a huge region called Great Ukraine - the grain barn of the then Kingdom of Poland and Russia together. The region of Greater Ukraine stretches along the banks of the Dnieper and Dniester rivers - with the capital of the country in the center being the city of Kyiv and the Volyn region in the west.

Southeast of the border between Poland and Russia, which existed between the two world wars in the area of Volyn, Lutsk County, near the city of Rivne, the town of Stepan is located.

The town is located on a plain along the banks of the Horyn River. According to the legend, the name Stepan was given after the name of the king of Poland Stephen Bathory, who fortified in this town and conducted fierce battles against the Russians and the Tatars. There are indeed remains of a castle - a fortress on the river bank. This castle was surrounded by massive artificial sand hills, man-made, and a deep-water canal around it. The access to the castle was via a rocking bridge.

This place is nowadays called the "Wall" and has become a kind of park for recreation and hikes.

A vestige of another protective castle on the riverside remained below the synagogue, which was probably built in a later period, and whose walls reached three meters thick. Under the synagogue there was also a tunnel that continued through the center of the town and connected two fortresses for protection against attackers coming from the east and across the Horyn River.

The town was small and was situated nineteen km away from the Malynsk train station, on the Rivne-Vilna railway line. There were no particularly developed public institutions in the town; apparently there was also no community register; and if there were any records, they were destroyed together with the destruction of the entire community.

According to historical documents, there was already a settlement in Volyn in the 12th century. Among the communities of Israel, which in 1388/89 received letters of existence from the Lithuanian Duke Witold, is also included the community of Lutsk, near which the town of Stepan is located.

In the first half of the 15th century, one of the richest Jews leased properties in the city of Ladmir, and even received an estate from the duke. Also, in the second half of this century, Jews with estates in the Lutsk district are mentioned.

[Page 10]

In 1507, the authorities reconfirmed the old letters of existence of the Jews, and since Volyn was annexed to the lands of the Polish territory, in 1569, the Jewish population in the area grew.

The main occupation of the Volyn Jews at that time was trade, and they also engaged in crafts such as tailoring and furriers. In the second half of the 16th century, the Jews began to lease bars and various branches related of the estate economy.

Stepan in the Historical Records

In "The World Chronicles" by Sh. Dubnov (vol. 2, page 260) it is written:

"During the reign of the king of Poland and Lithuania Jagiello Witold in the year 1386, there were significant Jewish settlements in all the big cities of the Principality of Lithuania and Volyn, which is connected to it". It can therefore be concluded that Stepan's Jews were also among the first residents of the town, which is one of the oldest urban settlements in Volyn, on the banks of the Horyn River.

It is also stated by Sh. Dubnov in the same book:

"During the rule of the Turks in the Crimea in the middle of the 15th century and their subsequent takeover of the Volyn areas, the commercial connection between Crimean Jewry and the Jewish center in Volyn was allowed, and there were movements of Jews from Crimea to Volyn".

The assumption is that at least some of the town's Jews came to Stepan and settled there at the time of the "movements of the Jews from Crimea to Volyn", as stated above in "The World Chronicles" by Sh. Dubnov.

In the book "Geographical Dictionary for the Kingdom of Poland and Other Slavic Countries" that was published in Warsaw in 1890, pages 326-327, it is told about Stepan: -

"Stepan - a town near the Horyn River and near the Vilna-Rivne railway. It is 68 versts from Rivne and 240 versts from Zhytomyr. The town has 512 houses and 3,384 residents, of which 47% are Jewish. There are three churches, a Catholic church, a great synagogue built in Gothic style, two Jewish prayer houses, a primary school, a brewery, two flour mills, six markets and a wax candle factory. Along the banks of the river rises artificial hills containing the ruins of an ancient fortress. There is a train station in Stepan that connects Woltsch station and Sarni station. The place is 68 versts from Rivne, 111 versts from Vilna".

[Page 11]

In an ancient document, the Stepan estate is mentioned as belonging to Prince Ivan Chalavovich already at the end of the 13th century, and afterwards to his son - Volodzimyzh. In the 15th century, the place belonged to the Dombrovitsky princes. According to a record of tax collection from 1577, the settlement counted twenty-eight cultivated agricultural units, and in the years 1583 and 1589 there were thirty-six cultivated agricultural units. In this last listing are already stated artisans and merchants in Stepan who contribute their share of the tax burden, and it can be assumed that a large part of them were Jews.

In 1648, Stephan Khmelnytsky subdued the Cossacks near Stepan. In the year 1775, the town had 521 residents and it was handed over to the ownership of Prince Josef Pototsky.

The town of Stepan is one of the oldest settlements in Volyn. The "Yevreyskaya Encyclopedia" indicates about it (page 567, library reference of Tel Aviv University, 114.56):

"Stepan in the time of the Zeshtypospolita was a town of Wibodstavo Volyn Fobiat Lutsk. It is one of the oldest urban settlements of Volyn. In 1765, there were 1138 Jews in Stepan and the surrounding villages. In Stepan an ancient synagogue in the Gothic style was preserved".

This synagogue is described as an ancient historical site in registration no. 947 of Blinski-Lipinski: "Strozschitna Polska" (Old Poland).

According to the 1847 census, the Jewish community in Stepan numbered 1,717 people. According to the 1897 census, the population of Stephan was 5,137 residents, of which 1,854 Jews.

Stepan Chassidism

Volyn, together with the nearby Podolia, was also the place where Chassidism developed. Some of the people of Volyn were already included among the members of the Baal Shem Tov's group. In the generation that followed, Chassidism in Volyn spread at a rapid pace. In Yitzhak Alfasi's book "The Book of the Rebbes from the Baal Shem Tov to the Present Day" it is told about the rabbis of Stepan.

Rabbi David the son of Rabbi Shmuel of Stepan, of blessed memory, passed away the 11th of Tishrei 5571 (in the year 1811), he was the brother-in-law and a student of the Magid Kadosh Rabbi Yechiel of Zolochiv. Rabbi David the son of Rabbi Shmuel was also one of the students of the Baal Shem Tov, as well as one of the students of Rabbi Dov Ber of Mezhyrich. One of his well-known works is the book called "Seder Hanahagot Adam". In the old cemetery of the town, it was possible to see the tombstones of Tzaddikim. There was a stone structure with

[Page 12]

a tin roof above it where the descendants of Reb David of Stepan were buried. Before the Days of Awe and in times of trouble and distress, the townspeople would prostrate on the graves of the Kadoshim and bury "Kvitlach" between the tombstones.

In the book "Degel Machane Ephraim" by Rabbi David of Beit Halachmi, Torah words are quoted on behalf of Rabbi David. And these are his descendants: Rabbi Israel Dov of Stepan who was the father-in-law of the tzaddik Rabbi Levi Yitzchak of Stephan. Rabbi Levi Yitzchak from Stepan had many Chassidim in Stepan and the surrounding area. He passed away on the 14th of Tevet 5684.

Rabbi Yosef Yoel of Stepan was one of the first students of the Baal Shem Tov and his father's successor on the throne of the Rabbinate in Stepan. He passed away in 5530.

The tzaddik Rabbi David Shmuel Halevi of Stepan and his son-in-law Rabbi Shmaryahu Weingarten of Lubeshov.

Rabbi Aharon Shmuel of Ostroh the son of Rabbi Naftali Hertz HaCohen of Sade Lavan served as the Rabbi of Stepan. He passed away in 5574. He served as the Rebbe in Ostroh and was the son-in-law of a rabbi Yosef Yoel of Stepan.

The tzaddik Rabbi Levi Yitzchak of Stepan and his father-in-law Rabbi Israel Ber (Dov) who was the son of Rabbi David Shmuel the Magid of Stepan.

Rabbi Yechiel Michal of Berezne, the son of Rabbi David, the son of Rabbi Shmuel the Magid of Stepan. He passed away in the 15th of Kislev 5609.

Rabbi Meir Chaim of Stepan. He was the son of Rabbi Levy Yitzchak of Stepan, who was an only child of and his father. Rabbi Meir Chaim's daughter, Raizela, married Rabbi Baruch Tversky, originating from the Maggid of Turisk dynasty.

Rabbi Baruch Tversky, his wife and all their family members perished in the Holocaust.

From the tenth century until 1918, Volyn was a political or administrative unit: a Russian principality, Lithuanian province, Polish "Vybodstavo", Russian province. During the 14th century, Volyn was annexed to Lithuania, and with the union of the latter with Poland, in 1569, Volyn was annexed to Poland and became a Polish "Vybodsatvo" province. During the period of the Counter-Reformation, when Catholic Poland succeeded in imposing the authority of the Pope on hegemony of the Orthodox Church in its domain, an Orthodox reaction arose in Volyn.

In the second partition of Poland in 1793, the eastern part of Volyn was annexed to Russia and in the third partition, in 1795, the western part, including the town of Stepan, was annexed to Russia as well.

[Page 13]

In the summer of 1915, the western part of Volyn was occupied by the German and the Austrian armies. In accordance with the Brest-Litovsk peace treaty (March 1918), Volyn was annexed to Ukraine. During the Russian Civil War, battles broke out in Volyn between the Red Army and the Ukrainian and Polish armies. According to the Riga Peace treaty (1921), the western part of Volyn, with Lutsk and Rivne (including the town of Stepan) was annexed of Poland, while the eastern part remained in the hands of Soviet Russia. In September 1939, the Soviet army occupied Western Volyn. In July 1941, the area was occupied by the Germans, who held it until 1944.

* * *

From the thirteenth century until the twentieth century, in a period of eight hundred years or so, Jews lived in Stepan, took root in it and contributed a lot to its development and advancement. In the course of those generations, the Jews of Stepan suffered a lot during the constant and frequent times that were Volyn's lot. The rule of the princes - the Polish-Russian landowners from the 13th century to the 19th century. In the days of the Polish monarchy, Czarist Russia, Khmelnytsky riots, the Hedmak, Tatars and Cossacks gangs. The upheavals of government after the revolution in Russia - Petliura riots, Denikin, the Poles, the Bolsheviks, etc.

But it should also be noted that during the history of the Jewish settlement in Stepan there were also acts of protection and sympathy for the local Jewry on the part of the Ukrainian population, especially during the pogroms of the Petliura and other gangs that did not pass over the town with the change of governments. But this was not the case during the total destruction of the town's Jewry by the Nazis and their Ukrainians helpers.

[Page 14]

Volyn Jews

Y.L. Yonatan

Translated by Mira Eckhaus
Edited by Daniel Shimshak

A

They were not nurtured in the same clear and smooth Talmudic mind of the Lithuanian Jews and the wise Torah scholars.

They did not have the same mental breakdown and Chassidic gaiety of Polish Jews, Shabbat and Yom Tov Jews.

There was not even a single greatest rabbi among the Jews of Ukraine, as well as throughout Volyn.

It was a special division in the Jewry of Greater Russia, a blend of these two together, they were, if it can be defined that way, the Jews of Chol HaMoed.

The mental realm of the sacred and the secular was close, and the spiritual border between them was narrow, in terms of back and forth, changing forms constantly. This is also how the Ukrainian Chassidism of the Baal Shem Tov explained the secret of the mikveh in simple terms as "to undress and dress", or in its language: "kanan zikh aoystun aun antun".

The Jews of Ukraine were like the waters of their rivers, flowing slowly and pleasantly between verdant shores, blessed in a transparent, deep blue, and they were anonymous person for many.

The names of the Horyn, the Pripyat, and the Sluch rivers come up and are remembered only in Gittin, the books of Kritot (divorce), "Mata Dibata (the place of the divorce) is on the Sluch River and on the waters of other rivers", those are swallowed up and lost in the abysses of the Vistula and the Dnieper.

The Jews of Ukraine were like the cedar trees of their forests, which surrounded hundreds of cities and towns, like a green belt. In secret and hidden places is stored the essence of life, which nourishes and revives the branches in depth and the top above and outside, the bark is whitish and soft, and can be peeled with a fingernail.

There were many cities and towns for Volyn, there were Medzhybizh and Mezhirichi for the Chassidism, there was Berdychiv for the love of Israel, a city that only by mentioning its name explicitly awakens kindness and mercy in the world. There were Zhytomyr and Kremenets for education, there were Ostroh and Pinsk for learning, there were Sudylkiv and Slavuta for the for the printing of the holy Hebrew letters, shining letters on a blue paper, there were those whose reputation preceded them, and there were many, many more of those, that no one knew about their existence. Remote and far-flung places, tiny dots on the map of the world.

[Page 15]

B

There were hundreds of towns in Volyn, most of them were built in the Polish-Ukrainian style. They were all similar to each other, as if they were the ruble coin, all of whose coins are similar to each other. The same ruble that they fought every day, from morning till night, to get it in order to bring home a living.

The shape of the towns was of one main street with wooden sidewalks and several other side streets that diverged from the main street. All the streets led to the market. In almost all of the towns was the same water pump in the middle of the market, which in the winter was covered with a thick layer of ice blocks all around and in the summer with yellow rust stains.

In all of them was the same Polish-Catholic "cloister" is one strait, and it dominated the whole environment. And on the other side of the town or near it was the "Preboslav" church - for the Ukrainians. Both of them had bells, which frightened and threatened on the eves of Easter and the day of Christmas: "Din - - din – we're sharpening the knives".

And so, more or less, was the order of the day for a Jew, a simple Jew, in the towns of Volyn - Ukraine.

In the morning, they woke up at dawn and ran to synagogue. There was a Beit Midrash, a new synagogue, as well as the old synagogue, there were artisans in the city who had their own small and poor synagogues: "Po'alei Tzedek", "Yegi'a Kapaim" and the like, where they prayed at sunrise. The great synagogue was closed all week, and in its space echoed the prayers of the dead, as the children used to call them.

In the morning, they woke up at dawn and took out the cows. This duty was the duty of the man, the duty of the man in the house, and it was usually done with the tallit and tefillin under the arm.

When they're done, they entered a synagogue and prayed quickly: they crouched, kneeled, danced in "Kadosh" and here - "Aleinu". As well known, the prayer of "Shema kolenu" on the "Shmone esre" prayer is broad in heart and soul, and there one can add a personal wish such as daily livelihood. And so, they prayed every day, without worrying about tomorrow.

In the meantime, the hinges of the store doors creaked, iron rails were taken down and the barrels with salted fish were rolled in, floating in a musty and murky stock, next to the door.

The goods in the stores were mostly for the farmers, and they were hanging on hooks and ropes: kerosene lamps with blue, think glass containers, shiny rims,

[Page 16]

with and without awnings and their accessories around them. There were also hoes, shovels, rakes and the three-pronged pitchforks. Also, were there sacks of grits and mushrooms emitting the smell of damp forests and on the selves aside were placed textiles, toys, soap, perfume, knives, purses for money, and colorful handkerchiefs for the housewives of the peasants. A department store! And the grocer sat and waited for buyers from morning to evening.

There were only a few stores in the town and they were all owned by the dignitaries of the town. Among the goods sold were textiles for the Jews, types of velvet and satin fabrics for the clergy and for wedding clothes for the girls of Israel. The important Jewish buyers enjoyed the costumes for Passover and Rosh Hashanah and enjoyed even more when in the synagogue they explained the meaning of the acronym of satin in Hebrew: "Only good for the people of Israel forever".

There were Jewish craftsmen for all trades in the towns of Volyn: tailors, shoemakers, welders, hatters, carpenters, lathe operators and blacksmiths. The blacksmiths' faces were black, sooty with flying jets of fire, their workshops were located at the end of the street of the gentiles. There were no signs for the tailors' workshops. In the distance, melodies that pinch the soul were heard, such as "HaBen Yakir li" and "Kevakarat rohe edro" and from somewhere was also heard the oath of the "Bund", "Mir Shvaren zu Kempan".

C

As a child, I knew how to distinguish by the smell of the garment the profession and the stock of the goods in the store. Their Shabbat and holiday clothes were also perfumed by the secular smell. This smell accompanies me to this day. The livelihoods were different, as mentioned, but the majority of the livelihoods were from stores.

The store owners had their own laws of justice and honesty, their own "professional ethics" - unwritten but binding laws. The area was rich in hundreds of villages and farmers and each one of them had its own Jewish store. They sold goods for credit and in each store, there was a thick and greasy notebook - - "I gave to Ivan on - -", "I took from Ivan on - - It was customary that a farmer will not exchange his store for supplies, and a Jewish grocer will not accept a new gentile client without investigating and receiving an explanation for the cause of living the neighbor's store.

Generally good neighborly relations prevailed between the store owners ("shared destiny and brotherhood" as it is called nowadays). On summer days, when they weren't buyers, they would sit outside their stores on top of boxes, talking and exchanging opinions about events in the world and in the town: the riots, the dead,

[Page 17]

robberies, blood plots, Grossenberg's speech, and is regular days they would talk about the cantor and the poets of the last Shabbat (these were divided among the homeowners and sang sad hymns while gazing at the host's daughter).

On winter days, they would sit inside their stores. The husbands were dressed in sweaters and tattered furs, and the women would sit next to a boiling pot, while their hands are put in wool gloves with no room for fingers, a special patent of theirs.

They would eat lunch in a hurry and nap slightly while sitting and nodding their heads. At this time, the women would take care of the house. In the evening, the movement of buyers increased, and the mother, the housewife, would appear to help, and the husbands disappear to pray Minchah and Ma'ariv prayers.

The husbands would return home late at night, suffering from the frozen winter or the heat of the sun in the summer, look through the book of debts, which is written in tiny letters, a virtue for a good sleep after a dull and hard-working day.

There were also few Jews who made a living in the forests. They would cut the trees, tie them together and ship them of rafts to Danzig. These were mostly among the affluent people in the towns, but no one was jealous of them. They were cut off from any Jewish community all year round, living without prayer and religious life, without a home and a family, why anyone should be jealous of them?

The Jews of the towns would also go to fairs. They traveled mainly in the winter, wearing warm clothes that were prepared ahead of the travel. They would travel in their carts all night and in the morning, they parked next to the stand and unloaded all the cargo. If they were lucky enough, they earned a living from the trade.

They did have great aspirations; they were always satisfied with only a little.

The saying uttered by the Jews of Ukrainian towns when they were asked about the livelihood situation was – "With God's help, we don't eat fried meatballs, but we eat enough to be satiated". The "cutlet" was a symbol of delightful food, delicacies of a king.

The food that a Jew in Ukraine liked the most was black rye bread, spread with homemade butter, with tea sweetened with plenty of sugar. Oh, the Ukrainian black bread! From these meager livelihoods, from a miserable life outside - they maintained a home, "did Shabbat", took care of all the holiday needs, supported the Torah scholars and the rabbi and at the top of their concerns was the payment of salaries to the melamedim.

The study was in a known method and order. First, a child studies with a young melamed until he finished the Chumash, then he goes to another melamed, at a higher rank than the young melamed, for the study of Rashi and

[Page 18]

Gemara and afterwards, he goes to the great melamed for the study of Gemara and Tosafot and study of the Maharsha. In comparison with the ordinary education system - a primary school, a high school and a university. Out of these meager livelihoods they supported the marriage of their sons and daughters, the girls grew up in the faithful education of their mothers, until their time to get married.

The matches were mostly between the families in the town. Each one was matched with several families with the help of a local matchmaker and with a little "love". And if the match was with someone from a distant or near town, then the local matchmaker in this town took care of it.

D

What was the worldview of these righteous Jews?

First, that the world is beyond understanding. Man of letters among the Jews of Ukraine - Volin, who were among the Chassidim of Chernobyl, knew by heart Rashi's interpretation of "Tamim ti'ye im elokecha", which is: "Walk with him innocently and wait for him and do not inquire about the future, but rather accept innocently whatever happens to you, and then you will be with him and a part of him" - this is all the people of Israel. And secondly, they all knew that "Genesis" does not begin with them, and the reckoning does not end with them. All the generations walked in their understanding in one chain linked by hand and arm: Moses, the Holy Zohar, the Rambam, the Baal Shem Tov and his Rabbi is - of the Chernobyl race - the Magid of Trisk, the Rabbi of Talana, the Rabbi of Stulin, etc.

Their worldview was simplicity and innocence, without knowing that from the philosophical aspect, it was a supreme clothing for wisdom and nobility.

They knew that there was a need for this panicked running, always worrying about livelihood.

The Shabbats placated the six weekdays, and the holidays filled the gap. And with the end of the year arrived also its mission and purpose - the month of Elul, the Atonement, ten days of repentance, Yom Kippur and Hoshana Rabbah – a good ending.

From the first Atonement prayers on Shabbat night at midnight, until after Hoshana Rabbah – with a short break of the days of Sukkot - the appearance of the town and its people had changed.

There were Jews who had special customs for excessive piety: one had the custom of the staying "to sleep" the entire night of Yom Kippur in the synagogue. The second used to pray in the night of Kol Nidrei

[Page 19]

and on Yom Kippur all day standing. The third - the custom of his ancestors in the ten days of Atonement was to finish the psalms every day, and he begins the reading in the synagogue and ends the reading in his store, in the spare time between serving the buyers, and everyone alike is cleansed and purified on the Holy day of Yom Kippur, as the words of the poet "Tired of fasting, barefoot, wearing white clothes and feeling exalted."

After they managed to get the "good note" - they returned as new creatures to the regular world and its nature, and the calculation began anew.

They knew that a Jew must negotiate with the faith, that even though he is the one responsible for providing for the family, he is obligated to do charity from time to time. And they knew, and their souls were gloomy and grieved secretly about it, if from time to time they did not stand up to the test and failed in measure or weight, in a price or in speech, and their prayer "and bring me livelihood to support my family in a decent way and not fraudulently" was not always answered. In all the towns there were societies of "Magidei Psalms" and on winter Saturdays they would get up at four o'clock in the morning, go to the mikveh, dip and go to finish reading the Psalms. On Shavuot, King David's day of celebration, they would hold the Kiddush, a Kiddush with man people.

No guest was left alone, God forbid, on Friday evening by the stove in the synagogue. Distinguished guests, "grandchildren", emissaries from the Land of Israel, those who serve in religion, were invited to the dignitaries of the town, passers-by and beggars were invited to the common people, often to butchers.

E

The world of these Jews was not much different in the attitude and the perception of the essence from the world of the same Ukrainian people in which the Jews lived. The main difference derives mainly from the first reason. The Ukrainian people were farmers who worked to enjoy the pleasures of life, while the Jewish people were satisfied with their lot and trusted God. The strong belief was that the boys should be educated to continue in this way. "The continuation and continuity order" as we call it today.

The more common and accepted greeting was "May we be privileged with a lot of pleasure from our children and not be ashamed of their actions". Pleasure meant that the chain would not break.

Ukrainian Jews loved and cherished life in simplicity and innocence, and the women, the mothers in the pleas of the good Sarah2, and in the Jewish prayer "God of Avraham", which was composed by Reb Shmuel of Kamianka in Ukraine.

Strong was the faith in the hearts of these Jews that the Messiah would come. Not only the tzaddikim of the generation would prepare the "zesipitze" and the "pantofel" by their bed so they would be ready to go

[Page 20]

towards him because the masses of the people were eager for every hint and acronym from the Torah and the scriptures to reach "Tarsav", because then "she took off her widow's clothes", etc.

In this way many generations lived and died. The two world wars agitated this life, rioters and robbers plundered, bursts arose here and there, the roots were exposed but the tree remained on its trunk, the branches grew and part of them tended to the dark sides, but even these did not drop and fall until the evil of this world came upon the people of Israel among the people of the place.

These knew well the homes of the Jews, they were aware of every exit and entrance, every hiding place and hidden corner, they knew the place of the silver candlesticks for Shabbat and the cup for sanctification, they knew the names of many of the boys and girls and they executed them.

The tree was uprooted in anger and fury on all its branches and roots.

[Page 21]

Judaism of the Heart

Yitzchak Lamdan

Translated by Mira Eckhaus
Edited by Daniel Shimshak

The communities of Israel in European countries that were wiped out of the world by gentile executioners - although their framework was usually one, the framework of "people that shall dwell alone" among the gentiles - were not at all equal. Each community and its character, its life style, its features and virtues. This diversity has many origins, some of which are visible and some of which disappear and are hidden in past generations and in mysteries of landscapes and climates. What was lacking in the character of a certain community was given to an unknown other community, a community that was rich in one area was poor in another, and vice versa. And so, the communities complemented each other and together formed that great Knesset of Israel in Europe, which for a long time was not only the majority of the nation but also its main source, the source of life and revitalization of the nation.

Volyn Jewry, as a significant part of the greater Ukrainian Jewry, contributed a great part to this diverse tract of the assembly of Israel. Its precious qualities persistently fertilized the lives of the people of Israel in the diaspora generation after generation and the signs of its actions are clearly visible in the ways of the new returning to Zion and in its vision. Volyn Jewry was not glorified in its sharpness in the Torah and intellectual as the rest of the Lithuanian Jewry; it was not adorned with crowns and did not have certain manners like the rest of the Polish Jewry. Instead, it was blessed with good faith, with a common and rooted simplicity, which adhere in the foundation and essence of things and not in their ornamental decorations and embellishments. It was a Judaism by heart that was full of love and loyalty, that poured its virtues into the sea of ??the great Knesset of Israel quietly, with constant loyalty and without standing out, like those bustling streams in Volyn that make their modest way in the shade of forests. The element of the heart was the main element that is evident in all the spiritual works of the Volyn Jewry. This element is the recurring motif between the sad lines of "Yeven Metzelah" of Rabbi Nathan-Nata Hanover and is expressed in the ethics and proverbs of the Nagid of Dubno. It was the background to the way of life and teachings of the ancestors of the Chassidism; It also was not damaged with the Volyn education, which, in contrast to the sullen face and the rationalistic strictness of the education in other places, was revealed in Volyn in the honest, noble-hearted character of Ribal; and it was the thing that inspired greatly Bialik's work and was reflected in the sad and dreamy eyes of Fierberg.

Judaism of the heart. And how many beating hearts overflowing with life and creativity could this Judaism bring out of itself! And here came this gentile heartless monster and trampled with its claws this precious heart along with the great living heart of the assembly of Israel in Europe.

[Page 22]

The Education in Polish Volyn

Shmuel Roznak

Translated by Mira Eckhaus
Edited by Daniel Shimshak

Volyn region was divided at the end of the First World War between Russia and Poland, and under the political conditions of those days it was possible to develop and maintain Zionist Jewish institutions only in Western Volyn, which belonged to Poland.

Some of the educational institutions of "Tarbut" were founded back in the days of Ukrainian rule, and when the Poles occupied the western part of Volyn, they did not hinder the existence of these institutions so much, since they considered the Jewish institutions in general (both Hebrew and Yiddish) as a "dirosifictory" factor until the time of Polonization.

Also, the D.D.K. funds (The Aid Committee on behalf of the Jews of America) supported the educational institutions directly and indirectly during the times of distress that passed in those days on the Jews of Volyn, after the riots of the Petliura troops and other forces, and thus, with the resumption of the normal life of the Jews of Volyn, various Hebrew educational institutions were established almost in every Jewish settlement.

The driving force in all the educational institutions in Volyn was composed mainly by two movements - the Zionist and the socialist, in all their shades and ramifications, The war between them externally was on the question of the language of instruction, that is: Hebrew or Yiddish.

The Jewish institutions, where the language of instruction was Russian, continued to exist for some time until their complete elimination by the Polish government. Their place was taken by the high schools in the Polish language - whose Jewish teachers were brought mainly from Galicia and the heart of Poland.

At the end of the First World War, many of the teachers who fled from Bolshevik Russia because of the political pressure from the "Yevsektsiya" arrived in Volyn. They laid the cornerstone of the Hebrew Ulpan by bringing with them the little experience of the Hebrew and Yiddish schools, which were built in Ukraine and Russia for the children of the refugees. Within a short time, Hebrew children's schools and nurseries were established in many cities and towns that attracted the children of Israel; the teachers' seminars in Kyiv and Kharkov, which were founded by Kahanstam and Tasharna, indirectly influenced the goals of education and their fulfillment. There have also been attempts by pedagogical newspapers that were published there.

And although at that time there was no direct connection with the Land of Israel, the schools in Israel floated before the eyes of all the teachers and founders. The curriculum of the Hebrew High School in Jaffa

[Page 23]

was copied, improved and adapted for the schools in Volyn, and the teachers from Russia also brought with them textbooks from the "Omanut" publishing house, founded by the Persitz family in Kyiv.

The study of Hebrew as the language of Jewish studies was common even before at the "reformed cheders". Some of the teachers moved to the new schools out of an effort to adapt to ambitions that filled their hearts as early as the days of the Tsar's rule and which came to full fruition with the German occupation, especially after the Kerensky Revolution.

With the foundation of the Hebrew high schools, excellent pedagogical forces who were educated in Western Europe (mostly - in Austria) were added, and their influence on the education in general was evident both for better and for worse. Over the years, the ambitions and ways of the East and the West merged and the schools received their desired character with the help of the "Tarbut" center in Warsaw, which was established in 1922 at the conference of the proxies of all Polish districts.

In 1920, the Hebrew high school "Tarbut" was founded in Rivne by Leibel Garboz (now Aryeh Avatichi), Meir Kodish, David Baharel, the three of them live in Israel, and their friends. With the help of Moshe Kiefer from Kyiv, who was invited to serve as the first director of the high school, the district committee for the territory of Ukraine, "HaKivush", was established which gathered around it the best working forces and expanded the educational network with the support of the D.D.K. The number of Hebrew educational institutions then reached approximately eighty, but with the cessation of American support, the institutions continued to exist, amid intermittent political disturbances, in those places where the activists, the parents and teachers bore the burden of the expenses.

The "Tarbut" high school in Rivne served as a center for the entire cultural movement in western Volyn and became a pillar and support for all the schools that were founded before and after it in the vicinity, such as: Zdolbonov (1917), Barstachka, Alexandria (1918) and more. The Jews of Volyn, like all the Jews of Russia, who aspired during the Tsar's rule to educate their sons and daughters in high schools despite all the restrictions, came to their satisfaction to some extent, and around the same time two more high schools of "Tarbut" were established in Kovel and Kremenets, which served as stimulating centers for the Hebrew primary schools and kindergartens within their districts.

With the formation of the Polish government in the borders of the districts, the difficulties and obstacles for the private schools in general and those of the Jews in particular multiplied.

Many of the Yiddish schools in Volyn were mostly closed, most of the schools of "Tarbut" did not receive their government approval, and even though the education legislation was supposedly liberal, it was still difficult for the Jews to meet

[Page 24]

the requirements, which were: a building that complies with the hygiene laws, teachers with general and pedagogical education, as well as Polish citizenship and political legitimacy. The buildings that remained from the days of the Tsar's reign were populated by the government's Polish schools and other buildings with large rooms connected by a corridor, were not at all available in the cities and towns, and even if a large building that could be adapted to the function of a school was found, it did not quickly receive the approval of the government doctor and architect and the affairs would roll from one office to the other. Nevertheless, the schools were not usually canceled, because the activists and the teachers knew how to get along with the local police. Over the years, with the help of the parents and the American support, many special buildings were built for the "Tarbut" schools.

Harder than the order of the buildings was the political legitimacy of the teachers in the primary schools. Most of the local teachers were registered in the civil registers in the towns of Greater Russia and it was enough if a teacher was registered in one of the places outside the occupied Polish territory that he would not receive a certificate of political legitimacy from the district government. A large part of the teachers in the primary schools did not have certificates that were accepted by the Polish education authorities, and it was necessary to bypass them indirectly and certify them as religion teachers only, for which the requirements of the authorities were more lenient. In fact, these teachers secretly taught general subjects, but when the government inspector came, all of a sudden, they became religion teachers, which included all the studies of Judaism: Bible, Israeli history, the geography of Israel and alike. Over the years were added to the schools' teachers who graduated the teachers' seminars of "Tarbut" and Tsharna in Vilna and Grodno, and even many teachers in Galicia with certificates from government seminars who also knew Hebrew. In the high schools, the certificates issue was easily resolved, since most of the teachers came from Galicia with official qualifications and in certain cases, and sometimes, certain subjects were taught for one or two years in the Polish language.

This whole affair proved even more the wonderful dedication of the parents of the pupils of the schools, who voluntarily gave up the government schools that were offered to their children free of charge in spacious buildings, equipped with laboratories and equipment, while in the "Tarbut" schools they were forced to support financially the teachers and bear all the expenses related to the institutions at their own expense, and on top of that, they even erected, as mentioned, over the years, their own buildings such as the buildings in Rivne, Kovel and even in small towns.

The financial condition of the teachers was poor. The financial support from abroad stopped and the tuition, although it was high and above the ability of petty traders and artisans, did not cover all the expenses. The "Tarbut" center tried to help pedagogically by supervising and publishing a pedagogical press, but its existence was also tied to the taxes it demanded from the schools. The government did not grant any aid to the schools, and only in the last years before the Second World War, small supports from the municipal institutions. During those years, the "Tarbut" center also managed to obtain from the D.D.K. (The American Committee)

[Page 25]

certain sums for the benefit of erecting school buildings in Volyn. From these funds was established also an agricultural school in Volodymyr, whose influence on the primary schools gave its signals in the trends of the pioneer education, which resulted the foundation of the "Association for Education and Culture" in Poland and throughout the Diaspora.

And these are the cities and towns in Volyn where in 1939 there were "Tarbut" institutions: Ostroh – high school and kindergarten; Olyka- primary school and kindergarten; Aleksandria- primary school and kindergarten; Berezne - primary school and kindergarten; Dubrovitsa - primary school and kindergarten; Derazhne - kindergarten; Vysotsk - primary school and kindergarten; Trochenbrod - kindergarten; Turiisk - primary school and kindergarten; Lutsk = two primary schools and kindergarten; Volodymyr - primary school and agricultural school; Mezhirichi - primary school and kindergarten; Murawica - primary school; Mizoch - primary school and kindergarten; Mlyniv - kindergarten; Maciejów - primary school and kindergarten; Stepan - primary school and kindergarten; Sarny - primary school and kindergarten (started organizing the building for the high school); Kovel - high school, two primary schools and two kindergartens; Kostopol - primary school and kindergarten; Kivertsi - kindergarten; Kremenets - primary school and kindergarten (the high school there was closed); Klewan - kindergarten; Radziwilow - primary school and kindergarten; Rozhyshche - primary school and kindergarten; Rivne – high school, two primary schools and three kindergartens.

These institutions formed the network of the Hebrew educational institutions of Volyn and most of the Jewish children of the listed settlements and their surroundings acquired their education in these institutions. The influence of the institutions among the Jewish population was significant, most of the opponents of the new Hebrew education at its beginning reconciled with it recently, and there were those who became its supporters.

[Page 26]

Part of the class of "Tarbut" school in Stepan in 5694. The school teachers with their students. These young children were indeed exterminated by the malicious hand of the Nazi oppressor and its murderous Ukrainian accomplices

Details of the names of the teachers and students who appear in the picture - on the next page:

[Page 27]

In the top row from left to right: Munya Zelberberg, the son of Karpel the painter - Sheftel Yokelson, Tzudie Derech, Munya Eidelstein, Zvi Rosenfeld, Zalman Geller, Herschel Bebchuk, Henya Filkov, Fanya Tachor, Batya Becker, Sheva Bebchuk, Duchi Guberman, Sheindel Eidelstein, ?, Herschel Geller, Nehemiah Gerber, Michael Weinstein, Shimon Rosenfeld, ?, Shlomo Stern

In the second row from left to right: Yosel Bebchuk, Zeev Gorinstein, Nahum (Weidelguiz) Gordon, Monya Kolodny, Baruch Green, ?, Freidel Kanonitz, Hinda Dov, Mindel Weitznodel, Henya Berm, Mila (from the Axelrod family) Stov, Yaakov Koifman, Shabtai Bass, a member of the Chodler family, Esther Becker, Runya Sorkin, ?

In the third row from left to right: ?, Hana-Ettel Volinsky – the daughter of the dayan, grandson of Zalman the shoemaker, Der Yeyt of Rovno, the son of Avraham the carpenter,

Avigdor Kendal, the daughter of Yehiel Weitznodel - one of the twins: Pasal or Mindel, **?** , Filkov, the daughter of Spialkov, a member of the Sorkin family, Tanya, Genya Kogot, Mindel, the daughter of Avraham Hengo, a member of the Hamer family, **?** , the son of Gershon Weitznodel, Shaul (Sheilyk) Prishkolnik

In the fourth row from left to right: Sonya Weiner, Haya-Pearl Volinsky, the daughter of the dayan, Malka Hochman, the daughter of the shochet, Henya Tsiyas, Deborah Goberman, Moshe Zilberman, Shayke Kagan, the son of Rabbi Avraham Machles the melamed, **?** , Shmariahu Bebchuk, Beba Shfilsher, Pesya Weitznodel, Mottel Hayat, Shefa Goz, **?** , Tzudik Geler, the son of Moshe Yosef Dragoff, Shayke, Yitzchak Bebchuk

The teachers of the school from left to right: the prayer teacher, the melamed Rabbi Avraham Mechalei Feldman, Moshe Koifman, the school principal Yaakov Averbuch, Sheindel Shechterman, Shnerer. Behind the teachers stands the dedicated janitor of the school Mottel der Bobes Kirzhner

Fifth row from left to right: Yentel Becker, Baila Shimshak, **?** , **?** , Shlomo Goz, a member of the Morik family, Sonya Toyeb, Buziya Eidelstein, **?** , **?** , **?** , Yaakov Gorinstein, **?** , Freidel Bass, the daughter of Avraham the carpenter **?** , **?**

Sixth row from left to right: **?** , **?** , Yona Rassis, Beba Kerzhner, **?**

Seventh row from left to right: **?** , a member of the Karpel family, Yitzhak Bronstein, Malka Grossman, Breindele Becker, Rosa Berm, the granddaughter of Zalman the shoemaker, Esther Hemo, **?** , Sonya Hayat, Haya Rassis, Yehudit Bebchuk, **?**

Of all the young boys and girls and teachers appearing in the picture, survived only Herschel Geller, Zeev Gorinstein, Nahum (Weidelguiz) Gordon, Monya Kolodny, Minz Weitznodel, Mila (Axelrod) Stov, Zvi Rosenfeld, Sonya Weiner, the son of Reb Avraham Feldman the melamed, Shmariahu Bebchuk, Pesya Weitznodel, Yona Rassis, Yitzhak Bronstein, Malka Grossman, Batya (Becker) Sheinboim, Tzudie Derech - may they all live long life

[Page 28]

Stepan Before World War I and the Period of the War

by Chasya Zoller

Translated by Daniel Shimshak
Edited by Mira Eckhaus and Daniel Shimshak

Chasya Zoller was the daughter of Shlomo Zoller and a teacher in Stepan.
She immigrated to Israel in 1933, and nowadays with Kibbutz Negbah.

Stepan my dear town, the despoiled. It is my desire to raise up a few thoughts about you, thoughts from a distant time.

I was born in Stepan and there spent my years of childhood and youth, years of happiness and pleasantness. We lived in an atmosphere of selfless love and good heart. The people of Stepan were good and cordial. Despite the differences in status from namely those who were educated and those who were illiterate, those who were rich and those who were poor, no jealousy or hatred was felt. When one family had a happy occasion – all the town was happy; when someone was sick with a serious disease – the whole Jewish population was worried; when there was a tragedy, everyone hurt and cried. The well-to-do helped those of lesser means with day-to-day life or during the time of holidays, at the time of sickness, with income, etc.

The name Stepan is a historical name that was taken from the name of Stefan Boturi. So the administrator of the Polish school, Parantzeshik Chodzik, told us. The source of Polish history from the author on the Polish king Stefan Boturi stated that he had palaces and fortresses. He would sometimes spend time in Stepan, and the kind Kazamir Yagelonkski would come there to hunt. This was during the period of brilliance of the Polish kingdom. After the division of Poland in the 17th and 18th centuries and annexation to czarist Russia, everything was destroyed following the wars. Only remnants remained, known to us formerly as a fortress ("The Volh") and the synagogue, whose construction used the walls of one palace or fortress. All of these places are known and remembered. The Volh, that served as a place of recreation and meetings between pairs of lovers, was a beautiful place, all covered in trees on two sides, the east and the north, enclosed by two hills forming half a circle. They would tell us that the hills were the graves of brothers from the time of the Polish war with her enemies.

There were occasions when bones of people were discovered in this place, primarily skulls, but they didn't research these things and didn't know to what era these belonged. Also, in my time, there was within the woods a small opening that, according to the story, led to an underground, secret passageway. According to the story the path continued through the whole town until the synagogue where there were many hidden treasures.

It was known to us that below the synagogue were basements, three of them that were used for different purposes. For example, it was used for watching of fruit in the summer by the merchants, ice in the event of sickness in the town, and others.

[Page 29]

The fourth basement was full of beans and had only a low, very narrow opening, built in the form of half an arch, that remained visible. But it was impossible to enter there.

After World War I, the lands of our city and region returned to the sovereignty of Poland, but no one explored what was told nor carried out any archeological dig to discover the truth.

It appears that the synagogue was built from the remains of a fortress, its walls were very thick and they were made from strong material, and also the ceiling. It was said that the walls were 4 arshon thick (1 arshon = 72 centimeters). The ceiling was very high and in the form of an arch. The part that was called "The Grosse Shul" was built within the ground and they would step down there. There were other wings, like "The Veibershe Shul" – two floors, and in the same shape there were two beit medrash and a large meeting hall.

In the course of generations, the name of this town was corrupted by the Ukrainian population and changed to Stepan (now with a dot in the Hebrew letter "pay"; formerly called Stefan).

Stepan was a beauty spot for nature. In the surroundings – forests, fields, fruit gardens, and to the northeast side – the Horyn River. Many pleasant farms are reminders of the Horyn.

[Page 30]

In the summer – the bathing, since the water was clear like crystal, and fish, fish of all kinds and sizes. When we were small, we would take off the dresses and fish with them. They were very beautiful and silvery. After we satisfied ourselves, we would release them with great mercy. When I got older, I would take part in fishing with a fishing rod (then I no longer released them). We would arrange fascinating trips in boats on the river: guitars, balalaikas, and mandolins – an orchestra with the accompaniment of singing. Many boats traveled and the echoes of the songs and the music carried in the distance, and trembling went through your body from so much pleasure. The wide river with the three bridges, the moon spraying its silver light on its waters, the trees bracketed on the river – they would instill happiness in the heart and youthful dreams.

Also in the winter we would get enjoyment from the beautiful nature. For example, sliding on the ice on the Horyn, gliding on a sled straight from the hills of The Volh to the river covered with thick ice – overturning, receiving hits, the heartening jubilation and laughter all around. Getting up and continuing. Also, sliding on skis or only on shoes. This was a pleasant sport, and until you learned how to do it you would get many hard bruises on the body – but it made no difference. The forests – they were also like a friend to us. A hike in the forest, in the snow, this was something fantastic and breathtaking. When you entered the forest in the winter, you stopped before the unusual vision of nature. The trees covered with snow and the white surface of the ground all created a picture of majestic splendor. The feeling was as if you entered a holy place. The forest would resemble an enormous, respected old man, quiet and holy. We would not dare speak in a loud voice, not before the sensation of majestic splendor. We would pick common berries on hikes only in winter, and always leave this place unwillingly. In the summer the forests would sprout different kinds of berries and mushrooms for food. But we were afraid of the forest watchmen, because we didn't want them to bring complaints and fines to our parents. Nevertheless we went – and really was it not possible to enjoy the abundance of good things and the pleasure of the picking?

But you can't draw a conclusion from the fact that we always spent time and hiked. We would utilize only the free hours for this pleasure. There were lessons to prepare, many lessons; we read books and helped in the house, knitting, embroidering, sewing, and the like.

On holidays and Shabbats almost all of the houses would empty. Families of young people hiked to The Volh or to "Hoyfen". The days of the holidays were very pleasant. The atmosphere in the house, courtyard and in the streets was festive. Everything was clean and polished and there were traditional foods for all the holidays: Pesach, Shavuot, Sukkot, Simchat Torah, Purim, etc. The children enjoyed the additional pleasure – always new clothing and types of games.

The adults would converse about worries of livelihood or successes in life, and visit relatives or acquaintances. We also loved the prayer hours, the time when almost everyone went to synagogue, especially the aforementioned holidays, since also the women would go to pray.

On these holidays, our house, close to the synagogue, was full of girls (the boys would go to pray) from every end of the town. Every woman who passed merited a thorough criticism of her outfit, her manner of walking, and her hair-do. A worthy imitation was done and the happiness was great. On Yom Kippur we would restrain ourselves from not desecrating the holiness of the holiday because on this day even "the fish tremble in the waters". Our parents were devout in their religion and educated us in this spirit.

It is impossible to tell about Stepan without mentioning the fires that occurred. Stepan was famous for them. As was said before, on every Monday and Thursday a fire would break out. Frequently the ringing of the church bells would wake the sleeping in the night to alert about the fire that broke out. The majority of the population would leave the house and run in the direction of the fire, to help to save what was possible from the burning house. It would happen that at the time that they would be busy with extinguishing the fire from one side of the town, that a fire on another side would break out, and then there was running back. After every fire, there was no lack of excited and thrilling stories about the cause of the fire, its course, its extinguishment and its damage.

Our House

We had a small family. Father, mother and three sisters – Panya, Manya and I, and one brother – Leibke. Father and mother were not born in Stepan, but they came from another place.

[Page 31]

Mother, with the name Blumah, who was from the family Morik, was born in Tchertorisk to a large family of students, teachers and merchants. The family was spread among many cities and towns in Wolhynia and Polisia. Also in Stepan she had relatives: Chaim-Simcha Morik and his family, Pinya

Goldstein, owner of a flour mill, and the Wachs family, who also owned a flour mill. Who among them remained alive after the Shoah? I don't know.

The Morik family worried that their children should learn and receive a good education. They sent the girls to an outside place, to Russian schools. Despite the limitations on the acceptance of Jews, the girls received, with thanks to G-d, their talents and industriousness. The exception was Jewish customs, prayer, reading Yiddish and the like which they learned in the house. The house was traditional, and in this spirit the children were educated.

The boys didn't learn in Russian schools for religious reasons. They learned in other schools with private teachers and acquired the knowledge for all professions.

The spirit of the learning – the will to learn and to know – was passed to us by mother. She was devoted to us without bounds. Despite the burden to manage the house with four children, she found much time for us. Father was always busy with his work and carrying out mitzvot for others, and mother bore the burden of our education. For us small ones, she taught the Russian alphabet and the multiplication table. By the age of 4 or 5, we already knew how to read Russian.

Father, Shlomo Zoller, also he, like mother, had a family that very much branched out to Wolhynia, Polisia and the Ukraine.

From the dawn of my childhood, I remember my father in the capacity of a teacher. After the reign of the czars, there were no Jewish secular schools – the schools carried the name "cheder", as it was called "traditional schools". Father could not make do by teaching tanach, gemorah, etc. He was a realist and humanist, par excellence. He had broad knowledge of many professions. He would teach accounting, Russian, geography and also singing. He knew notes and songs on the violin. He would answer and explain the students' questions that pertained to daily life, from a social educational point of view, etc.

From morning until the late evening hours he was busy. After he finished the hours of learning, we ate midday. At the time of eating, he would read the paper. Without getting up from the table, he would sleep a few minutes, and after continue with work. He never prepared the lessons for he knew everything by heart. Without difficulty he was able to point to the place, page and sentence, and the required material was found. He was also able to be devoted to his additional work. He was an insurance agent. They would also come to consult with him on construction matters. They would turn to him to write letters to relatives who were found in outside places, particularly in America. They would write the letter with their own hands but came to father to write the address, since they believed that only an address written by his hand would bring the letter to its destination.

[Page 32]

A shidduch was not arranged without the advice of the parents of the bride or the parents of the groom. In the event of this, they would seclude themselves in the dining room and litigate. The children did not have entrée to this room. Only when the parents were outside the house, at the theater, or visiting with friends, would we open it and go wild without bounds. We watched that we would not cause damage or disorder. Frequently the religious judges would invite father to help them with the issue of a Torah judgement, not because he taught defense or prosecution, but because of his expertise and good memory.

In the year after the outbreak of World War I great distress was felt in the city. Many fathers were drafted in the army and the students dispersed. We were left without livelihood. Father turned to trade, and bought two horses, because from Stepan to the train station was almost 18 kilometers. He would arrive at the station, leave behind the horses and continue by train to all corners of Russia, to Kiev and to the Crimea (we had an aunt there, the sister of mother).

Not a lot of time passed and he was supplying wholesalers in a few towns in the area. The livelihood was plentiful. We became rich according to the standards of that time. Seldom would he come home. The education and care of the children fell on the shoulders of mother. She did her best to try for us not to have distress over father's absence. Only now do I understand what she did for us. We yearned for father. The feeling in the house without a man was the feeling of fear and lack of security. As far as I remember, there was never a murder of a Jew in a house by goyem, nevertheless there was eternal fear that perhaps something like this would happen. When night came, the Jews would close their doors and windows; the fear was to such an extent that for extra safety, the men prepared instruments of defense such as an axe or hammer by the bed. The knifes were hid that they should not be ready for the murderers, if they came.

This feeling changed when the army came to Stepan. The houses of the citizens were filled with soldiers and officers who were brought in to live together with the tenants. To our house arrived an officer, a person likeable in his manners and his exterior. Our Russian language was fluent (despite that we were still small). The officers, who were changed once in a while, would play with us, and bring candies and games. To our good fortune, they were all amiable. They never bragged as was customary of people with high rank in the Russian army. Their servants would help mother with the household.

That was the situation until the outbreak of the revolution in the year 1917.

Then started chaos. Father returned home. He seldom traveled, because of the great danger on the roads that he traveled. Our great sums of money remained in places where father received his merchandise. The situation was made difficult. The people lived in tense expectation – what would the day bring.

[Page 33]

Before I continue with the story of events, it is my desire to briefly review the population of Stepan and the relationships between the goyem (Ukrainians, Chocholem) and the Jews. The population of Stepan at that time was made up of Jews, Ukrainians, and a few Polish and Czech families.

We felt anti-Semitism always and in every place. In the streets, in the offices, in the schools (that was turned with the entrance of the army of Petlura [Simon Petlura, leader of independent Ukraine from 1918-1920] from a Russian school to a Ukrainian school). The teachers were steeped with anti-Semitic feelings; they still mourned for the czar, remained in their places and continued to teach. The administrator Andre Dmedyok displayed his hatred towards us more than they did. More than once did it happen that he honored us with the words "Zeyde du Palestini" (Jews go to Palestine). And this at the time of the lessons, in the presence of the goyem students who were poisoned with hatred for us Jews, which was absorbed from their teachers. Dmedyok "didn't see and didn't hear" when the goyem hit us, accompanied with words of shame like "Zid Parchati" (leprous Jew) and the like. There was not a chance that one of us dared to harm a goy. All of them were filled with rage and vindictiveness. I will tell one episode from the many.

We had in class one student, not a Jew, by the name Zogrolski. He was the worst of all of them. His father was a low clerk in the "zamastve" (the local council) and he was not liable for any punishment. He was permitted to do with us as he pleased. After he annoyed Itzak Sheinboim (son of Shroolik), he called him a "goy". He, Zogrolski, complained about Itzak to Dmedyok. Dmedyok, as if a snake bit him, spanked Itzak and decided to dismiss him from school. He imposed a punishment on all of the Jewish students in every class. He left us locked in the classrooms after the learning was finished and didn't permit us to return home. The atmosphere was electrified, as if before a pogrom. Itzak claimed that the word "goy" was not an obscene word, but he didn't know how to explain this. He asked for permission to clarify this with his father at home. Dmedyok agreed. And while we were locked in the classrooms, Itzak ran home, a way of a few kilometers, and returned with a Yiddish-Russian dictionary. After Dmedyok read in the dictionary that the word "goy" was a nickname for all people who are not Jews, he agreed to leave Itzak in school and released us to our homes.

It was not a good heart that led the administrator to this agreement. Were it not that we Jews were the advanced people intellectually and economically in the school, this matter would not have ended like this. Generally, we would not have the possibility of a foothold there. We were the glory of the school. When the person in charge came, we would be called to the blackboard. We answered questions and not the Ukrainians. They were at a lower level. The good students from among them, were at most a small number.

[Page 34]

Shlomo Zoller, his wife Bluma, the daughter Manya and her husband, the daughter Paniya, on the grandmother's lap, the grandson, Manya's son

As I mentioned earlier, these were the years of the rule of Petlura in our area. Fate decreed that there was found in all of this a few "tzadikim" among the goyem. The generation of age 25-30 years old befriended the Jews, because they earned a living from the Jews, they received advice and guidance in these difficult times and also medicine and medical help. Thanks for this came from the "somoboronah" (self-defense) from the cooperation of goyem and Jews. Two goyem, representatives of the somoboronah, were Onkah, who lived not far from our house, and Michal, son of Fruska Zadatzki.

The two of them were nice men, tall, and humane. From the Jews, from our street, I remember the first born son of Levi Hashochet (the slaughterer), it appears to me that his name was Yosef. With the appearance of the army of Petlura, the Jews hid in their homes under lock and bolt. They heard the murder and disorders brought about by the Petlurans on the Jews, and their pranks on the Jews. Eye-witnesses told of their sadistic actions. For example, passing a Jew with a beard, seizing him, standing him in the middle of the street, and plucking the hair from one half of his beard with their hands, as he twists in pain. And if he screams out, he receives a severe beating. And another story, that they undressed the Jews of their clothes and shoes and forced them to run naked and barefoot in the streets. Also small children and babies were stabbed to death with their bayonets.

[Page 35]

As stated, the Jews were closed in their homes. The streets were empty of people, the stores were closed. The sad Jewish eyes checked the acts from behind the curtains.

We arranged learning tables in the entrance room, a board with chalk, and the door was locked. From outside, the house appeared like a school.

The Petlurans appeared all the time. They approached the houses, knocked on the door, screaming that they should open. No one answered them and no one opened the door. They didn't use force, and they went from one house to another and so on and so forth. They approached our house a number of times, peeked inside, and said: "zdyes shkoolah" (here is a school), and departed. We watched them closely through the windows in another room.

One day three officers appeared and marched straight to our house. Maybe what attracted them was the pleasurable balcony of benches that was in front of the house. They approached the door, saw that this was only a school, and didn't try to enter. It was the time of the summer holidays and it was understood that schools were closed. Father identified their ranks and said that they were high officers. They sat on the benches to briefly consult. Father and mother told us to listen to their conversation. They were very angry with the Jews and their seclusion in their houses. One of them said: "be zydov safsei roosev"(beat the Jews and save Russia), and they departed from the place. We passed on to our parents what we heard. They took us out through the window, so that the Petlurans wouldn't see , and they sent us to Onkah to inform him that he should come.

Not much time passed and Onkah appeared armed with a rifle. The Petlurans received him happily and told him what they decided to do. Meanwhile, two other goyem from the defense came, armed with rifles. Without hesitating they informed the Petlurans that here, in this town, there will not be any hostile actions taken against the Jews. "Zdyes me vasye bratye" (Here, we are all brothers), and the Ukrainian population will defend the Jews. The Petlurans were forced to relinquish their malicious plans and thus we were saved from a great disaster. During this time it happened that the Ukrainians assaulted the Catholic priest and wanted to slaughter him. I don't remember how this happened or who intervened, but the priest remained alive with a great injury to his neck. The Jews hastened to his aid and watched over him day and night. I tell about this event, because with the continuation of my story there will yet be told about the priest who came to our aid in a time of sorrow.

The Jewish Sacrifice

I don't remember the order of the chain of events, but I will tell what I remember.

One day a rumor spread that a giant army would come from the direction of the village of Korets, and it was not known who they were. The people went out to the streets to see who this was and if it was necessary to be afraid or not. When they entered the town,

[Page 36]

it became clear that this was the Polish army, "Hellertzikim" (based on the name of the commander, the Polish general Heller). We heard about this army from time to time from people who returned home from the war, or who visited in other cities. This was an army unrestrained in their hatred for Israel. Upon their entrance to the town, they decided to rob. They entered the house of the sandalmaker, one of the soldiers selected a pair of the nicest and best boots, measured them, took them and turned to go without paying. The children of the sandalmaker demanded that he should pay, and the soldier didn't agree. They took the boots from him by force. The soldier said that he would take revenge on them, and went out. The children fled the house and hid. The elderly parents remained in the house. A short while later the soldier came accompanied by an officer. He took the boots without paying. The officer demanded that the children should come, and if not, they would kill the father. They took with them the elderly man and left. His wife went out to search for the children with the help of the neighbors, but they didn't find them.

For pleasure, the youngest boy of the family was sailing on the river, without knowing what had happened. His mother found him there and he presented himself to the officer. Without a judgment or words, he stood him by the door of one of the stores (the house of Bebchuk?) that was in the marketplace and a party of soldiers fired at him and killed him in that place. The Jews came from the marketplace square and from all other places and secluded themselves in their houses, all of them, except for a few who remained to take care of the burial of the murdered victim.

We saw the dead person when he was brought to the synagogue (our house was next to the synagogue) in order to eulogize him, as was customary before the burial. Unto this day I can see that picture. He was carried on a board (not a death bed) in his clothes, his right hand hanging down. Great sorrow filled our hearts. Tears flowed over the death of the young boy who was murdered in cold blood due to no injustice from his own hands. But this didn't bring an end to the murderous actions of the Hellertzikim.

After the murder, they imposed a monetary fine of 50 million rubles, of this 5 million in gold coins. They imprisoned a few houseowners as guarantors, among them two religious judges, and they announced that if the money was not paid within 24 hours, they would take out all the guarantors to be killed (it appeared to me to be six men). My father was among them and already I considered him as dead. At night, father returned home. According to the request of the Jews, they released him. The Jews explained to the authorities that father was needed to help in the collection of the money. They knew that father would give from his money a great sum, because he was considered among the rich who were in the town.

As I mentioned before, the financial situation was bad and those with money had hastened to invest it in merchandise, because its value went down day by day. The demand to give 5 million rubles in gold was indeed a nightmare. There were not many gold rubles in the town. Feverish consultation was arranged and in the meanwhile the hours passed. Night came. Nobody closed an eye. It was difficult to obtain the money. Then the delegation turned to request the intervention of the Catholic priest Haksyondz (priest in Lithuanian) on our behalf (Haksyondz, whom the Jews saved at the time from the slaughter by the followers of Petlura). The request was that they should give an extension of 24 hours until paying the money. Haksyondz promised to do everything. In the meanwhile, they prayed, said passages of tehilim, went to prostrate themselves

[Page 37]

at the graves of the fathers who would request from G-d to have mercy on us and save us. It was announced that there was a general fast. In the morning Haksyondz announced that his request was accepted by the Hellertzikim and they agreed to the extension.

In the meantime, they turned to the non-Jewish population in order to borrow money. One who complied with the request was the Polish sandalmaker by the name Degmont. He agreed to give a great sum of money on the condition that he would receive an expensive pledge in pawn. There was not time to consider too much and there was deposited in his hands the gold crown from the sefer torah (by the way, it remained with him a few years until it was redeemed). With great toil, without a moment of rest, with fasting, exhausted and depressed, they collected the money. The guarantors returned to their houses. The spirit calmed down, but the fear didn't vanish. The Hellertzikim got up and left the town suddenly, in a rush. Their departure was deeply pierced in my memory.

Jews came out from their houses, rushed around and informed one another which army approached the town. I didn't go to buy the meat that I was sent with mother to buy, and I ran home to tell the news. There was great happiness in the whole town. The Jews went out to the streets after days and nights of sitting in the houses. The Red Army – the Bolsheviks – entered. We saw them for the first time. Not all the

Hellertzikim succeeding in escaping, and among them was the officer who commanded the taking out and killing of the boy (so said the adults). Also Haksyondz was frightened of the Bolsheviks and he joined the officer. Together there were six who did not succeed in fleeing (so it was said). Haksyondz turned to the Jews to save them (because the goyem would certainly murder them). All other peoples, not the Jewish, would revenge themselves on them as it is fitting "for these dogs", but a Jews, will he be a murderer? Also the fear, that perhaps they will return and make carnage on the Jews, prevented all acts of revenge. The Jews did the opposite of this, and they saved their lives (according to the request of Haksyondz). Despite the fact that the Jews endangered their lives, they hid them in their houses (of Aharon Shlimtzya, and others).

The Bolsheviks made searches for the Poles. They also entered the houses in which they were hid. The Jews told them the horror story about what these people did in the town. Upon hearing this the Bolsheviks expressed their sympathy and they left. It didn't enter their minds that after all this the Jews would save these murderers. With the coming of night (it was very dark) they dressed them in woman's clothes and a number of our young boys led them to the lines of their army. They feared for the lives of the boys, because they suspected that the Hellertzikim would liquidate them. But they returned safely.

The Bolsheviks behaved all right, except for a few incidences of opportunities to take things (not to rob!), such as velour of armchairs (of Rabbi Twersky) and things like this. They heard about the "somoboronah" (self-defense) in the town and they had regard for it. With all of this, when they tried to enter any house to take things, a few shouts of "gevalt" were sufficient to chase them away. There were two characters among them that I remember. One "Das Rotte Kvittel"

[Page 38]

(the red flower) – an officer who always had a red flower on his hat. The second character, a woman whom they called Torishkah Leyova. They always went together and they were the first to visit the houses. Usually they didn't bother us, not even the rich. The Bolsheviks gave the impression of an unorganized army, without uniforms. Each one dressed in his own clothes. They didn't have shoes and they earned the nickname "Borvesa" (barefeet). After some time the Poles attacked the city from the other side of the Horyn "Hakolonia". We experienced the taste of war. Bullets flew like rain. The population started to seek safe places to escape the death.

All the buildings' basements were filled. The synagogue, as I mentioned at the beginning of my words, was in fact a fortress that was used as a place of safety by hundreds of people. Even the echo of shooting didn't enter inside. Thanks to this there were no victims. The Bolsheviks (and after them all other armies) discovered that this synagogue was an excellent place for an army position. It towered high over the bank of the river and from here it was possible to observe in the distance. They stationed cannons and shooting machines and they tried to repel the enemy. The enemy noticed this and attacked the synagogue. Cannon shells injured it, but didn't pass through the ceiling. Stepan suffered from the war for three years, so it seemed to me. Battles occurred, but only in the summer. During the winter, the Bolsheviks always remained in the city. In the summer there were changes, some entered and some retreated, and the opposite. The suffering was great. Things to eat and to wear were lacking. The disease typhus broke out in almost every house, like the majority of the parts of warring Europe. The typhus was rampant, and toppled many victims. This event shook the entire Jewish population. One day Chana died, the wife of Bentzia Yonas (Weitznodel) and their only son Moshe, and who was the mother and sister of Slobah (Weitznodel) now Min, who can be found in Israel in Kibbutz Mesilot. As I mentioned, the shortages were great. In the summer they would buy from the goyem a few vegetables or fruit, gather seeds in the forest and collect mushrooms. In the winter, there wasn't even this. The value of money went down or went out from usage (like Hakerenskalach and Hakarvontchki).

My family suffered, in addition to financial hardship, also from war damages. In this sense, we were the only family in town. Already from the first day of the war our cow was killed (the majority of the homeowners in Stepan had cows) in the path from the pasture to the house. After a number of weeks passed a cannon shell fell within the house, exploded and destroyed everything that was inside – the walls, the stove, the dishes, clothes, bedding, and furniture. Father repaired the house with his own hands (there was no money to pay for the work), including the roof and the windows, in order that it would be possible to make it through the winter. With the last money we bought another cow. Summer followed, and again everything was destroyed, like the first time. Again the cow was killed from a cannon shell that fell within the house. After this people were afraid to cross by our house at the time of the battles, because the place was prone to hits.

After three summers (so it seemed to me) came the end of the battle for power between the Bolsheviks and Poles. The Poles won ultimately.

[Page 39]

New times began. The Poles who suffered during lowly generations and much persecution from their foreign rulers, announced that they would treat us, the Jews, with understanding and tolerance in all the territories. You Jews, they said, you are experienced in suffering, torture and humiliation, and we will not treat towards you any different than towards ourselves. Majorities of your people paid with their property and their lives when they helped us, the Polish people, to fight for independence against the invaders. The Jews believed that this is what would be.

And in truth, at the beginning it was very good. The lives of our society and culture received new character. They were unrestricted, mainly in the cultural area. My father fulfilled his dream of many years and he was the founder of a "Tarbut" (cultural) school whose language of teaching was in Hebrew. Father invited Esther Tzasys-Halpern as a teacher, and also Borak, a relative of my mother, not a citizen of Stepan. The parents sent their children to learn there. The method of learning was "Hebrew in Hebrew". The other cultural area that livened up our lives was the theater. We organized two troupes of amateurs, one mainly of adults, and their participants were Yoel Prishkolnik, Baruch-Moshe Siegel, Yosef Siegel, Mirkah (daughter of Baruch Mordechai), Tzippah Chasias, Chanale, Sosel Bebchuk. From the repertoire that they came out with was: "Das Pintele Yid", "Maidele Afrat", and others.

The second troupe was composed of young people who aspired to follow the adults. The participants in it: Tzirel of Yosef Mirles, my sister Panya, Faygel Kagan, Avraham Feirstein, the son of the pharmacist Mendel (he moved to live in another city), Berel Siegel, Zeivel Kopel, the Kerzners, and others. They presented: "Koni Lamal", "Chassia De Yesoma", and others.

There was not an auditorium fit for a play in the town. The Ukrainians would perform in their schools (two in number), but the Jews were not permitted to perform there. Without a choice they started to perform in the synagogue for women (the Veibershe Shul). For illumination they used kerosene lamps. Of course, there was no electricity. Once it happened that a fire broke out during the play. Apparently, the reason was that the kerosene was diluted with benzene, and only by a miracle were there no victims. Great panic arose. It was hard to flee outside, since there was only one door, and a path through the windows was impossible to take because it was at a height of two stories. Since then we didn't perform there.

After great effort they succeeding in obtaining a license to present in the shack of the "pazsharne" (from the firemen). For us, the children, a movement named "Scout" was organized. The founder and guide was a young girl named Bracha Sheckman, the bride of Pinya Gaz. Our meetings were always at The Volh. The Ukrainians didn't give us any peace. Every time that there was a meeting, they would assault us and stone us with rocks. Upon one assault, my brother Leibke succeeded in hurting the head of Pintchuk with a stone that was thrown at him. The assault stopped for a time and was again renewed in a manner that was dangerous to our lives. Since there were no other places fitting to meet, our movement was dismantled.

[Page 40]

A local entertainment group of Jewish youth in Stepan, 1931

In the year 1921-22 they opened a Polish school. An order came out that all Jewish children who learn in the Ukrainian school must transfer to the Polish school. The teachers and administrators arrived from Poland. All of them were officers who participated in the war for the independence of Poland. Dmedyok fought with the authorities for freedom of choice. He said that a Jewish student should be able to choose between a Polish or Ukrainian school. He asked that we try to remain with him. Suddenly he saw us as necessary and wanted students. The Poles didn't agree and moved us to the Polish school. So a separation was implemented between students, the young Jewish and Ukrainian. After that, only a few preserved a connection between them.

Father was invited to teach in the Polish school. We experienced the sense of a good, free life, a balance between rights and nationalism. The economic situation was good.

Only with respect to the youth did the situation remain as it was. There was no employment. There were no high schools in the town. There were no factories and no workshops. The youth didn't know what to do with themselves. The situation was particularly difficult for the children of the low-income families.

[Page 41]

They suffered, because they were not able to help with the subsistence of the family, and every young boy and girl had a yearning to help their parents and to be moderately independent.

Students of a Polish public school.
Among the teachers, teacher Shlomo Zoller stands out (marked with an X)

In the course of time the relationship of the Poles towards the Jews changed. Anti-Semitism, that was latent, started to be revealed. They started to impose high taxes that were largely passed onto the income and onto the value of property. The police gave tickets for every small thing. Jews were squeezed out of every governmental financial position.

In the year 1924-25 father was transferred to the town of Osovah in the role of teacher in the Polish school. In addition to this he gave private lessons. (Father, despite being religious, founded a cell of the Shomer Hatzair [leftist Zionist youth movement] and was its guide and representative to the authorities).

After father bought a forest besides Osovah, he created a place of work for my brother, Leibke, and he joined father. At the same time father bought a store in Kostopol and the plan was that my two sisters, Panya

[Page 42]

and Manya, would journey there to work in commerce. The plan didn't captivate them, because they didn't want to separate from home.

In the year 1927 our house was burned by the great fire that punished the town. We didn't have the desire to build life from new in Stepan and we moved to live in Kostopol. We always yearned for Stepan. Sometimes we visited there and also people from Stepan would visit us, primarily our friends. Intentions to immigrate to Israel came to our house. We received our passports in Kostopol, and this was a good opportunity to visit us. Also not just Jews: Ukrainians, Poles, and others who chanced upon Kostopol came to visit us. Both young, who at the time we learned with in the Ukrainian school and we remained friends, and also adults came to visit. Thanks to these visits we knew about things in Stepan. Polish anti-Semitism grew. The Poles utilized every possibility in order to harm the Jews. They also looked for ways to deepen the hatred of the Ukrainians that was, in any case, very much ingrained in them. The Ukrainians were haters of the Poles and Jews together. A Ukrainian nationalistic movement arose when the Poles arrived.

Meetings were arranged in the private home of a Ukrainian family who were friends. They invited me after I promised them not to reveal what I would see or hear. The words of Srootnik were filled with venom and plans of action. His words so influenced me that more than two times I was not able to listen to them. I felt that the sky was going away and darkening.

In the years 1932-33 the organized Ukrainians went out, group by group, to the forests to act against the ruling power. In Wolhynia, their actions were more widespread. The Poles, the police and the army, fought against them. In the newspapers they would publicize that gangs of "robbers and murderers" carried out actions in the forests and that they had liquidated them. I tell these things because they have a connection with Stepan Judaism.

At the end of the year 1933 (exactly before I immigrated to Israel), two Ukrainians visited me who had been friends from school. They told me, bitterly, about the liquidation of the Ukrainian rebellion by the police and army with the help of the Jews. They treated me with complete confidence and they told me that they were sent by the decision of the organization to secretly research a burial in Kostopol for three of the rebels who were killed in Stepan. I told them that I didn't believed that the Jews of Stepan would have cooperated with the actions of the Poles against the Ukrainian population. So they told me about the event that happened.

A group of rebels were attacked by the armed Polish force in the forest. The rebels succeeded in escaping to Stepan. Despite that they were surrounded, they succeeded in hiding. The Poles placed guards on every road outside from the bridge beyond Stepan. The Poles lacked people, so the Jews volunteered to guard, so goes the story according to the Ukrainians, to watch the bridge and to catch the escapees.

[Page 43]

There was no limit to the bitterness of these two Ukrainian boys. They asked: where were the years of the "somoboronah", our common self-defense, when we succeeded in saving you – the Jews – from death? Is this how you repay us?

I, who was surprised by the story of these deeds, lost my thoughts, and didn't know what to answer. It was very unpleasant for me, and I was embarrassed. My poor common sense told me that it was not possible that the Jews "volunteered" for these actions. I explained to them that this was a provocation by the Poles intending to arouse the two parts of the population, one against the other. After all, you know us, the Jews, I said to them. Did it ever happen that we caused you trouble? Do you know us as people thirsting for blood or for enmity? Please, journey home and explain to your people the truth, that the Poles forced the Jews to help them capture the people, forced them to guard the bridge. I am certain, I said to them, that if they guarded, then certainly they didn't bother them from crossing, if by chance they came. The Jews are not stupid, I said to them, and they aren't cruel and they don't tolerate murder.

To my astonishment and to their surprise, as I had guessed, that was the case. They actually became confused and they admitted that indeed the escapees succeeded in crossing the bridge and hiding within piles of straw, but they didn't know how it happened that the Jews didn't catch them. I don't think that my words helped with anything. Certainly not. The awareness that the Jews helped the Poles in situations like these remained with them. So I know, because we are found between a hammer and an anvil.

All that is written here belongs to the past. What remains is only to mourn and to cry for you, my dear town, the despoiled, the wounded. In my imagination you are buried together with your Jewish sons and daughters and their elderly, who were annihilated by thousands of different and strange deaths by predators in the form of a man – the Nazi animal with the cooperation of the animal from the Ukrainian race.

My dear Jews, you who are not still alive. Your bodies are spread everywhere, in the forests, in the rivers, in pits, crematoriums, gas chambers. My dear family, mother, father, my sisters, my brother-in-laws and the children – where did the cruel death find you, and where are your holy bones? I will never know. There is not a day, not a moment that I am not reminded of you, the six million who were annihilated.

G-d remember them, and bless and watch them for generations!

[Page 44]

Stepan: 1910-1920

by Moshe Woschina

Translated by Daniel Shimshak
Edited by Mira Eckhaus and Daniel Shimshak

The author was known in the town by the nickname Minikel. During World War II he was imprisoned by the Soviets and exiled to Siberia. At the end of the war he arrived in the United States. His first wife and his three children perished in the Holocaust together with the large number of his remaining relatives.

As it is known, it was forbidden for Jews to acquire land during the time of the rule of the czar. But, in the town next to Stepan there was a Jewish neighbor by the name "the Parantzuyiz". He was known as a well-off Jew. In his desire to acquire many estates, also in the area of Stepan, he was forced to convert to Christianity and to carry a cross on his chest, but this only for appearance sake. In fact, he was a good-hearted Jew and loved to help his people, and once he even dared to scorn the cross and wore it on the neck of his dog. The widespread rumor about him was that he paid a great sum of money in order to be saved from a severe punishment. He was very famous and rich and worked primarily in the production of brandy from potatoes. In order to prevent himself and his wife from being buried among the Christians, he bought himself and his wife a burial place beside his house and requested to be buried there after his death.

In the year 1910 a Polish landlord by the name Golboski acquired all of the plots of land around Stepan. A Jew named "the Giller" managed the estates of the Polish landlord. In this period the economic situation of the Jews of the town improved. He erected narrow railroad tracks to a sawmill. He issued papers for payment to the non-Jewish workers and concluded with the Jews of the town that they would honor these papers in place of money. After a period of time he would redeem the papers in exchange for money. Once the goyem tried an attempt on his life, but his servant, a goy, revealed it to him when he was drunk, and so a disaster was avoided and his assassin was caught and jailed.

At the end of World War I, a group of Jews organized: Berel Yeluvitzky and Moshe and Itzik the Milner and after they contacted relatives in America, they organized a benevolent charity fund and established a "Talmud Torah". This was a kind of progressive school that was managed by Shaul Shachnes.

Berel Yeluvitzky donated his house for the establishment of a "Tarbut" school that was managed by Mr. Ohrvoch and Mr. Moshe Koifman and another group of people their age who showed an interest in Zionism and the Hebrew language.

[Page 45]

The aforementioned donated from their money to the needy for the mitzvot of Passover, for the survival of the poorhouse, for keeping ice in the summer for medicine, and for other things.

At the start of the Polish rule in town, Yitzchak Greenbaum visited with Malviv Brovneh, while he was the Jewish Polish representative in the "Sejm" (Polish Parliament). This was in the year 1920. The Jews in all the towns met and laid out their complaints. He clarified to the Jews what their legal privileges were and requested that they turn their complaints into writing about every exceptional event, unnecessary taxes, demands for bribes and other troubles.

In the Stepan region lived those released from the Polish army who were called "Osadnykas". With the establishment of the Polish government, authorities settled those former Polish legionnaires in these places and they established agricultural settlements and here they were employed in governmental positions, involved with forestry and the roads – which were public governmental property.

On every Polish national holiday, the "Osadnykas" cavalrymen participated in the holiday parade in the town and they demonstrated riding while they were decorated in pennants and sparkling brilliant uniforms.

Settlers who came from Germany also lived in the area of Stepan. In the beginning they worked in nomadism, and they were very industrious in the work of agriculture. The majority had settled on plots of land from felled forests, that they had acquired dirt-cheap. During the years they invested great effort in pulling out the roots that remained in the area and they improved the land. After years of labor they succeeded in developing model farms and in marketing excellent agricultural products. Primarily they were known for clean, excellent milk products, that merited great demand. All of the rulers, the czars or the Poles, treated these Germans with great suspicion and whenever a conflict or war broke out with Germany they exiled them, in the time of the czar, to the depths of Russia. And thus they made things difficult for them and kept them under observation in the time of the Poles.

After World War I, at the time that various armies captured Stepan, it happened once that a Polish army took over the town. Of course the scapegoat was first and foremost the Jews: robbery, beatings, rape and the like fell on our lot. Once, three armed soldiers entered our house and asked to eat. My mother served them a meal fit for a king and also honored them with whiskey. Prior to this my father was worried about hiding my sister in a side room with a disguised opening that was hidden by a swollen clothing closet. While they were eating, the soldiers noticed the hideaway closet from beyond and asked to move it in order to arrange a search. My father stood opposite them and resisted. One of them waived the butt of his rifle and hit him in his head. That led to a big fuss. My father's face was covered in blood and he fell stunned. The Polish soldiers approached to move the closet, but my three brothers and I intervened and we attacked the soldiers, we unloaded their weapons and tied them up. In order that many people would not know about this matter, we brought them down to the basement of the house. After a day, again the Polish army fled the town and the Bolsheviks entered, and then we delivered the Polish soldiers into their hands.

[Page 46]

To the Jews of the town it was hard to distinguish between one army and the other. For example, once a group of Bolsheviks overpowered the town. With respect to their clothing, they were identical to the uniforms of the Polish army. And behold, one of the Jews of the town started to converse with one of the officers and complained about the Bolshevik government together with his praise of the Poles. Understandably, in the end he received serious blows from the Bolshevik army.

During the time of the Petluran government (Simon Petlura, leader of independent Ukraine in 1918-1920), 50 ruble banknotes were issued and none smaller were found. This hardened the lives of the town. A Jew named Itzik Marcus-Wastchineh arose and established something like a bank. He issued signed notes with his signature and every note was equal to a specific value. Thus in accumulation of a quantity of notes (kvitelech), 50 complete rubles was given in exchange, thus solving the money problem.

The Slaughterers

Among the slaughterers of Stepan was one who was famous as a cantor with the most pleasant voice – Levi Hashochet (the Slaughterer), cantor of the great synagogue. It was pleasant to stand close to him during the holidays and to enjoy his pleasing and skyrocketing voice. And in our hearts, the hearts of children, there was no doubt that the voice of the cantor penetrated the heavens, and the prayers of the people of the town were received willingly and compassionately. We the children, who lived close to the synagogue, enjoyed standing behind the eastern wall of the great synagogue during the evening hours to listen to the voice of Rabbi Levi Hashochet (the Slaughterer), at the time that he would prayer the counting of the omer. Rabbi Levi Hashochet was well liked by the majority of the Jews of the town and to a certain extent even by the goyem. He was a shining face to everyone, big and small. Always a smile spread over his face. It was possible to see him at most of the celebrations of the Jews of the town, including weddings, Bar Mitzvahs and circumcisions, and of course even funerals, at the time he ran a memorial service. Rabbi Levi would even accept the celebrations of some goyem, despite the criticism of the orthodox circle. It was understandable that his visits to these events were courtesy visits – acceptance of a guest invitation and nothing else. Rabbi Levi continued as a slaughterer and as a cantor in the legacy of his father, Rabbi Shmuel Hersh Hashochet.

Among the other slaughterers was Rabbi Yoel Hashochet, who came to the city as the son-in-law of Rabbi Yoel Hashochet, who was the son of Rabbi Moshe Hashochet. In addition, in the city was Rabbi Hershel Hashochet, who was accepted in the town as a refugee from Russia and who found livelihood in town as a slaughterer and as a reader of the Torah.

The slaughter house of the town was found in the neighborhood of the goyem. There they would slaughter the animals according to the laws of Israel with the help of the butchers and according to a specific rotation, in order to promise livelihood to all of them. In addition, there was a small slaughter house on the street of the Jews to slaughter fowl. The house servants or their children would bring the fowl there for slaughtering in exchange for payment to the slaughterer. Again the slaughterers would work according to a rotation during the regular work hours. In addition, they would also receive

[Page 47]

in their houses those who turned to them at irregular hours for the sake of slaughtering the chickens. The slaughter was carried out in the slaughtering corner that was by everyone's house. The main burden of slaughtering chickens was, of course, on Shabbat eve, Fridays, and primarily before Yom Kippur for the sake of kapporet (atonement), and in general before the holidays.

The family of Yitzchak "the doctor" – who was the father of Shmuel Sorkis the barber – the Tzyrolnik – the Falsher. I remember him because at the time of need of the Jews, and mainly the goyem, Shmuel the barber gave medical assistance – for healing diseases: he used leeches for bloodletting, he extracted teeth, etc. And certainly his father was famous for during his time Stepan had no doctor. After all, at the time of the activities of Shmuel, there were general doctors and also dentists, but despite all of this, still people were helped by his good service.

The mother of Shmuel the Tzyrolnik was called Fasya – Rochel the Bobbe – the midwife. She was famous for taking care of the majority of the town's births, both those with means and those who were very poor. She would answer the call in every hour of the day, in every season of the year, and in all kinds of weather. She was known as a righteous person who visited the land of Israel once for a few years. She accumulated a little money and fulfilled the mitzvah of visiting Israel and she visited besides the Western Wall. On her return, she brought news of Israel to the Jews of the town. In Stepan there was another midwife, who I remember, who continued the tradition of Fasya-Rochel. She was Sosel the Bobbe, who was known for her good heart and good service and that she served all of the needy.

The students of the Polish preliminary public school with their teachers

[Page 48]

Town Life during the Period of the New Poland

by Slobah Mann

Translated by Daniel Shimshak
Edited by Mira Eckhaus and Daniel Shimshak

Slobah Mann, from the Weitznodel house, was the daughter of Ben-Zion Weitznodel. She immigrated to Israel in 1939, and today is a member of Kibbutz Mesilot.

The population of Stepan was comprised of Jews from the Ukraine and from Poland. The Ukrainians, who were the majority, worked in agriculture; the Jews worked in commerce and small crafts, and the Poles worked in office work, agriculture and teaching.

In the city council there was a majority of elected Poles, a small percentage of Ukrainians, and very few Jews. The bank was in the hands of the Jews, the post office and the courts in the hands of the Poles. Also, there was a Jewish community.

The election committee of Jews, Poles and Ukrainians for the municipal council.
(The Jews are marked with an X)

[Page 49]

Despite that our generation descended from devout homes, we were influenced by the currents and the new spirits that were blowing then in the world in general and by the way of the Jews in particular, such as: the revolution in Russia. In the same period the Zionist movement arose and a free Poland was established.

The memories of Stepan, my town, never left me. Different characters arise in my mind, and all of this so alive and close to my heart as if it was the day before yesterday. I ask myself: how and from where did this town produce the kind of people that it produced. There were no schools for high levels of Ulpan, no libraries, motor transportation, electricity, etc. Despite all of this, the adult generation – three generations before – succeeded in organizing and creating a dramatic group that performed plays before the Jewish population with great success, such as: The Witch, The Dybbuk, and others. Also the primary teachers of the "Tarbut" school were from this generation: Moshe Koifman, Esther Kolodny, and others. Also the manager of the bank, the bookkeeper and many others were enthusiastic Zionists who donated to Zionist fund-raising drives with generosity. I found much sympathy among these people, and they willingly delivered their children to our hands for guidance.

We acquired our little education through self-teaching, and even tutorial books for study like this were not found in Stepan, but only in surrounding big cities, and a book like this would be handed over from hand-to-hand with the fear of holiness. Thus we succeeded in acquiring a little knowledge, everyone according to his abilities. Also the Zionist movement gave us very much. During that time we grew and we needed to worry about our physical existence. The boys, after they completed school, joined the profession of their parents, and only three boys left for advanced studies far away, but they never completed their studies because the war broke out. The girls went to study sewing or to become homemakers with their mothers.

We were three loyal and friendly souls. We were together during our studies, and after the finish of the course of studies, with the recommendation of the teachers, we tutored children who had difficulty with their studies – something that served us as a source of our livelihood and as financial assistance for our family.

Only death succeeded in separating two of the friends from me. Berta Krakover of blessed memory, who died in the prime of her youth in Nes Ziona and was a member of Kibbutz Negbah, and Bella Geller of blessed memory who was killed in the Shoah. I feel their absence until today in every step of the way.

In the course of time Stepan turned into a household name and a magnet, and children from surrounding villages started to flow to her, in order to study Torah. And so I befriended children from two neighboring villages – with Raizel Scheyns from the village of Stodin and with Leah Rodnik from the village of Kosmishtov, now Mrs. Leah Chashvia, and her sister Pankah.

The Horyn River very much served the population of Stepan, who derived great benefit from it. First it was the main transportation artery, it served to float felled trees from the forests, for water for drinking,

[Page 50]

and for washing clothes. The farmers who lived on its banks would bleach the linen cloth that they produced themselves. How pleasant and interesting it was to see the picture of 100 meters of white linen cloth spread out on the edge of the river. On the warm summer evenings we spent hours in sailing, in swimming, in singing and in playing music.

Especially engraved in my memories is one of the nice events that I observed – it was a Polish holiday that they called "the holiday of the sea." The Poles would come to the river with big wreaths and would light candles on them, they would sit in boats and they would cast the wreaths into the current, and accompanied by song and music they would return at the time that the wreaths would disappear from sight. We would stand on the shore fascinated with this wonderful sight.

From Thursday until the start of Shabbat the river was bustling with woman and children who were busy with the cleaning and polishing of copper utensils, samovars (tea-urns), candlesticks, plates, and pots. And it was a kind of competition to see whose vessels were brighter. And of course, in meetings like this, it was impossible not to have gossip: who was getting married, who got married, who was getting divorced, who died, and who was dying, who was born, who was going to give birth, etc. And on Sunday it was possible to again see the convoy going to the river with the empty utensils from the cholent in order to wash them in the waters of the river.

Neighboring the town, from the direction of the river, was a settlement and within the settlement was a forest within which we would conduct activities of the cell of "Shomer Hatzair" (leftist Zionist youth movement), and also carried on interesting conversations while hiking. There was also a convalescent home ("Datshe") there, where people of means from the towns would spend time during the hot summer days.

The times were tranquil. Slowly we grew and progressed and integrated into a Jewish cultural circle that was the peak of accomplishment in Poland.

The first of the steps in studying was the cheder, like the rest of the children of the town. After, I moved to the Polish elementary school. There were Polish children there who were happy for Poland's freedom from foreign yoke, and we were certain that they would willingly and enthusiastically receive our outstretched hands in order to help to restore Poland, but our outstretched hands remained hanging in air. And how deep was our visible disappointment over their arrogant patronizing and their anti-Semitic relationship towards us, to their friends from yesterday! And now the idea of a return to Zion penetrated our hearts, and also for us our essential homeland. In addition to this we were knowledge-thirsty, therefore we overcame all the obstacles, and we excelled in our studies and always we were the first in the class.

I especially was impressed with the continuous battle of the Poles over one hundred years to free their land from foreign yoke, and this brought me the idea of our national liberation.

[Page 51]

On the Jewish Street there were many different currents. One believed in a strong hand and regal pomp; and there was a current that believed in "a dunam (measure of land) here and a dunam there" and self-realization; there was a current that believed in the collection of money and in the sending of others to the land of Israel.

My friends and I searched for a society and a movement in order to serve as an outlet for our seething aspirations of youth's excitement, and this we found in the Shomer Hatzair. In it we also found an answer to the Jewish anomaly question, that is to say: without land and a national house the Jewish nation doesn't exist. Joy of youth, dances, singing until the last breath, loosened the daily gray concerns.

The devout Jews did not look upon all of this favorably, and we had a difficult struggle against them. As I already said above: we not only would dream, but also fight, men of action, fulfilling that which was proclaimed. And the action: fund-raising drives, educational operations, and holy work for the sake of the Jewish National Fund, and in addition, the crowning achievement: self-training towards the realization of our dream – to arrive in Israel and a kibbutz!

Carrying out the preparation was not an easy thing. Breaking off from the house and resistance of the parents to our side – all of this was foreign to their spirit as if we are severing ourselves from Judaism and from the family, but at the time we saw that we were right, and not they. The Shoah that came upon our people proved us to be correct. From the start we chose training the hard way, towards our lives in Israel and in a kibbutz, because we knew what waited for us, and certainly we were not disappointed…the reality proved itself.

After my return from training, the remaining family was without any means of livelihood, and I sensed that my first worry was to find a source of livelihood for me and for my family. Very quickly I found a source of my former livelihood, tutoring students having difficulties with their studies.

Slowly I started to prepare to immigrate to Israel, which lasted for two years, owing to the lack of financial means. But thanks to the help of my sisters in Canada I succeeded in collecting the needed sum. These were the last moments and the last opportunity to go out from Poland.

When my dear father saw this tragic reality, he said to me: Slobkeh, there is no choice, go your way and perhaps I will also succeed in going out from this exile! My father was a Zionist, a lover of farming and he never bothered me to follow a way that he chose. Just the opposite, he would say: If only I was able to be like you.

We almost missed the bus, and on the brink of World War II, on August 18, 1939, we escaped from a Poland that faced destruction.

[Page 52]

This was an illegal escape, by off roads. The long trip to Israel took more than two months and was on board the famous freighter ship "Tiger Hill". After we suffered from hunger and after much flinging about, we arrived on the coast of Israel.

On the way, on board the ship in the middle of the sea, I would allow myself thoughts about finding a way to quickly bring my father and my family to Israel. Even during the most difficult and most tragic moments that I had along the way, I didn't stop from planning and portraying the meeting with my family.

Two weeks after our sailing from the port Konstentz, in which we were confined for four days in very bad conditions, and while we were in the middle of the sea on September 1, 1939, we heard on the radio the horrifying news about the invasion of the German murderers into Poland. All my dreams and plans were smashed into splinters. I would not be fortunate to see my family again.

When finally we arrived on the beach of our motherland and our feet tread on the firm land, the English met us with handles and rubber clubs and escorted us to the detention camp in Sarafond. There we were under guard for about two weeks, and only after this were we transferred to the Jewish Agency, and then we felt ourselves living with our brothers in the land of Israel. At long last we arrived at our destination. I arrived at my kibbutz, Mesilot that is near Beit Shean. Here I built my family nest and here I live until this day.

Hashomer Hatzair activists in Stepan

[Page 53]

The Synagogues

by Y. Pery

Edited by Mira Eckhaus and Daniel Shimshak

The great synagogue was the central structure of the town. It was built on the foundation of the ancient fortress from the period of the Polish king Stefan Boturi.

Before the entrance to the great synagogue was the "polish". It was used as a room that allowed secular conversation among the congregants. In the entrance to the "polish" was two thick, rusty iron gates that were not being used in our time. Apparently they were used in the past to serve the defense needs in case of trouble. When the people of the town assembled in the synagogue, these heavy gates were closed and locked for the defense before the rioters who penetrated or expected to penetrate the town and the synagogue itself. Also, there was a thick wooden door with thick colorful glass panes. From the main opening, spacious steps led to within the synagogue.

From the center of the synagogue was a high platform that was used for reading the Torah and for sermons and people went up on it by steps on two sides. The ceiling of the synagogue was concave and spread out onto thick iron tracks were bowls, and a portion of them were engraved with dates, like 1635.

There were thick iron chains and on the ends hung heavy copper chandeliers for the insertion of candles. On the last two chandeliers the electricity for the synagogue was connected. The hall was spacious and many of the windows had colored glass. The Ark (Aron Kodesh) was along the central wall and steps led up to it in the middle.

The Ark was carved in the thick wall. The walls of the synagogue were several meters thick. The Ark was very beautifully molded: there were two tablets of the commandments, along side were two gold-plated lions, and there were columns.

The architecture of the Ark was performed many years ago by artistic experts who were brought from outside the area or from a nearby town. Serving as the chazan was Rabbi Levi Kreizer, of blessed memory, who had a pleasant, beloved voice.

Apparently in a much later period, additional synagogues were built around the great synagogue. The upper and lower synagogues for women bordered on the common wall with the great synagogue. In this wall were built many arched openings and through these openings penetrated the voice of the chazan of the great synagogue, and thus the women were able to follow his prayers. Devorah Brunner served as gabbai of the women's synagogues.

[Page 54]

Along side the "polish" of the great synagogue was a small synagogue for the working people – shoemakers, tailors, carpenters and others. And also there was an additional room that was used as a storeroom for scrolls, prayer books, prayer shawls (tallit), and used phylacteries (tefillin). We, the children, saw it as sort of a storeroom for hiding places that existed during the time of Rabbi Yokel the old shamash (beadle), who served like a general shamash for all the synagogues. He was very old and white and he had great strength in his arms, despite his extreme age. He would go around with his large bound keys and he would worry about the arrangement of things, the cleanness, the candles, the heat and other things. We, the children of the street, never volunteered to help Rabbi Yokel, of blessed memory, with transferring the benches and such, except on the condition that he would give up his habit of pinching us (out of affection, of course, but it caused great pain).

**Rabbi Yokel Rassis the shamash against the background
of the Ark of the synagogue in the town**

[Page 55]

From the second side of the great synagogue was the "supreme" synagogue – there would pray big shots (business people), from the followers of the religious judge, Rabbi Ben-Zion Volinsky, of blessed memory. From under this synagogue was a small synagogue that was used for praying by big shots, a portion of them were from the Chassidim of the religious judge, Rabbi Pinchas "the good natured" and a portion of them of Rabbi Ben-Zion the religious judge. Attached to this synagogue was another synagogue for women of these big shots.

Before the entrance to each of these synagogue was the "polish" (the same spacious room that was used for secular conversations and for rest).

[Page 56]

My Town and My Homeland

(In memory of my grandmother Rivka Shmuel Leibs)
The author immigrated to Israel in 1934. Today he is a member of Kibbutz Negba.

by Gershon Krokover

Translated by Mira Eckhaus

Edited by Daniel Shimshak

During her best years, Grandma Rivka was widowed. Although she was able to rebuild her life and have a happy family life, she didn't. Whether it was because of her love to her only son, or because of her compassion for the defect that was inflicted on him at his childhood, she decided to devote her life to him and his descendants.

Her life with us was not easy. I remember her always busy and worried about managing the household and its finances, which were under her responsibility.

Mother, who was confined to her bed, and on summer days would travel to places of healing, could not devote much of her attention to us, so our grandmother took care of our education as well. We, the children, did not make it easy for her, and especially I, who have been pampered since my childhood, was not grateful to her. Later, when I grew up and understood the magnitude of the sacrifice and actions of Grandma, I no longer had the option to correct the deformity. After my immigration to the Land of Israel, I dreamed about the day when I can bring my grandmother and the family to me, and honor her old age. But the exterminator came and ruined all my plans and my best dreams, and for that my heart is sorrowful.

I vaguely remember the end of the First World War, when the town was subject to a change of government. The shots were heard outside, and the Jews were crowded in the basements from the terror of the shots and hooligan attacks. Every family was crowded with its bundles under it, pale-faced and bearded young Yeshiva students were hiding, trembling like fallen leaves from fear of soldiers entering and taking them to work in the fortifications. When the door opened, the soldiers jumped out and with their rifles and their daggers pierced the glass to reveal men hiding. The screams of the children who were in the hands of their mothers increased the noise, and rushed the soldiers outside.

When the battles ceased, we came out of the darkness into the light, and the vision that was revealed to us was the destroyed bridge, which retreating soldiers had burned and sturdy villagers sailing barges across the wide Horyn River, and serving as a transportation for people and horse-drawn carts, which aim to reach the other side of the river. We, the children, who used to stay by the river all day, were happy in the opportunity to sail a little across the river.

[Page 57]

Many families were impoverished by the war and aid institutions were established to help those in need. In the mornings they would give out a cup of cocoa and a bun to poor children. I, whose family used to have their own cow and we didn't need help, was not allowed by my grandmother to enjoy it, but the cocoa attracted me so much that without permission I would run and hand out my cup to receive the desired drink.

The war was over, but its aftermath signaled the spirit of the children and the organization of warrior gangs. On one side the children of the Jews and on the other the children of the gentiles, with the area of the market square serving as the battle field. We the little ones served as assistants for the older children, we were collecting stones for the catapult war. More than once, someone came out of this war wounded and bleeding. But even the adults who dared to pass through the market square put their lives at risk and more than once someone was hit in the head by a stone. But the days of idleness ended quickly and the time for the Torah studying came, because we are not like the children of the gentiles! This Torah is being taught by young melamedim with the assistance of beatings with the "Kantchik". These young melamedim don't have a lot of knowledge, but to their credit it must be said that they were the only ones at that time, who provided the first foundations for the spiritual and moral development of the children of Israel in the town, and constituted a foundation for imparting a wider education with the establishment of the "Tarbut" school.

The rabbi's kantchik was a threat to the children, but it did not prevent them from doing mischief. And since the rabbi was the one who distanced them from the world of games and imposed his teachings on them, he served as a target for their revenge. Their pranks were many and varied.

The monotonous hours of memorizing the Torah for the children put the rabbi to sleep for most of the day, and then the children's spirits came back to life and the time for pranks began, whether by tying the rabbi's tzitzit to a stool or by scratching with a straw under his ear (and it was a great pleasure to see the rabbi waving his hands in the air to punch the flies), or by adding salt to the glass of cholent that the "rebbetzin" served to the rabbi. But there were also days when the rabbi was kind to us, and those were the days when he took us out of the stuffy air of the cheder, whether it's on Lag Ba'Omer, when the rabbi took us to walk in the field, or when the rabbi taught us the "Shema" prayer; when the rabbi with his kapota walked at the head, followed by all the children in noise and bustle to bless the woman giving birth, and especially to receive the delicious honey cookies…

A child went through several cheders until he reached the mitzvah age. Every rabbi and the nickname they gave him, every rabbi and his influence on the child. But all of them alike, apart from the necessity of making a living, were good Jews, they liked the child in their own special way and wanted to see them to grow to be good and God-fearing Jews. I have a special fondness for Rabbi Benetzia. Whether it was because of his extreme old age or due to the fact that he was also my father's rabbi. The children arrived to the cheder willingly in the long winter evenings, when the children learned the Chumash; each child came with a lit flashlight and the stove in the cheder spread its heat. The light of the candle did not dispel the darkness in the end of the cheder and the bartering of buttons among the children flourished, while the rabbi was immersed in the Chumash and the tiny letters.

[Page 58]

Shabbats and holidays with their special delicacies were bright spots in the routine of life. Every holiday with its special dishes, which only the Jewish grandmothers knew how to prepare. Over the years, when we abandoned the tradition of our ancestors, we left the warm nest and prepared ourselves for the eastern sun, or according to grandmother's version, we fell into bad ways; when we sat and sang and also ate the soup that consisted mainly water, the smell of grandma's cooking still rose in my nose. On the morning of Friday, the preparations for the arrival of the Shabbat Queen began, with the baking of challahs, the frying of fritters seasoned with geese fat. And at noon, grandma sliced the fresh challah with her hands and dipped it in the tasty steaming and fragrant Russel Fleisch. After Birkat Hamazon, God-fearing Jews ran to the mikveh with bundles of clean underwear under their armpits. The children of Israel, with washed heads and wearing bright Shabbat clothes, were going out to the streets of the town. The time of lighting the candles and the time of prayer in the synagogues was near, after which, led by Father's hand, you would return home, bless everyone with "Shabbat Shalom", and Father would make the blessing over wine while we were all sitting around the table with bright faces.

On Friday night, I was often unable to fall asleep, wanting not to miss the call of the shamash to recite Psalms, and more than once I was able to hear the banging of his stick on the door of our neighbor, a God-fearing Jew who got up in the wee hours of the night to recite the Psalms. The shamash would strike with his stick and his melodious voice was heard late at night – ("Merciful Jews, wake up, wake up to the service of the Creator"). I also hurried to get up. It was dark and silent outside, but the windows of the synagogue were lit and Jews were reciting the book of Psalms. At dawn they would return home and read the weekly parasha.

Grandma would take out the pot of milk that has been in the oven since yesterday, take off the three-finger thick milky crust, and fill the glass. The crispy Shabbat cookies remind me of barter trading.

Yitzchak Moshe Avrahams lived next door to us. He was a Jew with many children whose livelihood was not abundant. He had a grocery store where sweets were also sold. His son, Moshe Avraham, was my friend and he had a special fondness for grandma's Shabbat cookies. Every Saturday I would fill my pockets with cookies, whether it was with permission or without permission, rush to the Polish of the Beit Midrash, where Moshe was waiting for me. The cookies quickly entered to his pockets and my pocket was filled with a thick chocolate bar that Abraham took from his father's store.

If these were the preparations for a regular Shabbat, it is obvious that the preparations for the holidays were much more meticulous!

When the Passover holiday was approaching (at that time, we did not know about all those sleepless nights our parents went through due to their worries about how to get the money for the preparations for the holiday), there was a great commotion in every Jewish house: sewing of the new clothes for the children, going out to buy hats and shoes, without all of which the feeling of the holiday was not complete. The special ritual of baking matzah.

[Page 59]

The taste of a purchased matzah was different from the taste of a matzah that was baked especially for you, when every houseowner supervised and helped with his own hands to bake his matzah; the specific noise of white-washing the walls and the koshering of the tools. And when the holiday came, the house was clean and tidy, the chametz has already been eradicated and the corners of the house were scented with honey as a virtue for the sweet year that will come upon us for the better. Children who were clean and dressed in new holiday clothes with their pockets full of nuts, filled the streets of the town. The Jews rushed to prayer, after which the Passover "seder" began, in which the child also had a significant role the four questions, finding the "Afikomen" and opening the door to the prophet Eliyahu. The preparation of the holiday delicacies did not begin until the next day, with the baking of the "kigalach" and all those dishes that grandma was busy preparing all day. I remember that even on weekdays I wanted to eat the holiday dishes. Grandma, who used to pamper me a lot, would sometimes rebel and say – "Madarf nit nachnaben di shmed", then Father undertook to do the job with a hearty smile on his face. There was no job that Father didn't know how to do properly - from repairing a shoe, to sewing a garment, and even doing a very delicate job. Everything he got his hands on came out properly repaired, even if he had never dealt with it before. He also excelled in cooking.

But not only holidays were in the life of the town. For many of the weekdays the residents were troubled with the search of sources of livelihood. The town was not blessed with extremely rich people, although there were people who made a living in abundance, but in contrast there were mostly destitute poor people. The craftsmen hardly earned a living, but they were "happy beggars", whose joy accompanied their handiwork. Most of the town's people were small traders, who made a living by trading with the villagers of the town, and especially with the rural people who would come to the town for the market days once a week. Market days were a special experience in the life of the town.

The commotion in the market started early in the morning. Stalls were quickly set up with industrial and agricultural products from all over Poland. Before dawn the villagers had already begun to arrive to the town, some by transportation and some on foot, villagers wearing "posteles" on their feet, so in case they would have a successful trading day, they would return to their village with fresh tar boots, the smell of which wafts into the distance, draped over their shoulders. Wide carts drawn by oxen or labor-weary horses came one after the other. Winged creatures of all kinds stuck their necks out and filled the space with honk, honk and cock-a-doodle-doo. A two-months old piglet also added his squeal to the chorus, to the chagrin of God-fearing Jews. A fat rural woman was sitting in the middle and with countless eggs in her lap, which were laid this week in her chicken coop. Sacks of potatoes, vegetables and fruits of all kinds, all the agricultural produce of the land was packed into the wide villager's carts. The market was filled in this way to the limit and in the narrow passages Jews ran with their kapota sleeves rolled up, touching, bargaining, swearing and buying whatever was available. There, a well-versed seller from the capital city loudly announced that only that day, practically for free, three items for only one Zlotowka. All the defective products of the factory

[Page 60]

in Lodz were being sold legally at the cheapest price. Jewish housewives and broad-shouldered villagers assembled together and took whatever was available. There was noise and commotion everywhere, and also there was no shortage in tricksters in the market.

There was Grishka with the card table, quickly turning over the cards in the game "who noticed, who saw". His partners gambled and won sums of money and innocent villagers did not resist the temptation, spending their money, which should be used to purchase the tar boots, a colorful dress for the woman and gifts for the children. In a moment their money was stuffed into Grishka's deep pockets. He quickly left the place so that the policemen wouldn't see him and then appeared in another corner, where the passersby had not yet figured out his acts. The sad villager scratched his forehead, he sat down, but he remembered that inside the kichma there was still some money for drinking that he had placed there ahead. In a short time, he would sit in the wine house, get drunk and forget his sadness. He would only sober up in his little hat when he would see the look of the sullen eyes of his deprived and accusing wife. But sometimes also an innocent Jewish woman was tempted to test her fate and lose her money, the livelihood of her family, and went away crying. But to Grishka's praise, it must be said that he was not eager for the money of a poor Jewess, and he sent it back to the Jewess by his messengers, receiving God's blessing that this will surely atone to some extent for his many iniquities.

It is said that during the days of "Odepost", when a crowd of believers were crawling on their knees and praying to the Father, the Son and the Holy Spirit, Grishka also crawled hesitantly. More than once, some of the believers found that their pockets were empty and their money was stolen when they got up on their feet, while Grishka, satisfied with his lot, was already on his way to the city of Alexandria, and to his expectant and concerned wife.

By noon, the hustle and bustle of the market decreased, the carts were emptied and the villager women would hurry to the stores and the merchants who were waiting for the buyers. They would buy the needs of the house with money from their merchandise. Grandma would stand excited in the store with the measuring tool made of metal, "Harshin", in her hands. She would measure and add a bit more for the sake of friendship. She tried to persuade pleasantly and remove all the doubt of the buyers to "buy it"! This colorful dress fits you so well that all the girls in the village will be jealous. Father used to help her, he would take down the fabric rolls, fold, pack and count the money. The same situation repeated in the other stores as well, until the evening arrived and the last of the villagers left to his home.

The Jews obtained their livelihood after much toil and over the years the taxes increased and the small merchants lost a significant share of their livelihood. The rolls of fabric shrank and there was a need to enlarge them somehow, like the pale girl who pinches her cheeks so that the blush will rise in them. The worry of livelihood troubled the lives of many of the town's residents. Sometimes, the "Creator of the Lights of Fire" came to their aid, and the fires that often befell the town relieved their despair. They would receive the insurance payments that were enough for them to rebuild their house and still have a sum of money left over to support the house for a while.

[Page 61]

The times of civilization and technology approaching the town continued slowly. The only transportation that connected the town with the outside world was a pair of knightly horses harnessed to spacious carts, with sturdy coachmen sitting on their seats. The profession of coaching was held by several families, and it was customary for it to be inherited. These sturdy Jews had a good livelihood, but they achieved it with great effort. Only in the last year, before I left the town, a motor vehicle was brought in, and the carts served as their alternative. As a child, I envied the children of the coachmen who would go down in the evening to the bank of the river to water their horses, or would sit on the seats of their fathers.

There were only two roads that led to nearby train stations.

Because of the condition of the road, there were not many travelers to Antonóvka, however the road that connected Malinsk with the town of Rivne was paved because of the town's Jews were involved in trade and transfer of goods. Even in the dead of night, the cart would set off with a lantern beside it, a lantern that only illuminated the horses' hooves, and inside the cart Jews curled up in their furs. The road was mostly in a thick pine forest. Silence and darkness were all around, only the lashing of the whip in the air and the voice of the cart owner calling "Onward" broke the silence of the night and the sound of the conversation of the cart occupants, telling stories about robbers and burglars or the wolves of the forest that attacked a cart. In the darkness of the night, the figures looked like animals among the trees and branches in the forest. Sometimes also a real forest wolf was walking through the forest and his eyes seemed as glowing coals. A shiver ran through your body and you curled up tight to minimize your figure and blur it. And then the dawn broke. The forest woke up from its sleep, birds sang from every branch, the smell of the resin of the pine trees rose in your nose, black berries glowed with dew peeked out from under the bushes on the roadside, and a pleasant Ukrainian singing was heard in the distance. These were the villager girls who collected berries of all kinds: black ones or those called "brosnides" that explode with any contact and spread their sour juice, or those "siniches", red berries whose taste was so delicious when they were mixed with sweet cream. A few more hours and all the full baskets would arrive in the hands of Jewish housewives and would be served as delicacies on the tables of Jewish homeowners, who were not familiar with the way these berries grew or were picked.

In the field of cultural life, the town was not blessed with great wealth. The "Tarbut" school did expand the horizons of popular education and imparted Hebrew culture to the youth, and Zionist activity even developed within it. But it was mainly the pioneering youth movements that stimulated the youth to develop extensive Zionist activities: to go beyond the routine life of the town and tie their future to the Land of Israel that was being built.

The "Hashomer Hatzair" movement was established in the town while it was still a scouting movement, and then brought together the best of the town's youth and was a lively and vibrant cultural center throughout its existence. It educated the youth for pioneering and personal fulfillment. Some of the youths were attracted

[Page 62]

to the Beitar revisionist movement and a constant war was taking place between the two movements over the hearts of the young generation.

**Some of the activists of "Hashomer Hatzair" and "HeChalutz"
movements against the background of the bridge in Stepan**

The "HeChalutz" and "HeChalutz Hatzair" movements that arose afterwards also made their welcome contribution by bringing together mainly that part of the youth who had not yet found their way to the existing movements. It is regretful that only a few of the youth reached both personal fulfillment and salvation.

The cultural life of all the residents of the town was quite poor.

A theater and cinema did not exist, and only rarely would a traveling theater group come. For several days or weeks, it would stir up the life of the town and leave, leaving behind many debts and broken hearts. Rarely a local group of amateurs would get up and put on a play on stage, and then quickly disperse. The municipal library contributed a lot to broadening the knowledge, although the number of books it contained was not large and it did not satisfy the "quick" readers like my Father. Father was the first to read every book that reached our house, but he would not be satisfied with that and would spend many hours reading at Pinia's "Der Macher", in whose house he would also purchase books as well as press.

The urban promenade "Di Hoifen" (the courtyards), as it was called (which was filled with travelers every evening) served as a place of entertainment. The promenade continued from the market square to the post office, with "bez" trees from the nearby gardens spreading a fragrant smell all along the way. I would be remiss of my townscape if I would not mention the lovely corner "Der Wahl", which was a small grove surrounded by hills, covered with a lot of grass like a velvet carpet. At the foot of the hills flew the broad Horyn River, which returned a fresh wind. In the evenings of the hot summer days, old, young and children would come here to rest and revive their souls.

[Page 63]

Farewell party for Zeev Weitzengois, the first immigrant to the Land of Israel from Stepan. The year was 1932

Family members, members of the movement, acquaintances and loved ones near the grave of the head of Beitar and a teacher of the "Tarbut" school in the town, the late Yeshayahu Neiman, who died in the prime of his life

[Page 64]

The House of Rabbi Baruch Twersky of Blessed Memory and the Rabbis of the Town

by Yeshayahu Pery

Translated by Mira Eckhaus

Edited by Daniel Shimshak

Description of the Rabbi's House

On Shkolna Street, near the synagogues, was located a spacious house with many rooms and long corridors.

Compared to the Jewish houses in the town, the house was unusual both in its unusual size and in its exterior shape. It had many large windows, a large number of entrances with stairs were leading to the them, because the house had a high foundation. As for the interior of the house, it was divided into many rooms and halls and long and dark corridors. The handles and bolts of the doors and windows were of a fine kind – at that time - shiny bronze. In this house, there were also sinks, faucets and bathtubs, which was unusual compared to the other houses in the town, as well as heavy bronze chandeliers.

We, the children, pictured this house as a palace from fairy tales. (In the days I remember as a child, starting in 1936, it seemed to me like a royal house that had gone down from its greatness).

The house was empty and there only one of the descendants of the Magid of Stepan was living in it, an old, unmarried woman named Gittel, and she had an assistant named Raizel, a red-haired woman who, among other things, worked in knitting socks from which she made a living.

When we, the children, dared to enter this house (out of curiosity) through one of the entrances, everything seemed to us full of mystery and holiness. Out of awe and fear we would often flee outside, in most cases, even before Gittel or her assistant Raizel noticed our presence.

At the back of the house, towards the river, stretched a spacious lot and traces of rickety wooden stables along the entire length of the lot, right on the verge of the Horyn River, still visible.

Description of the dynasty

Until 1936, Rabbi Baruch Twersky of blessed memory and his family lived in this house. He is a descended from the dynasty of the Magid of Tarisk. Rabbi Baruch Twersky was the grandson of Rabbi Avraham of Tarisk of blessed memory, who was the son of Rabbi Moshe of Kirshov, of blessed memory, who was the grandson of Rabbi Motel of Chernobyl of blessed memory.

[Page 65]

Rabbi Baruch Twersky married Raizela, the daughter of Rabbi Meir Chaim of blessed memory and that is how the Stepan dynasty continued. Rabbi Meir Chaim of blessed memory was the son of Rabbi Levy Yitzchak of blessed memory and he was the son-in-law of Rabbi Israel Ber of blessed memory who was the son of Rabbi David the son of Rabbi Shmuel Halevi known as the Magid of Stepan.

The other son of Rabbi David Shmuel Halevi, the Magid of Stepan, was Rabbi Yechiel Michael of blessed memory, one of the founders of the nearby Bereznit dynasty. The Bereznit dynasty was well-known in all of Volyn and had its origins in the early 19th century.

The Magid of Stepan, Rabbi David Shmuel Halevi, was one of the students of the Volyn Magid of Mezhyrich, Rabbi Dov Ber of blessed memory, who was a direct successor of Rabbi Yisrael, the Baal Shem Tov of blessed memory.

From what I remember from the stories of my father and my uncle Yaakov Prishkolnik, who was a passionate Chassid of Rabbi Baruch Twersky and even served as a Chazan in the synagogue of the rabbi's house, it seems that he had a very rich past in this Rabbi's house. The name of Rabbi of Stepan was famous and Jews flocked to him from all over Volyn: some for consultation, some for healing and some to receive his blessing or just to be in his presence, near him, to touch and see him. Crowds were waiting for weeks until they were privileged to see the Rabbi and talk with him.

At that time, the rabbi's house and courtyard were like a beehive, they were full of Gabbaim, servants and guests. In the courtyard, stables stretched along its entire length near the river (the traces of which are still visible today), where the Jews would house their horses and carts.

The Chassidim of the town and the surrounding area, in all the generations, and especially in the period before the First World War, adored the rabbi, and made sure that the rabbi and his family members had financial support and financial welfare.

The intention was to allow the Rebbe to pray and study Torah (without worrying about livelihood) for the sake of his community and his people. The tzaddik rabbi would bless his Chassidim, advise on healing the sick and in matters of livelihood for the miserable, widows, and barren women of the community. In addition, he strengthened, supported and encouraged in times of trouble and disturbances, which were not lacking at all times for the communities of Israel among the gentiles in general and to the Stepan community in particular.

The rabbi's tenure was passed from father to son and when there was no son to inherit, the daughter married a descendant of the dynasty of a nearby town or a city. Thus, the groom continued his predecessor's family and the families of the tzaddikim multiplied as dynasties of kings in all of Volyn.

[Page 66]

Rabbi Baruch Twersky of blessed memory had an only son named Moshe. Moshe married the daughter of the Rabbi of Stolin. As the son was educated, he worked for a while as an insurance agent in addition to having Semichah. After that he served as a rabbi in Lubimol and probably perished there along with his family members by the Nazis.

Rabbi Baruch Twersky served as the Rabbi of Stepan until 1936, when he separated from his Chassidim in the town. Below is a description in the newspaper "Volyniar Zeitung" No. (733)30 about the rabbi's farewell from his Chassidim: -

"Several days before Rosh Hashanah, Rabbi Twersky and his family left the town permanently. Most of the town's Jews gathered to say goodbye warmly to the rabbi. The rabbi who will serve as the Rabbi of Lublin. As reported, the Jews of Lublin gave him a warm welcome when he came to the city".

Rabbi B. Twersky left Stepan and was appointed as the Rabbi of Lublin. From there he would travel to nearby towns in Volyn and occasionally he would come to Stepan. Here he was received by his Chassidim with great splendor but with longing for the old days.

At each such visit there would be a magnanimously feast, with the rabbi's Chassidim dining together with the rabbi. At the end of such a meal, there was a ritual with the leftovers (I witnessed it when my uncle Yaakov Prishkolnik, of blessed memory, who was among the rabbi's ardent Chassidim, took me there). I saw the snatching of the leftovers of food from the rabbi's plate, in order to win at least some crumb, when the holy and admired rabbi got up from the table.

During the rabbi's visit to the towns of Volyn near Stepan, he was received with great splendor by the crowd of his Chassidim in every town. The Chassidim in these towns also had their own synagogue and was called the synagogue of Stepan's Chassidim (Di Stepanier Shul).

It is known that there were synagogues of Stepan's Chassidim in the following towns: in the nearby town of Olyk - Rabbi Mordechai Glick served as the Gabbai of the synagogue there. This Gabbi instituted vows in favor of the Jewish National Fund, which was an unusual thing in those days

**The Chazan Yaakov Prishkolnik, of blessed memory, one of
the Chassidim of Rabbi Baruch Twersky**

[Page 67]

Also, in Sarny, a district town located north of Stepan, there was an independent synagogue for Stepan Chassidim that was founded by a Jew named Roizenberger. The founders and worshipers of the synagogue were mainly Chassidim of Rabbi Twersky from Stepan who moved to Sarny due to financial reasons. In the town Ratna, which was about fifty kilometers away of Kovel, was also a synagogue of Stepan's Chassidim.

Rabbi B. Twersky had also many Chassidim in the USA and he occasionally went on a journey there, to stay among his Chassidim, to cheer them up and excite them.

In the ancient cemetery of the town, it was possible to see tombstones of tzaddikim who were descendants of the rabbis' dynasty.

Family members on the graves of ancestors in the cemetery.
In the background are typical tombstones of the cemetery in Stepan

[Page 68]

There was a stone structure with a tin roof above it where the descendants of the Magid of Stepan were buried. Before the Days of Awe, on Ninth of Av and in times of distress, the townspeople would prostrate on the graves of the tzaddikim and hide notes - "Kvitlach" - between the gravestones, hoping that the credit of the tzaddikim would protect them and that they would find attention to their pleas.

The members of the Kotler family next to their father's-grandfather's tombstone,
behind the tombstone, Rabbi Levi Kreizer - the Shochet and Chazan

[Page 69]

The Tzaddik Rabbi David Halevi
- the Magid of Stepan

by M.Sh. Geshori

Translated by Mira Eckhaus
Edited by Daniel Shimshak

"A supreme Kadosh as one of the seraphs, Tzaddik Yesod Olam (a great tzaddik) and famous in his generation" - this definition highlights the exceptional personality of Rabbi David Halevi of Stepan, that the book "Baal HaDorot HaChdash" (the new generations book), which is considered to be a lexicographic book of the first three generations in Chassidism, considers him among the thirty nine distinguished students of Rabbi David Ber the Magid of Mezhyrich, and according to the book "Degel Machane Ephraim", which was written by one of the grandsons of the Baal Shem Tov, he is described as one of the students of the Baal Shem Tov.

In the third generation of Chassidism, a Maor Gadol (a great rabbi in Israel) was discovered in Stepan. Reb David Halevi was an excellent preacher, or according to the nickname given to him in the Chassidism books - "Magid Mesharim". Being a Magid was then considered to be the top step in the ladder of

Chassidism in particular and Judaism in general. He was very honored in the town and his name was known as a man who was well-versed in the matters he handles, and whenever it was possible, he would preach before the people who delighted the pleasantness of his speech with his fierce and loud voice.

He glorified the name and respect of Chassidism in public and he was liked by the audience, because in addition to his speaking talent and his pleasant personality, he knew how to spice up his words and melodies.

It seems that the tzaddik Reb David behaved with excessive modesty and humility, even though his origin was from a privileged family, he was the son of the fifth generation to Rabbi David Halevi (5306-5427), the author of "Torei-Zahav" (16?) for the Shulchan Aruch (from Ostroh). However, despite the fact that the rich imagination of the people liked to adorn and crown its beloved heroes with many legends and sprinkle them generously with virtues, they did not treat Reb David that way. "All the tzaddikim and rabbis of Poland mentioned his name with great honor and fear of God, endless wonders were told about him, and he was considered among the important students of the Baal Shem Tov" – wrote about him the author of "Shivchei HaBaal Shem Tov", which is the most common classical book in Chassidism, without any further details. These few details are not enough to give a correct description of his personality, and therefore the written words about his life and his actions remained obscure to a great extent.

Some of the known details which are of great importance, that are mentioned in the books, are: that he was a Magid Mesharim in the holy community of Stepan; that his book "Seder Hanhagot Adam" was printed, a book full of holiness and purity; that is his second marriage he was the son-in-law of Reb Michal the Magid of Zolochiv, and that he passed away on the ninth of Tishri (and some say on the eleventh of this month), 5561.

[Page 70]

Stepan, his hometown, was one of the remote places of Volyn, mostly inhabited by Jews and steeped in Judaism, which came, under the influence of the tzaddik, a place of Chassidism and music. The role of the Magid was most common during the foundation of Chassidism, and it seems that the Magidim were the emissaries of Chassidism, its chosen ones who were tasked with bringing its word to the masses of people.

The Magidim, as is known, incorporated into their sermons the melody or niggun, which constitute a significant part of their speeches and served as an important means to attract the masses. After all, the melody does not just caress the ear, it lifts the heart as well.

The great-grandchildren and descendants of Rabbi David Halevi provide details about him that have not yet been published publicly. From them it became known that he was the Rebbe of many Chassidim. And his house, which he founded in Stepan, was the clan of the dynasties that branched off from him, such as: Dubrovitsa, Berezne, Sarny, and others. He was gifted with a talent for singing and playing, and with his pleasant voice he could both sing and accentuate the words. On Shabbats, a strong song full of light and joy emanated from his house, which sometimes alternated with the sounds of sadness and devotion. Evidence of this can be found in the many melodies attributed to him, sung to this day by his great-grandchildren and his many righteous descendants.

Reb David of Stepan got close to the Magid of Zolotchov, and finally married his only daughter, Yentel, whose father the Magid said of her that she possessed the Holy Spirit, and while the angels were singing, she sang with them and jumped: Holy, holy... Reb David was already forty years old at the time, a widower from his wife and the father of four sons, and the bride, the daughter of the Magid, was only eleven years old at the time, and when the rebbetzin protested in front of her husband about his desire to marry his only daughter with a man who is the father of four sons, the Magid told her: let's call the girl and ask for her opinion. The girl, without thinking much, answered: Yes, I see that he is my perfect match...

As a student of the Magid of Mezhyrich, he would always walk to the Magid from his town. At the Magid there was a custom that all his students would wear a "Shtreimel" (a hat made of fox skins) on their heads. Reb David of Stepan was not able to purchase such a hat for himself, and this caused him great sorrow. And here in Stepan one of the townspeople passed away and left behind a Shtreimel, and the deceased's sons gave it as a gift to their Magid, and he was very happy about it, even though the deceased was known as a violent and a criminal. This was not considered a serious fault in his opinion. Reb David took the Shtreimel, walked to Mezhyrich and arrived there on a Rosh Chodesh day before the prayer. According to the custom in Mezhyrich, they would wait before praying the Musaf until the Magid gave a signal to begin the prayer, and the person who passed before the holy ark would wear a Shtreimel on his head. On that day, the Magid ordered Reb Aharon of Karlin to go in front of the holy ark to pray the Musaf prayer, but when he went to pray, he found that he had forgotten to bring the Shtreimel with him. The students searched and found one at Reb David, they borrowed it from him and gave it to the Baal Tefillah. Reb Aharon began to pray in the repetition of the Shatz and immediately felt that some hidden factor

[Page 71]

prevented him from talking, his voice was hoarse and his throat was snoring. Those present were amazed when they saw how hard Reb Aaron labored in his prayer until sweat covered his face, something they had never seen before. After the prayer Reb Aharon took one of the Magid's students and together they walked around the Beit Midrash when they reached Reb David, and after he told them how he received this Shtreimel, they already understood who caused this evil. And when Reb David spoked about the history of the Shtreimel, he added: but after everything that he went through, Reb Aharon of Karlin praised the Shtreimel, until it became an appropriate vessel for the ascension of the souls of its previous owners.

One of Rabbi David's sons, Reb Yehezkel Michal Pechnik, who lived in the town of Stolin in Polesia, where he studied Torah and worked, settled at the beginning of the nineteenth century with his family in Berezne and became known as "Rabbi Michal of Berezne". From him began the dynasty of the righteous from Berezne, which prospered and flourished in particular by his only son, Reb Itzikel of Berezne, the son-in-law of the tzaddik Rabbi Aharon of Chernobyl, who was well-known as a holy man with magical powers, and from whom branched out many dynasties in Dubrovitsa and Sarny (the Toichman family). The last rabbi of Dubrovitsa, Reb Nahum Yehoshua HaLevi Pechnik (5640-5702), the son of the tzaddik Reb Avraham Shmuel of Berezne, perished by the Nazis along together with sixteen thousand Jews from all the surrounding towns in the city of Sarny on the fifteenth of Elul, 5702. In those days, the other descendants of Reb David, the Magid of Stepan, were also perished in tragic death, may God avenge them.

[Page 72]

Atmosphere and Way of Life

My Father's House

by Yeshayahu Pery

Translated by Mira Eckhaus

Edited by Daniel Shimshak

Family origin

I was born in Stepan in 1927 to Yoel Prishkolnik (nickname - Di Gates). According to one of the rumors, my father's grandfather of blessed memory, Yeshayahu, served as a gabbai and passed before the holy ark in the synagogue. And on one occasion, when he finished the prayer "Shema Yisrael…" by unintentionally chanting loudly "I am your Lord, your God. True", instead of the accepted and customary saying, "your Lord, your God. True", when the "I am" is not uttered at all. Hence, he probably received the nickname. As for the family name Prishkolnik, which means - by the synagogue, or by the school. In our case, my grandfather's house was indeed located near the same ancient synagogue that, according to legend, existed since the time of the Polish king Stephen Bathory, for whom that the town served as his fortress and was even named after him. Therefore, it can be assumed that during the middle of the 15th century, the Jews who came from Eastern Crimea also settled there, that is, to the extent that our family settled with the founding of the town and the ancestors of this family, like other families with Slavic surnames or without surnames at all, came in the migration of the Jews from Eastern Russia, Crimea to the West, this nickname - the surname - Pri-Skolnik, probably stuck to the family since its house was in the vicinity of synagogues.

For generations, this family continued to live on the same lot near the synagogues, and this despite the vicissitudes of time and rule, and despite the many fires that have consumed the house many times, it was rebuilt in the same place.

In most of the towns and cities of Volyn near Stepan there were Prishkolnik families, and according to information that passed by word of mouth in the family, all of them originated from Stepan, but over the years they changed their residences in their search of sources of livelihood. Indeed, my father had cousins, one in the city of Rivne - David Prishkolnik, in Sarny - Israel Prishkolnik and his sons: Aryeh and Yaakov Prishkolnik, of blessed memory, and their descendants, some of whom are still alive, and they are: Yeshayahu Prishkolnik who lives with a family in Tel Aviv, Yechiel Prishkolnik and his family who live in Petach Tikva, Yeshayahu Prishkolnik with his family in Givatayim, Yaakov Prishkolnik in Kibbutz Ashdot Ya'akov, Berel Prishkolnik with his family in France, and his daughter named Neita of the Prishkolnik family lives in Tel Aviv. In Luninets also lived one member of the Prishkolnik family from Sarny named Shamai Prishkolnik. Also lived in Sarny my father's brother, Gedalyahu Prishkolnik and his family members. In the town of Matchilik, lived my father's sister Reizel from the Prishkolnik family, with her family. There were also members of the Prishkolnik family in Zdolbuniv.

[Page 73]

The example of the branching out and migration of my family members from Stepan is more evidence of the roots of Judaism in Volyn.

The assumption is that until the time of my father's grandfather, Rabbi Yeshayahu Prishkolnik, the entire family lived in Stepan, and since then the branching and dispersal of the family's descendants in the towns and cities of Volyn began. And as evidence of this, in every family from the Prishkolnik family in Volyn, there is a member in the name of Yeshayahu, after the same grandfather.

Although I was uprooted from my family, my home and my town when I was only 14 years old, I am filled with memories of my father's house, my grandfather, my uncle, my friends and all the people of my town. I remember that we lived in an apartment at grandfather's house. The two-room apartment was at the back of the house and faced the direction of a large barn. There was also a garden which was cared for in the spring and summer and neglected in the fall and long winter.

Next to our garden was a neighbor's orchard, with fruit trees, apples and juicy pears, some of which bordered our garden fence (the garden belonged to our neighbor Itzik Weitznodel the Butcher). The garden was cultivated by our late step-grandmother Sarah (her origin was from one of the surrounding villages, I think Zhelezna). She was knowledgeable in all the methods of agricultural cultivation and with the help of her gentile assistants she would hoe, rake, sow, uproot the weeds and water only sometimes in the summer, because it usually rained in our area during the summer season.

For me it was a special experience to work in the garden together with my grandmother, who was very kind to me and willingly and patiently explained to me the nature of the work, the types of growth, and the treatment methods. More than once I damaged the garden while "studying", by uprooting some plant instead of a wild grass, but after a slight reprimand, my grandmother would forgive me.

I remember that my grandmother used to go out to work in the garden in the early morning hours and return at sunset. During this period, my grandfather was not among the well to do breadwinners, so my grandmother helped through the agricultural produce that she used to grow: garlic, onions, tomatoes, cucumbers, beets, horseradish, etc. As for me, I was always happy to join her, and I enjoyed her company very much when she worked in the garden and I tried to help her as best I could.

I had a brother who was three years older than me, Shaul of blessed memory, and a sister who was three years younger than me, Sesil (who now lives with me in Israel). My father, Yoel of blessed memory, was the youngest son from my grandfather's first wife (grandmother Sesil, who died, as it was told to me, at the time of my father's birth). My father had brothers and sisters, these are my uncle and aunts: Yankel Prishkolnik the chazan, who lived in a house next to ours on Shkolna Street, next to the synagogue. Aunt Raizel of blessed memory, who lived in a nearby town and would rarely visit Stepan. Uncle Gedaliah of blessed memory, who lived in Sarny and sometimes visited Stepan. I also remember one or two visits together with my father to their home. They were very pleasant hosts, especially his wife,

[Page 74]

aunt Rachel. My uncle was a sewing machine dealer. He was not rich but made a decent living and had three children: Hannah, Yeshayahu (who was very gifted) and Haya. I also had three aunts from my step-grandmother, who actually raised my orphaned father. The firstborn daughter, Adele, who was very kind, was like one of the family in our house and was very loved by my father and mother, and Teibel of blessed memory. We, the children, loved her and were very attached to her, as if she were our real sister. The family ties with the sisters Genia and Miriam, the little sister, were also very close and we were connected to them.

The livelihood of my mother and father, of blessed memory

I remember my father as being of medium height and thin. He was busy from early morning to late evening in his shop, a tobacco and cigarette shop and alcohol in concession. I remember my mother always went to the shop right after she sent us to school to help my father, and she was not always at home when we returned from school. She was still in the shop, helping my father. As far as I remember, the livelihood was relatively not bad, but my parents invested many efforts and nerves and took many risks for earning a living and the take care of the household.

I particularly remember the days of the market on Wednesday, when the town was filled with gentiles from all the surrounding villages, who concentrated in the market square and the nearby streets. As a curious boy, I liked to squeeze in and look at the deals being made in the market: the sale of the produce of the villagers and the purchase of products from local peddlers, and the more professional ones who came from nearby towns or cities to offer their goods on market day. I loved listening to the peddlers' ridiculous statements and the many pranks that were often played on the rural gentiles, most of whom were innocent and ignorant. Our store was also very crowded, especially on market days, because tobacco and cigarettes were an accepted and extremely popular commodity among gentiles of the surrounding area. On market days, my mother had to help my father in the shop from morning to evening. More than once, when I was in the store in the afternoon, I noticed that my father was liked by the many gentile buyers who visited the store. Most of them called him by the name Suchoi (dry) meaning: thin. They sometimes consulted with my father about contacting the authorities and submitting requests. My father was very proficient in the procedures of applications to the authorities and in formulating requests in the Polish language. I remember that my mother also used to find a common language with the people in the store and especially with gentile women, whether they were smokers or came to buy tobacco and cigarettes for their husbands. Most of the time my mother would advise on health, hygiene and household issues. And of course, without any payment, but out of a good intention to help others regardless of class or nationality.

My mother is from a town near Stepan - Berezne. My mother's origin is from the extensive and respectable Zuckerman family in this town. None of my mother's immediate family survived, except for cousins, the children of my mother's brother, Ephraim Zuckerman of blessed memory, who live in the USA.

[Page 75]

The way of life at my parents' house

My mother showed a very fair attitude to the two gentile housemaids – one in the role of nanny, who spoke Yiddish fluently as she stayed in our house more than in her own, and a second one whose role was to pump water, do the laundry and clean the house. The relationships were excellent, the gentile women would treat my mother with complete trust, would leave their savings in her hands, consult with her, and my mother would treat them as if they were an integral part of our family. My mother used to give charity to the needy and poor, and there was no lack of such in our town. I often saw her sneaking out of the house in the evening, especially on Thursdays, carrying a bowl of wheat flour and various supplies to give to the needy who lived in the neighborhood. In a later period, after 1939, we purchased a cow, and then my mother would give milk and its products to the needy by bringing it to their homes personally and secretly. When I asked her many times why she does this in secret, I was answered that giving charity in secret is the most real help, without talking about it and publicized it, and thus insults and shame are avoided from those in need.

My parents used to host a "guest" every Friday, in most cases - a beggar, one of those who occasionally came to the town and stayed in it for the Shabbat. Father would invite him when he left the synagogue and he would sit at the table with us and have the Shabbat dinner with us. Such an act was a source of pleasure for my parents and us, the children.

The figure of my grandfather of blessed memory

The image of my grandfather, Ben-Zion Prishkolnik, or "Benzigot", as he was called, is well remembered. An old Jew, bent over, with a short beard, often walked with a cane for support. From the time I remember, he owned a small butcher shop selling non-kosher meat - only to gentiles, of course. His business was not very flourishing, and he would be assisted by his daughters in running the store. A unique phenomenon that I remember is that my grandfather had many debts owed to him by his gentile buyers who were landowners, and his desk drawer was crammed with notes, on which the debts were written, but very few would repay him their debts. When one of the landowners accumulated a large debt, my grandfather would rent a wagon or sleigh with horses (and I would often join their journeys) and travel to the landowner's farm to receive what he deserved. As payment for a debt, he would often receive sacks of grain, flour, potatoes, onions, garlic, and the like. He would bring the goods home and store them in the basement - for home consumption in the winter.

One of his famous habits was drinking a lot of tea. After the water boiled, they poured five or six cups of strong tea and arranged them in a row in front of him, the tea was, of course, unsweetened. My grandfather would sip cup after cup while sucking a hard sugar cube and smoking a cigarette at the same time, which would give him a lot of pleasure. This phenomenon was repeated

[Page 76]

every evening. I remember my grandfather's walks on Shabbats after lunchtime, when he used to walk around the house and the nearby garden, with his hands clasped behind his back, surveying his property and enjoying it. At lunchtime my grandfather used to sip some alcohol before the meal, but moderately and with limits, only for the purpose of Kiddush and to delight the soul.

My grandfather had a sense of humor and often used to joke and tease the gentiles passing by or visiting his shop. Being a believing and God-fearing Jew, but not a fanatic, he used to visit the synagogue near our house on weekdays, Shabbats and holidays. I was happy to join him from time to time, especially on winter evenings, to sit by the hot stove in the Beit Midrash. On Shabbat evening, I would willingly accompany him to the third meal, and enjoy by the cheerfulness of sitting together, and by the pleasure that the meal brought to most of those present. Some of them probably because they were hungry and that they had a good opportunity to break the hunger by eating a piece of challah with salted fish, and some of them for no specific reason. Sometimes, I would also accompany my grandfather to the Selichot prayers at night or early in the morning (with my parents' permission, of course) with great reverence but also in fear of demons and wandering souls.

The Image of my brother Sheilyk -Shaul of blessed memory

From my father's house I remember my brother Shaul- Sheilyk, who was three years older than me and studied at the "Tarbut" school. He was thin and somewhat indecisive, but kindhearted. He learned to play the violin by a Jew named Moshe der Klezmer, who came to our house and taught him. I was very jealous of his great ability and success in playing and singing. I especially remember the melody "Der yald is meer mekane". I would try to imitate the playing by rubbing stick against stick or by drumming, and I remember how they used to make jokes about me because my hearing was not developed enough. But I was better than him in running, swimming and all kinds of mischievous acts.

My years as a student – youngster

As for myself, I was a student at the "Tarbut" school until the 5th grade and I mastered the Hebrew language well. The spoken language was of course Yiddish. I was an active member of the Hebrew Speakers Association and even though we lacked daily useful words, we kept a vow, and at certain times we only spoke Hebrew. I was considered a good student and had a lot of free time for games. I had many friends and in most cases I was the head of the gang or the deputy. We used to organize into a group to fight and defend ourselves against the gentile children in the streets near us.

[Page 77]

Description of my living environment

My home was near the synagogues and the square in front of them, as well as near the houses of the rabbis and the shochets - the center of ethnic and community-religious activity of the Jews of the town and the surrounding area. Both the poorhouse and the bathhouse were nearby. As is well known, most of the chuppahs (marriage ceremonies) were held in our town in the square of the synagogue, and the funerals were also held by the synagogues. Most of the beggars of the town and its guests were concentrated near the synagogues and in the nearby poorhouse. Most of the Jews, when they came to slaughter their poultry, would pass by the street of the synagogues, as the three shochets of the town lived nearby: the shochet Levi of blessed memory- the chazan, the shochet Yoel of blessed memory and the shochet Herschel of blessed memory, who was also Baal Kore. When they wanted to turn to one of the town's dayanim for a ruling, consultation, divorce or any other reason, they would pass by the synagogue street, because the two rabbis - Rabbi Benzion Volinsky of blessed memory and Rabbi Pinchas Gorinstein of blessed memory, lived near the synagogues. In short, I grew up and lived in the heart of the vibrant life of the town. I did not miss any wedding or funeral; in any case of a ruling, I would stay near the courthouse and out of curiosity swallow any information about the outcome. And so, I was well versed in all the practical processes of chuppah arrangements, funeral and burial, circumcision, Torah law and divorce, ritual immersion in the mikveh and bathing in the bathhouse, poorhouse procedures, shechita and more.

View of the synagogue street after the great fire in 1925

[Page 78]

In the synagogue square, farewells were also held for immigrants who went to America, and I particularly remember a case of a mass farewell for a couple from the Beitar movement, who decided to immigrate to Israel -Rozka Bebchuk and Tzelia Shpritz (both of them live in Israel today). I also remember parades of organized Zionist youth in their costumes.

Beitar headquarters in Stepan – 5682

In Stepan, most of the youth were organized in "Beitar" and the rest in "Hashomer HaTzair|, "HaPoel HaMizrachi". Older adults also belonged to the Zionist movements.

I enjoyed all the Zionist organizations in the town and from time to time I would change costumes and visit the nests of "Beitar", "Hashomer HaTsair", participate in entertainment evenings, dances and trips to the wonderful pine forests around Stepan. On days off, on Shabbats and holidays, we would go out into the deep of the forests near the town, equipped with food and also with sticks for self-defense against the attacks of gentiles. In addition, I was an enthusiastic donor to the Jewish National Fund within the framework of the "Tarbut" school. My classmates and I used to compete on the filling of the stamp notebooks with the plants and fruits of the land that we used to buy and the proceeds from selling the notebooks would be a donation to the Jewish National Fund.

When we used to go out into the woods, we would reach a certain place and wave a national flag there - that we created. There we would set up in a camp and train in drilling exercises, with rifle sticks, like the senior Beitar members in our town. We spent many hours in watching drilling exercises, marches and self-defensive training and beating with sticks by Beitar seniors.

[Page 79]

"Jabotinsky" group, first rank in Stepan, 5682

On Lag BaOmer, we would go out, of course with our parents' permission, equipped with tasteful food, such as colored hard-boiled eggs and various foods that were accepted at that time, on Shavuot eve we would go far across the river to pick a variety of green rush (in foreign language "Lafcches") to decorate the house for the holiday. This involved the risk of attacks and beatings by the gentiles, but this did not prevent us from repeating this process every year. As for the mature youth, they were mostly organized in the "Hashomer Hatzair" and "Beitar" movements, the Zionist movements, as well as considerable activity in sporting events of volleyball and sometimes also football, swimming and river boating. From time to time there were sports competitions between the teams and sometimes also competitions between the volleyball teams of the Poles and the Jews. I remember that in most cases our young people would defeat the Poles and this would upset them to the point of gnashing of teeth, cursing and calling the Jews by derogatory names. Sometimes this would cause real fights, and in any such case, the Poles would take a serious beating, because the entire Jewish youth would unite. We, the children, enjoyed watching them hit and defend themselves, we admired them and this encouraged us to unite and defend ourselves in case of attacks or teasing from the gentiles. In case of a fight in one of the corners of the town, the news would be passed by word of mouth very quickly and we, the children, would run after the adults, equipped with the defensive sticks.

[Page 80]

Stepan's river and the bridge over it

Stepan's river, the Horyn, was one of the important branches of the Pripyat River. The river flowed from the east of the town at the foot of a hill on top of which the town of Stepan was located. The waters of the river were quiet and flowed calmly, except for the place by the wall, where the flow was extremely strong. From stories I learned that in the past a flour mill was built in this place that was powered by the current of water. Remains of thick wooden pegs were still stuck in the same place at the bottom of the river. In the spring time when the snow and ice melted, the river would overflow its banks and flood extensive pastures (Lonka) across the river. This flood usually lasted until the beginning of summer and then the water level of the river decreased and the river would return to its normal course. The pastures would be uncovered again, except for a number of water lakes that would dry up only by the end of the summer. Travel to the town from the east was over a solid wooden bridge, which was about a kilometer long. The bridge was built of wood, including its thick foundation pillars, and all its beams and sides - all of these were connected by long screws and iron hoops. The bridge towered above the river at a height of over ten meters. As boys we often wondered how the wooden bridge was able to carry all the load of the carts passing over it and sometimes even individual cars. When the Red Army entered in 1939, even tanks passed over the bridge and it held on. We were always afraid that the bridge would collapse and then we would be cut off from the world and especially from the lovely pine forests, to where we would escape in the hot summer days and spend there on vacations and Shabbats.

Out of curiosity, we would go down under the bridge and climb on top of its pillars and go along and across it and check every peg and plank for rotting and cracks, and we checked every connection and every screw to make sure they were tightly closed. After such a tour, we would return home satisfied, that the bridge was indeed strong and that the authorities had really taken care of it, and would have fastened the screws and smeared its pillars with tar to protect the wood from the summer heat and winter humidity. The bridge was a cause for a special concern to all the townspeople and the authorities at the beginning of spring, when the snow and the thick ice that covered the river in the winter melted. Large icebergs were shaking the thick foundation pillars of the bridge and it seemed that the entire bridge would be swept away with the huge surges of the flow and the floating blocks of ice. The authorities together with the volunteer fire brigade, as well as other volunteer citizens, would break up the blocks of ice approaching the bridge using huge wooden beams that were sharp at the ends. After the danger passed, the townspeople would breathe a sigh of relief and the authorities would inspect, strengthen and fix what was required to ensure the firm standing of the bridge for the future.

I remember is that in 1939, when the Polish army retreated from the Russian border, they made all the preparations to burn the bridge by laying dry straw along its entire length, but in their panic, or for any other reason, they did not burn it. Before the retreat of the Poles, the Russians even threw a number of

[Page 81]

bombs into the river near the bridge, but the bridge was not damaged and this allowed them to enter the town easily with their weapons and heavy vehicles, including the tanks. When the Soviets retreated in 1941, they made sure to blow it up and burn it almost entirely and that was probably in order to prevent the Germans from catching them during their panicked retreat. The Germans built a temporary bridge, taking advantage of the forced labor of the town's Jews and based on some of the foundations and the remaining parts of the old bridge.

The view of the bridge over the Horyn River in Stepan

The river was destined for important tasks in the life of the town. Being rich in fish, it provided the Jews of the town with delicious fish, such as carp, a great variety of small fish to be eaten in weekdays and large fish such as wolf fish for Shabbat. And of course, those fish were caught by gentile fishermen who lived along the river and this was their livelihood. They fished with rods and small nets and in seasons when the catch was plentiful and the fish appeared in large concentrations, the fishermen would spread out a long trawl net and sink it to the bottom of the river. After a night, or sometimes after several days, they would go out in light rowboats, surround the trawl net from all sides and pull it out of the river with all the fish. The fish would be marketed to the Jews of the town through the Jewish "fishermen". I remember Reb Yerachmiel the "fisherman", who used to provide the Jews of the town with the best fish for Shabbat and holidays. Among the Jewish boys and young men there were also amateurs who engaged in fishing with fishing rods and sailed canoes and fishing boats as sport and pleasure (kikim).

The townspeople used to bathe in the river during the summer days. It was not customary to bathe in swimwear. Most of the young men would slip into the river naked and swim for their pleasure, some of them wore some kind of special underwear that resembled bathing suits. Those who were ashamed would move away to remote corners along the river and slip naked into the river from among the thick willow (horva) trees on the river's banks.

The gentile women enjoyed bleaching linen fabrics day and night by soaking them in the river for a long time, laying the cloth on the banks of the river to dry in the sun and rewetting in the river. Women and girls, residents of the town, would go down to launder in the waters of the river.

[Page 82]

In winter we used to skate on the thick ice that covered the surface of the river. We used to concentrate in special plots from which the snow was cleared and they were prepared for skating. The river water was pumped for drinking both in summer and winter. In the winter they would make holes in the ice (polonka). At the end of the winter, the Stepan community, with the help of hired gentiles, used to collect blocks of ice from the frozen river waters and store them in a deep pit on a nearby river downstream, near the house of the late Levi the "Smoller". The pit was covered with a low small roof with multiple layers of straw to preserve the ice during the summer and preventing its melting. The ice was used for healing needs of the entire community and even to the gentiles of the town.

The bathhouse

Down the river, near the street of the synagogues, was the bathhouse, which took its water from the river, and the river received the sewage water of the bathhouse. The bathhouse was a rather shabby and neglected structure in both its exterior and interior appearance. Its exterior walls were made of red burnt limestone and the roof was made of dilapidated rusted tin. It contained a system of pipes and boilers, a room with a heating stove that was fired by wood, a room with taps for cold and hot water, mikveh and a nearby room with high stairs and a sweating room (a shvitz baad). On Thursdays and Fridays, the Jews of the town, especially the old people, accompanied by their sons and grandchildren, used to dip in the mikveh, bathe in the bathhouse and grab "a shvitz baad". We, the boys, used to compete who would manage to last and reach the highest level of "a shvitz baad". To ease breathing and refresh ourselves, we used to splash cold water with a special wooden bucket and beat with a special twig broom. As far as I remember, the bathhouse was provided free of charge, and it was maintained by the entire community, Reb Herschel Der Baader operated it with the help of his family members, probably for a fee from the community.

"Jewish folk musicians"

The Klenikes family branch of Stepan composed the well-known orchestra group: Reb Pleiah with the bass, Moshe with the fiddle - the violinist, Herschel with the violin or the trumpet and there were also drummers among them. They would entertain the guests with their Jewish tunes at Jewish weddings and were also invited to gentile weddings. The chuppahs were usually arranged under a tarpaulin in the synagogues square, accompanied by most of the townspeople and of course the orchestra. Some of the Jewish folk musicians served also as violin and trumpet teachers for the youth of those who had the financial means. At the end of the chuppah, a generous feast was usually held at the home of the bride's parents, to which most of the townspeople were invited and, of course, all the poor of the town were given the opportunity to enjoy generous hospitality and a special feast for the poor.

[Page 83]

The market – the fare

The selling of the produce by the villagers and purchase from the peddlers, grocers and artisans was carried out in the market. There were no fixed prices for the agricultural produce and the prices were set according to the demand at the same fare. If the demand was high, they would raise their produce prices immediately and if the demand was weakening, they would settle for discounted prices. Also, the power of persuasion was of great value and a continuous and frequent buyer, who acquired the trust of the villager, would receive his produce at a price that was sometimes lower than that accepted in the market. Many of the rural and suburban villagers of the town had reliable persons among Stepan's Jewish merchants and craftsmen and these were faithful to their Jewish friends, advised them in times of need and poured out their hearts to them. But in the disaster that befell Stepan's Jews, these acquaintances were estranged from their Jewish friends, abused the trust placed in them and in most cases, betrayed their Jewish friends. Most of them were looking forward to the moment when they could inherit the property of the Jews who were eliminated.

**The view of the market in the market square in Stepan.
In the background is the Pravoslav church**

There was a secret language between the shopkeepers so that the gentiles or the Polish officers would not understand - words of clues in the holy language: "This gentile understands everything", and the meaning is that he understands Yiddish. And indeed, there were among them several who understood and even spoke Yiddish, from their continuous service with the Jews. "Arlakhans" means "he steals". One hundred and six or five hundred zlotys means refusal to give a discount. "Agony" means negative. "A Shreiers" (narrators) - the peddlers and haberdasher from outside the town - of Galician or Warsaw origin - would stand in front of their elevated stand wearing leather jackets and would announce loudly in the Polish language mixed with Ukrainian. Their speech was firm and fast and they would praise their goods and explain their use. The price was standard and equal to everyone, everything of one gold coin. They would fill the villager's cap with all kinds of cheap haberdashery stuff, miracle cures for all kinds of ailments. The visitors of the fairs were gypsies, fortune-tellers, habitual gamblers, and fortune-tellers. The innocent villagers would fall into the trap by participating in the games of fate and lose all the money

[Page 84]

they received from the sale of the produce. The villagers would return to their homes drunk. The fairs were in part an important source of income for the merchants and artisans of the town because it was a day with a decent income.

A wedding

A wedding was not only the matter of the two families, but almost the whole town shared in the joy. In rare cases there was "a stila chuppah" - marriage of a widower or marriage when one of the parties was not satisfied with the match.

The clothes of the town's Jews

The elders of the community and its dignitaries wore traditional clothes, the men usually wore dark fabric and woolen pants, gray kapote for the weekdays and dark and bright-shiny kapote for holidays and Shabbat.

Most of the town's Jews wore unusual headdresses which were adapted to the different periods of the year. The women wore long dresses, usually with headscarves. The women's holiday clothes were, of course, different from the everyday clothes, being more multicolored and the types of fabrics were more expensive.

The middle generation and young people wore more modern clothes than the fashion accepted at that time in the cities and towns of Poland. And indeed, there were a selection of tailors and seamstresses in Stepan who were very professional and sewed according to journals accepted at the time. Those with the financial means could afford themselves to sew suits and dresses from fine pieces of wool that could be purchased in the fabric shops in the town. At the same time, it was possible to find a selection of fashionable shoes in the shops in the town as well.

Almost every family took care arranging holiday clothes and new shoes for his family members and children, especially before the holiday, as well as a suitable coat for the winter days.

Compared to the clothing of most of the Jews of the town, the villagers of the town and the surrounding area were dressed as follows: the villager wore a linen shirt and pants, roughly sewn, which were prepared by his wife. The Jewish and the gentile women wore dresses and cotton shirts with colorful embroidery, a work of art. The shoes were worn only in winter. In the summer they walked barefoot, in the winter they wrapped their legs in diapers and wore pastales - sandals made of strips of tree bark and attached to the feet with strong leather laces dipped in tar to make them soft and flexible. In the summer days they wore various round hats with a glittering lacquer-coated forehead or casket hats

[Page 85]

from a coarse cloth. In the winter, they wore warm sheepskin hats with extra fur on the sides to cover the ears and the nape of the neck, and there were also cylindrical hats made of sheep's wool, known in the language of the gentiles as "kutzme". The men wore vests and pants with cotton linings and long coats lined with sheep's fur and they wore boots larger than the size of the feet, because they wrapped bags called "onices" and straw around the feet in order to protect the feet from the intense cold.

The clocks were really expensive and many guessed the time according to the position of the sun. Most homes had wall clocks built into cabinets. There were only a few wristwatches. The wealthy and the dignitaries had pocket watches that were given as a wedding gift and were stuck in the front pocket on a long chain dangling from the pocket. The women often wore earrings, some women wore gold watches on a gold chain. Most of the women had jewels that were kept guarded and in times of need they were secretly used as collateral along with gold coins in the value of five rubles.

Foods and hygiene practices

The water was supplied from wells with each house collecting it in wooden barrels or in a tin for regular consumption. To fill the barrels, they would be assisted by the gentile women who would carry the water buckets on their shoulders in yoke (Koromyslo). The houses had cooking stoves, baking ovens and heating ovens, all of them were built of mud bricks or granite stone with great skill. In a small house the tenants were content with only one oven, while in the houses of large families there were two or three ovens. Most of the housewives would bake bread once a week, usually on Sunday. They kneaded the dough with clenched hands inside the special bowl for this and then created the shape, put the dough on a board covered with a thin layer of bran and sprinkle cumin or poppy on the surface of the bread. The bread was usually enough for a week.

On Fridays, they usually baked challahs and cakes for Shabbat. As early as late at Thursday night, they would turn on the fire in the baking oven so that it would heat up to the required level and they would prepare challahs, cakes, bagels and other types of pastry, including delicious pita bread called papalikes, which are very popular among the children. On Fridays, the children would take hot paplik or hot fritters, dip them in milk and eat with a hearty appetite. The houses were lit with candles and oil lamps and a large part of the Jewish houses were lit with electricity supplied from the power station of the Tachor family.

There were dairy foods, ladishkes, made with cream that they used to fill on Tuesday or Wednesday and then use them for the third meal. There was a creamy and delicious layer on top and leben (sour milk) on the bottom. The cream was spread on the challah and the dish remained the

[Page 86]

"Zoyer Milch". The poor would enjoy thick bread on the crust of which fresh and spicy garlic would be spread. The smell of garlic wafted from afar but did not bother anyone. Salted fish was considered a delicacy and especially with the addition of potatoes boiled in their skins.

For lunch there was soup with hirsh (millet) - grits with bones - or beetroot and cabbage borscht. For Shabbat there were fish and meat dishes also for the poor, challah and cakes. For Friday noon there was Russell-Fleisch - cooked meat with beans and garlic dipped in challah.

Shabbat and holiday meals: fish, chopped liver, tsibeles mit eyer und shmaltz as starters, followed by cholent containing potatoes and grits called kotie, kishke filled with flour and grits, flakes of meat and fat as well as chicken and beef, noodle pies with raisins and tzimmes of spiced carrot and plum and cherry compote as a dessert.

Both the poor and the rich were strict about the festive meals on Shabbats and holidays. The difference was that the quality of the types of meat or the drinks and fruits were different.

The preparations for the holiday

Before Passover special preparations in the town were noticeable. Immediately after Purim, the parents made sure to buy new shoes and, in many cases, new suits were even ordered for Pesach and at the very least new hats. Near the holidays, the Pesach dishes were brought down from the attic, washed in boiling water and placed in clean cupboards lined with shiny new papers. In front of every house there was dish immersion – every housewife made sure to heat stones in front of her house and to properly immerse her dishes in the boiling water in preparation for Pesach. The act of preparing the matzah and baking it was a special operation. Each family took care in advance to purchase fine wheat for themselves and under the supervision of family members, it was taken to one of the flour mills that were kosher especially for Pesach. This sometimes involved standing in line for a long time, and family members often spent half a day to a day supervising and personally assisting in kneading the dough and preparing the matzah using the primitive machines, baking them in an oven heated by burning wood. The matzahs were stored in a special box for this purpose, and in any case, the quantities that were prepared were sufficient for use for a long period even after Pesach, in order to ensure a sufficient supply for the holiday. In the winter, many housewives made sure to prepare goose fat with griben kosher for Pesach, as well as a homemade wine made from raisins for the holiday. Very often, stocks of fine potatoes, beets, eggs, meat, poultry and everything needed for the holiday was prepared ahead.

[Page 87]

Public activity and aid institutions

It is clear that as part of the preparations for the holiday, the town's residents who were with means remembered the poor and donated to Kamcha Depascha Factories, helped the needy as they did before the other holidays by providing loans from the Gmilut Chassadim Fund, or by signing them on "giving charity in secret" deeds. There were always righteous women who, at their initiative, would go from house to house and collect on Shabbat evenings challahs for the needy, clothes for the winter, charity for the dowry of a bride, donations for preparing firewood for the winter. In severe winters, the youth would spontaneously organize themselves and pass between the town's houses with a horse-drawn cart to collect firewood from those who had a stock of firewood and deliver it to the needy. As was customary in every town, there was a Chevra Kadisha in our town as well - those who were engaged in this work considered it as a great honor. The committee and the public activists did their work voluntarily, of course, except for the gravedigger who performed his work with a small fee that was barely enough to support his family. Yosel the gravedigger, who also perished in the massacre is well remembered.

The center of community life and spiritual activity of Stepan's Judaism was concentrated on "Shkolna" Street, the synagogues street. In this street, as the name explains, the synagogues were concentrated. On this street, near the synagogue, lived the rabbis of the town, the dayanim, the shochets, the "Tarbut" school. Here they held celebrations, chuppahs, funerals, processions and often even debates between political parties. In this vicinity were the bathhouse, the poorhouse and the poultry slaughterhouse. In the evenings of the Days of Awe, an atmosphere of reverence and anxiety prevailed in the town. Most of the town's Jews, who were dressed festively, came to the synagogues from all parts of the city with their children accompanying them. The surrounding rural Jews stood out accompanied by their boys who also came to pray and spend the Days of Awe with their relatives or friends in the town. They were a little different in their dress and customs and for some reason were considered inferior "Dorfs - Jungen". During the Days of Awe were seen in the synagogues also Jews who would otherwise have avoided coming to it. In the ladies' section there were women, most of them wearing foreign wigs, who were praying without many of them even understanding what the prayer meant. Among them were women who were more knowledgeable about the prayers in the original language and in Ivry Teitsch (Yiddish written in Hebrew letters) and, in advance, these women would inform about an important prayer and then the women would bitterly cry and utter heartbreaking sighs.

On the eve of Yom Kippur, the act of collecting donations in bowls began. The activities of the communal public institutions in the town were based on volunteering, except for the Shamash and the gravedigger, who would receive a small fee from the public fund for their activities. The collection of funds for public institutions on the eve of Yom Kippur was made by donations using the bowl method. Every Jew paid his debt to the public and its institutions. Large bowls would be displayed on a long table in the polish before entering the prayer halls. Each bowl was marked in handwriting, clearly stating its purpose. Next to each bowl sat the gabbaim or the officials on behalf of the institution that the bowl belonged to. Everyone was obliged to contribute according to their ability to the big bowl, that belonged to the gabbai of the synagogue. The funds that were collected were used

[Page 88]

to cover the expenses of maintaining the synagogues, for cleaning, furniture, repairs, heating, and more. After the obligatory main donation, the donors went through the rest of the bowls and donated according to their ability. The purposes of the rest of the bowls were varied: mikveh, gmilut chassadim, maintaining the poorhouse, and there was also a bowl for the Jewish National Fund.

Special buildings in the town

I remember two churches close to the center of the the town and one or two more outside the town - in the suburbs. The external shape of the churches was a stone structure rising to the height, followed by a tin dome painted green, the bases of the domes were wide and pointed at the top, a cross made of gold was fixed at the top of the dome. Inside the domes were the bell chambers where heavy copper bells hang. The bells were used to call the crowd of believers on holidays, and to alert during fires or any disasters. On the roads, there were crosses with icons - pictures of Jesus and Maria that were used by the crowd of believers to kneel and pray on their way to or from the town.

There was also a Catholic church that resembled the Pravoslav church, except for the color of the dome, which was reddish brown, and besides being more conical and sharper. The sound of its bells was less loud. Smells of perfumes emanated from the churches and they were surrounded by grass and ornamental trees for the most part. There was also a Ukrainian cultural house - the Prosvita, where the Ukrainian intelligentsia used to meet for cultural activities. There were rumors that there were anti-Semitic and nationalist incitements there. At both ends of the town there were also the two primary schools built of burnt stone, which had large courtyards. Next to the city council was a nice fire station, opposite to it was the courthouse and on the same street was the police station with a detention room. There were two hotels in the town owned by Jews. The town had three flour mills powered by steam engines and driven by wood, all owned by Jews. One of the mills was also used as a power station that barely provided light to most of the town's houses that were connected to the electricity grid.

[Page 89]

What Was in the Past and No Longer Exists

Zeev Gorinstein

Translated by Mira Eckhaus
Edited by Daniel Shimshak

The late Moshe Stern - the head   of Hashomer Hatzair in the town

Before I write a few words about my town Stepan, I would like to commune with all the beloved and dear Jews of Stephen, who were tortured, massacred and led to slaughter and that their ashes were scattered in all the surrounding fields.

But I ask myself, where should I go? Is there a grave, is there a cemetery where I can pour my heart in front of them?

Yitgadlu v'yitkadshu our teachers and rabbis, our brothers and sisters, the children, the members of the Stepan's community, who were massacred and slaughtered by the damn Nazis and their helpers.

The memory of our dead will always be with us, may their memory be blessed!

Life in the town

The town of Stepan was a town like the other towns in the Volyn region. Stefan was located on the banks of a wide river called Horyn, in which we, the children of the town, used to bathe in the clear waters during the summer days and during the winter days we skated on the ice that was on it.

Most of the town's Jews were merchants, shopkeepers, craftsmen and a few were engaged in free professions. There were Zionist movements to which most of the youth belonged, such as: Hashomer Hatzair, HeChalutz, Beitar.

Who does not remember the experiences in the nest of the youth movements, in the camps that were established on holidays or the events they made in the forest near the town? Inside the camp there were an iron discipline and a strong desire to fulfill every role as well as could be, there were various exercises, games, singing and dancing and at the end of the camp, there was a festive parade

[Page 90]

to the town. And only few were privileged to go to training and later to immigrate to the Land of Israel.

Members of the Hashomer Hatzair movement in Stepan

My town, Stepan, was a town where Torah, craft and trade were intertwined. For example, the synagogues and Batei Midrashot. And who does not remember the great and ancient synagogue, with the magnificent Holy Ark. The great synagogue served as a place of prayer for all the Jews of the town and the permanent cantor was Reb Levy the shochet who had the pleasant voice. Public meetings also took place in synagogue.

[Page 91]

The education in the town was divided between: the "cheder", Talmud Torah, "Tarbut" school and two Polish state schools called "Skola Pawshechna".

Most of the town's children started their first steps usually in the "cheder" and later moved to the other educational institutions that were in the town.

The history of my family

I was born in Stepan. My family was a large and rooted family in the town and its surroundings. My parents Naftali and Sosel Gorinstein (or as she was known by her name Naftali-Yankel Simes). The family numbered ten people: the parents, six brothers and two sisters, some of them left the town and father's house after their marriages. We stayed three brothers and one sister at father's house. Our brother Yassel, who was older than us, lived with his family in father's house - part of the spacious, two-story house, the side facing the yard, served as his home. We, the three youngest children (from his second marriage), my sister Feisel (Pnina), my brother Moshe and I (the youngest son) continued to live in our father's house and we were educated first in the "cheder" or "Talmud Torah" and finished our education at "Tarbut" school. My sister Feisel (Pnina) graduated from the Polish state school, and at home she received lessons in prayer and Hebrew. Also, lived in our town the older brother of my late father – the dayan Reb Pinchas Gorinstein, who was known by his nickname "Der yetzer tov". His three sons were shochets and each one was in a different city.

About a year after the death of our parents, in 1933, my sister Feisel immigrated to the Land of Israel, my brother became a teacher in a village near Stepan and I went to the large district of Rovno where I studied the profession of printing.

In 1937, my brother Moshe served in the cavalry in the Polish army and fought in the Polish-German war in 1939 against the Nazis in East Prussia, and thanks to his military skills and his good command of the cavalry, he was able, after many hardships, to return home when the Russian army was already in the western Ukraine region. Since our town was also in this region, it also fell

**The head of the family, Naftali Yaakov Gorinstein
(passed away in 1933 at the age of 85)**

[Page 92]

under the Russian occupation. My brother Moshe was appointed as the responsible for the cooperative in the town, and I continued the printing work in the town of Rovno.

However, with the outbreak of World War II and the "Blitz" occupation by the Nazi armies of Poland and everything that belonged to Poland until 1939 (Western Ukraine), our town of Stepan fell into the clutches of the Nazis and their helpers in 1941, after an interim rule by the Soviets, from 1939 to July 1941.

In 1942, the Jews of Stepan were massacred - men, women and children - by the Nazi murderers and their Ukrainian murderous helpers.

We, the remnants of the Stepan community, meet every year to reminisce the memory of our loved ones. Like threads hidden from the eye, we are drawn to a place called "Volyn Hall", we stand in groups and reminisce about the past, from the warm house, from the "cheder", from the school and the youth organizations. We remember the Shabbat nights and the holidays, we bring up the figures of our family members, our friends, our neighbors, who are no longer alive. In my mind I see my old father wrapped in a tallit, with the checkered crown at the top of the tallit; I see my mother sitting in the synagogue during the Days of Awe in the ladies' section, praying for the safety and welfare of her family.

The Organization of Stepan's Expatriates and the Surrounding Area in Israel

Dear member,

You are invited to participate

At a Memorial Assembly

In memory of the Keddoshim of the
Stepan's Community and the Surrounding Area
Who perished in the Holocaust

Which will take place on Tuesday the 12th of Elul 5736, September 7, 1976,
at 8 o'clock in the evening, in "Volyn Hall", in the hall named after A. Avtichai
of blessed memory, at Korazim St., Center for Crafts, Givatayim
    Buses:
No. 52 from the central station
No. 55 from north Tel Aviv, Sderot Ben Gurion by the sea
No. 57 from Ramat Gan

The Committee

The hall will be open from 6 o'clock in the evening for a friendly meeting.

[Page 93]

Sadness surrounds all those gathered at the sight of the few that are left. Where are our beautiful and honest in heart brothers and sisters. In vain will I look here for a neighbor in the yard, but everyone perished. Only one person from every street was left. Wrapped in grief and with bowed heads, we commune with the memory of our town's people.

It is impossible to describe in words the depth of the grief and sorrow in memory of all the dear families who were tortured with terrible cruelty in an impure land, who died with holiness and purity - the beloved and the pleasant, who were not separated in their life and in their death.

We will carry their memory with love in our aching hearts and will not forget them forever!

[Page 94]

The occupation of Stepan's Jews

Yeshayahu Pery

Translated by Mira Eckhaus
Edited by Daniel Shimshak

Those who were engaged with the sacred and religious matters and public figures

All those who were engaged with the sacred and religious matters and public works such as rabbis, dayanim, shochets, chazans, gabbaim, Torah scholars, melamedim and teachers received financial support from relatives and acquaintances from Stepan who immigrated to the USA, and maintained contact with the townspeople. As for the shochets, they engaged in their main occupation of slaughtering poultry and cattle, and would receive wages for their work. In addition, most of them served as chazans and the most prominent among them in this area was Rabbi Levi, who had a clear and pleasant voice and served as the permanent chazan of the great synagogue.

As for the dayanim, they received grants from the houseowners, especially on holiday eves and Shabbats. In addition to this, they would receive a commission fee when they served as poskim in matters that were raised by the housewives regarding kosher matters, as well as during Torah law, divorce, Levirate law and more. Each one contributed to them according to his ability.

As for the teachers and melamedim - they would receive tuition fee from the children's parents and in addition community support. The "Tarbut" school used to receive financial assistance from the center in Rivne.

Some were engaged in the management of charitable giving and the Chevra Kadisha, mostly on a voluntary basis, and this in addition to their regular occupation.

There were also people such as the gravedigger and the administrators of the poorhouse and the Shamesh, who were employed by the community and received their wages from the community board.

The houseowners - shopkeepers and merchants

This group includes houseowners, among them were shop owners, cattle and grain merchants, flour mill owners (and there was even one power station), oil press owners, peddlers, pharmacists, a dentist, a doctor, a dairy owner, fish sellers.

Among all these there was a small group of wealthier people, who lived in spacious houses and had nice furniture and more elegant clothing. The shopkeepers would stay in their stores from morning until evening and were often at the mercy of the policemen who were harassing

[Page 95]

them in imposing fines for cleanliness offenses and the like. Obviously, in order to stop the harassment of the police, the shop owners had to give them special grants from time to time such as to write off debts. Some of these police officers were called "di fiabka" (leech).

The craftsmen

The group consisted of the following professionals: carpenters, tailors, shoemakers, photographers, potters, butchers, builders, plasterers, painters, rope makers, tinsmiths, brush makers, glaziers, blacksmiths, cart wheel makers. These professionals served the entire Jewish and gentile population alike. Each of these was a craftsman in his area, and to the extent that there were similar professionals among the gentiles, they studied or were apprentices with the Jewish professionals, and their profession level was usually lower than that of the Jews.

Peddlers

There were traveling agents and peddlers who wandered between the surrounding villages during the week and sometimes for weeks selling their wares or buying pig's hair for brushes, rags, grain, cattle and more.

The Zionist activity in the town

Zionist activists began to get involved with Stepan's Jewish circles from 1920 onward. Some of the houseowners, shopkeepers and merchants,

"Jabotinsky" group rank A. in Stepan, 5693 [1933]

[Page 96]

devoted themselves to the matter of selling shekels for Zionist congresses, donations to the Jewish National Fund and financial support for the establishment and maintenance of the "Tarbut" school. The activity in this area would increase at holidays and festivals. During these times, they would gather at one or the other's house, partake of refreshments while donating themselves and collecting donations from others.

Beitar youth in Stepan

Later, at the end of the 1920s, Zionist youth movements arose: "Hashomer Hatzair", Beitar, which was the strongest and largest organization in the town, and "Hapoel HaMizrachi". These groups had branches and highly active leaders. In the branches of the organizations, youth meetings were held according to age groups, and there were talks, lectures, order drill training, stick fighting, trips in the woods and fields, sports, etc. There was also operation of collecting donations to the Jewish National Fund and the Tel Hai Fund. One of the famous leaders of Beitar was Yeshayahu Neiman, who died prematurely in the 1930s.

[Page 97]

Some of the first activists of "Hashomer Hatzair" in Stepan, year 5685 [1935]

The Zionist and public activity in the town was expressed in a series of articles during that period by our townsman Mr. Bezalel Shpritz and published in the Volyn newspapers at the time, which were translated into Hebrew and included in this book in the section "On the Way To Zion and Zion is On the Way".

[Page 98]

Stepan in Retrospect

by the late Yitzchak Weismann

Translated by Mira Eckhaus
Edited by Daniel Shimshak

It is still difficult to describe in the right colors the appearance of this town. Although ten years have passed since its destruction, the wound is still fresh and the blood no longer clots, and there is no one who will come to console us for the destruction. Therefore, from this point of view, we describe what can be described by a human being. (Written in the year 1952).

The town of Stepan was located on the banks of the "Horyn", a quiet and clear river, from which the fishermen who lived in houses along the shore made their living as they would sell the fish to the Jews. Some Jews ate fish every day, and others enjoyed the fish only on Shabbat. There were also families whose livelihood was from the fish: they would put them in large crates and take them to nearby Rivne.

In this river, the residents of Stepan used to bathe for pleasure during the hot summer days, stark-naked, without understanding why they should be ashamed at all.

The town was rich in simple Jews, without cunning, but with total devotion. Muscular Jews, strong like oaks, from whom even the gentiles were scared. Those who will be remembered favorably are: Mordechai Weismann (they called him Mottel Sarlis), Asher the blacksmith, Leib the shoemaker - each of whom is a chapter in himself. There were also in the town Jews who could use their strength for self-defense as well as defense on their Jewish brothers against the haters of Israel.

In addition to the simple people, there were also inspirational people: the Magid of Stepan who was famous and well-known in the vicinity, and left behind a dynasty of rabbis and a rabbinical throne with a "courtyard". The Chassidim of the last heir, Rabbi Baruchel Twersky, reached as far as Luboml as well as the well-known Chelm.

There were Chassidim who immigrated to America and even there they did not leave their Chassidism and during the Days of Awe, they rushed to the Rabbi's table to "grab" leftovers from the Rabbi's hands, to dance at his table during the meal, to lead the Rabbi to Tashlikh accompanied with religious songs and psalms. There was an ardent Chassid named Katriel. The whole town knew that if Katriel would come - joy and happiness will prevail in the town.

There were also two rabbis in the town, who were called dayanim, one by the name of Rabbi Pinchas Gorinstein (who was called "Der Yotzer Tov") and the other dayan, Rabbi ben Zion Volinsky, both of them were like two cats in one bag: what the one permitted, the other sometimes forbade, and vice versa.

[Page 99]

The old shochets, among whom there were also God-fearing people, such as Eli Moshe and old Rabbi Moshe, were also considered as intellectual people. The youngest of them were Levi the shochet and the chazan of the town, Rabbi Zvi Hochman, and Yoel the shochet. The shamashim of the synagogue were also considered as people who were engaged in the service of religion, among them were: Nachman the shamash, whom I remember with the tobacco box in his hand, Rabbi Yokel, a muscular Jew, who lived until the Holocaust and was over eighty years old. Until his last years, when he squeezed the hand of a young man, it was impossible to free the hand from his grip. He loved little children and every child he met shook his hand to say hello. The youngest among the shamashim was Novogrotsky Eli. In the morning and evening, he would serve in the holy work and in the afternoons, he would mend shoes.

Jewish youth against the background of typical houses in the town

[Page 100]

Memoirs
by Yeshayahu Shpritz

Translated by Mira Eckhaus
Edited by Daniel Shimshak

It is very difficult for me to come to terms with the idea that the town where I was born, Stepan, no longer exists. A short time after we arrived in Israel, we received the tragic news about the destruction of everything dear to us in our town of Stepan at the hands of the cruel Nazi enemy.

It is hard for me to forget the place of my birth and the place where I spent my childhood and youth together with my dear and loyal friends: Shachna Wachs, Mottel, Senderka Dem Dayans, Shmuel Zvi Kreizer, and Chaim Hochman. We showed initiative and ability and organized a youth club for us so that we could read newspapers, books and even listen to the radio, because there was no other entertainment in Stepan in those days.

There was a dear Jew in Stepan named Rabbi Hershel the watchmaker. His house served as a meeting place for us, and he was willing to listen carefully and was always ready to help. This Jew had three sons and three daughters. One of the boys, whose name was Lipmanke, survived and currently lives in Israel. The wife of the watchmaker was an outstanding hostess.

There were two expert photographers in town: Aharon Stoller, who was dark-skinned, thin, with a long, pale face and dark eyes. He loved his profession and had the talents of an excellent craftsman.

The second, Matityahu Mottel Weismann, was well-versed in his profession, was very energetic and punctual.

Each of these photographic artists had a specialized assistant. Aharon's assistant was my friend Shachna Wachs, who was one of the best guys in town. And I, the writer of these lines, worked as the assistant of Mottel.

**Aharon Stoller,
the expert photographer in
the town**

Although between the two artists, Aharon and Mottel, there was no idyllness, mainly due to competitiveness, and friendship prevailed between the two of us, the two interns.

[Page 101]

The Jews in our town took pictures only on special occasions: when they had to send a photo or portrait to relatives in America, or when they intended to immigrate to the Land of Israel. Of course, from time to time there were also photographs of schools and of Jewish youth groups organized as part of Zionist movements. But most of the work was photographing the Poles and Ukrainians, mainly on their holidays.

It is hard to believe that all those dear and beloved people were exterminated by the Nazis of Hitler and are no more alive. Much of their hard work and art, which were expressed in the pictures and portraits, must have remained to this day in the hands of our Ukrainian neighbors from Stepan, some of whom helped in the extermination of the town's Jews.

———————

[Page 102]

The Youth and My Family Activities in Stepan

by Zvi Zilberman

Translated by Mira Eckhaus
Edited by Daniel Shimshak

In 1930, when I was a sixteen-year-old boy, I graduated the "Tarbut" school in Stepan. At that time, as a young guy, I was debating about my future plans. Since there were no options for continuing studies for a profession or for higher education in a small town such as Stepan, I, like most of the boys of this age, wandered around idly.

In this year, youth organizations were founded, such as "HaChalutz", "Hashomer HaTzair" and "Beitar". I was attracted to "HaChalutz" even though during the day there was nothing to do there, but in the evenings, we would gather in the branch and we would spend the time talking, dancing, etc.

On Saturday or on a holiday, we used to sit on the Val that was on Poshtova Street, in front of Stepan's police station, and we would also take walks in the Galach garden (in Galaches garten). In addition, we would walk on Shabbat to Stepan's forest which was near the cinema, we would visit relatives and acquaintances, go swimming in our stream, and that's how we spent our time.

Most of the residents of Stepan, who were mainly shopkeepers and merchants, would stand in the doorway of their shops for entire weekdays waiting for a buyer, except for Thursday, which was the market day (mark). On Thursdays, hundreds of villagers from the villages near Stepan would come and sell what they had produced - milk, cheese, eggs, etc. We, that is, those among Stepan's Jews who dealt in peddling, would arrange entire rows of stalls in the market and would sell our wares and this process would continue continuously. During all the years, every Sunday of the week in the morning, all the Christians and gentiles would go to the Cloister (Church). They would walk proudly and with their heads held high and pass by our houses with hatred for us was evident on their faces.

In 1934, I went to training and finished it in 1938. At the beginning of 1939 - I immigrated to the Land of Israel with a group of pioneers from all countries. At the end of 1939, the war broke out and in 1944, in the winter, we heard the tragic news about the great Holocaust of all the Jews, among them residents of Stepan and members of my immediate family.

My late father, Yitzchak, was from a God-fearing and privileged Chassidic family. I remember that my grandfather Moshe and my father were well-known merchants, greatly admired by those around them. The Ukrainians called my father "Yitzhak Zlotnik", which in Ukrainian means "man of gold", because of his kindness, sincerity and understanding towards the Ukrainians with whom he traded.

[Page 103]

My late mother, from a family of rabbis and shochets, was an exemplary housewife. My mother's brother was Levi the shochet and the chazan, one of the beloved and admired figures among all the Jews of the town. He was the chazan and the one causing happiness at all the simchas in Stepan. My mother had another sister in the village of Stodin and a cousin named Etka Sheines, who emigrated to Canada before the war. One of my mother's brothers was Rabbi Kreizer who lived in the USA and passed away there close to World War II. His descendants live today in the USA and most of them serve on the throne of the rabbinate.

My father was a wealthy Jew relative to the other residents of the town. This continued until 1914, the period of the First World War. At that time, he became impoverished when the gangs of Petliura looted all his property.

The survivors of my immediate family include my brother Shlomo, who lives in Kyiv, Russia, my sister Gittel, who immigrated forty years ago to Brazil, and myself, who immigrated to the Land of Israel before the Holocaust.

My brother Dov, who served as a shochet in the city of Kremenets, and his family, and my brother Chaim who lived with his family in Rafalovka all perished in the Holocaust, as well as all the other members of my family near and far. May their memory be blessed forever!

Yitzhak, the son of Moshe Avraham Zilberman

[Page 104]

The Dacha
(Convalescent Home)

by Yeshayahu Pery

Translated by Mira Eckhaus
Edited by Daniel Shimshak

After crossing the Horyn River through the same wooden bridge that is over one kilometer long, you reached the gentiles neighborhood called the Kolaniyeh. Further in this neighborhood was a sandy road that led to a dense pine forest and in the entrance of this forest were a number of wooden buildings with many rooms, which were used in the summer season as a convalescent home - dacha. The convalescents in this dacha were not necessarily people from Stepan, but from nearby cities and towns. This dacha was famous and had a great reputation and people would come to it from central Poland as well as from abroad (more than once people from Paris stayed there).

The dacha was owned or leased for a long time by the Magid family. Its managers took care of fresh and clean food that was brought from the town every day in carts. The food was mainly dairy products from gentiles' farms as well as fish. It was the air of the pines forests that attracted many of the convalescents from far away.

We, the townspeople, would come to stay in this forest on Shabbat afternoons and have a picnic there and swing in a hammock, and we would visit the dacha and even go deep into the forest in search of mushrooms and berries.

These trips were held throughout the weekdays during the summer vacation and not always with the permission of the parents.

The Jews of Stepan, who would come near the dacha, would look at the convalescents from central Poland and abroad with great curiosity, at their different behavior, their clothes and the like.

In addition to the aforementioned dacha, a hot mud healing spring was discovered near the Polish village of Huta - Stepanska, and the place began to become famous in the area.

[Page 105]

Memories

by Ethel Shimshak

The place of my birth, my dear town, you appear before me in all your happiness and joy, with all the goodwill and friendbetween one and another, and with all the will to help one another. I am sad to say that there quickly came a horrible, bloodthirsty time when an animalistic attack destroyed all that was precious in the blink of an eye. May the name of our enemies be destroyed, those wild animals descended from Amalek.

I am my parents eldest daughter. My name is Ethel, born in Stepan. After I got married, we lived in Rafalovka. With the help of G-d, we were fortunate and I was saved from the claws of the Nazi war. My parents were Aharon Mordechai and Hennia Shimshak. My sister Tzippah and her husband Pesach had 3 daughters, Beila, Rachel and Rivkah. Her husband, Pesach Plotnick, was a genius in Torah and with the help of my parents was able to devote himself totally to learning Torah. He brought joy to my parents and the whole family. All of them perished in the Holocaust. Also, my brother, Dovid, his wife, Channah, and daughters, Beila and Sarah, and their son, Avraham Altral, perished.

My parents and my brother were very capable people and in their financial lives they were very successful. They produced oil (Alearneal ?) and they always helped others. As I remember in their house, normally Motzei Shabbat, the big shots, shochets, and the Rav gathered for a Melava Malcah of song and dance. My mother always attempted to host all the important guests in an appropriate way. And I remember a special incident when they were burning coals, on top of which was a special warmer (samovar – Russian coffeepot). After a while the samovar melted because my mother never put water into it. After the moment of disappointment, everyone continued with the joy as if nothing happened and the guests enjoyed the other goodies and niceties of the party.

[Page 106]

Our House in the Village of Kosmachov
(Memories from My Father's House)

by Leah Rudnik-Hashavia

Translated by Mira Eckhaus

Edited by Daniel Shimshak

In Kosmachov, a small and poor village on the road between Stepan and Kostopol, in which lived about a hundred Ukrainian families of Israel haters, lived only one Jewish family – the family of Yankel der Kosmichover.

Our house differed from the rest of the village houses in its size and shape. It had four rooms, while the neighbors' houses were built of no more than one room and an entrance and their roofs were covered with straw. Since our house was located on the main road, it was used as a hostel (without payment) for any Jew who passed from one town to another. They would stay in our house, eat with us and very often sleep in our house. We were always happy to see Jewish people visiting us because we were very lonely.

In this house we were born, grew up and for a certain period we also studied. We were six children - three boys and three girls. Ever since I can remember and until the bitter end, our grandmother, Grandma Scheindel, lived with us and took care of us. Those who knew her would say that she was one of the thirty-six righteous people. I share the same opinion.

There was no school in the village, however the children had to study. When we were little, our parents would bring a melamed to our home, usually he was a very old and lonely man and we didn't manage to learn much from him. Young guys were also brought to us, such as Gedalia Koifman and Silberman.

When we grew up a little, they loaded us - four children - on the cart - and brought us to Stepan, to a family such as the family of Moshe der Kovel, Machla Melamud, or Dudel Kriegel, where we lived and studied at a Polish school, and we studied privately Yiddishkeit with Moshe Koifman.

And here I must mention with trembling and great respect, the supreme, superhuman efforts that our late mother made to allow us to study. I will never forget how my mother mortgaged her last candlesticks so that she could pay for us the rental fees.

Every Sunday, my mother would show up with my older brother or with my father and bring us food for the coming week, which included potatoes, beans, milk, lettuce, and the like.

My late father had many businesses, but he had very little success in them. We had an olive press (oliarna), a machine for combing wool, and a large plot of land. We all worked very hard

[Page 107]

and despite this, great poverty prevailed in our home. Ever since I can remember, I saw our father wandering in his boots to look for loans to pay all kinds of taxes. We were always in debt and couldn't buy a pair of shoes. I will not exaggerate if I say that we lived in malnutrition.

Our life in the village was without purpose and without hope. Our whole dream was to get out of this valley of tears, to live among Jews, to manage somehow.

And indeed, with great efforts I was able to arrive to Vilna, to the "Tarbut" seminar, and while I was there, I was able to join my little sister to "Gordonia" and she left with the first group of illegal immigrants to Israel. A year after that, I also arrived in Israel, and here we began to plan how to get the rest of the family out of there.

Unfortunately, we were not able to do it on time and the Holocaust came upon them quickly and they all perished. May their memory be blessed forever.

Yaakov Rudnik, his wife and their
grandchildren

[Page 108]

Miserable People and Passers-By

by Yeshayahu Pery

Translated by Mira Eckhaus

Edited by Daniel Shimshak

As in every town, there were a number of mentally ill and disabled people in Stepan. These were mostly poor, wretched people, who did no harm to anyone. But of course, they were well known to the townspeople for their strange and unusual behavior. Most of these would to go from door-to-door begging for alms and were supported in one way or another by the Jews of the town. Some of them lived in houses of their relatives-their families and some in the public poorhouse of the town. Those I remember are: Pearl - with her fantasies, Dinka, Raizel, Gitel-Kafka.

There was no shortage of disabled people of all kinds in the town as well: mutes, cripples and more. All these wretched people were supported by the townspeople, everyone was ready to come to their aid and even provided them with material assistance; but of course, first and foremost they were a burden on their families and relatives. However, at the same time as expressing sympathy to the situation of these wretched people, the mischievous people of the town enjoyed joking at their expense and harassing them with pranks, albeit in a restrained and limited way. The hand of the German and Ukrainian murderers did not spare them either.

In addition to these wretched and supported local people, different and strange types of people would regularly visit the town more than once a year. The most prominent among them was Rabbi "Messiah-Pali-Pali". He was an old Jewish man, usually with a long beard, strong with muscles and unlike the custom of most Jews in the town and the surrounding area, he walked around bareheaded. This man would go from door-to-door begging for alms and food. One of his weaknesses was burning cloths and weaved things. He used to take underwear and clothing that were hanged on the rope or the fence for drying, and stuff them into the sack that he carried on his back. He would burn all the clothes he had gathered in the oven of the bath house and every burning of a rag would give him great pleasure which would be accompanied by shouts and cheers of happiness and joy: "Pali-Pali" (burn, burn) and hence his nickname.

We, the children of the town, would run after him and follow him so he will not steal rags or clothes from the homes of our relatives or friends. We also used to sneak up while he was sleeping and check his bag of things. When he would wake up, he would chase us angrily like a predatory animal and we would run away and drop his rags during our escape. On the other hand, we would gather around him every time he would burn the cloths and we too would enjoy his crazy happiness.

And we would not fulfill our duty if we do not mention the image of the other miserable people in our town. These were needy people, who would go from door-to-door begging for alms, who would come to Stepan several times a year until they had become familiar faces in the town. The Jews of Stepan treated them with good hospitality and invited them to sit in their homes or gave them alms and food.

[Page 109]

The Way to Zion

Founding the "Tarbut" School

by Shlomo Sheinboim

Edited by Mira Eckhaus and Daniel Shimshak

In the year 1923/4 a teacher from the nearby town of Rechelovka was brought to town to be the Hebrew conversation teacher. His name was Gerber. Later on Mr. Gerber made aliyah to Israel and served as a principal of a school in Petach-Tikvah for many years. This teacher taught only a small group of students whose parents could afford payment. Also, the parents were patriots to the Zionist movement and considered learning Hebrew as a major part of the Zionist national education.

The teachers and students of the "Tarbut" school in its first year
From right to left: Teacher Burstein, Principal Kunst, Teacher Rotblatt and Teacher Moshe Koifman

Study took part at Stesel Waldman's house. It was the hardcore that served as the base of enlarging language studies, and with the help of some activists from town, they established the "Tarbut" school. At the beginning, they had students from 3rd through 7th grades. The first teachers were: Moshe Koifman, who started this as his mission and contributed greatly to the school's existence, development and standards for many years until the war broke out; also, teachers Rotblatt, Burstein and Chasdai.

[Page 110]

The way to get permission from the authorities to establish the school was to get a certified teacher of the Polish language. Therefore, they hired a teacher whose name was Kamerman and the permit was obtained. Teacher Kamerman married a woman from Stepan named Dovah Waldman.

Later there arrived in town the school principal by the name Auerbach and the teacher Shnerer. Also they hired local teachers by the name Yeshayahu Neiman and Baruch Kreizer, the son of the butcher and cantor Rabbi Levi Yitzchak Kreizer. The building that housed the school was donated at first by a Jewish man named Berel Nodel and his family who immigrated to the United States. This building was remodeled with a few years to meet the needs of the school.

"Tarbut" school students and their teachers
Moshe Koifman, Yeshayahu Neiman, the school principal Auerbach and his wife, the kindergarten teacher, Pesya

[Page 111]

The Beginning of Zionist Activities

by Shlomo Sheinboim

Already by the year 1911, the Zionist movement had come to town. Zionist youth activists started selling shequels for the coming Zionist congress. Also they established a drama class.

In the year 1917, the Zionist Histadrut (union) was established and also the JNF (Keren Kayemet).

The Keren Kayemet L'Yisroel council in Stepan

The Zionist youth movement also organized other public activities. They established a group for "Linat Tzedakah: in which volunteers spent days and nights with sick people who could not get up from their beds.

The Zionist activity moved to the next generation and that was how the political party started.

In the early 1920s a young woman arrived in town from the city of Kovel by the name Bracha Shickman. This woman later on married Yitzchak Goz.

[Page 112]

Under the umbrella of "Hashomer Hatzair", Bracha collected young people from the town. This movement was characterized as the Zionist scouts. Many youngsters were attracted by the impressive uniforms and to the scouts' activity in general. This activity included trips to the countryside, to the fields and to the forests. These activities lasted for almost a year and then stopped for a while. Later on the teacher Chasdai from the "Tarbut" school restarted the movement "Hashomer Hatzair". For most of the youngsters belonging to this movement their main goal was to make aliyah to Israel.

"Hashomer Hatzair" activists in Stepan

After a few more years, there were mostly political party activities in town and the "Hachalutz" and "Beitar" movements were established. Most of the youngsters left "Hashomer Hatzair" (which was characterized as a left-political party) and joined "Beitar" under the leadership of the teacher Yeshayahu Neiman, z"l. The "Hachalutz" and "Hashomer Hatzair" movements were still active but had a low profile. Some from these movements left town and were active all over Poland and then made aliyah to Israel as part of the "Aliyah Bet" (second immigration) based on the certificates given to them.

These activities of the young Zionists lasted until the war started in 1939. Right before the war, "Beitar' took a few members – Motel Rassis and Nunya Hochman – and smuggled them through "Aliyah Bet".

[Page 113]

From the organization "Hashomer Hatzair" in Stepan

The National Fundraisings

"Keren Hayesod" mainly directed its efforts towards the wealthy Zionist people in town, while "Keren Kayemet" (JNF) was directed to everyone else who wanted to donate. Almost every Jewish house in town had a JNF blue box. The JNF box served an educational value for the young generation.

The Zionist Council in Stepan

[Page 114]

In addition there were all kinds of activities involving the collection of money and the selling of JNF stamps at every holiday or family event. At the beginning of every month, the JNF people walked from house to house in order to empty the blue boxes.

The Zionists had a separate minyan on Simchat Torah and the income from the aliyot was donated to the JNF. Also the income from the drama class was donated to the JNF.

A nature trip by the students of the "Tarbut School" in Stepan led by the teacher Shnerer

[Page 115]

Publication about Stepan in the Yiddish newspaper in Volyn, "The Mentsch", that was written in the 1930s by the local journalist Betzalel Shpritz

[Page 116]

Reflections of the Volyn Press on Public Activities

by Betzalel Shpritz

Edited by Mira Eckhaus and Daniel Shimshak

Mr. Betzalel Shpritz, from Stepan, was a writer in the Wohlyn newspapers. Today Betzalel Shpritz and his wife, Rozka-Shoshana, also from Stepan, are living in Tel-Aviv. They both made aliyah in 1935 as "Beitar" activists.

In the "Wohlyn-Nayes" the establishment of "Brit-Yeshurin" in Stepan by the "Beitar" commander is written. In total, 50 members arrived at the beginning. The first speaker was Sender Volinsky, the Rabbi's son, from the head activists of the Brit. They continued with a very interesting and serious discussion. At the end they elected Tzvi Segal as general manager of the board, Levi Yitzhak Kreizer as president, and Sender Volinsky as secretary, and the following board members: Yehuda Woschina, Dov Zelberberg, Nechemia Gaz, Yaakov Petashnik, Avraham Zelberberg and Yoel Baruch Becker. This committee was in touch with the headquarters in Poland and they expected a visit from the president of "Yeshurin" in Poland, Dr. Rabbi Treisman, to Stepan.

Big Success in Selling Shekels for the 18th Zionist Congress

In spite of the economic recession, they succeeded in selling shekels for the 18th Zionist Congress to 550 families in town. The Revolutionists sold 270 shekels, the "League" sold 200 shekels, and the General Zionist sold 80 shekels. This was a lot more than for the 17th Congress in which they sold 180 shekels, in total, in the town.

An article in the "Wohlyner Tzaytung", number 30 (733)

There is a story about the departure of Rabbi Baruch Twersky from Stepan. He left Stepan for good a few days before Rosh Hashanah with his family. Most of the Wohlyn Jews came together to offer a warm goodbye. The Rabbi was going to become the Rabbi of Lublin. It was told that the Lublin Jews gave a warm welcome to the Rabbi when he arrived.

An article in the "Wohlyner Tzaytung", number 13

It reported about the elections for the 18th Zionist Congress in town when the results were known at 9:30 in the evening. There was great stress among the political party activists, but in general there were no clashes. The Revolutionists showed the most initiative and the election results were the following: General Zionists – 64 votes, "Et Livnot (Time to Build)" – 16 votes, Mizrachi – 12 votes, Hitachdut (Union) – 10 votes, Grossman Group – 2 votes, the "League" – 80 votes, and the Revolutionists – 248 votes.

[Page 117]

An article in "Eber Wohlyn", number 23 (726) on expanding the number of students in the "Tarbut" school in town

It was 5 months after the death of the active teacher and great Zionist Mr. Yeshayahu Neiman. This was a big loss for all the citizens of the town and for the routine activities of the "Tarbut" school.

A meeting was held in order to increase the number of students in the "Tarbut" school and to ensure for a proper National-Zionist education to the young generation in town. This meeting took place at the beginning of the school year. Among the participants were the teachers and representatives from all of the Zionist youth movements of any kind. The meeting took two hours in which they established a youth department at "Tarbut". The following members were chosen to be members of the department: the teacher Moshe Koifman, Rafael Yokelson, Betzalel Shpritz, Yitzchak Weismann, Shlomo Sheinboim, Chaim Slavotsky and Gershon Krokover.

The same newspaper published an article that had the eulogy of the passing of the great philanthropist Melyah Woschina at the age of 67. Most of the people of the town took part in her funeral. The widows and orphans who Melyah Woschina supported with donations during her life were crying and very sad. Of the rest, she also contributed much money to yeshivas in Israel.

An article in "Eber Wohlyn", number 181 (721) on the memory of Dr. T. Hertzl

Traditionally they had a memorial ceremony in which all of the Zionist representatives took part. This time it was the 28th year since the death of the leader Theodore Hertzl. Many times in the past, there were clashes between the different youth parties. Even this year there were attempts by the leftist groups to interfere but the presidents of the groups succeeding in quieting the people and the ceremony went on without interruption.

The ceremony was organized by Avraham Weitznodel from Rovno and other speakers were: Yitzchak Weismann from Beitar, Zev Woschina from "Hachalutz (The Pioneers)", and the very impressive speaker Dr. Gorin. The member Hershel Shpelsher read a protest against the obvious intention of the British not to keep their promise to establish a national Jewish home in Israel.

The ceremony was concluded with the singing of Hatikvah.

[Page 118]

An article in "Eber Wohlyn", number 32 (735) on a fight between political parties on Simchat Torah

Traditionally, for the last few years, the young Zionists of the town would get together to celebrate Simchat Torah in the auditorium of the "Tarbut" school.

From the auditorium of the school you could hear loud and happy singing from the Zionist youth. But suddenly a fight broke out between parties that were restrained by the strong discipline of the Beitar youth who prevented fighting among brothers.

Here is what happened. The youth of Beitar, Group A, happy in celebrating the holiday, started to dance the hora. Immediately, curious people from the town clapped hands and encouraged them. Unfortunately there appeared a number of youth from "Hashomer Hatzair" who interrupted the singing and dancing with yells and screams. And so it went from words to fighting. Adults from Beitar got involved and succeeded in separating the youth and stopping the fight.

Most of the Jews of the city in attendance protested the provocation by the youth of "Hashomer Hatzair". Many of the parents decided to take their children out from this movement.

An article in "Mament" from December 1933 on the big petition against the British mandate decree in Israel

In the big synagogue in town there was a protest against the British mandate decree in Israel. In memory of Leo Mitzkin every assembled stood on their feet for a few moments of silence.

During the event there were speeches by: Yitzchak Weismann, deputy leader of Beitar, Betzalel Shpritz, and Yaakov Petashnik. The cantor, Rabbi Levi Yitzchak Kreizer said the "me sheberach" prayer for the Zionist prisoners in Zion and Betzalel Shpritz read the decisions that came out of the gathering:

"This great general gathering expresses its deepest protest against the British mandate decrees in Israel which reverses the former promises to help establish a national home for the people of Israel in the land of Israel, and calls on the Zionist leadership to act immediately to prevent these drastic consequences."

[Page 119]

Illegals to Israel: Stepan 1939

by Yeshayahu Pery

Edited by Mira Eckhaus and Daniel Shimshak

When the Soviets entered the town in 1939, Beitar activists understood that they could no longer function under the Soviet authorities. So, some young Beitar activists decided to do everything possible to get to Israel.

Among them were Motel Rassis and Nunya Hochman, who turned to Romanian border and after much difficulty made it to the land of Israel. Nunya Hochman, z"l, later on died in battle fighting the Germans in the Italian frontier. Meanwhile, Shimon Rosenfeld, Zvi Rosenfeld, Chaim Hochman and Zvi Gorinstein crossed the border from Russia to Lithuania. First they lived in Vilna and then they moved to Panevezys.

Right after Lithuania was captured by the Russians, some immigrants tried to contact the western embassies before they evacuated Lithuania, hoping to get out of Lithuania through their borders. Those who did that were captured by the Soviets and sent to Siberia. Fear of this caused many others to avoid this option. Shimon Rosenfeld tried to contact the British consulate in Moscow and request a visa claiming that he had a certificate from Turkey. But the Soviet authorities caught him and put him on the train to Siberia. This was in 1941 after the war between Russia and Germany had started. This train was bombed and he succeeded in running away but later he was beaten to death by nationalistic Lithuanians.

בית הכולל בייתר ד' יאיר סטעפאן/וואהלא

Activists in the Beitar Organization in Stepan

[Page 120]

Additional Details about the Illegals from Stepan – Shimon Rosenfeld--
From the Book by Chaim Lazar, "Destruction and Resistance"

Rosenfeld, Shimon, a Beitar member from Wohlyn.

A Polish refugee who came to Lithuania in 1939. He was a counselor in Beitar of Panevezys. He was arrested by the Russians and was about to be sent to Siberia because of his Zionist activity. When the war started he was liberated from the Lokisky prison in Vilna. He was in touch with the Beitar member of Vilna. He died during the provocation in the summer of 1941.

One day I met Shimon Rosenfeld, a young man who ran away from Stepan in Wohlyn to Lithuania in 1939. I hadn't seen him for more than a year. His pants were torn and his upper body was covered with a worn shirt. He was nearly barefoot and he looked very hungry.

He tells me that a few months earlier the Russians arrested him and suspected him of Zionism. They put him in the Lokisky prison and interrogated him many times. Two days before the war started, they put him on a train with a few dozen other people who were about to be deported to Siberia. They never had the chance to make it there because the Germans started to bomb the town and particularly the train station. Bombs fell from every direction and the prisoners thought that they would die from the bombing.

After two days silence prevailed and the prisoners noticed that there were no guards. They broke out of the train car and escaped for their lives. Shimon was hosted by one of the Jews who was a prisoner with him on the train. He lived on Rechov Hazagagim – The Street of Glaziers (Galezer Gaz).

[Page 121]

After two days, Shimon Rosenfeld came to me completely wounded. Two days earlier he and some other Jews were captured by the Lithuanians and were brought to Lokisky prison. At the entrance to the prison, they passed between two long lines of Lithuanians armed with iron and rubber sticks, and they hit them brutally with no mercy. Whoever didn't have the strength to withstand until the end, was beaten to death.

They repeated the beatings between the gates and between the inner courtyards. After a basic inspection, they were pushed into a courtyard which was crowded with Jews. It was so crowded that you couldn't move. Anything that you had to do, you did in your place. The suffocation was great.

Shimon Rosenfeld z"l

From time to time the Lithuanians opened the gates demanding gold and money from the prisoners and each time they kept beating the prisoners on their heads. The prisoners started to run away but there was no room and they crashed into one another.

The next day they took the prisoners to the main yard and ordered them to climb on trucks that were ready to go away. Shimon was already on a truck when suddenly a fancy car stopped by and a German came out and read names of Jews from a list in his hand. These Jews were separated from the others. When the German called a name that wasn't answered, Shimon decided to answer as it was him. After a few minutes, the German took out "his" Jews from Lokisky and he sent them to work. Shimon was very happy that he survived a definite death. But the miserable man didn't know that this was a temporary relief.

[Page 122]

There is no evidence about the rest of the group of members, except for Zvi Rosenfeld who fled to Russia before the Germans entered Vilna. He survived and lives today with his family in Israel.

The Beitar Group in Stepan during the 1930s

Our Fathers' Homes

Our Fathers' Homes: Where They Were in Stepan

by the Editorial Board

Edited by Mira Eckhaus and Daniel Shimshak

[Page 123]

1. Shkoolna Street

Shkoolnah Street was the center of the spiritual life of the town. On this street stood the synagogues and lived the rabbis, the religious judges, the slaughterers and the chazans. On this street were the central public institutes like the schools, the Tarbut (cultural), the Yeshiva "Talmud Torah", the bath house and the hostel for the poor. Most of the town's Jewish-Zionistic events took place on the street of the synagogues: wedding ceremonies, meetings and political quarrels, funerals and eulogies, protest rallies and emergency assemblies in time of trouble. Most of the street served as Jewish dwelling places and only the other end, like a quarter of it, served as dwelling for Ukrainian goyem. This street continued to the Jewish cemetery and the other end led out of the town by the famous bridge that crossed the Horyn River. This street and its adjoining narrow streets, mainly those in the direction of the river, served as the town's Jewish ghetto. Here were concentrated the Jews of the town and the Jews of the villages that were in the vicinity of Stepan in the days of the rule of the Germans.

The Chait Family

Father of the family: Binyamin Chait. His wife: Meral. His sons: Yisroel, Avraham and Moshe. His daughters: Shoshanah, Rochel and Sarah.

Benjamin was busy with tailoring. Near the outbreak of the war he moved to live with his family in the railway station in Malynsk, nearby Stepan. Binyamin and his family escaped from the claws of the Nazis at the time of the slaughter to the forests and they lived among the goyem. His wife found her death in the forests from the ambush attack of the Ukrainian nationalists, while he and his children, who were saved, returned to Malynsk with freedom by the Soviets, in the year 1944.

Binyamin volunteered to serve in the special Soviet police to purge the area of Ukrainian nationalists. In one incident he fell during his guard watch.

Two of his sons, the first born Yisroel and the young boy Avraham - live nowdays in Russia with their family while Moshe and Shoshanah live with family in Haifa; Rochel lives with her family in Tel Aviv, Sarah lives with her family in Be'er Sheva.

In the same house near the bridge over the Horyn, also lived Binyamin's brother, Hershel, his wife and daughters, Raizel and Rochtcha, and another daughter and son. In the same house lived also the old mother of Benjamin and Hershel Chait, and she had another four daughters and a son who emigrated to the United States before the war.

[Page 124]

Israel Nodel - A Widow

His daughters: Nachamah, who lived in Korets with her husband Lazar Rom; her sons Moshe Bear and Shaul and her daughters Chana, Dina and Rochel; the daughter Beila Yostein and her children: Perel

Zalman, Yosef, and Moshe Dovid - her son from her first husband; the daughter, Elka, was married to Leibel Pakowitz and bore his children Shaul, Yisaschar, Nachum and daughter Manya. Shaul had a wife named Chana and children. The son Yisaschar had a wife, a son Hertzl and daughter Chana. Leibel had an additional son named Nachum and daughter Manya, who was married to the son from the Chait family.

**Rabbi Israel Nodel, his daughter Beila and his grandson
Moshe, may he live a long life**

[Page 125]

Rabbi Israel, who was nicknamed Sroolkah, lost his legs in the Russian-Japanese War. He was a devout Jew and feared G-d, he enthusiastically supported the hostel for the poor and did a lot in order to enclose the old cemetery that was in the town. From this large extended family, the one who remains alive was the daughter of Beila, who was recruited by the Red Army and lives today in Israel, in Holon, with the children of his family.

The House of Nechamia Geller

His wife: Chaya. His sons: Zalman, Tzodek, Shmuel and Hershel. His daughters: Beila and Tziporah.
Remaining alive: The daughter Tziporah and her husban Konot from Stepan, who immigrated to Israel before the war, and also the son Hershel and his wife Tessie, from the family Wachs, who live in Israel.

Nechamia educated his children in the Zionistic spirit. His daughters and his sons were active in the Zionist youth movement in the town and they had many initiatives to instill the Hebrew language in the young children in the town. Nechamia, with his great diligence, was one of the few in the city who tended and grew a vineyard of grapes in his garden and this in addition to his daily troubles to sustain his family with honor.

The House of Yitchak Moshe Weinstein

His wife: Dovah. The married daughter Raizel, her husband and three children. The married daughter Ainda Torek, her husband and two children. The son Berel, his wife Yocheved and their two children. Sons: Chaim and Nechamia. Daughter: Rochel.

The sons, Chaim and Nechamia, escaped from the killing pits, but Chaim was shot to death in the forests whereas Nechamia lives with his family in Russia.

The daughter Rochel was saved while she was in Russia and lives today with her family in Netanya. The name of her family is Gottfried.

[Page 126]

The House of Altar Novak

He, his wife, two sons and two daughters, his son-in-laws, his grandchildren - all lived in the two story house, one of the few in the town.

Altar was a respected Jew who served as a Stepan representative to the Polish rulers. He was the owner of a store in manufacturing.

The House of the Twersky Family

From the offspring of the Magid from Stepan. In most of the rooms in the house lived Rabbi Baruch Twersky before he left the town. Afterwards, there lived in the house Gittel and the helper Raizel. This house was also the Beit Medrish in which the Chassidim of the Rabbi learned and prayed. During the time of the Soviets, the house was used by his followers as a Yiddish school. In the ghetto, the house was used as the central kitchen for preparing the meager food for the citizens of the ghetto (see the separate report on the Twersky family).

The House of the Kreizer Family

The father of the family: Rabbi Levi, his wife Chanya, four sons: Shmuel Hirsch, a Yeshiva graduate, Yaakov, Moishele, and Baruch, who served as an officer in the Polish army and used to be the authorized teacher in the Tarbut school. The daughter Gittel was married to a Jew from a neighboring town.

Rabbi Levi Kreizer was the slaughterer and chazan in the great synagogue. He was a well-liked figure and very popular among most of the citizens of the town, Jews and goyem alike.

His son Baruch also used to be the policeman of the water cistern in the men's camp in the ghetto. He was different than the other policemen by his knowledge of how to behave when fulfilling his duty according to the Judenratt and together with this he would be careful not to harden the lives of the confined in the ghetto. His behavior was a shining example and he even curbed the degree of wild behavior of those who served as policemen who didn't know from restrained behavior.

Shmuel Hirsch Kreizer, one of Rabbi Levi Yitzchak's sons

[Page 127]

Rabbi Levi Yitzhak Kreizer, the shochet and chazan of the great synagogue in the town

[Page 128]

The House of Yoel Hashochet (the Slaughterer)

In the continuation of the hill that was used for playing by children in the neighborhood, and primarily during the winter for skating on the ice and snow, was found the house of Rabbi Yoel the slaughterer, his wife and two daughters. The name of one of them was Henda.

The House of Berel Rassis

The house of Berel Rassis, his wife Dovah, their son Motel, who was married to Esther, and was born to him Shayna, Abalah and an additional small child.

The daughter of Berel, Sosel the very beautiful, was married to Gavriel Feldman and she moved to live in Kostopol. Berel was the son of Rabbi Yokel the main shamash (beadle) of the synagogue in the town. He was the owner of a carriage, industrious, peaceful and honest. His son Motel, who was an activist in Betar in the town, immigrated to Israel on the eve of the outbreak of the war and he lives at this time in the Moshav Bnai' Zion in Sharon.

The House of Rabbi Chaim Weinstein

His wife, his son Yosef and his daughters Malka and Chayka, who was married to Berel. Rabbi Chaim (his nickname was "L'Chaim - To Life") used to be the teacher of small children and was a person full of smiles and beloved. Most famous in the family was his wife, who was engaged in buying and selling with the goyem in the neighborhood.

The House of Chana Tzasys

This widow had a family of three married daughters and their husbands: Blumah, Sosel and Beila.

The House of Hershel Gelman

Hershel Gelman, his wife, two daughters and his son.
Hershel was a peaceful Jew, a laborer, who served as night watchman in the flour mill of the Graz family.

The House of the Widow Freida Gelman

Freida Gelman lived together with her married daughter. The nickname "Kaloosh (thin)" stuck with the widow's family, who was busy with peddling and also served as a cryer (at funerals). Remaining alive is the grandson Yaakov "Kaloosh", who spent the war in Russia and apparently lives in America.

[Page 129]

The Tzokar House

The shaky, small house of the Tzokar family, who had the nickname "Bon". The father of the family, Rabbi Avraham "Bon", his wife Elka and three sons.

Rabbi Avraham was known to the Jews of the town by his pleasant voice, while he roused the Jews to say Tehilim and the work of the Creator (prayers) on Shabbat at dawn. Besides this, Avraham worked in peddling.

The House of Hershel Stratz

His nickname was "Tzotzman". His wife and three sons: Choneh, Yosef and Velvel, who served in the Red Army at the time of the war and apparently lives in Russia.
Hershel Stratz was a butcher and supported his family from the strain of his occupation.

The House of the Widow Adele Weismann

Her son Motel married to the woman Feigel the daughter of Yitchak Weitznodel. A few of her children emigrated to Argentina and they or their offspring remained alive.

The House of Eliya Novogrodasky

Eliya Novogrodasky, his wife and their son and daughter. He served as a helper to the shamash (beadle) in the synagogues and proclaimed the arrival time of the Shabbat.

The House of Binyamin Wachs

As a tenant in the house of Hershel Wachs lived Binyamin Wachs, his wife Leah, his son and his very beautiful daughter Sofkah. Binyamin was an active partner in the flour mill and the power station with his brother Yosef and the brothers Tachor and Moshe Bebchuk. Binyamin was active in the Zionist-Revisionist movement.

Before this, they lived in the apartment of Miss Rivka Kemnschein, the first born daughter of Rabbi Moshe Yosef Sheinboim, and her daughter Aytzenka. After many days the two of them moved to a nearby city, Rovno.

[Page 130]

The Family of Dovid Chait

His sons: Berel, who married Sonya Tachor as his wife; Aharon, who married Perel Stratz for as wife; and Binyamin.

His daughters: Rochel who emigrated to Argentina before the war and Berel who lives apparently in Russia.

The Family of Yankel Chait

His wife Devorah, the daughters Sarah and Gittel and the son Shayka.

The Family of Zalman Hasandler (the Sandalmaker)

Zalman, his wife and his married daughter with the children of her family.
In Zalman's house lived the administrator of the school, Mr. Abarboch and his family.

The House of the Families of Hershel Leib Dov (Hatzerterisker)

His wife Esther (Ethel), his son Yisroel and his wife Roni, and their sons: Yitzchak, Chaim, Bobyl, and daughters: Leah and Perel.

Also there lived in the same house a family of additional relatives: Dovid Moshe Yosef and his wife Golda.

The House of Asher Shechterman

His wife: Chasya.

He served as an advanced teacher and he was even active in the Zionist movement. He was known for the fine preparation of the youth of the city towards their Bar Mitzvah.

Asher's sister - Shayndel of the house of Shechterman (today named Beck) - served as a teacher in the Tarbut school in Stepan. She immigrated to Israel before the war and lives nowadays in Haifa.

[Page 131]

The House of Rabbi Yokel Rassis

A house made of burnt brick, spacious, that before it extended a green, carefully tended garden. He became a widow and married a second wife.

Rabbi Yokel had four sons and they had their own families: Berel, Shmerel, Shmuel, and Yadel Leib, who died before his son Leib was born, who was called by the name of his father and lives today in Israel in Kfar Aviv.

Yokel served as the main shamash (beadle) of the synagogues.

On the area of the garden stood the house of Rabbi Shlomo Zolar during the period of the World War I and a little after that (see the separate section). The daughter Chasya and her brothers immigrated to Israel before the war and live in Israel in Kibbutz Nagvah.

In the second end of this house lived the son of Yokel, Shmuel Rassis, his wife Esther, his sons: Yonah and Sroolik, and his daughters: Chaya and Teyva.

Remaining alive is his son Yonah (about the ways that he escaped the fingernails of the Nazis - see the separate section). Yonah lives with his family in Kfar Aviv.

The House of Rabbi Moshe Hazelaznik

His wife, his son Leibel his wife and their children, and his daughter who married a boy from Rovno named Chona.

Rabbi Moshe was owner of an iron store. His house was used as the house of authority in the ghetto and lived in it the head of the Judenratt and his family.

The son Leibel was shot to death during his attempt to smuggle wood for heat while in the ghetto. He was the first sacrifice in the ghetto, before the general extermination. The event caused heavy depression to all of the people of the ghetto, who didn't foresee what would be their bitter future.

The House of the Religious Judge Rabbi Ben-Zion Volinsky, Of Blessed Memory

His wife and the sister of his wife Perel. His son Sandrel and two daughters. The oldest daughter Perel Chaya was married to a young rabbi from a neighboring town, who inherited the position of Rabbi Ben-Zion upon his death, and the daughter Ethel.

[Page 132]

Sandrel - despite that he was a genius in the wisdom of Israel and in Torah - never continued in the way of his righteous father as a scholar and was never attracted to judgeship. Sandrel was though an activist in the Betar movement and Brit Yeshurin, though not exactly with the consent of his father.

The House of Hershel Wachs (the Koroster)

A widow, his wife died at the time of the birth of the son of his old-age, Peretz. Additional sons: Shchana and Shaftal, and daughters: Chaya and Freidel, who was married to Aharon Stoller the famous photographer of Stepan and its surroundings, and another sister by the name Sarah.

The House of Ben-Zion Prishkolnik (the Gott)

A big house having three single, separate accommodations with balconies, and adjoining it a stable and a spacious, green garden.

His second wife Sarah from the nearby village of Zolozneh. The daughter Adele who was married to Zelik Weitznodel and his little daughter, and the sisters: Ganya and Miriam.

Rabbi Ben-Zion had children from his first wife Sosel. Sons: Yaakov, Gedaliah, who lived with his family in Sarny, and Yoel. The daughter - Raizel, who was married to Mitshilik.

The daughter Adele was an activist in the Betar movement. The husband of Adele, Zelik Weitznodel, remains alive. He married a second time and lives with his wife and his children in Stepan. Apparently the only Jew who remains there of the survivors.

The middle apartment of the house was rented out and the tenants would change many times. In the second end of the house, the apartment that faced the green garden, lived Yoel Prishkolnik, his wife Taibel from the house of Tzockerman from Barzna which was neighboring, the sons Shaul and Yeshayahu and the daughter Sosel-Sarah.

Yoel was a Zionist activist and in his youth he even belonged to the drama group of the town.

Remaining alive is Yeshayahu Pery, who lives with his family in Ramat Gan, and his sister Sosel-Sarah Kaplan, who lives with her family in Rishon L'Zion. The father of the family, Yoel, escaped from the ghetto, but was handed over to the Germans by a goy from the village of Zilna and taken out to be killed. The son Shaul was taken out to be killed even though he was in the work camp in Kostopol. The mother Taibel escaped to the forest, but froze to death during the time of a hard winter (see the separate section on this family).

[Page 133]

The House of Yitzchak Weitznodel Hakatzav (the Butcher)

Yitzchak Weitznodel, his wife his robust sons Avraham and Yonah, and his married daughter Feigel. Beside his house was a nice, cared-for orchard.

He was transported at the head of the Jewish convoy at the time they were taken out from the ghetto by wagon to the killing pits beside Kostopol, where the majority of the community of Stepan was ended.

The House of Tanya Weitznodel Hakatzav (the Butcher)

Tanya Weitznodel, his wife Chaya-Sarah, his sons Zelig and Yonah and his daughter Mindel.

Zelig was married to Adele and they had a small girl. The two sons - Zelig and Yonah - remained alive by serving in the Red Army and the two of them live with their families around Stepan.

The House of the Bebchuk Family

The daughters: Chana and Batsheva, who was married, and the son Yankel who was nicknamed Tchemach. '

Owners of an oil press and crushing mill that was powered by horses. The wheels of the crushing mill also served like circus amusements to the children of the neighborhood.

According to the best knowledge, the son Yaakov remained alive by serving in the Red Army. He lives, apparently, in Russia.

Three children from this family emigrated to Argentina before the war.

The House of Nachman Shenker, the Gabbai of the Synagogue

His wife: Yentel. The sons: Aharon, Reuven and Dovid, and the daughter Chana.

The father of the family, was a glazier by profession and the owner of a well-developed agricultural farm, he served as the gabbai of the synagogue and community representative in the town council.

The daughter Chana escaped from the killing pits and remained alive. She lives with her family in Tel Aviv. The name of her family is Gondelberg.

[Page 134]

The Korzek House

The wife and four sons: Gershon, Yisrael, Shmuel and Chanina, and married daughter.

The children of the family were busy with butchering and the selling of cattle.

The son Shmuel, of blessed memory, was saved and returned to Stepan at the start of the year 1944, with liberation at the hands of the Soviets. In his desire for revenge, he enlisted to serve in the special police to purge the Ukrainian nationalists and fell a hero's death on his guard watch.

The House of Moshe Sofer

His second wife, son by the name Noskeh and a number of additional children.
Moshe was a baker in the bakery of Bongart.

The Brothers Shmuel and Leibel Bazbasha

They were married with children. Among the children were two daughters: Beila and Zelda. The two brothers were butchers and cattle merchants. The families were poor and they lived with great difficulty.

The House of Yitzchak Bongart

His wife and three sons: Hershel, Shimon and Moniya.
Yitzchak was the owner of a bakery and bread store and other baked goods.

Hershel remained alive by his service in the Red Army and lives today in Russia. Shimon, who was a boy of courage and a good heart, was saved by hiding himself in the forests. In the year 1944 he volunteered for the special police to purge the Ukrainian nationalists by his desire for revenge. He continued to enlist in the Red Army to fight the Nazi enemies and from there he didn't return; apparently he fell on his guard watch.

In the house of this family lodged a young boy, a relative of the family, by the name Yerachmiel. He was saved by his service in the Soviet Army and apparently lives in Israel in one of the Kibbutzim in the Jordan valley.

[Page 135]

The Family of Benzion Weitznodel

His second wife Malka and his two sons - Yonah and Dovid.
Rabbi Benzion was a butcher.

His daughter Slobah immigrated to Israel before the Second World War and lives in Kibbutz Masilot. Another of her sisters, Ritzah, died not long after in Canada, and even her descendants and also another sister and her family live in Canada.

The Family of Meir Tzeizek

His wife Batya, his son Yankel, his daughter who was married to Motel Berel. Two additional daughters: Devora and Golda.

Meir was a sandalmaker by profession.

His son-in-law Motel Berel was imprisoned by the Polish authorities following Communistic activities that were forbidden in those times. Much later, in the time of the war, Motel Berel was called up by the Red Army, and according to the best knowledge, he lives today in Russia.

2. The Narrow Alleys Along Shkoolnah Street

The House of Rabbi Yaakov Prishkolnik (Yankel Gott)

He was widowed from his wife Margalite, of blessed memory. He had three sons: Yeshayahu, Moshe and Hershel, and five daughters: Chaya, Ethel, Raizel, Sosel and Ganya.

The father of the family was busy in cantorship and, as such, the primary breadwinner was the daughter Ethel, a well-known seamstress in the entire town. She also served as the manager of the household at the death of her mother. Together with her sisters, Raizel and Sosel, they raised the son of the sister Chaya. He was a beautiful child by the name Losik. Chaya herself was a sick woman and she lived in the village Bystrice with her husband Mendel. The sister Ganya studied and worked in the sewing profession in Barnovitz. Her brother Moshe studied in the technion of Vilna and he completed his studies as an authorized technician. The first-born brother, Yeshayahu Prishkolnik of blessed memory, immigrated to Israel in the year 1930 and served as a teacher in Jerusalem. He died from disease in the year 1935, was buried in the Kinneret and left after him a wife and son. Moshe and Hershel served in the Red Army.

[Page 136]

Moshe was injured in his fight against the Germans. He immigrated to Israel and lives in Netanya with his family. The traces of Hershel are not known and apparently he fell in the war. Ganya, who was an activist in Betar, immigrated to Israel and lives in Tel Aviv with her family. From the remainder of the children of the family, not one person remains alive.

In this alley was found *The Orchard of Yitzchak Weitznodel*. In the continuation of this orchard stood a building, not too big, that served as a slaughter house of chickens. In this slaughter house three slaughterers found their livelihood: Rabbi Levi Kreizer, Rabbi Hershel Hochman and Rabbi Yoel.

In the continuation stood the ***House of the Weitznodel Family***. The father of the family was Yechial and he had five daughters: Pasal, Feigel, Mindel, Sarah and Malka. The father of the family Yechial was a butcher and a cattle merchant. His family existed with great difficulty, but the family was strict not to be in need of help from strangers. Yechial himself was a modest Jew, overflowing with humor and even very much helped the theater amateurs in the town. He inspired the young people with his knowledge and talents in the area of popular Jewish folklore. His daughters: Sarah and Feigel emigrated to Argentina before the war and apparently they, or their descendants, still live in Argentina. From the remainder of the children of the family, not one person remains alive.

Facing the house of Yaakov Prishkolnik, on the side opposite the same alley, stood the house of the old, lonely Jew by the name ***Zeleg***. Zeleg worked in carpentry and he used to cultivate the small garden of his house. His one daughter lived in Zdolbunov and before the war he uprooted himself from Stepan to live with her.

The House of Ben-Zion, his second wife Raizel, his two sons: Zecharia and Leibel and his daughter Yacha. His two sons were married and fathers of children. Rabbi Ben-Zion worked in plastering and helped his son Zecharia, while his second son, Leibel, was a carpenter. Ben-Zion was a peaceful man, hardworking, modest and G-d fearing. This family was killed in the quarter by the bombing of the Germans before they entered the town, in the year 1941.

In the house of Ben-Zion lived the tailor ***Michel Shir***, his wife and his two sons: Berel and Heliya. Michel was the son of Rusya the Gabbait, who used to bake cakes in the house for customers for different happy occasions, like weddings and circumcisions. Rusya had a daughter by the name Nachah. Michel Shir worked many days of the week in peddling in the surrounding villages and his family existed with great difficulty.

[Page 137]

An additional house was the ***House of the Becker Family***. The father of the family was Yoel Baruch, and his wife Bonyah from the Tachor house, a son Avraham and daughters: Batya and Bryndele, the small, frizzy, curly golden haired. Yoel Baruch, the owner of a manufacturing store and an oil press, was active in public activity and was a supporter of the committee of the Tarbut school. An ardent Revisionistic Zionist. Batya his daughter was saved by hiding herself in the forests among the goyem and Polish and she live nowdays in Tel Aviv, while her sister was saved while she was in Russia.

The last house in the line of these houses was the ***House of Motya-Styof Weismann***. With him lived his daughter Sosel the redhead, wife of Fesya and their two children. Rabbi Motya the popular Jewish widower, was an unparalleled merry humorist.

3. The Alleys That Led to the Horyn Along Shkoolnah Street

The House of the Religious Judge Rabbi Pinchas Gorinstein, Of Blessed Memory

The owner of the nickname "The Yatzer Tov – The Good Nature", and his wife the Rebbitzin Malka Barucha. They had three sons: Shayka, Hershel and Lazar. The three of them were slaughterers, and the daughters Chasya and her sister.

The first-born son Shayka got to Basravya in the years of the First World War. Hershel with his family lived in Kostopol and Lazar left Stepan, the place of his birth, because of a dispute with the remaining slaughterers of the town and the constant clashes between his supporters and his opponents. He moved to Rovno and served there as a slaughterer.

The daughter Chasya emigrated to Canada during the 1930's. In the sunset of her days, she immigrated to Israel and died in Netanya.

Rabbi Pinchas was a short, chubby Jew with two shrewd eyes. He was very popular with his Chassidic congregation, most of whom were workers and very small merchants. Rabbi Pinchas died at the good, old age of 85, a number of years before the outbreak of the Second World War. His place was inhereted by a young Rabbi from Lonintz, the husband of his granddaughter Sorel.

The Adjoining Houses of Two Carpenters, Yaakov and Avraham and Their Families.

The father of the family Yaakov (Yankel) the carpenter, his wife and their daughter Chaya, an activist in the cell of the Shomer Hatzair (leftist Zionist youth movement) in the town, and also an additional small daughter and a son.

The father of the second family, Avraham the carpenter, his wife and their daughter Mindel, and talented son, an excellent, industrious student. Avraham was killed in a work accident before the war, at the time that he was busy fixing the dome of the Provoslavit church in the town. This caused heavy mourning for all of the town's Jews.

The two carpenters worked as partners with the understanding that through the work of their hands they supported their families, though with difficulty. Not always did an atmosphere of friendship exist between the women of the house and in the common kitchen, but the husbands overcame and therefore persevered in the active partnership between them in their professional work and their shared livelihood.

[Page 138]

The House of Pinya Motelikes. The father of the family Pinya, his wife and their two daughters and son Simcha. He was a G-d fearing Jew. In this house once dwelled the Yeshiva Talmud Torah by the management of the teacher Shaul, of blessed memory.

Their business: owners of a store of candies and soft drinks.

Not one person remained alive.

The Father of the Family of Rabbi Leibesh who died before the outbreak of the war, and this house was inherited by his son Levi, a widower, and his old mother. The daughter of Levi was Gittel Kafka.

Their business: selling lime, guarding the public ice pits of the Jews of the town. He would announce the time of the coming of Shabbat. Thus he roused the Jews of the town to do the work of the Creator (prayers) by his pleasant voice.

The Father of the Family of Baruch Rafal, his wife Fayge, and to them: a married son Velef Rafal, his wife named Blumah and their married children: Miriam, Chaya, Sarah and Sosel.

The daughter of Baruch Rafal, Masya, and her husband Baruch Kartzar lived in a nearby town, Kalban. They had three daughters. Baruch Rafal had an additional daughter, Rochel, and son Zelek. The wife of Zelek was Masya and their daughter Malka. Zelek Rafal the son was saved while he was in Russia. He lives today in Rishon L'Zion.

In this house there lived and died before the war a couple extremely old in years - Yodka and his wife. Yodka, a person of short stature, old age and white, would predict the rain in times of trouble and at every opportunity farmers would ask him and he would anwer them willingly. His wife served as a rebbetzin for the teaching of Torah and Mitzvot (commandments) to the girls of the town.

The House of the Widow Devora, the Gabbait, Brunner (see the separate report, about her public activity). Two sons: Yisroel and Avraham - remained alive due to their service in the Red Army and they live apparently in Soviet Russia. In the same house lived another son who was married with children.

The sons were in the tailor profession.

The House of Rabbi Aharon Baas, his wife Basecha, son Motol and three unmarried daughters. The husband and the son worked most of the days of the week in a tree sawmill outside of the town. The youngest daughter Shayndel remained alive and lives apparently in America or Canada.

The House of Hershel Habader (the Bath House Operator), his wife and his children. His first-born daughter Chaya and other sons and daughters. His house was on the bank of the river, between houses of goyem. Hershel was a hard-working, modest Jew, who maintained his large family with great difficulty while making a living from his public position - manager and operator of the Jewish bath house in the town.

[Page 139]

4. The Alley Adjoining Shkoolnah Street in the Direction of the Horyn River

In the Hostel for the Poor lived a blacksmith by the name Berel, his wife and their two daughters. One daughter was killed by disease when she was a girl of 18. The parents had bitterness together with all of their surrounding neighbors.

The House of Berel the Cleaner of Chimneys, his wife and their son and a number of daughters. This Jew was the only cleaner of chimneys in the town. This was an attraction in the eyes of the children when he appeared equipped with all of his special tools and accessories: chains together with weights, brooms and brushes. Berel was hard working and most of the days of the week he was covered in soot from his foot to his head. To see him clean was possible only on Shabbat and on the holidays.

In the House of Freida the Cryer Lived Her Son-in-Law, Koven, with the Nickname Kotek

The House of the Shenker Family - the father of the family Tzvi Shenker, his wife Zlata, the sons: Yitzchak and his family, Pesach and his family, and Shalom Shenker and his family who immigrated to Israel before the war and he lives with his family in Tel Aviv.

Berel Greenstein, his wife and daughters: Chana and Michla, and son Shlomo, who was saved by hiding himself in the forests among the goyem. He lives today in Israel.

Berel was a hard-working man and sustained his family with great difficulty. He worked as a watchman and miller in the flour mill of the Tachors.

Moshe the Invalid, the lame, married to one of the daughters of Yachneh. His profession was butchery.

The Zelberberg House - the son of Rabbi Berel Aharon Hershles, his wife and their four daughters and one son. The name of one of the daughters was Chaya.

Nearby the Slope of the River Lived the Two Sisters of Nechamia Geller

5. The Third of May Street (the Koroster Street)

One of the central streets of the town. This street continues from the marketplace until the popular state school, a continuation of the way that leads to the nearby town of Korets. This was a paved street with sidewalks and lighting, and on its entire length were dwelling houses with stores in front.

[Page 140]

The House of Rabbi Avraham Bebchuk (Bravaar, the Brave One), his wife Menucha, the daughters Sonya and Edele, and the son Ben-Zion. The father of the family, Rabbi Avraham, who was the owner of a grocery shop, was a G-d fearing Jew, peaceful and modest.

The son, Ben-Zion remained alive and lives with his family in Haifa, another daughter Edele, who escaped from the claws of the Nazis and was saved by hiding herself in the forests, arrived in Israel, and lived in Ramat Gan with her family and died in the year 1973.

The House of Leib Pach-Gruber - the owner of a carriage by profession. His wife and his three sons: Sheilik, Yeshayahu and Yosef. Sheilik and Yeshayahu were husbands of families. Remaining alive were

Yosef Gruber the son and Yosef Gruber the grandson, son of Sheilik. The two of them live nowadays in Russia.

The House of Tzvadya Garber - in the same house lived Aharon Leib the sandalmaker and his family. Berele, the son of Rabbi Tzvadya lives in Argentina - and even his two grandchildren, the son and daughter of Berele, live in Israel in Kfar Saba.

The Family of the Widow Maachlaya Malamud - the daughter Leah, her husband Dovid Gorman, their son Avraham and their daughters Esther and Sonya, lived in the nearby Kostopol; the son Yechial, his wife Rivka, and their sons: Yehoshua and Avraham, lived in nearby Rafalovka; the son Dovid and his wife Sima lived in Pietchyov. The son Yankel, his wife Zelda and their son Avraham and the son Moshe. Remaining alive from this family branch is the son Yehoshua Malamud, who was from the first activists of the Shomer Hatzair (leftist Zionist youth movement) in the town. He immigrated to Israel before the war and lives nowadays with his family in Haifa.

The House of Shmeiril Rassis, son of Yokel the shamash (beadle), his wife Bryndel and two daughters: Golda and Teyva. Shmeiril, the owner of a carriage, was industrious and well-off.

The House of Sander Leibes Bebchuk. The sons: Hershel, Motel and Yoalik. Hershel and Motel were married and heads of families. The family had a flour mill in a nearby village. Hershel was a fish merchant and Motel was a cattle merchant. The daughter of Motel, Perel, was saved after she hid herself in the forests and she lives nowadays in Ramat Gan. Yoalik, the son of Sander Bebchuk, lived, at that time, in Argentina.

The House of Yosef Wachs, and his second wife after he became widowed. His son from his first wife - Motek - a learned, intelligent young boy, and daughter from his second wife - Paula.

Yosef Wachs served as the head of the Judenratt upon the entrance of the Jews to the ghetto.

For details on his behavior and personality - see the separate report.

[Page 141]

The House of Shroolik Sheinboim, his wife Dentza, his sons: Shmuel, Dodel, Itzak, Zevel, and Yankel, and his daughters: Rochel and Golda. Shroolik was busy in commerce. Remaining alive are Zevel and Yaakov (Yankel), they live with their families in America; and also Golda died in Israel. The brother Yitzchak (Itzak) lives nowadays in Israel.

In the same house lived like a tenant ***the Teacher Kalat***, his wife, his son and his daughter. Mister Kalat served as the teacher in the Polish state school (see separate report on this family).

The House of Moshe Bebchuk, his wife Beila, daughter by the name Tzippah was married to a boy from Rovno, the second daughter was married to a Jew from Tchortorisk and they had two children. The husband of Tzippah lived together with the parents of his wife and erected in the back part of the house a factory for soft drinks. They nicknamed him "the Kobeches", based on the name of the goy from whom they purchased the plot. This Berel, at the time of his old age, had dimmed eyes, but despite this he continued in his work and as often as every day used to go slowly to the synagogue.

The House of Hershel Kola Hachavalim (the Ropemaker, the Shtikendreir) - he was a widower and had a daughter who managed the household and also a son by the name Yaakov. Yaakov was saved while he was in Russia and lives apparently there until today. Hershel was a craftsman at his work and despite the relatively primitive mechanization in his place of work, he supplied good-looking and excellent products to all of the neighboring goyem by investing the best of his of his energy and personal talents.

The House of Izik Grossman, his nickname Antek, the son of Rabbi Peseiah Harozenyahr. His wife Pasya and their two children. Izik was a cattle merchant. Izik died from hunger in the depths of Russia while he was enlisted.

The House of Motel Rocks, his wife and his sons: Hershel, Kotzik and Sander, and his daughters: Adele, Rivka and Raizel. Raizel, a well-known seamstress in the town, was the primary supporter of the family.

The House of Shlomo Rocks, the brother of Motel. His wife, son Yosef and his family, and daughter Adele. Shlomo was the owner of a grocery store.

The House of Shmuel Weisrashtrom, his wife and their son Lozar. Lozar was saved by escaping to the forests and he emigrated after the war to Argentina.

In the house of Shmuel Weisrashtrom lived a neighboring ***Family of Yisroel Lochselrod***, his wife Teiba, his son Pesach and his daughter Mila. Yisroel worked as a forester. The daughter Mila was saved and lives with her family in Hadera.

The House of Hershel Hecht, his wife and son, who lives in a nearby city - Kolk. In Israel lives the grandchildren of Rabbi Hershel: Simon and Boris Cheitchok.

[Page 142]

The House of Berel Aharon Hirsch, his wife and his sons: Avraham and Valka, and the daughters: Tzarna, Leah and Sosel. Rabbi Berel was a leather merchant. Sosel emigrated to Canada with her family.

The House of Rabbi Shlomo Hachazan (the Chazan), his son Yitzchak was married and the father of a daughter and son.

A relative of this family, ***Asher Glozman***, while he was a pacifist, refused to serve in the Polish army and therefore was imprisoned and tortured hard until Asher went out of his mind and suffered from mental depression. He lived nearby his family, in a secluded room.

The House of Rabbi Avraham Feldman (Machles), the teacher, his wife Chaya-Sarah, daughter Masha and three sons. Rabbi Avraham served as a teacher and thus he gave prayer lessons to the children of the town who learned in the Tarbut school. His last son lives currently in Argentina. In Israel lives two of his sons, Aharon and Baruch and the daughter Masha with her family.

The Family of Avraham Zelberberg, his wife Sarah, his sons Leibel and Monya and daughter Sosel. Avraham was a leather merchant.

The Family of Aharon Chait, his wife Perel, two daughters - Sarah and Minkah, and his son Zalman. Aharon was the owner of a shoe store. Perel traveled to America on the eve of the war and it is not known what befell her.

In the House of Yitzchak Chazan lived an unmarried teacher by the name ***Paparberg***, who descended from Warsaw. She worked as a teacher in the state-run elementary school.

The House of Shmuel Sorkin (Hatzyrolnik), his wife, his son Avraham and his daughters: Pasal and Ronya. The healing business was passed to Shmuel as an inheritance from his father, Rabbi Itzik, who was called "the doctor", because he was a druggist. Additionally, while Shmuel was a druggist, he was the owner of a barbershop and he worked together with his son Avraham.

The House of the Shpelsher Family. The father of the family Alter Males, the son Hershel, his wife Chana, son and two daughters: Manka and Sosel. Sosel remained alive while she was in Russia and lives currently in America. Alter Shpelsher was a tailor. His father-in-law Mops had a handsome son described by the name Pesach, who was married to a woman, Rozka, from the Neiman house. Hershel Shpelsher was an active Zionist and manager of the only bank in the town.

The House of Leibel Candle - the builder. He had a wife, son and daughter. His son was killed in his service in the Polish army in the year 1939, at the time of fighting during the Nazi invasion.

[Page 143]

The Hakozeles House - the brothers Moshe and Baruch Broder and their families. The two of them were iron merchants. Their sister Rivka had a daughter and son - Issar the lame, owners of a candy store. Issar, despite his deformity, was active and energetic. In his extra businesses, he would distribute the newspaper "Der Hint – Today". From this family one brother remained alive by the name Yosef, who emigrated to Argentina. A daughter by the name Zlatka lives in Petach Tikvah, and son Velvel, lives in one of the kibbutzim.

6. The Second Side of the Third of May Street

The House of Mendel Tveiktz Bostos, his wife Gittel, two sons - Yitzchak and Chilke, and a daughter married to Gedaliah Shaftrik. Mendel Bostos was a successful grain merchant. The son Chilke remained alive while he was in Russia. He immigated to Israel at the end of the Second World War, raised a family in Haifa. Chilke died in a sudden manner in the year 1973.

The House of Leibel Hastelmach (the Wheelwright) Rochblatt, his wife Feigel Pales, a married daughter who lived in Kostopol, and four sons. From them Avraham remained, who lives with his family in Ramat Gan, and Yitzchak, who lives with his family in Tel Aviv. The two of them immigrated to Israel before the Second World War.

The House of Peseiah Grossman (Harozenyahr) - a widower and his seamstress daughter, who managed the household, and sons: Moshe, Yonah and Izik. Moshe was married to Raizel and they had three children: Malka and sons: Avraham and Aharon. Moshe worked as a cattle merchant. He succeeded in his work and he was a seller to all of the surrounding villages. The daughter of Moshe, Malka, and his son Aharon were saved by hiding themselves in the forests among the goyem. Malka lives with her family in New York, and Aharon lives with his family in Tel Aviv. He is married to Rachel from the Chait house, who was also born in Stepan.

The House of Issar Hanimovitzar - in his house lived his son-in-law - **Hershel Salavotzki** together with his wife Chayka, their daughter Feigel and their son Velfel. They were the owners of a large grocery store.

The House of Yosef Shenker. Yosef Shenker and his second wife. Yosef had a daughter from his first wife by the name Yentel who lived outside the town.

The House of Mendel Hanapach (the Blacksmith), his wife Zelda and their married daughter and son by the name Yaakov. Mendel was a craftsman by profession and besides this he was known as a cheerful and amusing Jew. He would participate in happy occasions (simchas) and weddings as a comedian. Also he tried his best at the times of the Ukrainian dances and was also very successful, which brought proud pleasure (nachas) to the community. His son Yaakov succeeding in escaping from the killing pits, but he was caught after a few days in the forest in the neighborhood of Korost and was taken out to be killed.

[Page 144]

The House of Aharon Motel Shimshak, his wife and his two daughters who were married and moved to a town outside of Stepan. His son Dovid was married to a woman, Chana, from the house Kirshner, and they had a son and daughter.

This family had an oil press.

The House of Itzik Meir Kogot, his wife and his three sons: Arye, Gershon and an additional small son, and two daughters: Rena and Ganya. The son Arye immigrated to Israel on the eve of the war together with his wife Tziporah from the house of Geller. He currently lives in Tel Aviv with his family. Gershon served in the Red Army and fell in battle in the year 1944 in the area of Kovel, having exposed himself to danger in the war against the Germans.

The House of Peseiah Bebchuk, his wife Leah Esther and his sons: Moshe and Avraham, and his daughters: Chayka, Tzilah, and Rozka. The daughter Rozka immigrated to Israel in the year 1936 together with her husband Tzlia Shpritz. They currently live in Tel Aviv.

The House of Motel Becker, his wife Pasal and their two daughters - Esther and Yentel, and son - Shayka. Motel owned a manufacturing store. The son Shayka was saved by escaping to the forests; he emigrated to Argentina and lives there with his family.

The House of the Tachor Families. Meir, his wife Hennia, and his daughters: Brunia, Sonya, Panya and Batya, and their son - Monya. In their house also lived the grandmother Raizel Tachor and an additional son Michel Tachor, his wife Rivka and his two sons Avraham (Mosik) and Yitzchak. Avraham was saved at the time that he hid himself in the forests, while his father was captured and shot. Avraham currently lives in Tel Aviv with his family.

The House of Altar Bass, his wife Esther, his son Shabatai and his daughter Freidel. Altar was active in the Zionist committee of the Jews of Stepan. This family was killed at the time of the German bombing, on the eve of their entrance into the town, together with another family - relatives of Altar Bass - Motel Koifman, a sandalmaker by profession, his daughter Asal and sons: Shmuel and Yaakov. Yaakov was saved from the annihilating bombing together with the surviving Jews of the town.

In the house lived a relative of the family, mute but very intelligent, well-liked by his neighbors.

The son Shmuel fell as a German prisoner in the Polish-German War and his consequences were not known.

The House of Yerachmial Gesais, his wife Gittel, his son-in-law Shlomo Neiman, his wife Tzivya and their son Yeshayahu Neiman, a teacher in the Tarbut school and head of Betar in the city. The boy was head and shoulders above the others and served as a shining example for the children of the town. He died from disease at a young age. Shlomo Neiman also had three daughters: Rosa, who was married to Pesach Mopas, Ganya and Reva who was married to Kolodny and apparently lives nowadays in Russia.

[Page 145]

In this house also lived a second son-in-law of Yerachmial - **Moshe Koifman**. He had a wife named Adele and son Monya. Moshe Koifman was the veteran teacher in the Tarbut school since it had been established. He educated a number of generations in Judaism and Zionism. He was very active in the Zionist movement and in the Jewish National Fund.

The House of Moshe Vosrostrom, his wife and their daughter Tanah. He was a devout Jew and feared G-d.

In this house lived as neighbors the **Family Rovin** - the widowed wife (the Beznke) and her daughters - Raizel and Devora. They were owners of a small grocery store. Devora escaped to Russia, immigrated to Israel after the war and lives in Haifa with her family. Her sister Raizel emigrated to Argentina on the eve of the Second World War and lives there with her family.

The House of Kopel Hakovaon (the Hatmaker). In this house lived his daughter Mishka, her husband Aharon Kessler and their five children: Gittel, Miriam, Batya, Leibel and Michel. Michel was saved while he was in Russia and lives today in Israel, in Holon.

The House of the Brothers Nechamia and Motel Goz. In this house lived Nechamia, his wife and his three children. Likewise, Motel, his second wife Gansal, the stepmother to three daughters and a son - orphans who aroused the pity of the neighbors. The brothers managed a leather and shoe store.

The House of the Shpritz Family. Two brothers from the Shpritz family immigrated to Israel in the year 1936. They were friends of the Betar organization in the town. They were grandchildren of the grandmother Freida Shpritz.

In the house lived **Meir Dekelboim**, his wife Zlatka and their son. Meir was the owner of a grocery store.

The House of Rivka and Shmuel Leibes (Krakover) - the son of Rivka - Yosef. The wife of Yosef died at the time of the great fire in 1925. They had three children: Berta, who died in Israel, Gershon who lives in Kibbutz Nagvah (see the separate section), and Roza, who lives with her family in Holon. Yosef was married a second time to a woman named Zelda and they had a son named Alykim and a daughter Yentel.

The House of Yitzchak Woschina, his wife Mirka, their son Shmuel-Minikal, his wife Chaya and their three children: Yosele, Mirka and Ziskind. The brother of Minikal, Sholom, his wife Kalra and their daughter, an additional brother Yisroel and sister Sosel, who also died in the year 1925. Rabbi Itzik, father of the family, who was known for his pleasant voice at prayer time. His wife died before the outbreak of the war. The only survivor of this family was Minikal, who was expelled to Siberia during the Soviet reign. Now he lives in America with his second wife and their son and married daughter.

[Page 146]

The House of Yitzchak Zilberman - a widower and his daughter Chava from his second wife, whereas from his first wife the sons: Berel, Moshe who died in Israel, Hershel who immigrated to Israel and lives in Hertzlia, and Shlomo who was saved while he was in Russia and remains living there; also daughter Gittel, who lives with her family in Brazil.

The House of Shlomo Filkov, his wife and their three daughters. The name of one was Hennia, and also son Yosef, who lives in Israel after he was saved in Russia. Shlomo was gabbai in the upper synagogue. He was owner of a leather store.

The House of the Brothers Yosef and Betzalel Bebchuk (Hatzalyokim) - they were merchants. The brother Yosef, his wife Pasal and their three daughters: Raizel, Rivka and Perel, and son Hershel.

Betzalel, his wife and his daughter named Sheva and three sons: Shmiryahu, Yosef and Yitzchak. Shmiryahu was saved by hiding in the forests and he lives today in America.

The House of Fishel Solbotzky, his wife and their daughter - Manya, and son - Chaim who died in Russia during his service in the Red Army.

On the second side of this house lived **Moshe Chait** (the son of Altar Koters), his wife Raisel and their two sons: Motel and Monya, and daughter Sonya. Moshe was a successful tailor.

7. The Alleys Adjoining the Third of May Street

The House of Naftali Gorinstein, his wife Sosel and their sons: Ben-Zion, Lazar, Yosel, Yankel, Moshe and Zev; daughters: Pasal and Rochel. A merchant of manufacturing and ready-made clothing.

The son Ben-Zion, after his marriage, moved to live in Barzna. The son Yosel continued in the manner of his father in the manufacturing and ready-made clothing store in Stepan. Living in the same house with his family was: his wife Leah and their three daughters: Sarah, Yentel and Freidel, and two sons - Hershel and Yankel. Ben-Zion, Yankel and Rochel lived outside of Stepan. In the house of Naftali remained two of the sons - Moshe and Zev, and the daughter Pasal. The daughter Pasal immigrated to Israel through the Betar movement in the year 1934 and lives today in Netanya with her family. Traces of the son Moshe disappeared during the Second World War. The son Zev was saved while he was in the service of the Red Army. At the end of the Second World War

[Page 147]

he immigrated to Israel and lives with his family in Israel. The daughter Rochel emigrated before the Second World War to Brazil and lives there with her family.

The House of Moshe Yosef Sheinboim and his wife Mussia, they died in 1934. A merchant of grain crops. He raised sons and daughters - Rivkah Komonshein, Sroolik, Tanchoom, Shabseil, Abba, Esther Baram, Raizel Shuster, Golda Pearlstein, and Nacha Bleiy. In the same house lived the **Family Bleiy**, Nacha and her husband Berel Bleiy, a wood merchant and shopkeeper.

In the same house lived the family of *Shmuel and Raizel Shuster* and their daughter and son. A merchant of grain crops.

In the Narrow Alley Lived the Family: The Brother Banah and his Sister Chayka with her husband, whose profession was a painter. Banah and Chayka were albinos and they were called "The Weisse - The Whites". Banah was a familiar figure, mainly with the children of the town who loved to flirt with him in a good spirit. Banah, while he was short in stature, knew the entire order of the prayers and psalms by heart.

The House of Bonyah Hatoferet (the Seamstress). Banyah and her sister earned a living from the hard work of their hands.

The House of the Gerber Family - the widow. Her husband Izik died before the war. The widow Sarah had two sons. The name of one was Chaim - he also died before the war. This widow earned a living from the baking and selling of black bread. This family was the rentor of a room that was used for the needs of the Tarbut School. The daughters of Sarah: Beila, Devorah, and son - Nechamia.

The House of Teivel Hatoferet (the Seamstress) - her husband worked in the flour mill of the Graz's. In this family was a sister of Teivel with three children. Her husband emigrated to Argentina and after many years of waiting they were taken there. There is the assumption that they remain alive. There was also there an old grandmother who worked at baking bread. The nickname for this family was "Dreikop - Skittish".

The House of Rabbi Ben-Zion Gonik and his wife Zesol. An old Jew, a scholar, who served many years as a teacher in the town. In his classroom he educated a number of generations of children of the town.

In the same house lived his daughter Chana and her husband Shaul Pakowitz and their children.

His son Motel also served as a Rabbi and as a teacher in a nearby town and after that in Stepan. In addition to his great expertise in Torah and in Judaism, he acquired general knowledge. His wife Machla and their son Yosef.

Rabbi Ben-Zion had an additional daughter named Leibah, who was married to Leibka Kraf, a merchant, and they had a number of children.

Nunya Hochman, my God avenge him, with his friend Mordechai Rassis, may he live a long life

[Page 148]

The son Yitzchak Gonik immigrated to Israel in the 1930's. He died after a number of years, leaving a wife and children in Holon.

An additional son, Shimon Gonik, lives in Yugoslavia. It is not known what befell him.

The House of Rabbi Hershel Hashochet (the Slaughterer) Hochman, his wife and their four sons and one daughter. The son Nunya, who immigrated to Israel on the treshhold of the Second World War, fell in the battle in Italy against the Nazi enemy as part of the Jewish brigade (he was injured and transported to Israel by British airplane; the plane was brought down on his way to Israel).

8. Hatetarim Street

The House of Hershel Feldman (from Hakalenykes), his wife Sarah, daughters: Henda, Faygel and Rivka, and son - Avraham. Owner of a stand for selling fruit. His hobby was fishing with a fishing rod. He served as a violinist with the family of musicians (Hakalenykes) and also appeared as a merry humorist at the Jewish weddings and happy occasions (simchas) in the town.

The daughters and the son were activists in the Shomer Hatzair (leftist Zionist youth movement) and pioneer. The son Avraham was saved while he was in Russia and lives today in Kfar Saba with his family.

The House of Moshe Feldman, who died before the outbreak of the war, his wife, and sons: Gavriel, Avramle, Velvel - a bass player - and another brother. The daughters: Brendel, Rochel, Devorah, Sarah, Golda and Miriam. This family belonged to the musicians. The father Moshe played

[Page 149]

violin and gave lessons for playing the violin. The daughter Brendel was an excellent guitar player.

The son Avraham remained alive while he was in Russia. Nowdays he lives in Poland.

The Waldman Family - they called them Stisel the Mitzker. They had three daughters: Dovah was married to the administrator of the Tarbut school Mr. Kemerman, the daughter Rivka was married to one from nearby Kostopol. and the daughter Rochel immigrated to Israel before the war and lives in Tel Aviv. The son Hershel emigrated to Canada and the son Shmuel immigrated to Israel with the fourth immigration wave, but went to the United States.

The House of Moshe Golprin, his wife Sosel, the son Hershel who was married in Sarna and moved to live there, and daughter Gittel. He worked in the selling of yeast. The daughter Gittel was saved while she was in Russia, immigrated to Israel after the war, but died from disease. There remains the husband and two sons in Israel.

The Kanonitz Family, the son Michel and daughter Freidel. Michel worked as a miller in the flour mill of the Goz family. The son Michel was active in the Betar movement. One day he withdrew from Betar with Moshe Gorinstein and together they served at the head of a faction to the right - the Grossmanists. They even established a Grossmanist cell. This event happened in the year 1933.

The Family of Moshe Bebchuk, the son Hershel and daughters - Tchrana and Beila. He worked in peddling. The daughter Beila remained alive by hiding herself in the forests with the Polish. She immigrated to Israel with her family, but ultimately moved to the United States.

The Weismann Family (the Motelykes) - a very spacious house. In this house lived together in a friendly way a number of families who led collective lives in still waters. The mother Sosel Weismann, her sons: Motel, who was a superb photographer in his profession (see the separate report concerning this matter) and the son Yitzchak, the young intellectual who was active in Betar, and the sister Michle.

The sister of Sosel Weismann, Esther, was married to Avraham Shochet and they had a daughter and son, and the sisters Gittel and Michle. There also lived in the same house an unmarried adult uncle by the name Motel.

This family had an oil-press adjoining their house and they also managed a grocery store in the front of the house. The son Yitzchak Weismann remained alive while he was in Russia. He immigrated to Israel (see the separate report on Yitzchak Weismann, of blessed memory, and his family in Israel).

The House of Yechezkial Stern, his wife, two daughters - Shayndel and Chana, and sons: Hershel, Yankel, Moshe and Shlomoke. Stern had a medicine warehouse, resembling a drug store, and a perfume store.

The son Moshe was an activist and prominent in his activities as head of the cell of the Shomer Hatzair (leftist Zionist youth movement) in the town.

[Page 150]

The Family of Shimon Gorbitz, his wife, the daughter Chana, the son Pinyah and another son. Pinyah was active in the Shomer Hatzair (leftist Zionist youth movement). He was involved with the pioneering preparation of the movement in Lodz. The aim was to immigrate to Israel at the outbreak of the war. All traces of him were lost.

The Family of David Finkelstein, his wife from the house of Stern and their children. The owner of a store for writing instruments. He was a well-liked man who took care of the students with love and goodwill. He was most popular with the Jewish children of Stepan.

The House of Mordechai Wolpel Hakatzav (the Butcher), his wife and his daughter Esther, who was widowed, and her daughter Rochel Chamar and another sister Bryndele.

The House of the Rosenfeld Family- the father of the family, Dovid, of blessed memory, was killed in a work accident, and Mirel, who remained a widow, and her sons: Pinya, Shmuka and Avraham, and daughters: Raizel, Beila, Chana, Chaya and Fasya.

David, of blessed memory, was an industrious and energetic builder and by the labor of his own hands he owned a flour mill and an oil press of his own. After his death the factory was managed by his sons and sons-in-law.

The daughter Raizel, who lived in the same house, was married to Shroolik Sheintoch and they had a daughter, Chaya, and sons: Avraham and Mordechai. Shroolik Sheintoch was an owner of a grocery store and was successful in his business.

The daughter Fasya emigrated to Argentina before the war and afterwards immigrated to Israel with her family; they live in Banas Tziyonah. The son of Fasya, Michel, volunteered and immigrated to Israel in the year 1967; currently he serves as secretary of the kibbutz Ein Hashlosha. The son Pinya was saved while he was drafted in Russia. Pinya fought in the ranks of the Red Army and fell to German captivity. After great hardship as a Jewish captive in a concentration camp he remained alive. After the war he emigrated to Argentina and lived with his sister Fasya, but died by a fatal accident there. The sister Beila was married to a Jew in Broznitz and they had three children.

In the same house lived the doctor, Dr. Ashkenazi, an adult woman, unmarried and childless. She served as the doctor there in the town for many years.

The House of Aharon Rosenfeld, his wife Brynner and their daughter Leah and son Tzvi, who remained alive by ending up in Russia when he tried to illegally emigrate to Israel through Latvia, with the entry of the Soviets.

Aharon was a plasterer by profession and he supported his family by the labor of his own hands.

Tzvi lives with his family in Tel Aviv.

The House of Shmuel Silberman, his wife and their five children - sons and daughters. In his house was the only dentist in the town, Dr. Gorin. The permanent dwelling of Dr. Gorin and his family was in Rovno. Dr. Gorin was an active Zionist public worker.

[Page 151]

The House of Hatzevai (the Painter) Pontak, his wife and their son and daughter, and also living in the same house was his brother, Gershon Pontak, and his wife.

Excellent painters who by the sweat of their noses and by honesty they earned their bread.

The House of Itzchak Woschina, his wife Aydeh, the son Yossele and his small sister. He was the son-in-law of Rabbi Pinchas Goldstein and the owner of a flour mill. He worked in partnership with his father-in-law. The son Yosef was an excellent student, actually a child prodigy.

The House of Moshe Morik, his wife Gittel from the family Woschina, and their three daughters: Motol, Mirkah and another one. He was a successful merchant of grain.

The Family of Walkah Feldman - one of the sons of Falya the musician, his wife and his mother-in-law. They had children. The daughters: Maale, Yentel, Rochel, and the sons: Avramle and another son.

He was the owner of a restaurant and also manufacturer of kvass (a drink from pickled cabbage) – a soft drink. The grandmother, primarily, was a seller of baked items and kvass in the marketplace.

Along side their house was a spacious garden and orchard that was taken care of and fostered. It was prominent for its wonderful grapes that grew extraordinarily in the region of Stepan.

The Tarchtarman Family - the Virker - he was the owner of a grocery store in the adjoining Polish village, Virke. His wife, Chofka, and their two sons and a daughter.

The House of Shabbtai Schnoik, his wife, his daughter Manya and three sons. He was the owner of storehouse for wood. His sons, most likely alive, or their offspring, emigrated to Argentina during his time. In addition to his business in wood, he was supported by his sons.

The Weitziner Family, his wife and children. He worked in the forests and was not a Stepaner. He lived in Stepan while he was employed in the proximity of the forests. He arrived from a nearby town.

The House of Chaim Goberman, his wife and their two daughters - Dotzya and Devora, and also a son of their old age. He was the owner of a haberdashery and fancy goods store.

The House of Moshe Feldman, the son of Rabbi Falya the musician. His wife Haydel and their three daughters. He was the owner of a large grocery store. He was a successful shopkeeper in his business.

The Shoftrik Family, their daughter, Holah, and son, Ezrial. He was a merchant of pig hair and mushrooms.

[Page 152]

The House of Yossel Hakeveran (the Gravedigger), a lonely, childless Jew, owner of a large garden beside his house. He made a living as a gravedigger and fulfilled his public duties faithfully.

The House of the Teacher with the Nickname Moneval, his wife Veronica - his death at a ripe old age before the outbreak of the war. They had a divorced daughter, Faygel, and she had a single son, Shlomo.

Rabbi Moneval was the well-liked Rabbi by the students of his class. He was accustomed to take his pupils and lead them to visit the women who have just given birth one day before the brit milah (circumcision), for reading the Shema (prayer). At the same event, the woman who just gave birth would generously distribute cookies and candies to the children of the classroom. The daughter Faygel would collect the money for the lessons from the parents of the students. The son Shlomo remained alive while he was in a nearby Polish town. He currently lives in Poland.

The House of Hershel Gelman (the son of Freida the cryer), his wife and children. He was a merchant of rags. His son Yaakov was saved while he was in Russia. There is an opinion that he emigrated to the United States and lives there.

The House of Helenke Hakatzav (the Butcher), his wife and daughters: Tovah, Malka, and Hennia. Tovah was active in the Shomer Hatzair (leftist Zionist youth movement). The daughter Hennia was saved while hiding herself in the forests among the Polish. She emigrated to the United States and lives there with her family.

In the Unfinished House Lived a Bachelor, Berel Weitznodel. He had the nickname - Yehofetz. He was a cattle merchant.

The House of the Family of Kolodny Leibel, his wife and daughters: Hennia, Roza, and a son. He was the owner of a factory for soap and soft drinks - kvass and soda.

The House of the Ploshnik Family - Motel, his wife and their children. Yankel, his wife and their children. The brother Izak and brother Ben-Zion. A sister Adele who was married to Yankel Patshnik and lived in a nearby place. Yankel remained alive while he was in Russia, married a second time and he had a son.

9. The Second Side of Hatetarim Street and the Adjoining Alleys

The House of the Widower Moshka Brick, her son Eliezer. In the same house also lived a grandmother, whose business was peddling with the goyem of the town.

The House of Baruch Wolf Kershner, his wife, their son Avraham and his wife and the daughter Babah who was born in Israel. Avraham immigrated to Israel during the fourth immigration wave but returned to the town since they were never acclimatized to Israel. The sons Aharon and Benjamin emigrated to Canada and lived there,

[Page 153]

Nachum - a young man active in the Shomer Hatzair (leftist Zionist youth movement) was saved while he was in Russia and apparently lives in Russia. There was another daughter who emigrated to Canada, and the daughters: Esther and Chana, who was married to Dovid Shimshak.

In the same house lived the brothers of Baruch Wolf - *Motel - Mordechai Kershner* - his wife, the daughter Chasya and two sons. Motel served as the shamash (beadle) in the Tarbut school in the town and fulfilled his duties faithfully during many years, until everything was destroyed by the wicked hands.

The Eisenberg Family – a widower and his daughter Shayna and son Yosef. He was a builder by profession.

The House of Moshe Yosef Dargoff, his wife and his daughter Hennia and other children. He was a community person, who established charity funds in the town, and he served in charge of them.

The House of Yaakov Petashnik, his wife Hodel and their daughter Simma and sons – Sander and Michel. Michel was saved while he was in the forests among the goyem. He lives nowdays in Ramat Gan with his family. Yaakov was an enthusiastic Zionistic public worker for Brit Yeshurin, and he also immigrated to Israel but he returned again to his town because of difficulties with the acclimatization and the lack of work.

The House of Yisroel Zelishnik, his wife Chana and their four children: Pinchas, Miriam, Michla and Chaya. The daughter Chaya was saved while she was in a convalescent home in Russia at the outbreak of the war. Her father, Yisroel, traveled to search for his daughter but never found her and he returned to Stepan to the children of his family. Yisroel was a sheet-metal worker by profession and supported his family with great difficulty, but with honor, without the help of strangers..

The House of Leivik Tzeseis, his wife Shayndel, and the daughters: Machla and Hennia and son Berel. He was a cattle merchant.

In the house of Leivik Tzeseis lived a rentor *Hellia Weiner*, his wife and daughter Sonia, who was saved by hiding in the forests among the goyem. She immigrated to Israel and continued her emigration to Canada.

The House of Baruch Broder (from Hakozeles), his wife from the Shpatrik house and their three children. He was the owner of a store of iron products.

The House of Zev Chayot, his wife Chaya Leah (from the Dov house), the son Shmuel and the daughter Sarah. Zev was a witness of proof to the killing of the Stepan community in the forests and being thrown into the death pits near Kostopol. He escaped and was saved. He served with the partisons in the Tchepyav regiment. Today he lives in Tel Aviv with his family that he established from new.

The House of Itzik Gooteis, his wife and their son.

The House of Dovid Chamar, his wife Basel from the Srashtrom house and their four children, a son Lazar a daughter Esther and another two daughters. He worked as a glazier and seller of fruit.

[Page 154]

The House of Ben-Zion Peloshnik, his wife and a number of their daughters. He was a cattle merchant.

The House of Mendel Hakatzav (the Butcher), his wife and his children. With him lived in his house his elderly mother Fayga, who was busy baking black bread that was known for its quality. Also living in the same house was the sister of Mendel with her husband Avraham.

10. The Area of the Marketplace

The Zilbervelt Family – the mother of the family was a widow and her daughters: Raizel and Henda, and son Shmuel who emigrated to the United States before the war and died there. In the same house lived an aunt with the name Mindel. One of the daughters was married to a Jew from Kostopol, whereas Henda was married to Yonah Grossman and they had a daughter and son named Yossele, who remained alive by hiding in the forests among the goyem. He emigrated after the war to the United States and lives there today.

The Widow Dovah Weingarten (Dobroshkah). In Kolnya, on the other side of the bridge, with the goyem, lived the family of the widow Dovah Weingarten including her daughter Esther, who was married and lived in Manevichi,;the daughter Freidel, who was married to Yossel Magid and was saved with her two children – Hershel and Eliyahu, who live today in the United States; and also a son, Leibel, who was killed in Russia.

Dovah, of blessed memory, traded with the goyem and was very well-liked among them because of her good heart and giving goods in the surroundings to all the needy without discrimination. Because of this, she also had the nickname "Dobroshkah" – a good heart. But these good, human qualities were to no avail and she was killed together with the remainder of the Jews of the town in the awful Shoah.

The House of Falya Feldman – the musician, his wife who was famous for the quality of her cooking, especially stuffed fish, and also for her righteous concern for the needy. (For a description of the personality of Rabbi Falya, see the separate section).

The House of Zevel Press – hatmaker by profession. His son Avraham emigrated to the United States and apparently lives there.

The House of Yekutial Goldberg, gabbai in the supreme synagogue, and his sons: Nissel and Motke, who emigrated to Argentina and apparently live there, and also sons Michel and Hershel and daughter Gittel.

The House of Rabbi Yaakov (Zunieh) Koifman – a widower, a learned and G-d fearing Jew. (See the separate section).

[Page 155]

His son Dodel and his wife Bryndele and daughters: Malka, Shayna and Sarah. They lived in Dubno. His son Moshe, his wife Hodel and son Monya. His daughter Rivka was married to Michel Tachor, their son Avraham was saved and lives with his family in Tel Aviv. His son Reuven, his wife and their son

Mordechai perished in Terspol, Russia. His son Gedaliah – a bachelor. His son Yisroel – immigrated to Israel in 1933 and lives with his family on Kibbutz Ein Carmel. His daughter Nachah, was married to a boy from the town of Totchin.

The House of Moshe Wachs (who was known by his nickname Moshe the Giller), his wife, the son Dodel and his daughters: Rivka and Leiva. He was the owner of a manufacturing store.

The House of Yaakov Wachs (Bocheles), his wife and son Yisroel. He was the owner of a store of groceries and commodities, specializing particularly and well-known for the quality of his sour, pickled cucumbers.

The House of Shaul Weitznodel, his wife and their sons: Gershon, Hershel, and Yitchak, and daughters: Leah, Faygel, and Sonya, who live in Argentina. An additional daughter is in Brazil, and Chaya, who lives in Netanya. Shaul Weitznodel worked as a butcher.

Shaul Weitznodel , against the background of his house

[Page 156]

The Family of Michel Bardas (Kootzik –short stature). He was a manufacturing merchant. He had a daughter Rochel who was married to Yaakov Tzukerman from Barzna, a daughter Dovah and a daughter Gittel who was married to Chaim Takas and they had two children. His son Avraham married the daughter of Yankel Partch from the village Krechilsk and he had an additional married son by the name Leibel.

The House of Gershon Weitznodel, a plasterer and owner of a bakery. He had a wife, three sons and a daughter. His son Moshe was married to Golda Rassis, the daughter of Shmerel Rassis.

The House of Motel Tchodler – the owner of a soft drinks factory and a manufacturing store. His wife was an excellent seamstress of women's clothing, his son Yitzchak and daughter Gittel, who was married to a boy from the city of Rovno, and also there were another son and daughter.

The House of Shmuel Derech Harokeach (the Pharmacist), his wife Chayka, two daughters, the name of one was Sheva, and the son Tzodya who was saved by serving in the Red Army and lives today in Russia.

The House of Motzya Waldman – the head of the house was his daughter, a widow, Bryndele Weitznhoyz. The son Zev was the first immigrant from Stepan to Israel, in 1932, and lives in Kfar Sabah. There were another two daughters – Sosel and Chava. The family house was a spacious house that stood in the center of the marketplace.

The Houses of Blumah Kriegel, her sister ***Mirkah*** and her brother ***Aharon Stoller***. The widow Blumkah sold ice cream that was famous for its quality and special taste, primarily among the youth. Blumkah had a son – Yoskah Kriegel, who was saved by serving in the Red Army and lives today in Russia. Mirkah – owner of a shoe store – was married and had two daughters.

Aharon Stoller was a well-known photographer and owner of a wonderful studio. His wife Freidel was from the Wachs family, and they had children.

The House of Shmuel Tzodies Garber, his wife and his children. Shmuel was an excellent men's tailor.

The House of Velvel Shmeles Wachs, his wife, and two sons. He was a grain merchant.

The House of Michel Wachs and his wife. The son Yaakov who was saved while he was in Russia immigrated to Israel and lives nowadays in Beer Sheva. The daughters: Gittel and Freidkah.

The House of Nachum Magid, his wife, and his sons: Leibel who lives in Russia, Yosef who was married to Freida and their two sons: Hershel and Alyah. A son, Pinkah, who was saved while he was in Russia and lives in the United States. A son Bankah and daughter Dotzyah.

[Page 157]

Nachum was a grain merchant and owner of a wheat mill in one of the villages near the town. His sons and daughters were activists in the Betar movement.

The House of Milah Yostein, his wife and his children. The son Ponkah, who was enlisted into the Red Army, passed by the town immediately after its liberation in 1944. He fell in battle against the Germans in the lines of the Red Army in 1944.

The House of the Brother of Moshe Bronstein, his wife and their two daughters. They were owners of a manufacturing store. He also had another son, Yitzchak, who was saved by hiding among the goyem in the forests and lives nowadays in Germany.

The House of Moshe Bronstein, his wife Dovah and their daughter Chava and son Yitzchak. In the same house lived the mother of Moshe. Dovah was an energetic woman, who predominantly managed the manufacturing store, with success.

The House of Chaim Simcha Morick and his wife. He was active in Brit Yeshurin. He was a successful grain merchant.

The House of Yitzchak (Irotzikel) Bebchuk-Meyers, his wife Sarah and their children: Chana and Meir. Yitzchak was the owner of a restaurant and also a grocery store close to the center of the town.

The House of Chaim Wachs (the Varbetzer – he descended from the nearby village of Varbetze), his wife and their daughter Gittel and the sons: Valkah and Shaptal. The son Shaptal was saved while he was in Russia, and at the completion of the war he apparently emigrated to the United States and lives there. Chaim was a grain merchant.

11. The Alleys in the River Slope – from Potshtovah Street

In the House of Gershon Weitznodel lived Shmuel Goz, his wife Faygel from the Kagan family and their son.

In the Gorinstein House resided the widow Beila Koshner and her daughters. Raizel, who immigrated to Israel before the war, was married to Aharonov. She ultimately died. Her sister Leibah, also immigrated to Israel before the war, was married to Yagodeh and lives with her family in Tel Aviv.

[Page 158]

The House of the Sokolosky Family, close to the river. Most recently, in this house, lived the widow Pasal.

The House of Dovid Baram, his wife Esther from the Sheinboim family and their daughters: Chana, Roza and another two sisters, and the sons: Motel and Bobah. With the entrance of the Germans to the town, their house was hit by a direct hit from the German's bombings. Four of their children were killed in this bombing. Dovid Baram himself was blinded and remained disabled in the majority of his body; he and his wife and two children remained.

The House of Motel Weinstein, his wife Blumah and their only son Avraham. Motel was active in public activity. In the same house lived his sister Michlia and her son, Leibel Rassis, who was saved while he was in Russia, and today lives in Kfar Aviv with his family.

The House of Simma Yokelson, his wife and their two sons: Shpatal and his brother, and one daughter. Simma worked as a horse merchant.

The House of Velvel Hachayat (the Tailor), his wife and their only son. Velvel was a tailor by profession. He worked primarily by sewing large and heavy clothing for the villagers and from this he earned his livelihood.

12. Potshtovah Street

The House of the Yokelson Family – in this house lived three brothers with their families. Ben-Zion and his second wife, the daughter Faygel and another daughter and son. The son Raphael immigrated to Israel during the 1930's. He was the first of the commanders of Betar in the town. He lives today in Israel. Hershel and his wife, and their three children. Berel and his wife and their girl.

The three brothers worked in the iron trade and its products.

There also lived in this house, or nearby, a sister of this family – Chana – who was married to Eli Koifman and they had a single son, Shaptal.

The House of the Family of Tanchum Sheinboim, who died before the war, his wife Etta, the son Chaim and his wife Shifra and their two children, the son Ben Zion, his wife Bruniah from the family Tachor with the children Moshe and Tanchum. Ben Zion and his brother Shmuel were saved while they were in Russia and live in Israel with their families.

The sons Yitzchak (today Aron) and Shlomo Sheinboim immigrated to Israel before the war and live with their families in Tel Aviv.

Tanchum Sheinboim immigrated to Israel with his wife and daughter Bracha in the year 1934; a short time after they came to Israel he got sick and died in Israel after an operation. The wife and daughter returned to the town at that time and were killed in the Shoah with the remaining Jews of the town. (See a description of these personalities).

[Page 159]

The House of Chaim Gershon Goz, his wife, they died before the war. He was and intellectual Jew. The sons: Michel, Valkeh, Shaul, Shmuel and Motkeh. The daughters: Adele, Chaykeh and Rochel who was the graceful and active one among the daughters.

The majority of the children of the family were active in managing a big grocery store in the town. This store was active seven days a week and the owners of this store were known for their decency and their good service to all the citizens of the town and the surroundings.

The son Motkeh was an activist in the Zionist movement and an activist in the pioneer training of the Betar movement in Katowitz.

The Milstein Family – mother and her son Yitzchak. Yitzchak was a talented boy who worked as a mechanic in the wheat mill of the Goz family.

The House of Pinyah Goz, his wife, who died before the war. This was one of the spacious and pleasant houses in the town. In this house lived two of his sons: Yitzchak and his wife Bracha and their son Shabbtai. His brother Avraham, his wife Hennia and their sons Zalman and Yaakov and daughter Gitteleh. The daughter Pasyah from the Goz family, who was married to Gotzyah Toyev and their daughters Sonya (Sarah) and Gittel, who was saved while she was in Russia and lives today in Haifa with her family.

He was the owner of a large and modern flour mill and the owner of a concession for the selling of firewater (brandy). They were well-to-do people with generous hearts, pleasant Jews and active Zionists.

The House of Baruch Rassis, his wife, and their sons: Shroolkeh, his wife and their children: Zalman, and his wife and children; Erkeh, who was saved while he was in Russia and apparently lives there until today. The daughter Chaykeh and her husband, who emigrated to the United States, and the daughter Rivkeh and her husband Shagrar, a teacher in the "Tarbut" school.

Baruch was the owner of a wagon and a horse merchant. He was owner of a concession for hauling mail from Stepan to the train station in nearby Malynsk.

The House of Alter Zeliks, owner of a clothing store – he had a son Yaakov and three daughters: Manya, who was married to Yasha, and their children. Yasha was the owner of a restaurant; an additional daughter was the wife of Chaim Goberman; and Rivkah, who was saved while she was in Russia and lives today with her family in Israel.

The House of Pinchas Goldstein, the owner of a flour mill on the edge of town. He had two daughters, one who was married to Yitzchak Woschina. Pinchas was an active public servant, who represented the Jews of the town before the local Polish council "Hagmenah" in the town.

[Page 160]

13. Nearby the Marketplace Region

The Family of Hershel Siegel Hashan (the Watchmaker), his wife Beila-Gittel, and their sons: Chaim-Moshe and his wife Golda-Chaya; Yosef-Dov and his wife Raizel and their son, Ben Lipman who was saved while he was in Russia and lives in Givatayim with his family. The daughters: Pasya and her husband Noach Zolar, Freida and her husband Yitzchak Bostos, and Devosyah.

The son of Yosef remains alive and lives in Russia.

Hershel was a respected Jew and a great scholar.

The House of Moshe Woschina – a two-storied, spacious house, one of a few of its kind in the town. It's front literally faced the center of the marketplace. In the lower level of the house were stores that had big lots that were rented.

Moshe, together with his sons, worked in trading grain and was very popular with the goyem of the surroundings, in whom they gave complete loyalty.

In the same house lived his son Dodleh, his wife Beila (from the Yachniuk family) and their children.

The son Yitzchak was saved while he was in the forests among the goyem. He lives with his family in Givatayim.

In addition to this there lived in the same house one of the daughters who was married to Boaz, the owner of a grocery store and their children.

The daughter Ethele with her husband Dorotchinsky from Slonim – a Zionist activist. Dorotchinsky was saved while he was in Russia and lives today in the United States.

The son Aharon was saved while he was in Russia and apparently lives there.

The House of the Kagan Family – the widowed wife, who by her own resources and with the help of her children managed a manufacturing store. She had a number of children: a son Moshe and his wife and children; the son Pinya; daughter Faygel who was married to Shmuel Goz; the daughter Batya who was married to Avraham Rodnik; the daughter Bryndele who was married to Zevel Kopols Goldberg, the hatmaker; the daughter Raizel was saved in the forests among the goyem and lives with her family in Israel.

The House of Tziporah Gonik, the widow, and her bachelor son Shlomo. They managed a hotel that was distinguished by its cleanliness.

The House of Leibel Bardas, his wife Maltziya and their three children: the daughters – Zlatkah and Sheva, and the son Zalman. They were owners of a store for kitchen utensils in the center of the marketplace.

The Family of Zalman Parlas and his wife Etta. Zalman was an activist in the Zionist committee in the town.

[Page 161]

Feivesh Hasandler (the Sandalmaker) – a widower and his two daughters. One was married to a man whose name was Chanina.

The Family of Berel Brandfein, his wife Chana and their children. Berel was the owner of a barbershop.

Berel Rozen and his Wife – owners of a manufacturing store.

The House of Yerachmial Goldman, his wife Devora and their daughter and son. Yerachmial earned an honest living from his toil as a wagon owner.

14. In the Town's Villages

A house of broad measurements with a vacant plot alongside was the ***House of Pinchas, the Koroster, Wachs***, the brother of Hershel Wachs who lived in the proximity of the synagogue.

A devout Jew, pleasant demeanor, and quiet. His wife, two sons and a daughter. This Jew worked in commerce involving pig hair for brushes. One of his sons was saved while he was in Russia and immigrated recently to Israel.

A meager, short house and along side a spacious, horse stable, this is the ***House of Yisroel Hatzerterisker***, owner of a wagon. The man was widowed and a son and two daughters remained orphaned. Afterwards, he married a second time with a woman from outside Stepan, and contradictory to the general worry from the fear of the fate of the orphans under the rod of the stepmother, in the course of time it was well known that this woman cared for the orphans with a soft hand.

Shroolik, owner of the wagon, made a living from his profession: the transport of travelers and merchandise to Malynsk, the nearby train station to Stepan, and to the district city of Rovno. Also there were additional horses in his stable beyond the two in active service. These horses served for exchange and trade in the horse marketplace that was in the town. On the whole, this was a poor family, but they existed by their own resources.

In the Polish-German war, in 1939, Shroolik was recruited into the Polish army. This event evoked great worry over his fate. His relatives and acquaintances remember the departure shaking the family. The heart forebode evil. But this war ended quickly and the Soviets entered the town. After a short time, Shroolik suddenly appeared, having fled in some manner from German captivity. At this time when the Jews of the town were living in a state of an uncertain future, this thing brought happiness to the heart, that a completely healthy man returned from hell, to the bosom of his family.

The Family of Velvel Zev Feldman (from Hakalenykes) - short in stature, the son of Rabbi Moshe the musician. A barber by profession, but he didn't own a store. He would journey

[Page 162]

among the houses of the goyem and would cut hair as needed. In exchange he would receive small coins and commodities that were barely sufficient for his families existence. His wife Esther, and their four or five children.

The Single Jewish House in the Neighborhood of the Goyem with the addition of a spacious stable, was **The Shilik House**, the son of Leibel Gruber – owner of a wagon, and his wife. He earned a living from his profession and in addition they cultivated a plot of land, apparently rented, and they existed in some sort of fashion. They were very industrious people.

His son, Abba, was a talented and very industrious student. A second son, Yossel, was the most industrious, and also there was a daughter. The children of the house and the wife worked hard, particularly during the time of the harvest. This is the portion of goods that they promised themselves: potatoes, cabbage and carrots, during the winter period. The son Yossel was sent to professional school outside of the town during the time of the Soviet rule and all traces of him disappeared. There is the opinion that he lives in Russia.

To Akiba the Blacksmith Was a Young Partner by the Name Chaim Kotler – a young person, dynamic, with a wife and two children. He excelled in the profession as a superb blacksmith, and together with this he was an intellectual young person, with leftist tendencies. With the coming of the Soviets into the town, he was chosen by them to be the head of the town council and served in this capacity until the coming of the Nazis.

The House of Ariyeh Kotler Hastolmach (the Wheelwright) – a special carpentry for the building of wooden wheels for wagons, wheel rims for wagons, and barrels. Like the rest of the Jewish professionals in the town, he was an expert in his profession and the goyem from the town and the surroundings flocked for the delivery of the repair and manufacturing work. The name of his wife was Ronya, a son, Eliezer, and three daughters: Sarah, Miriam and Leah. Sarah immigrated to Israel in 1932 and lives today in Kfar Sabah, Miriam remained in Russia with her family, but died recently. Leah was saved while she was in Russia and lives today in Holon with her family.

The Family of Alter Pollack, his wife Beila, four children: Meir; Feivish; a daughter Manatzia; and a brother, by the name Yaakov Schwartz, who remained as a survivor while he was in Russia and lives nowdays in Israel.

Alter was an energetic owner of a wagon and his family carried on respectfully.

The Family of Simcha Pollack, his wife, and around ten children: Feivish, Berel, Itzik, Meir, Zelik and others. Baruch remained as a survivor while he was in Russia and lives in Israel with his family. A child was born in old age to this family by the name Yosele. The name was given to him based on the name of Marshall Filasodsky, head of the Polish government, who died at this time. This thing caused waves throughout the town. Simcha, the wagon owner, was from the wagon owners who made their livelihood with great difficulty by the performance of transporting within the town itself, because his horses were lean and too old to be used for transporting between municipalities.

[Page 163]

An Additional Wagon Owner in Stepan – The House of Mashke Goldenblatt – his wife and two sturdy sons – Avale and Izik. The two sons, and especially Avale, were strong-armed.

The brother of Mashke was ***Yaakov Hapotzter (the Postman)***, a wagon owner who lived on the river slope, his wife and a number of their sons and daughters. The name of the family was Goldenblatt, the nickname Potzter came to this family because, apparently, their father would transport the mail between Stepan and the train station in Malynsk.

Akiba-Kiba Gilbert Hanapach (the Blacksmith) – the owner of a large smithy nearby Hagoyem Street, his wife Rochel-Chaya and their children. The sons: Yechial, Moshe-Nissel, and Leibel. The daughters: Rivka and Devora, who immigrated to Israel before the war and lives in Netanya. The name of her family is Kemachi.

This Jew was an excellent skilled-worker and was known as such in this capacity among all the goyem who would flock to his smithy to shoe their horses or to fix their wagons, ploughs and other things. He was a man of labor who supported his blessed family by his talented hands, indeed not with excessive comfort, but respectfully.

15. The Jews of the Villages Around Stepan

The town of Stepan served as the center of trade for the close surrounding villages. In these villages lived isolated Jews, some of them originated from Stepan and some of them were Jews whose origin was from nearby towns.

These Jews worked in shopkeeping and trade and their lot was also as owners of flour mills, beverages, and spacious agricultural farms who cultivated their lands with great success and their products were up to the quality of the neighboring Ukrainian products. The village Jews were mainly miserably poor, although among them there were extraordinary capability and great means. At any rate, they preserved their living connection with the Jews of the town that served as the spiritual center. Their children were sent to the town in order that they would learn and absorb a little Judaism, whether in "cheder" or in the "Tarbut" school. The children would be lodged with relatives or with merely Jews, and the exchange of payment was expressed primarily in commodities and agricultural products. The children of the villages were courageous, robust and tanned in contrast to the children of the town who had pale appearances.

Sometimes the Jews of the villages would come and bring with them roosters to the shochet for slaughter; likewise they were accustomed to come to the town on the weekend or towards festivals and holidays, and this in order to stay with the Israel community and to pray together in the synagogue.

With the coming of the Nazi conqueror, his fiendish hands caught up with also these out-of-the-way Jews and gathered them together with their brothers, the citizens of the town, in the Stepan ghetto. Their bitter fate was not long in coming and they were liquidated by the Nazis.

[Page 164]

Jews lived in the following villages: North of Stepan – Korost and Krechilsk; Northwest – Varbetziah; Southeast –Verkhi; South – Kosmitzov, Zolotolin and Trostenets; East – Kazimirka, Zolozneh and Yavalinka.

In Korost there lived the following families: ***The Yachniuk Family***. Father of the family – Yaakov, his wife Ayde-Blumah, the daughters: Beila, who was married to Dodleh Woschina and she had a son by the name Yitzchak Woschina who remained alive and lives with his family in Givatayim; Shoshana, who was married to Tzvi Gondler and she had a son by the name Yosef; and also there was Sarah, Ayde and Leiba. There were four sons, the first-born Yosef and after him Aharon, Manya and Avraham.

Yaakov, the father of the family, was an intellectual and well-to-do Jew. He was the owner of a great amount of land and flocks of sheep. On his agricultural farm he would employ many goyem. Yaakov was also a cattle merchant in a big way. His cattle were known by the citizens of the nearby cities.

Yaakov Yachniuk worried about providing his four sons and his daughters with both a Jewish and general education. The four sons succeeded in escaping to the forest and were liberated from the yoke of the Nazis in 1944. Today they remain alive: Manya lives with his family in Israel in Kfar Aviv, and Avraham emigrated to the United States and lives there now with his family. Yosef was murdered by the Ukrainian craftsmen on his way back to Stepan, whereas his brother Aharon fell during the Second World War at the time he was serving in the Red Army.

The Woschina Family – the father of the family, his wife, and daughters: Leah, Sonya and Devora; and son Moshe.

Leah, Sonya and Moshe live today in Canada, whereas Devorah remains still in the Ukraine and lives under the Soviet rule.

The Bebchuk Family – the father of the family, Rabbi Sander, his wife, daughters and sons. The father was a relative of Rav Avraham Brauer of Stepan.

There were additional people from Korost: *Meizel Mordechai and Chana and their Family, Lazar Rim, Leib Bender, Sarah and Leah Bender*.

In the village of Trostenets lived a number of Jewish families –

The Litvak Family, the Schectman Family, the Nezben Family, the Family of Avrahm Wachs, his wife Rivka, his brothers and his sisters: Tesya, Pasya, Faygel and her husband Dovid Reichman. They had a son by the name Yitzchak and daughters: Blumah and Esther.

The father of the family, Mr. Avraham Wachs and his sister Tesya Geller, live today in Israel.

[Page 165]

In the village of Yavalinka were two Jewish families by the name Bebchuk.

The Family of Tanchum Bebchuk. Tanchum Bebchuk arrived after the war with his family to Israel and he died in Israel. His sons live today in Israel.

The Family of Moshe Bebchuk – the brother of Moshe, he immigrated to Israel before the outbreak of the war and lives today in Tel Aviv.

In the village of Zolozneh lived the sister of Sarah, the wife of Ben-Zion Prishkolnik from Stepan. This sister, whose name was Chemkeh, managed alone a flower farm.

In the village of Krechilsk lived a well-off Jewish family with rich assets – the *Family of Yaakov the Krechilsker Partch* – married off a daughter to the house of Avraham Bardas Kootzik from Stepan. This man succeeding in escaping to the forests with one of his grandchildren, but also there the cruel hands of the Nazis caught up to him and he was murdered.

An additional Jewish family that lived in this village was the *Family of the Wife of Avraham from Kortzon*. His wife Blumkeh, who was a relative of Sarah Prishkolnik, survived alive and lives today in the United States with her husband and children. The mother of Blumah – Perel – and the rest of the children of her family were killed in the Shoah.

In the village of Kazimirka lived the family of *Rabbi Peyseh Bebchuk* – his wife and first daughter were killed by the Germans, and also he himself; his second daughter Chana and his granddaughter escaped and remained alive. The daughter lives in the United States.

An additional family that lived in this village was the *Family of Chaim Trachter*, who was a relative of Rabbi Avraham Bebchuk, Bravaar (the Brave One), from Stepan.

In the village of Varbetziah lived the *Wachs Family*. This branch of the family was generally had many sons, the majority of whom were murdered by the Nazis. Two of the sons – Chaim and Avraham – were killed at the time when they chased after Nazi collaborators, the Ukrainians, in the year 1944, after their liberation. Two additional sons remained alive. Mordechai lives in Canada and Yitzchak in Israel.

In Varbetziah lived an additional family – the *Family of Golda Shwartzblatt* – the children of the family were Shaul and Asher.

An additional family was the *Zelishnik Family*. The father of the family was called Pesach Zelishnik, his wife Tzivyeh, his son Yosef and his daughters Beila and Zelda. Zelda was saved and lives in Israel.

[Page 166]

Memories: Images and Families

Some Images and Families

by Yitzchak Weismann

Translated by Daniel Shimshak and Yona Landau
Edited by Mira Eckhaus and Daniel Shimshak

1. "Usishkan" from Stepan

Next door to Irotzekal was Zalman Farlos's store. His mother was Malkah, the one who made millet and grits. When she became a widow, she opened a store for groceries and haberdashery. She had a daughter by the name of Rivkah, whose husband had immigrated to the United States of America. She remained in Stepan with her children. When World War I was over, they traveled to him, and Zalman remained with his elderly mother. He took care of her and supported her financially. Zalman got involved with Zionism and became one of the founders of the Zionist Federation in Stepan. He became very active in collecting contributions for the Jewish National Fund. He became so involved with this, that he neglected his livelihood and totally devoted himself to the JNF.

Zalman was a gentle fellow, he read many books, and he knew all the reports of the JNF by heart. If there were meetings in the town, Zalman was one of the participants and always was a speaker at the meetings. His voice was weak, and when he spoke, he was barely heard. Even when there was silence at the meeting, his words were not heard very clearly.

He referred to the name Usishkan many times because Usishkan was noble in the eyes of Zalman, and everything that was written about him or that Zalman read about him was considered holy by him. Therefore, before long, the people of Stepan began to call Zalman by the name "Usishkan". Here Usishkan is coming, Usishkan is going, Usishkan is sitting, Usishkan has not begun to speak, etc.

Things changed when Zalman got married, and had to make a living for his wife. His mother died and the store's business went downhill. Zalman Farlos opened an oil press with his relative Binyamin Farlos. The work was very difficult for them, and they were not suited for it. The competition was great. One day Zalman sold the oil press. He moved from Stepan to the town of Liobomil by Kovel. He was killed in the Holocaust along with the others.

2. Alter Bebchuk (Alter Zaligas)

Alter Bebchuk lived on the street of the non-Jews. He was bent down with a head of grey hair, with smart eyes that looked downward. He was nervous and short-tempered. He had a good Jewish and general education. Many called him in Russian "Piser" (the writer). It was told about him that in his youth, he read many books, and knew how to walk with authority. With regard to his nervousness, there were several reasons. He had two boys and two girls. His son, Zelek, a very talented boy, was killed in World War I, and it was not known where he was buried. His second son, Yankel, during World War I, traveled to America, and left his wife, Hannah and their four daughters at his father's house. He traveled to America to make money, but he returned after the war empty handed. (By the way, it was told about him that he was able to make some money and he bought clothes for his family. But he fell into the hands of swindlers, and they took all that he had.)

[Page 167]

His two daughters were very talented, and helped him a lot at home and with the oil press, until they got married.

Reb Alter Zaligas was an educated man, but he was not able to make a living from his education, and had to make his living from an oil press. The tools and the machinery in the oil press were very primitive and it was hard and slow work. Days and nights farmers, who came from far and from nearby, waited with their wives in order to receive their oil. Of course, the noise in all the rooms of the house, during the day and the night, added to his nervousness and his short temper.

Indeed his education did not turn into a source of income for him, but when you spoke with him, you immediately felt that he was an educated man. He would bring proof from books and writers, and also with regard to politics he was superior. He would read the important Russian newspapers, and nobody should doubt his opinions. Since he was knowledgeable and well versed, he would turn many times to the authorities on behalf of the community in Stepan.

Once the Polish Archbishop came to our town to visit the Catholic members in the community, and Poles from the neighboring areas came to enjoy his divine presence. Of course, people of the other religions came to receive him, including the Jews. Every community made a gate of honor, and came toward him with bread and salt, as was customary in those days. Amongst the receivers was Reb Alter Bebchuk, the representative of the Jewish community in Stepan. He blessed the honored guest in the pure holy language. The Archbishop understood Hebrew, and enjoyed the blessing very much.

Reb Alter lost his assets in his last years, and suffered from stress and poverty, because as time went by new technologies and machinery developed and ruined his livelihood.

He died before the horrible Holocaust that came upon the total community of Stepan.

3. Moshe Bebchuk

In the town, he was called Moshe Yankel Yishayahu Leibes. All his life he lived in alleys outside of the town, because he was not able to pay rent for an apartment in the town. He became a widower from his wife, Fraydel, at a young age, and he was left to raise three daughters and a son. Moshe was not a great provider, and perhaps did not have much luck, as he had good understanding of all of the products brought by the farmers to the market. He had bad eyesight. Below is a story that happened because of his disability:

[Page 168]

During World War I, a gang of brutal soldiers came to the town, and amongst them soldiers of the Polish army, who were known for their hatred of the Jews. Moshe Bebchuk was walking on the street, blinking his eyes as if looking for something…Suddenly he heard a voice calling him by his name in Polish: "Moshike, come here." It was a Polish soldier who saw the man with a beard from far away and decided immediately to bother a Jew. Upon hearing his name said clearly by the Pole, Reb Moshe thought for sure that it was an acquaintance or a friend who wanted to see him and did not notice that it was a Polish soldier who he did not know. Quickly Reb Moshe moved close to the Polish soldier, and the soldier did not hesitate much, took out scissors, and instead of making a handshake in order to say hello, he took hold of the beard with his left hand, and with his right hand cut the beard up to the chin. We children, when we saw Reb Moshe Bebchuk the next day with a handkerchief tied to his face without any sign of a beard, broke out in laugher. For many months, Reb Moshe Bebchuk was ashamed to go out to the street without a handkerchief tied to his cheeks, until his beard grew back as it was.

His eldest daughter, Sosel, was very tall. Nobody knew what happened to his son, Tzvi. The second daughter, Tcherna, was sent by the Hashomer Hatzair Movement for training in a kibbutz in Chelm. She never returned from there, and was killed by the Nazis along with all the Jews of Chelm. The third daughter,

Beila, survived in the forests and amongst the Poles. She made Aliyah with her family and from there moved to the United States.

4.   Meir Bebchuk (Pik) and his son, Yitzchak

I remember Meir Pik or Bebchuk by the name of his family because of a dream. He was a tall Jew, with an elegant beard, one of the leaders of Stepan. In the winter, he wore an excellent fur coat, like that of the rich, and all of his behavior was like that of a leader, ruler. His wife, Chanache, or as she was called in Stepan according to the name of her husband Meir, "Meirva", never carried the weight of the household, and she did not even know how to cook or bake. Try and imagine what Chanache's situation was when her husband, the lord, died in World War I, and she remained a widow, with her only son, Yitzchak, or as he was called in the village "Irotzekal". Their wealth came to an end and the days of poverty began. In addition, in 1914, a big fire broke out, and their big home burned down. They barely put up a poor shack at the market square. There they began to build their lives.

When I was a child, I always visited their shack. It looked very poor inside, especially during the winter, when it was very cold, and they used moist wood to warm the shack with the oven. The mother and the boy worked very hard in order that it would be a little warm in the shack, and how much smoke they swallowed into their lungs. They both were always sooty and black, and many times I would break out in laugher when I saw them. But life continues, and sometimes the family would have some satisfaction from their hard work.

[Page 169]

On Saturday night, when everything was already cooked and ready, the mother would turn to her only son in these words, "My son, take out the violin and play for your mother." The son would not turn his mother down, and immediately there would be heard from the shack tunes of the violin, as if he wanted to get out everything that was stored within.

The son, Irotzekal, an only son to his mother, was under her continual supervision until he grew up. When World War I broke out and the Jews looked for a place to hide from the shooting in their basement, we saw and heard much about the poor lives of the mother and the son. I still remember their basement and the way to go down into it through the wild weeds. The unventilated basement served as the home for many neighbors with their children and their belongings. For many weeks and months, they were afraid to leave the basement.

When the war was over and the basement became empty, everyone went back to their own lives.

The mother died and Yitzchak remained a lonely bachelor. People suggested to him a "shidduch" (match) with a girl from Stepan. In the house of Bracha Rozen, there were three daughters who were rather old. When the eldest daughter married a man, they suggested to Irotzekal the second daughter, Sarahle. Irotzekal accepted the match.

They had two children. The eldest daughter was sick with tuberculosis, but very smart. The son was not a heroic type.

As years went by, they built themselves a big house and also a store. They worked hard in order to live with honor.

5.   Yitzchak Bongart

In the town, Bongart was always considered a stranger. He was not born there, and his fathers did not live in Stepan. He came from other areas of Poland. He was a short Jew and his eyes were always tearing.

He came to Stepan in the year 1925-26, after a big fire that fell upon the town. He built a modern bakery according to the standards of those times. Up to that time, Jewish women would bake bread in the oven in the big house and would sell it in stores to everyone. There were families whose livelihood was from baking bread, challot, and cakes.

Bongart caused a revolution in the baking and selling of bread. First, he would turn to every store that sold bread and convince them and even pressure them to sell his products.

He had a family. His house and bakery were on the edge of the town, not far from the oil press of Aharon Mordechai Shimshak. His store was in the center, in one of the store

[Page 170]

on the plot of Roman, the sausage man. With the help of his wife and three sons, they worked hard in order to make a living with honor.

His oldest son, Tzvi, was drafted to the Red Army, and lives in Russia today with his family. The second son, Shimon, survived, but fell in the service of the Russian army. The rest of the family died in the Holocaust.

6. Michal Bardas ("Kotz")

He was called "kotz" or "kotzic" because he was short. He was a Jew with a majestic appearance, fat, and had a beard. He was a merchant of fabrics of the superior type. He had different consumers that trusted him, and they bought from him because of his "loyalty".

He had two sons: Aryeh and Avraham, and three daughters: Rochel, Dovah, and Gittel. When his children were young, the business went well. But when the children grew up, especially the girls, and he had to dress them well so they would be liked amongst others, the business weakened until in the end he went bankrupt. Bankruptcy was not usual.

On one of the charming spring nights, when dawn broke, a strange voice was heard that shouted: "Get up, shake yourself, why sleep, there is a fire in the town, not far, danger is expected for you!" The noise of all the neighbors of the street was very loud, and from the street the noise spread to the rest of the streets. Not but a few minutes passed and the whole town became bustling with activity.

In the meantime, men dressed in women's clothes were seen on the street, or just in their underwear. There were those who took his left shoe and put it on his right foot, and there were those who were barefoot, and everyone was screaming: Es Branet! The second would ask: Vas Branet? Nobody could decide where exactly, even though it was clear that the fire was close by. The doors were broken down noisily, and they started to take out the belongings, and one could hear the noise of boxes being taken out of the houses. In the meantime, the fire spread. One could hear the bells in the churches of the Christians, and the horns of the fire trucks. The cows in the barns smelled the smell of the fire and began to make sad noises. The pigs in the courtyards of the non-Jews began to scream in strange voices, and the dogs also did not stand by, but barked. It was very noisy.

In the meantime, it became known that the fire was in the house of Reb Michal Bardas. The Tanchum Sheinboim family, who had a store on the same row in the market, next to the building of Michal Bardas, looked from their window and decided that their store was in danger. Everyone left the house half naked and barefoot, opened the store, and began to take out the bags of produce. In the meantime, the fire spread to the whole area of the houses and stores in that area

[Page 171]

and became one big fire. Chaim, Ben-Zion, Shmuel, and Shlomo worked hard in order to take out their belongings, which were about to burn to the street.

But then something surprising happened. When the fire reached the pillars and they burned, the roof fell and covered the doors of the stores. Ben-Zion and Chaim were trapped inside, and they were in danger of being burned or suffocating. They wanted to get out of the place, but it was too late. They had no choice but to jump straight into the fire. They jumped. In the end, they were taken out burnt, and barely alive. Their bodies were covered with burns, and they could not talk because they were in so much pain.

There were those who cried over their belongings, their house, or their store, but the Sheinboim family cried over Chaim and Ben-Zion who were in a state between life and death.

The story of that spring night was not yet over. Ben-Zion and Chaim were brought to Lvov and lay there until they recovered. The rest of the families who were financially hurt because of the fire recovered, some how, over the years.

From this family, nobody remained after the Holocaust.

7. Chaim Guberman

He was the son-in-law of Alter Bebchuk, the husband of Raizel. He had two daughters. He came to the town from Brazna. He was an educated and smart man. He had a store for haberdashery, and was very accepted amongst people. He had a very polite and courteous attitude to every person, whether the person was an adult or a child. Such was the case even more so with women, as he turned to them with great courtesy. It was not surprising that many were drawn to him and his store. For this reason he had good revenue and honorable profits.

At any rate, there is no doubt that Chaim Guberman was an intelligent man, who was familiar with books, and thought of matters of supreme importance. We will not exaggerate if we will say that he was one of the interesting figures in Stepan, involved in Zionist activities and in public institutions, and he knew how to contribute in a nice way.

But his business grew and his revenue grew such that it was difficult for him to deal with it, and he became nervous. Of course, it soon affected his buyers and they began to leave him, and began to look for other stores. Then the opportunity came to my oldest brother, Mordechai, who was forced for security reasons to leave his livelihood of photography, to open a business in the same store that earlier belonged to Guberman.

[Page 172]

Even though he was a free spirit, Chaim Guberman spent time on Shabbat in the synagogue by the Rabbi Baruch Twersky. This added to his diversity and his noble character.

He passed on to his eldest daughter, Datzia, his nobleness. She was a tall, slender, and charming girl. At the time of the Holocaust, when the people of Stepan were lead to be slaughtered on the bridge of the Horyn River, she jumped from the bridge along with other girlfriends and sanctified the name of Israel as opposed to being passive to the German monsters.

There were no survivors of the Guberman family. Let their memory be blessed.

8. The House of Reb Pinchas Goz (Pini Dar Machar)

The house of Pinchas Goz was two stories high and had twenty rooms, except for the basements. The house was one of a kind in Stepan in its size and comfort. To this day it is not known if he built his house by himself, or not, because he was known as a professional in building. Whenever he saw a structure being built, if it was a factory or a bridge on a river, he would appear as an engineer, and express his opinion, and move on.

I remember once when a long bridge was built in Stepan on the Horyn River, and there were engineers and good professional people involved. Of course, the bridge was built according to the government plans, and it was necessary to build it in order that it would be possible for very heavy loads to pass over it without collapsing, and to make it safe from "tearing" (the flow of ice blocks after the thawing of the spring, without moving the bridge from its place). Months passed and they prepared at Dubinushka the necessary pillars from oak trees. These were placed within the river and the work continued up to the middle of the river.

Once Reb Pinchas Goz, out of curiosity, approached the shore and with his clear eyesight, looked at what was being done, and immediately said to the engineer who was supervising the work that between the rows of the pillars there was one pillar that was not placed straight, and that it would affect the continuation of the building. The engineer, a Pole, proud and arrogant, looked at who was talking to him, and this proud engineer, reluctantly, told the workers to take out the pillar that was deep in the water, and place another pillar in its place, as Pinchas Goz told him earlier.

His father, Moshe-Bar, made wood tile roofs. He was a poor and simple Jew, but honest and his whole life dealt with his profession. Days came and his son Pinchas saw his father's work as lessening his honor. Even though his son urged him that it was not honorable for a wealthy man that his elderly father was to deal with this work, his father did not leave this profession.

It is told of this Reb Moshe-Bar that once he was called before the Polish court to testify against someone. The Polish judge asked of him all the details that were related to his personal identity such as his name and his family name.

[Page 173]

But the name of his father he did not answer. The judge asked again the name of his father. Then he became resentful to the judge: "What does sir the judge want from me?" And then he said – "I am the father, and Pinchas Goz is my son."

Pinchas Goz became a widower from both of his wives, and in the end, married a third wife. He had two daughters: Faisel and Raizel and four sons: Avraham, Yitzchak, Ben-Zion, and Yankel. They all got married and lived by Reb Pinchas, except for Ben-Zion who lived in Kostopol. The third son, Yaacov, died in the First World War. The two older brothers, Avraham and Yitzchak, took initiative, and after their involvement in the alcoholic beverage business (types of wines made from the fermentation of beets, potatoes, or grains) that gave them good profits, they slowly began to build themselves by the house on the downward slope of the well known "Wolh", a superior flour mill that had a good reputation in the close and far surroundings. Their house was a place for receiving guests and they gave a lot of charity and supported the Zionist funds.

Yitzchak Goz's wife, Bracha, was from the city of Kowolh, and in her youth, was a guest in the house of the Goz family. She was one of the first organizers of Hashomer Hatzir, the Zionist youth movement in Stepan. Many of her friends are today in Israel.

There was only one survivor of the whole Goz family – Gittel Toib Shwartzblatt, the daughter of Pasya and Netzia Toib. The rest were taken as prey by the Ukrainian and German beasts.

9.   The House of Chaim Gershon Goz

Who did not know Chaim Gershon in Stepan and its surroundings? Amongst the Jews and the non-Jews, everybody, from the young to the elderly, knew him. The family of Chaim Gershon Goz had a grocery store, and except for fabrics and watches, it was possible to buy in the store anything that a person could want and at a cheap price. Everyone treated Chaim Gershon and his family with trust and support. The store was even open at twelve o'clock at night. On the Shabbat and on holidays, it was possible to buy anything needed, of course from the back door. In the town, Chaim Gershon and his family were known as educated people and as those who studied philosophy in depth.

When Chaim Gershon got old, one could see him wearing eye glasses, reading Jewish, Polish, or Russian newspapers, and in his hand, a "heavy" book, in a literal and metaphorical sense.

His wife was a sick woman.

The eldest son of Chaim Gershon and also his second son, Wolf Walka, also suffered from diseases. The third son, Shaul, was a learned fellow, well versed in world literature and in accountancy.

[Page 174]

He was a good and generous fellow. He was the internal manager of the business. Chaim Gershon had a daughter, named Chaya, a girl who finished high school, knew Russian well, was one of the active intelligent youths in the city, and of course, an ardent Zionist. After she was married, she made Aliyah. After a short time, they returned to Stepan with a set of twins of their own. The couple separated. She stayed at her parent's house and her husband left the town.

The fourth son, Shmuel—Shmulik, was a strong fellow, with an athletic body build. He read a lot. He was the manager of outside connections for the family business. Once or twice a week, he would travel to Rovno for commercial products. The merchants trusted him greatly, and he would bring merchandise that was sold wholesale and that was sold to grocers on credit.

In the later years, the business went down hill. Nevertheless, he continued to travel to Rovno. He would not only bring merchandise, but also spirituality. He would bring with him much reading material. I was the first to meet him on Tuesday mornings when he would return from Rovno, and he would give me reading material for the whole week until Friday. On Friday, he would take back the material from me, leave his business, go up to the attic in the haystack, or on the hill of the charming Wolh, and in a hidden corner would spend the whole Shabbat, along with me, and we would enjoy the splendor of the holy spirit.

Those hours had their affect upon us, and planted in us the love for the Hebrew language, yearning for the land of Israel, and desire to act on behalf of Israel. After many years of bachelorhood, Shmulik married Feigel Kagan, and they had two children. All of them died in the Holocaust.

It is impossible to tell all of Shmulik's merits. Many memories have weakened since then, but his character stands before me with clarity in all of its dignity.

After him, came the daughter, Rochel, or as she was called, "Oka". I don't know if it was a nickname in Russian or only a childhood nickname. She was a very beautiful girl who read a lot, helped in the business, was active in the Zionist youth in the town, and loved to take hikes in nature in her free time and on weekends.

After her, came Mordechai –Motke, the youngest and the agile. He also read a lot. He did not like the business. He befriended people who enjoyed tasting alcohol. They would meet in the evenings on the Wolh and sing songs in Ukrainian, and sometimes would join up with the Ukrainian youth, and become friendly with them. But this would not prevent the Ukrainian youth from giving them the cold shoulder, being cruel, and even killing their former friends at the time of the Holocaust.

Thus a large and enlightened family from the residents of our town, Stepan, was destroyed.

[Page 175]

10. Yekutial Goldberg (the Long)

He was as his name says, a tall man, as it was said about him "head and shoulders …". He had a store, and in the same place was his home. The entrance to it was from the back door, through a shack with a roof. His house was always dark, because the light penetrated only through a small window.

Reb Yekutial had tall and healthy sons, like him. He had a business dealing with alcoholic beverages, gathering honey, selling grain, and other things.

His sons were: Nissel and Mordechai (today both are in Argentina), Yaacov who married Antonovka, Hershel who died in his youth, and Michal who married Osova. There was one more son who was deaf and his name was Yisrael. He had two daughters – Raizel and Tzipa.

One time Reb Yekutial tried to go up to the attic of his house, and the rotten ladder did not carry his weight. Reb Yekutial fell from that height to the ground and broke his bones. For many days he lay in bed and was in need of long term medical care until he came back to himself. This ruined his health, and after some years, he passed away.

For many years, Reb Yekutial was the gabbai (the treasurer or beadle) of the high Beit medrish, and had much influence on the order in the Beit medrish. Thanks to his efforts, it was warm in the Beit medrish in the winter. It would enliven many souls to come in from the cold and snowy street and enter the walls of the warm Beit medrish, when Jews were sitting by the heater, learning Gemorah, taught by Reb Zelberberg. By Reb Yekutial's influence, there was a "seuda shilishet" (third meal) on Shabbat in the Beit medrish. It was very pleasant to sit in the dark and listen to the tunes of the holy Shabbat as it was coming to an end and the beginning of a new week was about to begin. There were also pranks performed in the dark by children against Walka the butcher (Zev), a short bearded man who had a bent back because he was old. He was always the victim of the naughty pranks of the children.

In general, Reb Yekutial was a serious man, and it was difficult to find on his face an expression of laugher or a smile. This was not the case on Shabbat, especially at the time of the reading of the Torah, or at the times of holidays. His face would beam, wearing his black capota, his beard combed, and his teasing eyes would follow after a person who could pay a high price for an aliyah to the Torah. There were always those, not just for the sake of heaven to make Torah grow and to glorify it, but simply to show the "world" who is a man who can pay a high price for the "Maftir". Reb Yekutial would then beam from happiness and his face would smile.

He died, several years later after the accident, even before the Holocaust.

[Page 176]

11. The House of Reb Sheftil Goldenblatt "Dar Putchter" (The Postman)

The family of Sheftil lived together with Yosef Zilberblatt. Their house was between the market on one side and on the other side was the Christian church. On the third side was the Horyn River. From this place, one could see the breathtaking view of all the surroundings. On the fourth side was the valley, or as it was called "Dei Dolana".

The entrance to the house of Reb Sheftil was on the side of the church, through the dark horse stables. It was dark there day and night. It was possible to find an entrance to the living rooms only by the light that came through a small window that was in the door. But one did not know whose rooms to enter because the rooms were divided between the sons of Reb Sheftil and their families. If you wanted to visit Avrahamachik, you entered into Yaacov's room. If you wanted to visit Yaacov, you entered into Moshke's room. One way or another, you entered into the house of the Sheftil family.

Amongst the grandsons of Reb Sheftil there was one who was my age, his name was Zindel, and his nickname was "Dar Deutsche" (the German) because his mother was of German descent. His father, Moshke, married her when he was in America. When they returned, and the woman did not know how to speak Yiddish, and nobody understood English, and she spoke German. His nickname came from this.

Zindel was a healthy fellow. He studied less than the others in the Cheder because all the time he would tell stories about the horses in the stables, these feet and these mains. He would tell about the demons who danced all night with the horses and when the horses would wake up in the morning, they would be covered with sweat and their plaits tied to their mains. It was impossible and forbidden to untie them, because anyone who would touch them would be punished by the pests. There were those who believed him and there were those who did not believe him. Nevertheless, the people of the town did not have too much desire to pass by the place during the evening. Everyone knew that it was not a good idea to be in the area of the church and the stables too often.

But the stables and the horses served for something special – to transport the mail from Malinsk, a distance of 18 kilometers from Stepan, through the forests. On a road that was not really a road, Reb Sheftil would drive with his horses with bells on their necks. The noise of the bells would echo in the air to the distance of hoofs, and would warn all sorts of terrorists and robbers who would not dare to get close. Be careful! Here the government mail is traveling.

On the way, close by the villages, when the non-Jews heard the noise of the bells of the mail, they would awaken on the long cold winter nights, and would light tar wood to light up the house. The women would begin to weave the flax and the farmers would harness their horses. They would go out to the forests to bring lumber. When Reb Sheftil would get close to Stepan with the mail and his bells, the Jews of Stepan would also awaken. The women would begin turning on the ovens, and the husbands would run to the Beit medrish to pray to the Creator. All this happened in the winter. But during the summer, the farmers of the villages went out

[Page 177]

to the fields to prepare their living and their animals for the whole year, and in the town, the Jews went to the market, to find their livelihood, and to lead their cows to the pasture.

When he got older, they hired other coachmen to transport the mail, and Reb Sheftil switched his profession and became a flour miller. By the Wolh, they built a dam for the water of the Horyn. The dam was built from branches, weeds, sand, and dirt without concrete and iron, but is still intact. By the dam, they built the flour mill with large millstones. The mill was tied with rope and with strong iron chains to the pillars that were by the shore, in order to watch that the flow would not carry away the mill. They would enter the mill by a wide board that was placed between the shore and the mill. The work in the mill went slowly. Farmers from the surroundings would sit days and nights, and would wait patiently for their turn. Reb Sheftil would sit with them, smoke his pipe as if one of them, and listen to their stories. The area of the mill with the board and also the other side in back of the entrance up to the big bridge, was called the "river of the boys", or as it was called "Dar Yengleshar Taich". The other side of the mill, under the Wolh was the "river of the girls" ("Dar Medelshar Taich") because in those times there were no swimsuits. Only at the time of danger, after swimmers began to drown, everyone forgot about their nakedness, and would mix with each other in order to save lives.

That was in the summer. In the winter, when it seemed that even the fish were shivering from cold, no one spoke of people going swimming in the river. But Reb Sheftil knew no fear. On Friday, he would make a hole in the ice on the river, take off his clothes, jump into the river, and dip into the water according to the law. Afterwards when he would go to the synagogue for Kabalat Shabbat in his festive clothes, he would feel refreshed and full of energy, as if he came out of a warm bath in a bath house.

At the time of World War I, the flour mill was destroyed, and Reb Sheftil stopped being seen as the flour miller in the eyes of the public. One could see him in the horse market with his sons as an expert. He lived several more years and died at a ripe old age.

His sons: Avrahamchik, short and with a black beard, was one of the quiet coachmen in Stepan, who made his living from his trips to Malinsk. He was not rich, but made an honorable living. Yaacov, the second son, was also a coachman who would transport cargo straight to Rovno, and sometimes would take travelers. Moshke, who we already mentioned, and his son, Zindel, would also transport cargo to Rovno, and on the market days would also sell horses along with his other son, Abba.

In general, one could say that the sons of Reb Sheftil were quiet men and were faithful, going to the synagogue and keeping the honor of the family. They worked hard, and with their own sweat, they made a living for their families with honor, even if it was not easy.

[Page 178]

12. Pinchas Goldstein

He was called Pinya Goldstein. He was a man with a red face, red hair, and a small beard. He was always covered in flour, and he was seldom seen in festive clothes, and when he was in festive clothes, it was not on Shabbat and holidays, but on Polish holidays, when it was forbidden to operate the flour mill according to the law.

Pinya was a very preoccupied man, and if he found a spare minute to stand and talk, he would open always in one word: "On my life." (Main Labein – in Yiddish), while extending his hands in order to catch his pants as if they were about to fall. The thing turned into a habit, and it was possible to see him as if he was always afraid he would loose his pants. The jokers added flavor to his name and called him "Pinya with the pants" (Pinya mit day mitkas).

Along with all of this, Reb Pinchas was a Jew with a warm heart, loved people, and drew them close to him. He would ask how each person was doing. He was chosen to the area council ("the Gemina"), and it was not known if he was chosen by the non-Jews, who also appreciated him and liked him, or if he was chosen by the Jews. After every meeting of the council, he would come to the town amongst his friends and begin to tell: "On my life, they want to increase the taxes and place it on the backs of the storekeepers and the craftsmen. I refused to sign and the decree was rejected."

During the days of World War I, when there was great hunger, he would grind flour almost free of charge, and was happy that a Jew received a "lottery" of rye or buckwheat in order to expel the hunger from his house for a week.

At the same time, they would sit days and nights and wait in line at the flour mill. During those days of calamity, many flour mills were destroyed, except water mills. Pinya served everyone tirelessly.

It was true of about Pinya Goldstein that he never in his life would get angry with someone, Jew or non-Jew, even though because of being very preoccupied, it was possible to get angry. He was very preoccupied before Passover when the Jews needed kosher flour for matzot. A month before the holiday he would invite the Rabbis to kosher the mill. All the Jews from the town and its surroundings enjoyed the flour that was kosher for Passover.

His wife, Manya, came from the big city, spoke Russian, and became friendly with Doctor Ashkenazi. Her two daughters, Ida and Sonya, were quiet and well mannered girls. It was almost impossible to say that their father, "Pinya, the miller" was always covered in flour. His financial situation was not always good. He would waste all of his income on wood for heating because his steam machine was like inferno, and it was impossible to satisfy its hunger. One would always see wagons harnessed to horses or oxen transporting wet wood to his courtyard all winter. This was for the coming year when they would dry.

[Page 179]

The situation of Pinya Goldstein was saved by his son-in-law, Yitzchak Woschina, the husband of his daughter, Ida. Yitzchak Woschina, a happy fellow who was vivacious and full of energy, was all of his days a storekeeper in a produce store. When he received half of a flour mill as a dowry, he entered it as a man of standing. He thought he entered a pit of fat. As a matter of fact, the fat was stolen from him and the pit remained.

On one clear night, there was an alarm of a fire and when the residents of the town ran toward the fire, they saw that the mill of Pinya was totally burnt. After several weeks, they received the money from the insurance. The business changed and moved to other lines. Even though the business grew and developed, Pinya Goldstein never changed his clothes covered in flour, as if it served to him as an attribute for livelihood…

Also of this family nobody remained.

13. Shlomo Gonik (Shloimke Mottias)

Shlomo Gonik – a special figure in Stepan, lived by the Christian church, east of the market. His house was built together with that of the Sheftil family and Yosef Zelberberg. The Gonik family had a hostel for Polish landlords and rich merchants. His father, Motel, or as he was called Motile, liked alcohol all of his life, unlike the way of Jews. This caused his wife, Tziporah, to separate from him, and he went to live alone in the apartment between Yaacov Buchliss and the tall Yekutial.

After the fire, when the Gonik house was burned with the rest of the houses that were opposite the church, the authorities did not give a license again to build the houses anew because they were close to the church. Shlomo Gonik and his mother, Tziporah, left their plot in the market place and went to build a house on a plot near Kagan and Wiantic the sausage man, the Pole.

Shlomo Gonik fought with the neighbors who did not see it nicely that they were building a house on a plot that all the years was empty, and that they used as a sanitary facility. In the end, they won in the struggle because of his connections with those in charge of giving licenses for building. Even though it was very crowded and that there were not proper sanitary conditions, the rooms were clean and orderly. Anyone who passed by did not hesitate to enter this motel. This was all because of his mother, Tziporah's conscientiousness and diligence.

Because he was close to the Polish authorities, he was not very involved in the life of the Jewish community.

[Page 180]

14.   Chaim Wachs (Dar Warbetzar)

Chaim lived all his life with his family in a nearby village to Stepan, Warbeche. After World War I, he left the village for the town, bought half a plot by Yitzchak Bebchuk and slowly began to build his home. His wife was Raizel, the daughter of Reb Sheftil, and he had two sons: the eldest, Sheftil, and the youngest, Zev, and one daughter by the name of Gittel. Their business was buying grains from the farmers of the area and transporting the merchandise in wagons to the city, Sarni, in order to be sold.

Chaim Wachs was a Jew who supported education. As a result of this, he was a lot more free spirited than the rest of the Jews. He did not pray everyday and did not go to the synagogue too much on Shabbat. Even though he did go to the synagogue on the High Holidays, he did not act like all the Jews, but would go from synagogue to synagogue to hear the different, nice melodies of the different cantors.

The two sons of the Wachs family, Sheftil and Zev, were in the Betar Movement in Stepan. When the war broke out in 1939, Zev, the youngest, was in the regular Polish Army, and he became a prisoner to the Germans. When Stepan was conquered by the Soviets, they received many letters from Zev from Lublin, until they stopped coming. His tracks were lost. He was probably killed by the Nazis along with the rest of his brothers.

Sheftil, the eldest, stayed at home with his parents. He was caught by the Soviets for doing crimes of illegal commerce. He came to trial and was sentenced to go to prison. His time in prison was not too long because in the meantime, the Nazis invaded Russia. Many prisoners were freed in different ways, and amongst them was Sheftil. He moved from place to place in Russia and ended up in Middle Asia. At the end of the war, he got to Poland, from there to Germany, and from there to Italy. In the end, he came to the United States, raised a family and lived there. The rest of the family became extinct.

15.   Yaacov Wachs (Buchalas)

It was never clear where the nickname "Buchalas" came from. But it should be noted that Reb Yaacov never was ashamed of his nickname, and he would always point out and say: "I am Yaacov Buchalas."

It can't be said that Yaacov Wachs had a majestic appearance. But it should be noted that his daughter, Shirka was rather pretty. She married a fellow from Alexandria, which was near Rovno. He had a son, Yisrael, who traveled to Argentina, to search out his luck. He did not find his luck there. On the other hand, he lost the fingers of his hand in an accident, and returned to Stepan.

Reb Yaacov Buchalas made a living from a store for household utensils. They were not the nice utensils that are found in most of the stores in our country. Those kinds of utensils were barely seen in his store, but simple pots from clay that were selected and painted with light lacquer.

[Page 181]

He had another business to add to his livelihood. In the summer, he would collect green cucumbers, pickle them in big barrels, and leave them there until autumn or winter. Everyday he would roll the barrels in order that the cucumbers would pickle and have a good taste and shape. When winter arrived and the good and superior fruits disappeared from the market place and the heart wanted something to revive the soul, then one would send a child with a plate in his hand to Yaacov Wachs and buy from him pickled cucumbers with some sauce. He who did not eat them with potatoes or as a spice with meat did not know from something with a good taste in all his life. The cucumbers of Reb Yaacov were famous in Stepan.

Nobody from this family survived.

16. Moshe Wachs Dar Galar ("the Redhead")

The father of Moshe Wachs – Reb Yaacov Wachs – was a redheaded Jew. Like his father, Moshe also was a redhead. It is possible that their family was called Wachs as its color was yellow. At any rate, in Stepan, they called him Moshe Dar Galar (the Redhead).

Many buyers came to his fabric store, which was one of the biggest stores for selling fabrics. They said of him that he bought his merchandise from Lodz, from the factory and paid with cash. Therefore, his had nice profits. They said that his son, Dodel, gave "an injection" to the store, and placed it on its feet.

This son of Moshe was a very interesting character. He was called in Stepan "Dar Lashakel" (the colt). He was given this nickname because in his childhood he would drag himself after his father to every place, like a colt going after a mare.

"The colt" professed to be an aristocrat. He always smoked superior cigars and gave off the smoke to distances, like a lord. He always tried to use words that he collected in lexicons, and he would throw out archeological expressions to his right and to his left without distinction and out of context.

He married a nice woman from Rafalovka, who gave birth to two girls.

It was interesting that even though he had an aristocratic tendency, in his house, he did not act with lavishness. Nevertheless, his house was orderly. His two girls, Rivkah and Liba, were quiet girls. They moved to Kostopol after they got married.

They were also victims of the Holocaust.

[Page 182]

17. Gedalia Weinstein

Gedalia's house was on the descent to the river. When one entered the house, it seemed that it lead to the depths of the earth. But from the back side, it looked like a two story house.

Gedalia, the shoemaker, was a Jew with a short beard. His beard was not anything special, but Gedalia's character was one of obstinacy, rebelliousness, and protest. He would express his opinion loudly, as if all that was important was to express his opinion, and that it was unimportant if his opinion was accepted or not.

The days of Chol Hamoed Passover and Succot were the days of Gedalia's "regime". Then it was customary that the craftsmen did not work. Then groups of people would assemble and smoke cigarettes while broadening ones mind and dealing with "high" politics. After that, they would go to activities at the synagogue and close "accounts" with the Gabaim (treasurers). Many times this kind of gathering would end in disagreements.

Gedalia had many supporters, especially amongst his friends, the craftsmen. He and some of his friends were active in the Chevra Kadisha, and did their tasks very carefully. Gedalia had a son, Motel (Mordechai). He also went in his father's ways with regard to picking a profession and his activities. Motel and his wife had one son called Avraham.

This family was also destroyed in the Holocaust, along with the others of the town.

18. Moshe Woschina (Mirkas)

Moshe's house was in the center of the city which was in the center of the market place. His house was two stories, and stood out more than all the other houses of the city. The living quarters were upstairs, and on the bottom floor there were many stores which were rented to Jews.

Moshe Woschina was a short Jew with a black sharp beard that was going grey. His speech was fluent and quick, and so were his movements. Despite his age, about sixty, he was very quick and very active. He would carry sacks of grain from the wagons of the farmers and he knew how to deal with them. His family was large and extensive – the girls: Gittel and Golda; after them, Yitzchak, Dodel, and Tania (Todros); after them, a girl, Esther; and after her, Aaron and Ethel.

[Page 183]

Moshe Woschina had special luck with his son-in-laws. The husband of Gittel, Moshe Morik, was a handsome, tall fellow, who was miserable that his wife gave birth only to girls. The second son-in-law, Boaz, the son of the Rav from Rafalovka, sat in one of the stores below and sold grocery commodities, while his apartment was above. The third son-in-law, Esther's husband, was from the village of Zalotzek, and his name was Zelik. The fourth son-in-law, the husband of Ethel, was the most handsome and intelligent of all, Avraham Dorochinsky from Salonim.

Moshe Woschina was successful with his son-in-laws, and his portion was not lacking with his daughter-in-laws. His first daughter-in-law, the wife of Yitzchak, was Ida Goldstein, and they lived on Listofada Street. The second daughter-in-law, the wife of Dodel, was the daughter of Yaacov Yachniuk from the village of Korist, and was from a rich and good home. The third daughter-in-law, the wife of Tania, was the daughter of Arakder from Rafalovka. The last daughter-in-law, the wife of Aaron, was from Rovno, was a widow after her husband.

Lately, there was formed in the stores of Moshe Woschina a wholesale commerce house in partnership with all of his sons and son-in-laws. They competed with the small merchants in Stepan.

Moshe Woschina was considered one of the honorable people in Stepan. He would sometimes pray as the cantor, especially on the Shabbat, in the morning and the afternoon service, and also on Yom Kippur. His house was open to give donations and contributions to causes in Eretz Yisrael.

From the large Woschina family, only two son-in-laws stayed alive, Zelik, in Russia, and Avraham Dorochinsky, in Argentina, and one of his grandsons, the son of Dodel, Yitzchak Woschina, who is in Israel remained alive. They say that his youngest son, Aaron, lives in Russia. All the rest of this large family was destroyed.

It is worthwhile to dwell upon the characteristics of Avraham Dorochinsky, who came to Stepan at the time from Salonim as an expert in the lumber business and worked as a clerk in the firm of the well known philanthropist, Paster Bernstein, who bought the forest estate in the surroundings of Stepan. Dorochinsky was a cultural man with character. He contributed to every cause nicely, and was very popular amongst the revisionist Zionists. He would take part in balls that were held in the town for charity purposes, and was welcome and accepted amongst all the parties and parliamentary institutions.

It is worthwhile to point out that as a clerk, he was not afraid of the income tax authorities, and he bought himself a sophisticated radio. It was the first radio in Stepan. Many of his acquaintances would gather in his house and would enjoy listening to the news and even music and orchestras.

When the Soviets invaded the area, something strange happened to Avraham Dorochinsky. The owner of the estate of the "forest of Stepan", the philanthropist Paster, was left without a means of existence. When this became known to Avraham,

[Page 184]

he met with the late Moshe Koifman and with Ben-Zion Sheinboim, may he live a long time now that he lives in Israel, in order to get financial support for Paster. The operation was done quietly, without any advertising. But the Soviets heard about this. The three were accused of acting against the revolution, and expected a severe punishment.

I do not know how the trial was canceled. But Avraham, who was before one of the people who ran the business of the municipal institutions in Stepan, was removed from the administration, and had to bless "the Gomel" along with his two friends because they came out alive from "the lion's den" of the NKVD (today called the KGB).

19. Meir Michel Vinik

There was a small house on the banks of the Wolh, between the Pinchas Goz family and the Chaim Gershon Goz family. In my imagination, this house was like a midget walking between two giants.

Meir Michel was a bright Jew. Jokes and brilliant ideas would be emitted from him like from his grits mill, where he would process seeds. The force that made the mill work was Vinik's feet. He was never rich, but his house was clean and orderly. I don't remember his wife, only him, his son, and his daughters.

I remember an incident that Meir Michel told about himself. At the time of World War I, when the front came near our town and the artillery began falling on the houses, thus Meir Michel tells: I heard from far away the noise of a cannon, I pushed myself to the nearest wall, and exactly at that moment, I felt fragments of stones falling on my body. I thought the wall was falling on me. I moved away from the wall, and by crawling, I found a second shelter, and thus I was saved from sure death. But not for long as after a few days, Meir Michel passed away.

He had one son, Avraham, and he also died at the time of the world war.

His three daughters were: the eldest, Rochtza, who married Natan Milstein; the second daughter, by the name of Reitze and the third daughter – Gittel. Milstein left Rochtza and fled to Russia, where he became a commissar. He left her with their young child, Yitzchak. The second daughter, Reitze, was a quiet and dedicated woman to her husband and children. Gittel, the youngest, was pretty with a round face and curly hair, and always reading in Russian. She did not leave the house without a book, and was considered one of the intellectual youths in Stepan. She left Stepan during the first years of the Polish regime, and immigrated to the United States.

[Page 185]

20. The House of Shaul Weitznodel (Shaul, the Butcher)

Shaul, the butcher, had a wide beard that showed his elderly age. He was tall, wide shouldered, and always serious. Nobody saw him argue with anyone or raise his hand to anyone. He would sell non-kosher meat only to non-Jews and Polish landlords.

Before the fire, he lived above on the row of houses, and below the residential houses was his butcher's shop.

He had three sons: Yitzchak, Gershon, and Tzvi, and several daughters: Yentil, tall and fat (she was called "the kozak"), Leah, Sonya, Shandel, and another two daughters whose names I do not remember. The younger children learned in school. Some of them became friendly with girls their age, and others stayed at home as if they abstained from enjoying life. Apparently the financial situation in the home was not very good, and there was no dowry in order to marry off the girls. Yentil married, and one of the boys, Yitzchak, married.

Gershon, the second son, was sickly. After he returned from his army service in the Polish Army, he spoke a lot about his life in the army. He would tell about it at any chance, whether others wanted to hear or not. Apparently, his army service influenced him greatly.

I remember the sight of Gershon carrying on his back a calf that he bought from a farmer, two feet on one side, two feet on the other side, and in the middle Gershon's head. He would walk, cursing in juicy Russian curses the cow, the calf, the farmer, and the buyers. Thus he would continue until he reached his house.

One daughter remained a survivor, as she was under a Russian guarantee. Today she lives in Israel. Also one of her sisters lives today in South America. The fate of the rest of this large family was like the fate of the rest of the people of the town – extinction.

21. Gershon Weitznodel (Peysis)

The home of Gershon Peysis was near the river. His house was a little higher than the house of Sokolosky, and was larger in area. There was a vegetable garden around the house.

Since the house was old, Gershon, the plasterer and builder, made improvements. He destroyed the old building, and built in its place a new building. He built a modern bakery there.

Gershon filled his position faithfully in the Chevra Kadisha.

[Page 186]

Gershon had several sons and daughters, amongst them were Moshe, the tall, and Tanchum (Tania). The two were quiet, hard working fellows who worked in the bakery. They were active in the "Zionist – Pioneering Youth".

Like others, they along with their families were killed in the Holocaust.

22. Yosef Zelberberg (Yosel Mirless)

According to his name, he was a Jew, and such was his origin. But according to his looks, with "a little beard" below his chin, and his customs, he was different from those of the rest of the Jews of the town. He was amongst "the learned Jews" (otshonei yavray) from the time of the Czar Nikolai. It was not known where he acquired his education, and especially the Russian language. All the years, he acted as a clerk for the Russian authorities ("the walast"), and everyone related to him in that manner. When the state of Poland was formed and Stepan, like all the Volynia area, became part of the new state, Zelberberg was chosen as the vice "Woit" (the vice head of the town council). When the head of the town council was absent, he would act as the head of the town council. He would wear a wide green ribbon with one side of it on his shoulder and the other side would hang down on his waist. The green ribbon was the symbol of the state of Poland.

In fulfilling his public-state job, he actually preferred helping the Ukrainians and the Poles. It was obvious that he did not visit the synagogue except on Yom Kippur for the Kol Nidre Service. That was primarily all of his Judaism, as he hid himself after the service until the next year.

His being Russian was expressed mostly in his drinking of tea that became a ritual for him. The samovar was placed before him on a table, and they would pour him four cups of tea at the same time. He would sit and would drink cup after cup until the samovar was emptied. When he was involved in this "holy" activity, it was forbidden for any of his children to enter the room.

His wife, Esther Malkah, was a storekeeper who sold fabrics for the farmers of the area. He had two sons. The eldest died when he was a lad during World War I from a contagious disease. The second son, Shmuel, immigrated to America. The daughter, Tzirel, married into the Feldin family from Kostopol. The daughter, Hinda, married Yona Grossman. One of her children, Yosef, went through the Holocaust and is in America today. The youngest, Raizel, married Yerachmiel Pearlstein, and they lived in Rovno.

Yofef Zelberberg and his wife died before the Holocaust, and the rest of the family died in the Holocaust.

[Page 187]

23. Zeivel Press – the Hatmaker

Amongst the row of stores was a store with living quarters without a window. The light in the room broke through the store in the market place. But in that one room, two boys and two or three girls were born, educated and raised. The boys are now in America. One of them, Avraham, a brave and bold fellow, was a member of the fire squad. When a fire would break out, he would run into the middle of the market place, wearing his steel hat with a horn in his hand, and would blow it and make noise in order to awaken the sleepy. How I was jealous of him and his great job.

Zeivel was already at that time elderly. His eyesight was defective. When he would sit and sew hats especially for the non-Jews, he would be engrossed in his work. He would place in the hat not only the needle, but also his eyes and his nose. It seemed as if he didn't sew with a needle, but with his nose. His wife was short. According to most, she was the one who sold the merchandise to the non-Jews. When his son, Avraham, grew up, he became the one who sold the merchandise.

At the end of his life, Reb Zeivel bought a better house in the area of the synagogue. The room by the store was used by Avraham. He would invite friends his age there in the evenings. They would have meals together and meet with friends. Of course, they were not lacking in good spirits, and they would go out to the "Wolh", and sing Ukrainian songs, according to the non-Jews' version. This way of life got them close to the Ukrainians who spent time with them as friends.

In the house of Reb Zeivel Press, a granddaughter of one of the girls was raised, and supported them when they got old, because the girls left their parents and they got married, and Avraham traveled to America. The elderly couple remained lonely.

Reb Zeivel died before the Holocaust. The elderly wife was left with her granddaughter, and they were murdered along with all the Jews of the town.

24. Velvel Tekes (Sokolosky)

His house was on the east side of the alley, on the down slope to the Horyn, standing as if it was dug into the mountain. The house was old and run down, just as was the head of the house, who would lie in bed all of his life.

Near the house was a stable with a wood shingled roof, which had weeds growing on it. One could stand on top of the mountain, and look into the stable.

I knew the house for other reasons: Firstly, in the summer, we would go swimming in the river, and how was it not to peek into the house that was by the river. How happy is the man that does not have to bother himself to go far on the boiling summer days in order to go swimming.

[Page 188]

Velvel Sokolosky was an old and weak Jew. His wife, apparently his second, was pretty, young, and nimble. They had one son, Leibeske, with glasses, and was amongst the intelligentsia of the town. He immigrated to America, and there remained with them one daughter, Fesil.

His second wife, who was the provider in the family from the beginning, got sick suddenly with a long term sickness and could not be healed from it. The daughter, Fesil, filled her place as the provider of the family. She married a fellow from Austria—Welin.

This family was also destroyed in the Holocaust.

25. The Sheftil Yokelson House

Reb Sheftil, a Jew with a white beard and with a majestic appearance, had several businesses: beer in barrels, iron products, and other businesses. He died at a ripe old age, and left after him six sons and two daughters. The eldest, Ben-Zion – his wife died when she was young and left him with a son, Rafael, and a daughter, Tziporah. The son is in Israel. After several years, Ben-Zion married another woman.

The second son of Sheptil was Baruch who lived in Dombrovitza. He was not very successful in making a living. He would come to Stepan to see how his family was, and in the meantime would get an "injection" of several hundred golden coins.

The third son, Shammai, was sober and independent. He dealt with selling cattle and horses. He never got rich from his business, but made a living with honor, and along with his friend, Baruch Rassis, he knew how to deal with the non-Jews. But during the time of the ghetto and the Holocaust that did not help him. He was killed along with the others.

Tzvi (Hirsh), the fourth son, married someone from Manivitza. She was a pretty and slender woman. They had children, and led a regular family life. The same was for Dov, who married a woman from Rovno. Only one son immigrated to the America, and lives there to this day.

The eldest daughter, Devorah, married a fellow from Keliven. The second daughter married Eliyahu Koifman. Eliyahu was from Russia, if I am not wrong from Odessa. He was learned, and knew many languages. After the wedding, he opened a store for fabrics, but he did not know how to direct the business. He always dealt with philosophy and politics and the business went downhill. One day, when he didn't have anything to do, he went to the forest to do physical work, which he did not have the strength to do.

[Page 189]

In the meantime, he met with a group of young people, and told them, in secret, that he invented a new arithmetic method that would bring a total revolution to economic policy and would bring great relief to the political crisis that took place in Poland at that time. He told that he wrote an economical pamphlet and sent it to the government as a patent. According to him, this revolution would bring forth the formation of the Jewish State which would not encompass an area from Madan to Beer Sheva, but from the Don River near the Volga to Warsaw. Of course, the fellows of Stepan had a lot of material to have a good time with and to make fun of this Eli.

In the black days of great suffering in the ghetto, Eli did a lot of his prophesies and fantasies, and as the calamities increased and decree came after decree, Eli Koifman would prophesy that redemption was coming near, in his desire to comfort and encourage those who were struck and chased after. He always knew how to find reasons and to explain his calculations on a complicated arithmetic basis. Indeed a great portion of the Jews of the ghetto, who were in great distress and despair, were a bit encouraged by the prophesies and fantasies of this Eli, even though they knew of him, that it was like "the person who is drowning holding on to hay." He was killed along with all his family and along with the rest of the people of the town in the horrible Holocaust.

26. The Nachum Kagan House

Before the World War I, Nachum and his wife, Sarah, lived by Moshe Woschina. His wife was diligent, had a feel for business, and was very religious. These were their seven children: Moshe, Yisraelke, Feigel, Batya, Brindel, Pinchas, and Shoshana (Reizel).

Reb Nachum was a very handsome man, with a black beard and good and caressing eyes. He was a public figure with every inch of his body. At the time of World War I, there were many people, especially women, whose husbands immigrated to America and who needed financial aid and a good word to be said. Reb Nachum was the address for all of them. When there came an announcement to a woman from her husband in America to join him and she did not know who to turn to and what to do, Reb Nachum would help her in order to make it easier for her to immigrate to America.

The son Moshe was involved in a clothing store, and by this he helped his parents. Yisrael was unusual. He would take to something after having a taste of it. If at home he would act according to the tradition, outside he would totally leave the ways of tradition. He was one of the most learned fellows in the town, dealt with Zionism, different plays, and of course, romanticism. Amongst the young people of the youth movement his age, there was one girl, also learned, who knew Hebrew well and was from a good home, and her name was Esther Galperin. She was the daughter of Reb Zalman Galperin. The two young people liked to spend time together.

[Page 190]

At the time of the war, contagious diseases spread in all of Stepan, and there was not one family that someone didn't die. Disease and bereavement did not pass over the Kagan house. Reb Nachum and Yisrael, his son, got sick and died.

Some years later, the son, Moshe, was walking by foot on Simhat Torah from the train station in Malinsk to Stepan. He came back by train from Rovno, where he had gone before the drafting committee of the army. When he came back from Malinsk, he did not want to profane the holiday and travel in a wagon. The distance between Malinsk and Stepan was 19 kilometers and the way was through forests, a place destined for trouble. In the middle of the road, robbers jumped on him, put a knife in his throat, and took what he had. But they did not kill Moshe. He tricked the robbers, and when they placed a knife in his throat, he pretended that he was dead. They left him, and he remained to bleed to death. He had luck and a neighbor of the Kagan family, Vatak, the sausage man, passed by, and recognized his neighbor, Moshe. He hurried to the town, which was joyous and happy because of Simhat Torah, and brought the horrible news to the Kagan family.

All of Stepan was bustling with activity. They harnessed horses and ran quickly to the place of the disaster. It did not take too long to take Moshe to Rovno with the knife stuck in his throat, and with the efforts of specialist doctors, they were successful in saving him. His condition was very serious and dangerous, but the doctors saved his life. Shortly after this, he married and his wife gave birth to one girl. Feigel, a nice girl, took on all the chores of the house, kept it orderly, and took care of the clothing store. She was amongst the finest girls of Stepan. She immigrated to Argentina, even though she was a dedicated Zionist. There she had to work hard in order to make a living, but did not stay in Argentina long and returned to the town. In Stepan, she met Shmuel Goz, and the shidduch did not take a long time to develop. They had two children, and lived quiet and happy lives until the Holocaust.

Batya was a tall and happy girl. She married Avraham Rodnik from the village of Kosmachov. They had children, and lived a quiet life in the parent's home. And also her sister, Brindel, was very pretty and charming, quiet and dedicated to the home.

The youngest, Rezel, or as she is called in Israel, Shoshana, was pretty and vivacious in her youth. I remember one time a band of actors came to Stepan, and did the play "Dei Romantishe Chatuna" (The Romantic Wedding). Shoshana took part in the play as the role of a young girl. The words of the song "Holiet Holiet Kol Z'man Iher Zit Yong" (They were mischievous when they were still young) vibrate in my ears to this day. Also Shoshana, along with Pinchas, did not have it easy in the later years. The mother got sick and died. The two were still young and had to run the house and the store. During the Holocaust, Shoshana hid herself in a far away corner. She took her fate in her hands, was saved, and lives today in Israel. All the rest of the family was killed in the horrible Holocaust.

[Page 191]

27. Rabbi Leib, the Shoemaker

The family of Rabbi Leib, the shoemaker, included his wife, Shprintza, his son, Zeleg, and his daughters, Tzipah and Yentel.

Rabbi Leib barely made a living for his family, and was one of the poor families in the town. Along with this, he was a proud man, and G-d fearing. He did not complain, even though he was close to starving. He lived with his family in a poor shack, with a mud floor and a leaking roof.

His son, Zelek, was drafted into the army, and was sent to the Russian-Japanese War in 1905. Since then, he did not return to his parent's home. There were rumors that somehow he got to Paris and lived there. But there was no connection with him through the years.

The daughter, Tzipah, married, and her husband immigrated to the United States before World War I, and she stayed with her parents. A few years after World War I, Tzipa joined her husband in the United States. Since then, she helped her father by sending packages and money.

The second daughter, Yentel, married a Jew from the nearby town, Osova. Thus Rabbi Leib and his wife remained alone in their house. By the aid of righteous neighbors, they were able to exist barely.

Even though his economic situation was very difficult, Rabbi Leib would not grumble, and at every chance, he would make jokes and make up imaginary stories. He was well liked by his neighbors.

Below is one of his stories:

On one of the nights before the Holy Holidays, Rabbi Leib woke up early for the Selichot Services. On the way from his house to the synagogue, he saw in the darkness a figure wearing white clothing, moving slowly and heavily toward the synagogue. The person carried on his back another corpse, who was also wearing white. (There were rumors in the town that spirits, demons, and dead people visited the synagogue at night.) Immediately Rabbi Leib became suspicious that these dead wanted to visit the synagogue. He was brave and decided to follow this mysterious figure. When he followed the figure, Rabbi Leib noticed that the figure was coming near one of the houses of the non-Jews, and dropped what he was caring on his back with a blow on the ground. Rabbi Leib came close to the figure, and what did his eyes see. It was a non-Jew that he knew, wearing white linen clothing, carrying on his back a log with white bark.

And the lesson to be learned, according to Rabbi Leib's words is that all the rumors about spirits and demons are groundless. One has to be brave and argue against these rumors.

[Page 192]

28. Nachum Meir

Nachum Meir was a short man. He had a red beard with grey hair coming out of it, but was still going strong. His business was selling merchandise to the non-Jews from the neighboring villages.

He had two daughters: the eldest, Maltchie (Malcha), and the second was Matel. They were part of the modern youth, who would take walks with boys to the "Pagolinka" (the promenade), and would take part in the amateur actors' troupe in Stepan. Maltchie married Nissel, the son of Reb Yekutiel Goldberg, and Matel married Dov Wachs.

The store of Nachum Meir was not enough in order to make a livelihood for his family, and they left the town.

Dov and Matel live today in Argentina, and the rest of the family died in the Holocaust.

29. Reb Fibish Feldman (Fali Dar Klezmer)

In the same crowded row of nearby stores and apartments without a window to the street was the apartment of Fali, a Jew with a wide beard who was short. His wife, Ita, was shorter than him. But the neighbors would say that she was a "Kozak woman". They had four sons and two daughters. The oldest son lived in Rovno.

The daughter Feigel had a husband who would make wheels for wagons. He was a quiet man who worked hard. Two of the grandchildren, Yitzchak and Avraham Rochblatt, are in Israel.

The second son, Zev-Veli, was an industrious man and a jack of many trades. He tried his luck with many livelihoods.

The second daughter, Sheindel, married a man who fled from Russia. He married in Stepan and returned to Russia with his wife.

The third son, Moshele, was an agile and slick fellow. He had a wholesale and retail store.

The youngest son, Avigdor, immigrated to Argentina.

What did a Jew like Reb Fali make a living from? As he was connected to the Kalenikas, the Klezmerim, he would play on a contrabass at weddings and joyous occasions.

[Page 193]

But the Klezmerim was not his only livelihood. He sold cooked and pickled fish, whose aroma was smelled from afar. His wife made them. Not only did the non-Jews enjoy his fish, but also many Jews bought from him. Fibish had another livelihood – making alcoholic beverages. He would hurry his wife to pour for the gentiles: "Ita, pour for this gentile a cup. Make a fat bill for this gentile." But he was never satisfied with the results. He always thought that he did not get a good price for his work, and would always be angry.

Despite all of this, Reb Febish and his wife reached an old age. But the atrocities of the Holocaust did not pass over them, and destroyed his family.

30. Yoel Prishkolnik (Yoelik Gatas)

The whole Prishkolnik family, including their elderly father, Ben-Zion and his offspring, were called by the name, "Dei-Gatas". I don't know where the name came from, but there were rumors that the name was stuck to Yoel's grandfather, Rabbi Yishayahu Prishkolnik because he emphasized too much "Lord, your G-d, of truth", as he was "a gabbai", a treasurer, and a cantor.

Yoel's house was on the street of the synagogue, under the same roof with his parents. The store was close to the house of Roman, "the sausage man", and in his ownership.

Yoel was one of the founders of the Zionist Movement in the town, and was part of the group of educated people in Stepan. When a troupe of dramatic actors was founded in the town, he became part of this troupe.

I have a distinct memory of the figure of "the witch" in the play of Goldfedan (in Yiddish, "Dei-Kishuf-Macharin"). The best actors took place in this play, and invested in it all of their strength and energy. They had rehearsals for many long days. I don't know whose idea it was to give the role of the witch to a man. But Yoel Prishkolnik played the role of the witch with great success.

Since then, many years have passed. But the calls of Yoel Frishkolnik, "the witch", to his nephew, Yishayahu Elikim in the play still echoes in my ears: E-li-kum-kim. E-li-ku-kim!

The impression of the play was very strong in Stepan. I saw the actors of "the Ohel" in Israel in the play, "the Witch", which was a great success. But it seems to me that this cannot be compared to the acting of the dramatic troupe in Stepan.

[Page 194]

Yoel Frishkolnik passed his years in Stepan like the rest of his friends. He married and had children. Amongst them were his son Yishayahu and his daughter, Sosel, today Sara Kaplan, who are alive today and live in Israel today.

Yoel turned from a great actor to an owner of a store of tobacco products, and was a man of standing. At the time of the Soviet regime, he worked as an accountant. He, his wife, Tivel (from the Zuckerman family from the nearby Brazna), and their eldest son Shaul were killed by the cursed Germans, and their local Ukrainian partners.

31. Chaim Kaminitz – the Great Tailor

He was from the city of Rovno. He learned in the cheder of the Talmud Torah. His family was poor and they could not afford to teach him any more. They turned him over to learn to be a tailor. He did not finish his studies to become a tailor. He was half-learned because he did not finish his studies and the other half, he was half a tailor.

When he came to Stepan, and married one of the daughters of Melech, the tailor, he announced clearly that he was a tailor of the highest level, and there could not be found anyone on his level in the area. It was clear, in comparison to his father-in-law, he was an excellent professional.

His father-in-law, Melech, a sickly Jew, who looked like someone with tuberculosis, was a tailor for farmers all of his life. Farmers from the area ordered from him clothes and they didn't care too much about exactness and the size. Therefore, when it happened that a farmer would insist on trying on the suit, we, the young people, would stand on the side and look on. We would comment that one sleeve was long and the other was short; every pocket was turning in a different direction and was a different size. Also the buttons were not sewn straight in the same line, but in a sort of zigzag. But what would a poor farmer do who barely had enough money to buy the fabric, and could not afford a better tailor? He would take the clothes and go home in peace.

This tailor saw the work of his father-in-law, and thought that all the tailors in Stepan were like his father-in-law. Therefore, he thought he was excellent.

After his wedding, he began to think about making a living, and there were people who advised him to join Shmuel Gerber, the best tailor in the area. There he could make a good living, and could gain experience in the field. After waiting a while and having doubts, he answered the request of his wife, and went to Shmuel Gerber to see what he was like. He entered the working room with measured steps, surveyed from above (even though he was short) all the people sitting in the room, and turned to the head of the shop, Shmuel Gerber with these words: "Will I have to sit and work with all these "shura-vantz" (vantz-bugs in Yiddish). A voice of laughter broke out amongst the people sitting on their work.

[Page 195]

Since then Chaim Kaminitzer was called by the name "Chaim Shura Vantz"), which did not leave him till the last days of his life.

He was a good man with good manners and responsibility.

32. Rivka Kamenstein

At the corner and central store was the store of Rivka Kamenstein (the eldest daughter of Moshe Yosef Sheinboim). She became a widow from her husband, Yehoshua, at a young age, and her one and only son, Yitzchak, stayed with her. He was called "Itchenke". He was a tall and handsome boy.

Yitzchak was accepted amongst the youth, and acted many years as the representative of the Keren Kayemet (the Jewish National Fund). He was active in the actors' troupe that performed in Yiddish.

Rivka married a widower from Rovno or that area. Itchenke also married and moved to Rovno or Zadolebonov.

Like many others, they also were killed along with their family in the Holocaust.

33. Baruch Rassis (Itzik Yokless)

At the age of fifty, Baruch became a widower, and remarried a second wife. He had four sons and one daughter. For work he had a wagon and he would take the mail between Stepan and Malinsk, and his sons would help him. Nevertheless, he was not successful in feeding his family. When he had to feed his horses oats, he would turn to the seller of the grain, place into his hand a coin, and the rest he would take on credit. But he always owed the seller of the grain money. Because he dealt with horses, he began also to deal with selling horses. On every market day, it was possible to see him checking horses, and all of this was in order to add to the livelihood of his family. But he never made this addition to his livelihood. After the market day, one could see him at the saloon, drinking spirits in great amounts. This was in order to flee from the difficult reality.

It was obvious that Baruch was not a very learned man, and such were his sons. Even so, in their childhood, he sent them to schools. But their father's business enchanted them more, and many times they would be seen with their father in the saloon.

Baruch Rassis could have spent his whole life in Stepan, and could have died without standing out, except for one incident that happened to him, that shook up the whole town.

[Page 196]

Baruch's daughter was pretty and charming. Her name was Rivka. She studied in a Polish school and finished a couple of grades. She matured at an early age, and was the target of the lustful looks of men, and even more so, of non-Jewish men. If the fellows of Stepan would let her pass by quietly without touching her, the manager of the Polish post office would take advantage of her innocence. One bright day, a voice was heard in Stepan that Rivka Rassis ran away from home with her lover, the manager of the post office.

Stepan was bustling with activity, because at the same time another girl fled from her home and converted. There were rumors that there were others girls in line to be converted.

Baruch Rassis, even though he was not amongst the more religious in the town, when he heard this horrible news, he turned white over night. He looked for his daughter days and nights. He went to different places, and asked his friends to follow her steps, until one day it become known by chance that she was found in a city near Warsaw, along with the manager of the post office and his family.

Baruch arrived at the place and pleaded with her to return to him and she said: No! No! Once he sent one of her friends who was very much attached to her, in order to influence her to visit Stepan for a short while and then return to her "husband". She returned to Stepan in order to visit her father's home. It was appealing to her to have the status of appearing as the wife of the manager of the post office.

Baruch Rassis knew how to take advantage of this opportunity and called all the youth to come to his house to visit. Perhaps they would succeed in influencing her to stay at her father's home.

This act will be remembered well, for the youth of Stepan of all age groups volunteered to come to Baruch's house, and spend there days upon days. Amongst the visitors was an educator and a teacher, who was very much influenced by this Rivka and fell deeply in love with her. Not much time passed and in spite of the objection of the teachers and the local parents' committee, Shenrer married Rivka Rassis and thus saved one Israeli soul from conversion.

For a long time after, many said in Stepan: what Tuvye, the milkman, from Katrilevka was not successful in doing, the teacher from Stepan was successful in doing.

No one from this family remained alive after the horrible Holocaust.

34. The House of Tanchum (Tanya) Sheinboim

The family of Moshe Yosef Sheinboim was a large and branched out family in Stepan. Tanchum Sheinboim was the second son to his father. It was accepted as if he was the eldest son of the family, and all the decisions received the approval of Tanchum.

[Page 197]

The boys of the Tanchum house, who were Zionists from their youth, received a traditional education, and afterwards also a secular education. They learned in Chederim with the best melamdim (teachers) in the town. Afterwards, with the opening of the "Tarbut" School, in the year 1923, that Tanchum was one of its initiators and founders, the boys went to this school. Along with this, they helped their father in commerce. Almost all the sons were brilliant salesmen.

Tanchum Sheinboim was the buyer and seller of all the merchandise that came into his hands, and almost always was successful. He would trade pig hair, grains, fresh and processed skins, harness equipment for horses, and all sorts of groceries. He would buy grain for animals, barrels of oil, kerosene, tar, bags of rice, dry alfalfa, and what would he not buy? Full days he would deal with commerce. He hated lazy people, and would always rush others, why sleep? It happened more than once that he would visit our home and would find me in bed in the early hours of the morning. He would scold me: "Are you still sleeping? Get up! It's time."

Tanchum Sheinboim had many good qualities and advantages, but the most important amongst them was his search for peace. Even though he was a Cohen, and it is known that Cohanim were short tempered persons, he would never get angry and in his house nobody would raise their voice. If it became known to him that in this house or another in the town there was a family quarrel, or a quarrel between neighbors, he would come without any hesitation, enter in the middle and force the fighters to make peace immediately.

Tanchum's wife, Ita, was from a cultured family. She was known for her education, her wisdom, and her influence on the education of her children (four boys and one girl) was great and decisive.

The eldest son of Tanchum and Ita, Chaim, a serious and intelligent fellow, learned accountancy, and read a lot. For a long time, he was the secretary of the Zionist Council in the town, the secretary of the Keren Kayemet (the Jewish National Fund), and would also worked in a store for manufacturing utensils with his uncle Heschel, until his uncle lost his assets. Chaim married Shifra Marcus-Makoritz. They had two sons. All of them were killed by the Nazis.

The second son, Ben-Zion, today in Israel, helped his father with commerce from a young age. He married Bronia Tachor, a young and nice girl. They had two beautiful and charming children, who were perfect in their beauty. Ben-Zion was drafted during the war into the Soviet army, which saved his life. His wife, Bronia and her children, were killed in the forests of Stepan, after she was successful in fleeing from the general massacre in Kostopol.

The third son, Yitzchak Sheinboim-Oren made Aliyah in 1934, after years of study in the secondary school in Vilna, and afterwards in France. When he arrived in Israel, he got a job in the Tel Aviv municipality. As time passed, he was promoted to a very high job in the municipality,

[Page 198]

the treasurer of the city of Tel Aviv. He held this high job until 1971. When he retired from the municipality, he was named the head of the board of directors of the lottery. He was also a member of boards of different public and financial institutions in the city. He is married to Sonya, and they have two sons and three granddaughters.

In 1935, Tanchum Sheinboim and his wife, Ita, made aliyah along with their only daughter, Bracha (Bozia). When anti-Semitism and the hate of the non-Jews got greater, he understood that he must leave the town and move to Israel. A year after he made Aliyah, Tanchum got sick and died. His wife, Ita, could not bear her sorrow, and retuned to Stepan along with her daughter, Bracha. Bracha married a relative, Shmuel Achtenbaum from Kalban, and they had one daughter. In the meantime, the war started, Achtenbaum was drafted into the Soviet army, and thus was saved. Ita Sheinboim, Bracha, and her daughter were killed in the Holocaust.

The father of the family, Tanchum Sheinboim, of blessed memory, died in the Land of Israel in the year 1936

The mother of the family, Ita Sheinboim, of blessed memory, was killed in the Holocaust

[Page 199]

The fourth son, Shmuel, made Aliyah after the Holocaust. He was saved from the Nazis because he was drafted into the Soviet army.

The fifth son, Shlomo, has been in Israel since 1936. He arrived in Israel before the war, married Batya Becker, and continued to deal in commerce.

The rest of the family who remained in the town was killed in the Holocaust.

[Page 200]

The Home of the Genius Ben-Zion Volinsky,
the Righteous Man of Blessed Memory

by Betzalel Shpritz

Translated by Yona Landau

The house of the Genius Ben-Zion Volinsky, of blessed memory, was known and famous in the town and its surroundings.

The Rabbi was known for his many talents and his knowledge of the holy books. He would sit day and night by his wide and big table and learn chapters in the Gemorah. At the time of his studies, his pleasant voice would reach many houses in the area.

The Jews of Stepan flocked to his house with all sorts of questions about Kashrut and other laws. His house was open all the hours of the day, and he would help all in counseling and guidance. Even though his economical situation was always difficult, he would invite Friday night dinner guests to his house. For the most part, the Rav would live from the support of his many followers from other countries, especially from the United States, where they appreciated their Rabbi as a great and wise learner.

His only son, Sandar, of blessed memory, was also a learned student, smart and of many traits. Despite his young age, he would solve all sorts of questions in Gemorah. Many yeshivah boys who visited Stepan would sit by the table of the Rabbi and his son, and would take in much wisdom and knowledge from the Rabbi and his son, Sandar.

Sandar was also active in the Revisionist Movement and would lecture and speak in synagogues in the town. When the news of the forming of "the Covenant of Yeshurun", which was a branch of the Covenant of Tzohar (the Revisionist Zionists), became known, he was amongst its first founders. Thanks to his talent in speaking and his strong clinging to the Torah of Israel along with Zionism, he was successful in forming "The Council of Supporters of the Covenant of Yeshurun", which was accepted by Religious Judaism in the town.

In the last years before the war, he also was a commander in Betar. His logic and energy contributed to the basis of the Revisionist Party, including all of its factions.

The house of the Genius Ben-Zion Volinsky and his son, Sandar, of great talents, and their family members, will always be remembered by the people of the town and by all who knew them.

[Page 201]

My Father, Reb Azriel-Yaacov Koifman (Zunieh)
of Blessed Memory

by Yisrael Koifman

Translated by Yona Landau
Edited by Mira Eckhaus and Daniel Shimshak

Yisrael Koifman made Aliyah as a pioneer in 1933. He was a member of Kibbutz Ramat Rochel. Today he is a member of Kibbutz Ein-Hacarmel.

There did not remain any pictures of my father. Because my father was afraid of breaking the negative commandment of "Don't make for yourself a picture or any stature", he did not have his picture taken a lot. The picture he gave me before I made Aliyah was burned in the battles of the Independence War in Ramat Rochel. But I can place before my eyes the pure figure of my father – tall, his face with a white beard, his soft eyes like the eyes of a child, which showed his good heart and pure soul.

My father was a man of the Torah, and every evening he would sit bent over his Gemorah until the late hours of the night and study. He tried to influence us, his sons, that we would look in the holy books, and that we wouldn't read all sorts of books that do not lead to the fear of G-d. Many a times I would sit with him and study Alshich, in order to make him happy.

Father was religious, kept the mitzvot, the difficult ones like the easy ones, and believed unreservedly in "Divine Providence". He was religious, but would not argue with others about religious matters. He tried to influence us in pleasant ways, so we would believe that "everything that G-d does is for the best."

Many times I was jealous of his great faith in G-d, of his ability to justify the judgment, even when fate was bitter, and his suffering was too great to bear. Till this day I remember the day of the death of my mother, Malcha of blessed memory. I was twelve years old then. All of us, including my father, cried bitterly over my mother's death. With great sorrow, we arrived at the cemetery. When the time came to say "the justification of the judgment", my brother, David of blessed memory, could not hold back and challenged the heavens by saying: "No, G-d is not right in taking our mother from us. I will not justify the judgment." Father was shocked when he heard these heretic words, and in a crying voice, he scolded my brother and said: "We must not ponder the actions of G-d. G-d gave and G-d took. He is right and his judgment is right." We all cried and said again what father said about the justification of the judgment, just as he asked us to do.

Father was a seeker of peace. He was very accepted by the Jews of the town as a righteous and naïve man of contributing attributes. More than once when a quarrel would break out between two Jews, they would come to him for "a din Torah" (a decision according to the Torah). When he would make his decision, nobody would protest his decision because all knew he was a symbol of justice. The love of Israel was a holy principle to him. He went according to the ways of Reb Levi Yitzchak from Bradichev. He would judge every Jew in a positive way. Even when the Jew did a sinful act, he would look for a way to justify his action, and to find in this Jew the "Jewish spark".

[Page 202]

I do not remember father speaking an everyday discussion. All of his free time was spent in learning Torah and Talmud. Only once a year, he would allow himself to become less serious and tell a joke, which was also related to the learning of Torah, and that was on the day of Simchat Torah.

Someone who did not see my father dance the Hakafot on Simchat Torah, never saw someone who could transcend materialism. When the Sefer Torah was in his hands, he would dance ecstatically before the Holy Ark, with his eyes closed, his face pale, and he looked like a man not in this world, as if in the upper spheres of spirituality. When they urged him to rest a bit, he would continue dancing as if "all his bones would say" to him it is not the time to be urged to rest and would sing: "All the Jews are happy on Simhat Torah, the Torah and Israel are one." Thus he would continue until his strength came to an end. Then he would return the Sefer Torah to the Holy Ark, sit in his seat, and his eyes would sparkle with precious light as if the Divine Presence was upon his face…

The year that mother passed away, a year of mourning, everyone thought that father would not dance his famous dance on Simhat Torah. But all were surprised to see him dancing greater than other years, the dance of "even though and despite it all", a dance that he had never danced all of his life.

Our house was a Zionist home. All the brothers knew Hebrew, and there was a period of time that Hebrew was the language of the home. Father was not a Zionist in the usual way. He was not a member of the "Mizrachi" Party or of "Agudat Yisrael", but his love for the land of Israel was great. He enjoyed hearing the "holy language" spoken by us, and on the Sabbath, he would use only the Hebrew language.

I will never forget the minute when father gave me his picture, at the time when I came to say goodbye to him before I made aliyah in 1933. With teary eyes and a shaky voice, he said to me: "I do not know if I will have the privilege to reach our holy land. I took my picture especially in order that my picture will be with you in the land of Israel, and let it be as if my body is also there." He requested from me that I visit in the holy places when his picture was with me.

Monthly I would receive letters from him full of yearning for Israel. He wrote his letters in Hebrew in the style of the Mishna, and every line expressed his great love for the pioneers that were building the land. I will never forgive myself for not helping him make aliyah. I was afraid that he would be disappointed when he would see me working sometimes on the Sabbath, and that I did not keep kashrut. Who would have dreamed then that the flood of the Jews of Poland was approaching, and that in a couple of years, the Jews of Europe would be destroyed, and along with them, my large family. My sister's son and I were the only survivors of the family.

[Page 203]

Also at the time of the Soviet Regime, I would still receive letters from him in which he would hint to me of the difficult life. But his heart did not predict what was to be expected under the horrible Nazi Regime.

From pieces of information that I heard from my father's life in the ghetto and his bitter end, it seems that until the last moments, he did not lose his faith in G-d, and did not let others arrive at heretic thoughts. He saw himself as the continuation of the chain of righteous that died in order to sanctify the name of G-d. He accepted his suffering with love.

All his life he lived a righteous life, and died as a righteous man.

[Page 204]

The Teacher, Moshe Kalat,
of Blessed Memory

by Yeshayahu Pery

Translated by Yona Landau
Edited by Mira Eckhaus and Daniel Shimshak

Mr. Kalat and his family were not born in the town. They came to the town from central Poland. Mr. Kalat was a teacher of Polish History in the public school, in which most of its students were Ukrainians and Polish and only a few were Jews.

In the school, Mr. Kalat was known as a short-tempered person, strict, not generous in giving good grades, and had high standards for discipline and order with no compromises. Amongst the Jews of the town, he was known as a Jew who kept his distance from the other Jews of the town. He and his family mingled with the Polish intellectuals and little with the Jews. They spoke Polish amongst themselves. Mr. Kalat and his family did not hurry to the synagogue to pray, except on Yom Kippur.

His children did not take part in the Zionist youth movement.

In summary, Mr. Kalat and his family were exceptionally different and heretic in the eyes of most of the Jews of the town, except for a few who were friendly with them.

Despite this strange behavior, I saw a totally different picture when he would join us (a small group of Jewish students amongst the sea of non-Jewish students) in a small classroom, and would teach us in the Polish language about the Jewish religion and its principles. Once a week, at the same hour, the rest of the Ukraininan-Provaslavic and Polish-Catholic students would receive religion lessons from a priest or his certified representative. Here the character of Mr. Kalat was totally different from his daily appearance in his regular classes. His face was lit up, and he was full of joy at his effort to instill in us our holy Torah and its principles. He always returned and stressed the importance of national pride, even though we were swimming in a sea of hatred and jealousy.

From a figure of a strict teacher, he turned into a friendly fatherly shepherd. He stressed the importance of deep learning of all areas in general, and especially of the Torah of Israel.

It can be said that Mr. Kalat and his family were on the inside very warm and proud Jews with regard to their Judaism, but because he had a state job, the needs of the livelihood obligated him, as it seems, from daily involvement with his people. On the other hand, when he was allowed in a formal framework as a teacher to teach the Torah of his fathers to his people, he was eager to speak and do his work faithfully. Mr. Kalat and his family suffered, like the rest of the Jews of the town, all the sufferings of the persecutions of the Germans even before the ghetto was formed and later in the ghetto. They were killed along with the rest of the Jews of the town.

[Page 205]

My Father, Reb Yoel Baruch Ben Yehoshua Halevi Becker of Blessed Memory

by Avraham Tachor (Becker)

Translated by Yona Landau
Edited by Mira Eckhaus and Daniel Shimshak

With great honor and love, here I bring forth the memory of my father, Yoel Baruch of blessed memory, "Reb Yoel-Boruch", as he was called in our town Stepan, the head and the crown of our family. I see him in my eyes: on his lips, a simple and pleasant smile, and his eyes showing warmth and goodness. He was short, had a high forehead which was a characteristic forehead for a talmid chacham (a learned student), and an educated man.

As a student of the Rovno Yeshivah, he immersed himself in the wisdom of Israel, and was well versed in the revealed Torah and the hidden wisdom. Along with this, our house was a traditional-nationalist home. Father would talk to his children sometimes in Hebrew. He had command of the language without any inhibitions.

As a lover of learning and knowledge, he was very committed to the existence and development of the local Hebrew school, "Tarbut". His concern for Hebrew education and Jewish tradition was of his greatest priorities. He was the head of the parents' committee and had close contact with the teachers of the school. He made an effort along with the teacher, Moshe Koifman, to pay the teachers their wages on time, something that was difficult at this time period.

Along with him being a well-off man, as a merchant of manufacturing utensils, and the owner of an oil press, he was a very popular person as his goodness was expressed on his face. He would say hello to everyone who came his way, and was very accepted by all levels of society.

Being of this type, he was accepted by all the religious judges of the town: Rav Ben-Zion Volinsky, the Rabbi of the working men, and "the good nature", the Rabbi of "the people" and the craftsmen.

Our house was an open house to all poor people in need of charity. There were cases of people who lost all of their assets. Father would not be quiet until they rose up again. He even would not be ashamed to pressure his friends, who had money, in order to help out. It is superfluous to say that he would practice what he preached.

In addition to his great work in the area of Hebrew education, he was the father of the founders of "the Covenant of Yeshurun" in Stepan, and was amongst the active people on the committee of the branch in Stepan.

In 1933, he joined the Covenant of Tzohar (the Revisionist Zionists), and in the last years of the 1930s, he was the head of it. He also acted as a delegate of the Tel-Chai Fund. Because of his great dedication and success in the area of his activity, he received a letter of thanks from Mrs. Z. Botinsky from Paris.

[Page 206]

Even though he was very involved in public activity, he did not neglect his childrens' education, and cared to plant in them good attributes and values, for instance: love for people, respect for adults, good friendships, not being arrogant, patience for others, and loyalty to the people and the land of Israel. When I would go with father to the synagogue on the Sabbath and on the holidays, father would say to me many times: "It doesn't matter how a man prays and where he prays. The main thing is the prayer in his heart.

This kind of prayer is more important than all." In general, we had a very warm relationship. I didn't only feel for him a relationship of a son to a father, but to an elderly friend with the wisdom of life. That was my sisters' feeling Brendele of blessed memory and Batya who should live a long life.

On Rosh Hashana, father would blow the shofar in our synagogue. He told me that this was something he inherited from his father, Yehoshua Halevi, my grandfather, of blessed memory.

On every Rosh Hashana, our synagogue would become filled with the usual people who prayed there, along with many visitors. Many of them were friends of father who came to hear him blow the shofar.

The fact that my father began, before the tekiot, the prayer "Min-Hametzar" by himself showed how accepted he was in the community. On his right, Reb Ben-Zion, the teacher who was very authoritative, would whisper in his ears: tekiyah, tekiyah, shivarim, teruah, etc. I remember this because I would stand by my father, with his prayer shawl over me. It seemed that his tekiot were stronger than the tekiot of the accusing Satan, and paved the way to heavens to the throne of the Creator of the World.

Along with this, my father was known in the religious circles as a progressive man and very far from religious fanaticism, and a keeper of the mitzvot in the true sense of the word.

Father was not a chassid, but was personally friendly with the rebbi, Reb Baruch Twersky, of blessed memory.

My mother, Bonia, of blessed memory, his helpmate, was very good hearted, and was one of righteous women of the town. She gave anonymous charity, and even my father and we did not know who she prepared the food for on the Sabbaths and the holidays. She was very honest, and always said what was on her mind. As a Jewish mother, she was very dedicated to her children, and she was considered as a good aunt on both sides of the family.

When we prepared for my Bar Mitzvah ceremony, the preparation of the cakes and the rest of the delicacies were like those of a wedding.

[Page 207]

One of the friends of the family, Sandar Volinsky, the son of Rabbi Ben-Zion, who prepared me for my Bar Mitzvah, said: "Bonia, we are talking about preparations for a Bar Mitzvah and not about preparations for a wedding." My mother answered him and said: "I am fortunate enough to prepare for my son's Bar Mitzvah. I am not sure that I will be fortunate enough to prepare for my only son's wedding." She said this without knowing that this would be the truth.

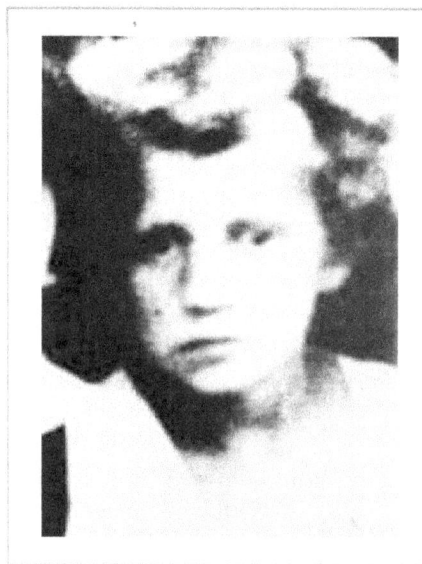

Brendele Becker

When World War II broke out, the Russians conquered the eastern area of the Polish State. In June 1941, the German Army invaded Russia, and within a short period of time, the Stepan Ghetto was formed. The suffering of the Jews in the ghetto was unbearable. The Germans, along with the aid of the Ukrainians, put the Jews of the ghetto on the wagons of the Ukrainians and led them to Kostopol, which was 35 kilometers from Stepan. They forced the Jews to dig holes, take their clothes off, and they shot them,

[Page 208]

as they fell on their knees into the holes. This was the last road of our dear friends, holy and pure, may G-d avenge their blood.

While they traveled in the direction of Kostopol, there were those who jumped from the wagons, and fled to the deep forests in the area. According to the advice of Uncle Meir (the brother of my mother), my sisters, Batya and Brendele, my mother, and my aunt, Henia jumped and fled into the forests. Uncle Meir refused to do so. My sisters, my mother, and Uncle Meir's family hid in the forest, and they ate what my sister, Brendele, who was twelve years old, would bring. She would go to the doors of the farmers to ask for bread for us.

In one of the attacks of the Ukrainians on Jews, they shot and killed some of the Jews of our town who hid in one of caves in the area. My sister, Brendele and my cousin, Sonya, were caught alive on their way to Stepan. They were brutally tortured until their pure souls died, may G-d avenge their blood. This became known to my sister, Batya, from a Polish woman who lived near our home, and who had even helped us during the period of time that we were in the ghetto.

Mother died of exhaustion in the forest, and was buried there. My father and my Uncle Michel were murdered in one of the nearby villages after they were deceived by a guard of the forest, an old friend of theirs. Before they were killed, they made sure that Mosik and Zina, the son of the sheet-metal worker, would flee into the forest and fight for their lives.

I will always imagine them before me. May G-d avenge their blood.

[Page 209]

The House of Reb Pesach Bebchuk and His Wife Esther Leah, of Blessed Memory

by Betzalel Shpritz

Translated by Yona Landau
Edited by Mira Eckhaus and Daniel Shimshak

The house of Reb Pesach Bebchuk and his good wife along with their children, Moshe Bebchuk, Avraham, Shmariyahu, and the sisters, Chaya, Miriam, and Tziril, were known in the town as a large family.

Reb Pesach was a fair merchant of manufacturing utensils, and was accepted by his many customers from the nearby villages.

When the war broke out, many of his customers and friends from amongst the Christians and the Ukrainians in the area turned to him and helped him and his family to hide in their homes. His eldest son,

Moshe, and his wife, Leah (from the Tachor family), and the two daughters, Yehudit and Sonya, were hid by a non-Jew in a nearby village for a certain period of time. When it became known that there would be searches soon for Jews in the village, Moshe had to bring his family back to the ghetto to his parents.

Moshe was known in the town as an excellent public dealer. He would support many orphans and people who needed help. In the years before the war, he was very active in the "Achdut Avodah" Movement. He organized many meetings, and would speak before the supporters of the movement. He planned to move to Israel, despite his age. Unfortunately, he was not fortunate enough to fulfill his dreams.

The Nazis murdered him along with his large family. Let their memory be blessed.

Their daughter, Shoshana, from the Shpritz family, is alive and lives in Israel. Their son, Avraham, lives in Argentina.

[Page 210]

Chayke Bebchuk

Pesach Bebchuk

[Page 211]

The Family of Yechiel Vildgoiz

by Nachumke (from the home of Vildgoiz) Gordon

Translated by Yona Landau
Edited by Mira Eckhaus and Daniel Shimshak

Their house served as a shelter in the town, a place for free sleeping quarters for homeless, and for passers by. It was the house of Yechiel and Reitza Vildgoiz. Yechiel immigrated to Canada in 1931, in search of a better livelihood than what he had in the town. His wife, Reitza (from the house of Weitznodel – the daughter of Ben-Zion Weitznodel) and her children, Nachum, Chava, Rochel, and Gittel stayed in the town until the husband got in order the new home in Canada and could receive them.

Thus they waited in the town until 1935. The mother, with the aid of her father, carried the weight of the family by herself, with some financial support from her husband in Canada.

The children were involved in the town life. They were students in the "Tarbut" School, and were active in the youth movements. It was difficult for them to say goodbye to the youth of the town. The son, Nachum, when he visited Israel, was surprising in his many and detailed memories from those days.

Yechiel, of blessed memory, died in Canada. Reitza, the mother of Nachum, died in 1972.

Nachum and his sisters, Chava, Rochel, and Gittel, live along with their families in Canada.

[Page 212]

Reitza (from the house of Weitznodel) Gordon of blessed memory with   her children Nachumke, Chava, Rochel, and Gittel, that they live long lives, when they arrived from Stepan to Canada in the year 1934

[Page 213]

The Holocaust

Death and Sorrow

(Memories from my father's home, Yoel Prishkolnik, z"l)

by Y. Pery

Translated by Yona Landau
Edited by Mira Eckhaus and Daniel Shimshak

The War between Poland and Germany (1939-1944)

In September 1939 with the outbreak of the war between Poland and Germany, the heavens darkened and the hearts of the Jews of the town filled with anxiety and fear. Already in the years 1938-39, anti-Semitism was well felt in Poland and also in our town, Stepan. Anti-Semitism was felt in every walk of life: in the schools, on the street, and it directly affected the economical lives of the Jews. In school, we suffered swears, threats, and derogatory nicknames, and sometimes even blows. The Ukrainians, because of the great hate for the Poles and the Jews, proclaimed clearly, that the end of the Jews was approaching and that Hitler is coming nearer. We, the Jews, were filled with apprehensions of what was to come, but we did not grasp that it would be so horrible.

The Decrees of the Polish Government

The Poles enforced different decrees, and the most outstanding decree was forbidding of kosher slaughtering which was something that affected the spiritual and economic life of the Jews of Stepan. This decree aroused many prayers and supplications. There was a prayer said on Yom Kippur Katan in the Central Synagogue to cancel the decree. Most of the people of Stepan took part in this service. I remember very well the words of Rabbi Levi, the shochet, who said: "We have reached the pinnacle of all decrees, the pinnacle of darkness, the accepted view from creation that it is the darkest before daybreak." This viewpoint was that redemption was approaching. On that occasion, we did not imagine that this was nothing compared to the decrees that would come in the future.

The effect upon the Jew's economy was felt by forbidding dealing in many areas of commerce, mainly with the monopolies that needed a special franchise. My father had a franchise for a store for tobacco and alcohol. The decree established that only a Pole was allowed to sell, and my father's franchise was cancelled with a warning of a half of a year to close the business. This hurt my father deeply as he was many years in the field and was very involved with what was going on in this area. He held a franchise for many years. He tried in many ways to convince the government in Stepan, in the district, and the King, by traveling to meet them and making many requests. But it did not help. My father even presented a notarized statement, certified by the court, with Polish witnesses, who claimed that in the years 1917-18, he helped the Poles and hid a group of their soldiers when the Communists

[Page 214]

suddenly entered their town. But this did not help, and his franchise was taken from him, and given to a Pole. My father was forced to deal with other areas of commerce, like a grocery store, but without much luck. After that he had a store for bicycles and building materials in partnership with Benny Bastus, the only store of its kind in Stepan. After a short time of success in this area, the war began. The children received a nice bicycle that my oldest brother, Shaul z"l learned to ride. I even learned how to ride it.

The Damage Caused to the Economy of the Family

Because of the damage to the economic situation, my sister and I were forced to leave "the Cultural" School, which caused us to pay a large monthly sum, and to transfer to a Polish public school, which caused us, the children, disappointment. I had just finished fifth grade and my sister had just finished first or second grade. This meant leaving all of our friends, and moving to a far away environment full of hatred. But we had no choice, and we adjusted after a beginning effort. We especially placed an emphasis on learning the Polish language and history. We became very good students along with some of our other Jewish friends who transferred to this school.

The Polish Defeat

A few days after the beginning of the war, there were rumors, which were verified within a short time, that the Poles were defeated, and that they retreated on all the fronts. The Ukrainians in our towns and in nearby surroundings raised their heads and with their great hatred for the Poles, they took arms and rebelled. They took over the police station, the government buildings, and the whole town very quickly. When they heard that the Russians were approaching, they raised red flags, even though their real intention was nationalistic. It turned out that the Polish guard force, which guarded the Russian-Polish border, retreated from the Russian border in the west direction, and had to go through our town. The Ukrainians, who did not have a great amount of weapons, organized themselves on the hills near the river on one side of the bridge, and came toward the Polish army, who retreated with gun shots.

The Night of Terror and the Shooting in Stepan

A night of terror fell upon the people of the town, and I remember how the bullets whistled by us. My father that was versed in the ways of war, apparently from personal experience since the incidents of WWI, ordered us to lie down on the floor behind a big heavy oven. We lied there all night until sunrise, the time the shooting stopped and the Polish army retreated

[Page 215]

to the town. We were closed in our houses and we did not dare to go outside. The Polish soldiers roamed the streets of the town in search of rebels, and they aimed their rifles at the houses of the Jews, on purpose or by chance. After one of the tenants of our house wanted to go outside to the bathroom in the barn, when he closed the door, the roaming soldiers paid attention to the noise. They approached the door of our apartment, and ordered all the tenants of the house to go outside. My father, my mother, my brother, and I came out with hands above our heads, and we walked to the Market Square under heavy guard. There we joined a group of Jews and Ukrainians who were organized in a long line in which there were on both sides of them rows of soldiers with rifles that threatened to kill. They aimed the rifles at the Communist traitors. Because of my great fear, I had the chills.

We stood there for hours, and suddenly there appeared a high officer accompanied by a Pole from Stepan, the son of Roman Hakolbasnik. He was the one who sorted out the guilty and the innocent. Because he knew us well, he said we were innocent, as he decided for most of the Jews, except a few young Jews. We fled when we still could, and we hid in a Polish store, and stayed there until the army left the town. The few Ukrainians and Jews that were not freed were chained and led outside of the city to be brought to trial for rebellion and treason. Their end was of course death.

Immediately after the evacuation of the army, the distinguished people of the town met: Poles, Ukrainians, and Jews. They thought how to save those who were taken who really had no part in the uprising. Then it was decided to send a delegation of Polish teachers and at their head the Catholic priest, in search of the army that had retreated, in order to convince the generals. The army that retreated moved quickly. The Catholic priest had a car, but there was a serious problem of gasoline. Therefore, they turned to my father, who had a store for building materials and gasoline. Of course, my father gave them the gasoline needed and they were on their way. This delegation was successful in releasing all the Jewish boys and even the Ukrainians. A number of Ukrainians were tortured and killed by shooting. This left a very heavy feeling upon the people of the town. A few days later, there was a large funeral in the town, in which most of the people of the town took part in. When the Soviets entered, the Ukrainians took revenge on the son of Roman Hakolbasnik and informed on him and expelled him and his family, including his father, his mother, his brother, and his sisters to Siberia. This was in spite of the fact that many had much sympathy for him as he saved many from death.

[Page 216]

The Soviet Regime -- 1939-1941
The Entrance of the Red Army into Stepan

Within a day or two after the Polish Army left the town, after the conflict with the rebelling Ukrainians, a rumor spread in the morning that the "Bolsheviks" were coming. We, the children, pushed our way to the head of a large group of Ukrainians and Jews toward the bridge to see the "Bolsheviks". We had heard about their appearance from our parents, about their clothing and behavior during WWI. And shortly we saw them approaching on their tanks (something we did not see with the Polish Army). They were not at all poor people. But their clothes -- boots, hats, and ranks -- did not shine or compare to the clothes of the Polish soldiers and officers.

A delegation of the honorable people of the town walked toward them and received them with bread and salt, as was the custom of the place. The crowd received them with cheers and clapping of hands. They were very pleasant and smiled to the crowd, and they were happy to explain about their rifles and their ranks. After the tanks, there were rows of walking soldiers and some of them were in trucks. In "the cavalry", there were horsemen of all types in their national clothing upon short horses, and there were also Cossacks in their national clothing. In the Red Army, there were soldiers of many nationalities -- Tartars, Cossacks, Uzbekistans, and others.

Our parents and the elderly were a bit afraid of the behavior of these soldiers, as they remembered their wild and undisciplined behavior during WWI. But things did not seem that way in the present reality, as the discipline was perfect.

Some of the officers lived in Jewish houses. A Cossack officer with the rank of captain lived in my grandfather's house. They taught us Russian, and taught us Russian songs. They tried to refill what was missing -- sugar, biscuits, and treats, even though it was clear that the lifestyle that we were used to during the Polish Regime before 1939 would not return.

We heard from them of the cancellation of private commerce, about the basic Russian rule -- "He who does not work does not eat", and about cooperatives. We began imagining to ourselves a first picture of what life would be like under the Bolshevik regime -- the Soviets.

[Page 217]

Civil Soviet Regime in the Town

Several days after the entrance of the Army, people of the civilian regime came and began to organize the town. The "small-Soviet" was formed. This was the town council whose real leaders were the craftsmen -- the proletarians amongst the Jews. A militia was formed which was headed by a Soviet police officer. An office of education and culture, an office of transportation, and other offices were formed.

The merchants and storekeepers amongst the Jews of the town understood that they could not exist under the Soviet regime. They began to eliminate the stocks of goods in order to assure their existence -- by trading with the non-Jews who gave them produce, potatoes, oils, milk, etc.

The regime did not look nicely upon these commercial deals and began to threaten and make arrests in certain cases. I remember at a later stage the bitter impression made by the arrest of the widow Sarah. She lived amongst the non-Jews. She was arrested for a long period of time for selling matches and salt. A rumor spread in the town that the rich Jews were being expelled to Siberia. It was always spoken of the possibility that the police could appear suddenly and expel people without any early notice. I remember that my parents, amongst the people of the town, also were very afraid. But as much as I remember, Jews from our town were not sent to Siberia. Another Jew was tried and sentenced because he was suspicious of looting as he tried to take for himself things at the time that he was dismantling the products of the rich estate owners amongst the farmers. He was sent to jail. Minkil, the Jew, thought that these were the times of the Communists from the period of WWI, and he did not realize that times had changed.

In our town, a cooperative store was opened, where they rationed the basic products for everyone: fish, salt, sugar, kerosene, and matches. There was the problem of standing in long lines for many hours in order to get the allocation. In addition, every Jew tried to privately organize for himself products like wheat – flour for baking bread, potatoes, meat, milk, and other agricultural products, in order to complete the necessary portion of food for his family's existence. Of course, under the given circumstances, the Jews had to cut expenses and to adjust to a different standard of living than they were used to under the Polish regime. But they did not suffer from starvation. My father, for example, bought a cow for milking, and this definitely improved our situation, even though it added work for all the members of the family to take care of her, to feed her, to cushion the barn with straw, to be friendly to her, and to milk her. My mother gave milk products to neighbors who were not as fortunate as we were. My father, who knew Russian and was learned, suggested himself as an accountant for the department of transportation. He became a government clerk with all the rights and obligations. This improved our situation

[Page 218]

as we received a monthly salary for existence, and there were several easier conditions for acquiring food products. We, the children, began going to a public elementary school, and within a short time, we knew the Russian language, with the help of our parents who already knew the language very well.

Education under the Soviet Regime in the Town

We, the Jewish children, stood out in our talents and became excellent students -- "Ottolichnikim", and at the end of the year, we received the report card -- "Pohbalenia Normota", which encouraged competition and caused us to want to continue to excel.

The preaching of equal rights with no difference of religion, race, or occupation, showed its results. In school, the non-Jews did not stop hating the Jews. But they did not even try to call us "Yid", but "Yori". This was not because they liked us, but because religion lessons were stopped in the school – for the Jews, the Ukrainians, and the Poles. On the other hand, there began lessons on Communism and on their great leader.

We organized political youth groups. There were organized groups for shooting at targets, learning defense against gases and bombings, and there were appropriate awards for those who finished the courses. We felt that as far as studies and advancement in studies, we had many opportunities. We had to make efforts, without our parents investing. Therefore, we were happy, studied, and studied more, according to the command of "Lenin". We were very happy, and our parents were already planning our college studies in the future. My parents wanted me to be a doctor.

Keeping the Jewish Image and Culture

Even though we had wide cultural activities, we did not go far from our Judaism. Our parents were sometimes sad that we could no longer learn Hebrew and keep a connection with the Zionist movement, as in the past. At the most, a public school was allowed where the language in which studies were taught was Yiddish with a public Soviet curriculum. As I became of Bar Mitzvah age, I studied the Shulhan Aruch, the Haftarah, and all that was necessary for my Bar Mitzvah party that took place secretly one morning in the synagogue. I remember that I prayed the Shaharit and put on teffilin for the first year early in the morning, without being forced to do so.

[Page 219]

On the Sabbath and the holidays, we would go to the synagogue, even though they began to bother my father about missing work on Saturdays. But almost always, he would switch Saturday for Sunday with one of the other workers of the office. This was possible since the head of the office was not a confirmed communist, but a local Pole, an acquaintance of my father from before the war.

The Implication of the Soviet Regime on the Nationalistic Feelings on the Jewish Street

The suppression of nationalistic feelings was stronger under the Soviet regime and showed even more as time went on. The united Zionist youth with deep consciousness and with a traditional Jewish education was pushed away from their Torah when the Russians took over in 1939. Through their special methods of threats to exile people to Siberia and suddenly sending people to jail for a small reason, they stopped the speaking of Hebrew and destroyed the youth movements and organizations. After 21 months of Soviet occupation in the town, the spiritual and social soul of the Hebrew language was forgotten. The subjects in school were taught in Yiddish, but they were not allowed to mention Zionism.

It seems that the spiritual suppression during the period of the Soviet regime contributed in negative due to the fact that the same Zionist united youth of the past who had self esteem and the readiness to defend itself in the past, refrained from doing so in an organized manner when the pogroms and the destruction took place by the Ukrainian and German enemy.

The Twists and Turns of Stepan During the Russian-German War – 1941

Immediately when the war between the Soviets and the Germans began, the Jews began to worry about their future. The Jews of Stepan learned from past experience that in any situation of instability of the regime, wars, changing of regimes, and times of transition, the security and rights for defense from the government was lessened. The fact that they were surrounded by Ukrainians who were "blood thirsty", searching for revenge, and desiring national independence caused the Jews of Stepan to understand that the Ukrainians would take advantage of the transitional periods in order to steal, to avenge, to hurt, and to do pogroms against the Jews. But despite all of this, the Jews did not believe or grasp that the Ukrainians would go so far in their actions and would become active partners even more than the Germans themselves in totally destroying the Jewish community.

Rumors reached the town that the Russian Army fell and that there was treason along the whole front. The German agents and of course the nationalistic Ukrainians began to spread rumors of German parachutes near the town. It is possible that here were several parachutes of agents and spies.

[Page 220]

The war began showing its signs in the limited allowance of necessary basic products like kerosene, soap, salt, and sugar. The lines by the cooperatives became longer and the allowances became less and less. Everyone tried to get products from every source. The black market began to flourish. The government began to draft men to the army. I remember how young men, Jews and non-Jews from the town went to an area before the courthouse accompanied by their close family: women, mothers, and children. The good-byes were filled with crying and kissing. The scene caused an oppressive feeling. We, a group of Jewish youth, accompanied the draftees up to the bridge on their way to Milinsk. We remember the sad expressions of saying good-bye between those who accompanied and those leaving.

As days past, we felt the existence of the war more and more. The war department in the town organized the youth and men who were not drafted to help in preparing wheat fields outside of the town to become an airport or landing area. My older brother, Shaul, was amongst the workers. I accompanied him out of curiosity.

On one of the days of the war, enemy airplanes appeared in the skies of our town. There was even a case that a Soviet plane was shot down in the skies of the town. The next day, the anonymous pilot was buried, wrapped in what remained of his parachute. During the burial ceremony, one felt that the Ukrainians were happy, but the Jews were very sorry and sad.

No more than ten days passed, and rows of defeated soldiers of the Red Army retreated through our town. The sight of the retreating soldiers was quite pathetic. They were tired, worn out, hungry, and battered. We, the Jews, tried to help them as much as we could. Our Ukrainian neighbors did not do the same.

I remember that in one case, one of the senior officers called an obligatory meeting in the center of town, and in his speech, he made clear that indeed the Red Army retreated, but the retreat was temporary and only for tactical reasons. He also made it clear, that it is known to the Red Army, who the Soviet enemies were amongst the civilian population who collaborated with enemy agents and placed knives in the back of the retreating Red Army. He added that the traitors should pay for their actions when the Soviet forces return to the area.

The panic and fear amongst the Jews of the town became greater. I remember very well discussions between my father z"l and neighbors who would meet in the evening in our apartment or in front of the house. The possibility of fleeing to Russia with the retreating army and with the civilian Russian officials who were in the town came up. My father had a personal acquaintance with them. We got a clear invitation from the head of the department of war, who was a high Jewish officer, to join him and his family in order to flee to Russia. He promised to help us get started there. But the doubts were many, and there were opinions for and against. The major consideration was if it was possible to leave an orderly house and property and to go with minimal things to another country. Was it so dangerous to stay in the town that it was necessary to flee? As we know, under the German regime, the Jews somehow lived as Jews. The decrees and the pogroms would pass in the end. That was an assumption. It was not possible that the Germans could destroy millions, since first, they must develop methods and means that one could not even imagine to exist in reality.

[Page 221]

Secondly, would the world be quiet when they see these extreme steps? In addition to these claims, we were influenced by the claims of the Jewish refugees who fled in 1939 from Poland when the Germans conquered it. These people claimed that after they lived under the conquering German regime and lived a little under the Soviet regime, that fleeing and leaving ones home is not worthwhile and it is better to take the chance and not to separate oneself from ones nest, ones home, ones town.

The Jews of Stepan did not catch the greatness of the danger. There were those who said he that meant to flee would flee anyways. But if salvation would come, why should we flee? There were those who said they did not want to die on foreign land, but in their home. But they were not granted this wish.

In the end, to our despair, the claims for staying won out. There began rumors that the Germany Army was approaching the town. From day to day, the numbers of retreating Red soldiers grew. The lack of order in the retreat was felt. It was clear that the Red Army received contradicting orders from time to time. There were rumors that the Red Army entrenched itself in the forests near the bridge, and dug trenches and stored hidden ammunition and artillery shells. Our Ukrainian neighbors began to walk around with their heads raised, and some of them, especially the farmers, began to appear and organize themselves in the town for places for robbery and pogroms. The feeling of insecurity grew, especially at sunset time, in the evenings, and at night. In the evening, we would shut ourselves in our houses under lock and key, with much fear and apprehension.

Two days before the final evacuation of the Red Army, the Germans began bombing the lines of the retreating soldiers. There were no arrangements for sirens at that time. I remember that we began to run outside of the town during the bombings and artillery against airplanes. We fled in the morning and returned before it became dark. We discovered that in our area, there was much destroyed. A large number of Jewish houses on the main street and a small street nearby received direct hits and this caused a large amount of human losses amongst the Jews of the town. Amongst the many, the entire Alter Tsiviis Bass family was killed. The next day, there was an enormous explosion in the town and the wooden bridge on the Horyn River was blown up. The retreating Red Army lit several places on fire. This brought the news to us that the Soviet regime had come to an end. We were cut off from the outside world and were under the control of the German Army and our Ukrainian neighbors.

The Ukrainians received the German conqueror with happiness and joy. The nationalists amongst them were happy because of their hate for the Soviets and their hope to receive independence from the Germans. The farmers, the simple people, were happy because it was now a time of lawlessness and they could rob the Jews and do pogroms without any interference. The Jews of the town hid in their homes, and trembled with fear thinking of what was to be.

[Page 222]

We, the children, despite the dangers and fears, dared to go out to the Main Street and see the victorious German Army. They looked different than the retreating Red Army, and not just the color of their uniforms and their ranks. They were more orderly and polished in their appearance. Convoys moved ahead on wagons with Belgian horses. Some of them moved forward on motorcycles and others on bicycles. I do not think that there were many automobiles, and this was because of the difficult dirt roads leading to our town. The army took positions in different places in the town. Platoons set up artillery, not far from one another, against airplanes. We, the children, walked around freely amongst the wagons and artillery without being bothered by the German soldiers.

The next day the town was filled with farmers that robbed the Jewish houses. In addition, these abominable creatures showed the German soldiers that one could take things from the Jewish houses that were of value to the army: material, produce, and bicycles. The farmers brought the Germans to our house and they went up to our attic and found our hiding place for bicycles. They confiscated the bicycles and their parts. German officers appeared and requested to stay in our house. We very happily gave them a large room to stay in as we thought they would protect us from the Ukrainian looters and rioters. When the farmers learned that German officers were staying in our house, they did not attempt to get close to our house. The German officers, who found out very quickly that we were Jews, said that they were sorry that the attitude of the regime toward the Jews was not good and that we would suffer in the future. They tried to help us. They gave our father cigarettes and a couple of other necessities. Several days later the soldiers and officers left us in order to advance to the front.

After them, the engineering corps came and began reconstructing the bridge on the Horyn River. The Germans even began in organizing the local government and formed a local Ukrainian militia, which was headed by one of the locals of the town, Shasha Kromenf. Their uniforms were granite blue. But since there were not enough uniforms for all of them, they went into the Jewish homes and confiscated from their closets any clothes with the same color of the uniforms so they could sew uniforms and hats. They also came to our house and took my school uniform and my brother Shaul's uniform, which were made of granite blue.

It was made public that all men up to age fifty must go to work in reconstructing the bridge. Therefore, my father and several other Jews of the town worked in carrying heavy logs of wood to the area where the bridge was being constructed. Several Germans in uniform who had working under them Ukrainian guards supervised the work. I remember how some of the Jews during their work were hit and pushed along. I remember how Yosef Wachs (who later was the head of the Judenratt) was hit when he failed to carry a log of wood.

[Page 223]

We, the Jews, were cut off from the outside world. We were not allowed to travel outside of our town, and we did not know what was going on in other Jewish communities. The non-Jews told us that the Germans continued to make progress and win along the whole front. They also told us that Jews in nearby cities and towns were kidnapped and were taken to work camps. All the rumors made us more depressed. A decree was made that every Jew must put on his sleeve a white band with a blue Star of David embroidered on it so the person could be identified. The Jews were only to walk in the middle of the street, and not on the sidewalks. The Jews were only allowed to go out on the streets during the day. In the evening and the night, there was a curfew for the Jews of the town. As time passed, the band with the blue Star of David was switched with a yellow patch on the chest and the back. It was forbidden to pray in public and in synagogues.

In this situation, the Jews of the town had to be concerned with their existence. Jews with workshops did work for Ukrainians and in return for their work they received basic necessities for their existence. Others traded their clothes and valuable articles for products like flour, potatoes, butter, milk, etc. Their standard of living went down extremely.

The Forming of the Ghetto and Living in It

After a few months, a rumor spread that it was decided to place all the Jews of the town and nearby villages in the area into a ghetto. The Ukrainian committee in the local government went through the houses of the town especially on our street, Shkoolna Street, the street of the synagogues, and nearby streets, to measure every room in order to decide how many houses would be included in the ghetto. Indeed, in a short time, an order was made that all Jews of the town must move to the houses on Shkoolna Street. The Jews packed their belongings, left their homes, and were expelled to our street.

Into each room, at least two families were placed to live, and this also included the kitchens. The crowding was horrible, and the result was that the hygienic conditions were run down, filth and dirt everywhere. At the beginning, there were not enough bathrooms. As time went on, they dug holes that were covered with boards and were used as public bathrooms. The Jews who were professionals were given the right to live in a group of houses by the fence of the ghetto. The Germans along with the Ukrainians began organizing the local government of the Jews: the Judenratt and police. Yosef Wachs was chosen to be the head of the Judenratt. He was tall and was well built. When he walked on the street, his head was upright, and it seemed that he loathed the whole world. This Jew was harnessed to aid the Germans. He was placed in the house at the opening of the ghetto, the house of Lazar Hazlazanik. He picked for himself a group of strong boys of the town, who would be policemen, and they began to rule the Jews of the ghetto. Of course, he looked out for his friends and relatives, and placed them as if they were professionals so they could live in houses on the border of the ghetto. Some of them were appointed to jobs in the ghetto,

[Page 224]

for instance administration the kitchen. One thing for sure, the head of the Judenratt carried out the orders of the Germans meticulously and very severely. The Jews carried the burden of the German decrees that were carried out by Yosef Wachs and his people.

The Structure of the Ghetto and the Decrees, the Work Camp in Kostopol

The Judenratt and at its head Yosef Wachs didn't really govern the Jews of the ghetto and its area, but there were those who carried out the decrees of the Germans and the Ukrainians. This institution decided the list of Jews to be sent to the forced labor camp near the town of Kostopol, and this was according to the number of workers needed from time to time by the Germans. The workers of the Judenratt dealt with collecting gold, precious stones, and furs. The amounts were set according to the needs of German and Ukrainian authorities. The head of the Judenratt, along with his close advisors, decided who will give what, and how much. If the person who was told to bring a portion of gold or an amount of fur did not appear or didn't bring the required amount, the Judenratt forced him to do so.

The methods were varied. First, messengers of the Judenratt were sent along with the Jewish police. They were usually simple people who used force. There were threats and surprise searches in private homes. In certain cases, they would place the head of the family, the father or mother, in jail in the ghetto. The jail was situated in one of the upper rooms of the women's section in the synagogue. If this pressure did not help, since some of the Jews thought they should keep some of the valuables belonging to themselves to use in exchange for food products in the future or for redeeming a member of the family in the future, the Judenratt sent the head of the family to the Ukrainian police for torturing by harsh beating and for solitary confinement, in order to get from him what was needed, as gold, furs, or precious stones.

I remember being a witness to a case when the head of the Judenratt himself slapped the face of a women who claimed that she was unjustly arrested and that she was not able to add anything to what she had already given. Also something happened to my mother. When my mother was asked to give up her expensive fur, after they had taken from us all of our other furs in the house, my mother successfully smuggled her expensive fur to a trustworthy non-Jew. This was in order to assure that we would have something of value in a time of need. My mother paid for her actions. She went through a series of interrogations and torture, stage by stage, first by the Judenratt and the Jewish police, and later by the Ukrainian police and their solitary confinement.

I remember very well, after not being able to sleep, that I woke up at dawn when my mother was arrested and taken to solitary confinement by the Ukrainian police. I jumped over the ghetto wall and ran

[Page 225]

to the Ukrainian police without any authorization. I stood before the entrance of the Ukrainian police station and whined like a baby. Just then the head of the Ukrainian Police, Sasha Kromenf, walked by and turned his head in my direction. He apparently recognized me from the days when he was a friend of my father from the good old days and would come to my father's tobacco shop. I was almost frozen because it was very cold outside and I was dressed very lightly. Sasha asked me what I was doing here, and how did I leave the ghetto without a permit. He said that I deserve a whipping and could go to jail. I answered that I was aware of this and that I did not care if I received punishment. I asked that my mother be released from jail and confinement since she was sick and would not be able to hold up. Sasha looked at me again, and told the police officer to take me back to the ghetto, and that I should not try to come to the police again because then I would be whipped and taken to solitary confinement. The policeman pulled me out of there, kicked me, and told me to run quickly back to the ghetto. I ran back to the ghetto and after a few hours my mother was released. She was exhausted, tortured, and wretched. I do not know if it was because of me or incidentally that my mother was released, but my sister and I were very happy to be with our beloved mother again.

In addition, the Judenratt and its workers dealt with filling the requests of the government with regard to street cleaning of the town, and work in the ghetto itself. When the Jews where taken from their homes and expelled to the direction of Shkoolna Street, the street of the ghetto, and the nearby streets, it was not clearly decided which families would live in which apartments or houses. Families chose their apartment through their previous acquaintance with the people who owned the apartment, or because they liked a certain apartment, or because there was no other place left and they chose the apartments that were still vacant. The people who lived in the apartments before on Shkoolna Street had to give in to the new reality, to crowd into one room of the apartment or even a half of a room, and to allow the refugees to get settled.

Into our two room apartment with a kitchen, two families moved in, in addition to our family. In the bedroom, my mother, my sister, and I lived, along with the wife and daughter of Berl Yokelson. In the dining room, the family of Ben-Zion Yokelson lived, his wife, his two daughters, and his son. The husband slept in the kitchen. The house was very crowded. My mother who was a very orderly housewife had to get used to it being disorderly as a result of it being very crowded. At the beginning, she would respond when there were damages done to our utensils and furniture that were caused by the other families. But slowly, we got used to the new grey reality, and new worries cancelled out those petty worries that we had at the beginning. The problem of food started. The stock that we had slowly decreased, and my mother, who was generous, let the needy people in our house use our food, like pickled cucumbers from the barrel and potatoes in the basement.

[Page 226]

Description of Life in the Ghetto

The authorities separated men from ages eighteen to fifty from their families. There was a fence between the camp of the men and the ghetto and passage was forbidden. The work camp of the men was situated at the continuation of Shkoolna Street. The men were housed in groups of houses. They did forced labor within the work camp and outside of it. From there, certain candidates were taken to the Kostopol work camp. In the camp, those who were craftsmen, barbers, tailors, or shoemakers gave service to the men. The men's food was rationed, like all the members of the ghetto, a small portion of bread and a light portion of soup. Most of the men were exhausted and suffered from malnutrition, filth, lice, hard work, being hit, and disgrace. A man who tried to leave the work camp in the evening to visit his family was heavily punished if he was caught by the Ukrainian police or by the Jewish police. In the cold winter months, means for heating were lacking and it was very cold in the rooms. After the residents of the ghetto and the camp finished taking apart buildings near the houses, like barns, storerooms, and stables, that were made of wooden boards, to get material for heating they had to steal in the night outside of the ghetto to take apart abandoned wooden structures for heating material. In one of these cases, there was a very tragic incident. One of the residents of the camp, Hone, the son of Hazlazanik, went out of the ghetto to organize wood. He was shot by a Ukrainian policeman even though he recognized him.

The First Victim in the Ghetto

The first victim who was shot in cold blood deeply affected the members of the ghetto and the camp. It became clear to us that Jewish blood was of no significance. Since it was forbidden to congregate, a small funeral was held with the members of the Chevra Kadisha and family members, which was different from the tradition of the Jews of Stepan to hold large funerals.

The Sending of Men to the Labor Camp in Kostopol

The effects of malnutrition began to show their signs on the residents of the ghetto and the camp as some turned partially blind. It was known that they would change from time to time the men who were sent to the labor camp in Kostopol. My father was sent there one time. This caused my mother and us to worry greatly, because our father was a skinny and weak man, and became even weaker in the labor camp. Even though we tried to convince those who were responsible for sending men to Kostopol not to send him, he was sent there. After several weeks there, my father was not able to hang on. One time when they went to work in the nearby forest, he fled and returned to the ghetto. The Jewish police immediately arrested him and placed him

[Page 227]

in jail in the ghetto. My father was exhausted and was near total physical collapse. After a couple days of jail, he was released and sent home to be taken care of. My mother tried to take care of him the best that she could, even though she was exhausted and lacking means to take care of him. I fled from the ghetto on several occasions to organize some food products for us from some non-Jewish acquaintances.

I remember very well an incident when policemen came to check how my father's health was in order to send him back to the labor camp. His response was that he fainted continuously and when I stood by his bed, he seemed like he was dead. I remember that after continuous care by one of the policemen, he barely gained consciousness. His situation convinced them that he was not a candidate for the labor camp, and they left him alone. But after a few days, they turned to my oldest brother, Shaul Shilik, who should be sent instead of my father to the forced labor camp. Shilik's physical condition was not much better than my father, and my brother was not very independent. This scared us. We tried to convince the authorities not to send him, but in the end he was sent to the forced labor camp. I remember very well his parting from us, especially from my dear mother. My mother cried along with all of us. She then bundled up his bundles, putting in several necessary food products from what was left in the house, and Shilik was taken from us.

The Routine in the Men's Camp and in the Ghetto

I would easily sneak into the men's camp through a hole in the fence, and would spend hours in my father's living quarters and sometimes bring him something warm to eat, from what mother prepared. I heard from the men's discussions that there were those who believed that the troubles would pass, and that in the end, salvation would come in one form or another. Others claimed that the end is coming and that there was no hope. They came to this conclusion as they saw that the Germans were prevailing on all fronts. I never heard discussion of rebellion or fleeing and joining the partisans.

In one case, I remember a remark of my past teacher, Baruch Kreizer, the son of the shochet Levi z"l. who was a Jewish policeman in the male camp. He was different than most of the policemen in that he would be very polite, and would only make remarks about order and hygiene. As far as I remember, he would never scream or scold. His comment was: "We are compared to feces in the public toilet and that will also be our end." He said this very near the time of the final destruction.

[Page 228]

I remember that a young fellow succeeded in entering Stepan, as it was forbidden for Jews to travel from one town to another. Perhaps he was sent by a partisan organization or a Zionist organization, with the purpose of organizing the Jews to flee or to rebel. He brought news of the organization and joining of young men from ghettos of different towns to the partisans. He told of the acts of killing of groups of Jews in the Volyn ghetto.

The fellow's activity in the Stepan ghetto did not last too long as in a few days he was arrested by the Jewish police by order of the Judenratt and he disappeared. There were rumors that he was turned over to the Ukrainian police and was forced to leave the town after being threatened by the Judenratt and the police that he would be turned over to the Ukrainians or the Germans.

Faith Regarding Salvation in the Ghetto

Because of the great hardships of the Jews in the ghetto, they began to believe in coming of the Messiah and salvation that was told by false prophets and fortune tellers. I remember one named Eliahu Koifman who would bring all different signs that salvation was coming and would say different dates when salvation would arrive. Even though he was a simple man, most tended to believe in him. This was a way of holding on to something like someone who holds onto straw while drowning in order to save oneself.

Finding Ways of Existence -- By Being Enslaved by the Non-Jews

Most of the residents of the ghetto could not exist from the small portion of food supplied by the Judenratt. Therefore they looked for all different ways of getting additional food. One of the ways was to be sent to outside work. They would sneak out to the non-Jewish merchants and bring them objects and clothes for food, or just would ask for help. Those residents of the ghetto who had relatives outside of the ghetto, or near it, would get help from them to receive additional food. Since the exit permits for leaving the ghetto were limited, most of the Jews sent boys or young men who would be successful in sneaking out of the ghetto without permits, and get to the non-Jews in order to get additional food products. Many times the boys or young men would stay with the non-Jews for the day or even longer, and take care of their sheep. They would get a decent portion of food for their work they did for the non-Jews. They would bring the food to their families to save them from starvation. When a young man was caught by

the Ukrainian police by the fence of the ghetto or on his way from the ghetto, he would get serious blows,

[Page 229]

they would take from him the food which he collected, and would throw him back into the ghetto. This deterred many of the youths from trying to get food in this dangerous manner.

I remember, a little before the ghetto was destroyed, most of the youths who were shepherds for the non-Jews would come home to sleep every night as they were afraid of what was to happen. I also was a shepherd for a non-Jew. I recall a story that shows how abandoned we were by the non-Jews.

One day my flock moved onto the land of one non-Jew. Before I could even move the flock from his land, the head of the land appeared. Without even asking if I did this on purpose or if the flock moved onto his land by mistake, he hit me with a heavy wood pole, until I lost the feeling of my senses. My friend who worked with me brought me to the non-Jew that I worked for, and he placed wet bandages on my whole body. The non-Jew said if I wasn't a Jew, he would hit his neighbor for his inhumane actions toward me.

Means of Heating in the Ghetto

As it is known, our cooking and heating ovens were heated by wood. Very quickly the residents' supply of wood in their storerooms ran out, because there were so many residents in each apartment. In order to find wood for heating, they had to dismantle storerooms and barns that were built of wood. As long as I could, I tried not to use this method. But the situation just got worse.

The Death of My Grandfather in the Ghetto

My grandfather, Ben Zion z"l, as I remember, reached the age eighty and died in the ghetto. It was clear that the main reason for my grandfather's death was not old age, but the distress caused by the difficult living conditions in the ghetto, and the hardships he underwent. I stood by his bed when he died. It was Friday night, and we had an underground minyan in my grandfather's house. On Saturday night, there was a funeral only for the family members, who were allowed to leave the ghetto. I was included in this. My grandfather was buried in the Jewish cemetery. We had to use wood from my grandfather's barn for the burial and for the gravestone.

In the ghetto, there were two young judges. There were differences of opinion between the two families of the judges. But in the ghetto, the two judges had a lot in common, and tried to encourage the residents of the ghetto that the darkness would end soon and the dawn would break.

[Page 230]

Because of the bad nutrition and living conditions, they tried to make certain laws easier on the people. I remember that they allowed the Jews to make matzot from rye flour and to eat legumes on Pesach.

The Night of the Annihilation of the Ghetto

Muffled but stubborn rumors about the partial annihilation of the nearby communities of Barobana and Kostopol spread somehow amongst the residents of the ghetto. There were those who believed it and there were those who argued that it was not true. But everyone was scared and they were sleepless as they thought about what was to come. There were rumors that a group of Ukrainian policemen from the town, headed by Evan Chatzik, was sent for special training to Kostopol. It was said that this was preparation for our annihilation. On one of the evenings of Elul in the year 1942, a rumor spread amongst the Jews of the ghetto that all the harnessed carriages of the non-Jews of the town and nearby towns were mobilized. But they said this was for transporting produce, but most felt that the end was coming and believed that it was for transporting Jews in the direction of Kostopol. The panic it the ghetto was great. Some of the men of the work camp were able to get into the ghetto in order to calm their wives. We saw that the guard watches around the ghetto were increased, and we heard shooting warnings.

I approached the building of the Judenratt and I heard screaming and threats in Ukrainian from the window of the building. Perhaps these were last attempts to blackmail money and jewelry from the head of the Judenratt, his clerks and family before being exiled. (There were rumors amongst the non-Jews that they were killed by shooting near the police building of Stepan). I was tired and scared and I returned home. I lied close to my mother and my younger sister and somehow fell asleep. But before dawn, we heard voices in German -- Jews get out of your houses. I looked out of the window and I saw three German soldiers with helmets and bayoneted rifles in their hands. They marched on the streets and hurried the Jews to get out of their houses.

Within a couple of minutes, I could see from the window a group of Jews with their wives and their children, taking their belongings with them on their backs, and walking toward the gate of the ghetto. From time to time, they would fight and the crowd would turn into a very scared group of people, or into innocent sheep led to slaughter. I remember how Yitzhak Weitznodel, the butcher, walked, being dressed in his dressy black suit, with his family after him. My mother, my sister, and myself, being very scared, jumped off our beds, without taking anything, barefoot, and in minimal dress, left our house in order to look for shelter. My mother suggested that we hide in a small basement at the opening of our house, until this would pass. I was against this as I thought that the next morning they would continue their search and we would be found. My mother listened to my advice and we climbed the fence

[Page 231]

to the outside of the ghetto. Near the ghetto lived a Polish non-Jew, Henger Yank. We jumped into his garden, and hid amongst the thick corn stalks. Suddenly we heard screaming from the attic of the Pole, that we should leave immediately, or he will call the police. Because of fear, we all got stomach aches and diarrhea. We had to leave the Pole's garden, and we turned to the main highway on the street May 3rd. When we got to the street, we discovered a convoy of carts harnessed to horses. On most of the carts, Jewish families sat, ready to be transported. The carts were facing the direction of the market, in the direction of Kostopol. On the opposite side of the street, many armed Ukrainian policemen stood in order to prevent people from fleeing from the carts, and to prevent any possibility or fleeing from the town.

Escape from the Death Carts

We tried to cross the street and to sneak away to one of the alleys, but every time the policemen prevented us from doing so with their bayoneted rifles and by shooting in the air. One time, my mother and I were successful in crossing the street and getting to a side alley near Sam's bar. But then we saw how my sister Sosel-Sarah was stopped by one of the policeman and dragged to one of the carts. Her voice and cries brought us back to her, and we took her and ran back to ghetto. Nobody prevented us because we were again in the trap. We saw several people still walking toward the gate, we heard crying from houses, and shooting from the area of the gates of the ghetto. We decided to go to the men's camp to see if my father was still there. We crossed the gate between the ghetto and the men's camp and went to the room my father used to be in. But the whole house was empty. We looked around in the house and outside it, and called my father a couple of times, but there was no response. It seemed that the men's camp was emptied beforehand, and the men were put on carts going in the direction of Kostopol.

As we were so desperate to find father, we turned to a bath house on the river banks. In order to get out of the ghetto, we had to go through water up to our knees which was filthy, full of sharp stones, and broken glass. We chose to jump over the fence of the ghetto in the area of the second corner of the bath house. In this area, the fence was high, and only with joint efforts were we able to cross the fence, helping each other, and get out of the ghetto. The minute the noise was heard when we fell to the ground after jumping the fence, there were shots heard from a policeman on a nearby hill by the fence. We heard the noise of the bullets,

[Page 232]

but we were able to crawl from the fence without being hurt. We ran very quickly along the river, toward the town Korost.

When we arrived at the house of Herschel that was situated between the houses of the Ukrainian judges, on the banks of the river, we heard again shooting and voices "stop" in Ukrainian. We lied under the pillars of the house and then we continued running along the length of the river. While we were running, we shook from cold and fear.

The surroundings looked very hostile, even though in the early hours before dawn, we saw groups of Ukrainians standing at the openings of their houses, in their yards, and in front of the stores. It was clear that most of these Ukrainians were waiting impatiently for morning in order to get from the commander the spoils -- the Jewish belongings that were abandoned. We got close to the house of our faithful non-Jew, Kozma. He was the person that we gave our most valuable possessions to be kept until this period of time passes. He came in our direction and said he did not want us to come into his courtyard. He suggested that we hid amongst the graves in the Jewish cemetery near his house. His reasoning was that there many other Jews hiding there.

My mother almost agreed to this, as she was tired and scared and thought that this hiding place would lessen our fears and stomach aches and our diarrhea. But my instincts told me to flee immediately outside of the town, in the direction of the villages and forests. I was afraid that we would be caught in the morning by the non-Jews in the area, and even by "our friend", Kozma. My mother listened to me and we continued to flee in the direction of Korost. When the sun rose, we were already in the fields of a village. We came to one of the hay bins. We hid ourselves in the hay and fell asleep. We suddenly awakened because we were hungry. It was sunrise.. Because of the great hope and yearnings to see father, it seemed that from far away father was approaching, but very quickly we understood the bitter reality. We decided to approach a village house to ask for a place to sleep and a little bit of food. We had luck and the farmer we turned to gave us bread, potatoes, and milk. We ate well and the farmer allowed us to stay that night in his threshing floor, and gave us some food for the journey. But he told us we must leave at dawn, so that no one would know that we were there. If it became known, he would be in trouble.

The First Night after the Escape to the Forests

We stretched ourselves out on the pleasant hay on the threshing floor. Thus we spent our first night outside of our home, being scared of every noise, and our hearts hurt from worry of what happened to our father, our brother, and the rest of our family. At dawn we awakened and left the threshing floor in the direction of the nearby pine forest. In the forest, we ran into several boys

[Page 233]

from our town who also escaped and were looking for a place to hide. We tried to get information from them about what happened to the Jews of the town, but they only guessed and were not sure what happened to them for sure. We asked if we could join them. But they refused, claiming that it was easier to hide in the forest in small groups. They left us, and continued on their way in the forest, apparently in search of food. Shortly afterwards, we heard shots from the direction of the village, and we understood that danger was approaching. Therefore, we continued running into the depths of the forest, without really knowing where we were going. Shortly afterwards, we ran into a village non-Jew. We asked how to get to Sarny. The non-Jew showed us the direction.

The News about the Destruction of the Community of Sarny by the Enemy

Our intention was to get to Sarny, as we assumed that the Jews were not hurt and that we could join our uncle who lived there. We started walking to Sarny, using the small amount of food that the non-Jew gave us the day before -- black bread and pickles. We were very thirsty, and since we did not find any other source of water, we drank from a puddle of greenish water.

As we were walking in the forest, we heard a cart getting closer to us. We walked all the time on the side of the road, between the trees, and we hid behind the thick trees in order to see who was coming near us. My mother saw that it was the non-Jew who we knew from Stepan. My mother turned to him to ask him what the distance was from here to Sarny. The non-Jew, who knew us, told us not to get near Sarny, because all the Jews of Sarny were taken yesterday to be slaughtered, and that we had no chance of finding one of our relatives alive. He said we might even fall into the hands of the Germans or the Ukrainians. He suggested that we flee into the depths of the forest, and not to get near the villages, as much as possible.

This made it clear to us that we would not find in Sarny any of our relatives alive, who we thought we could use to lean on and to hide with them. We had a very difficult problem: the struggle of existence of a widow and her two children who were in a hostile and strange surrounding, being persecuted, with no home, and no manner of existence. We were barefoot and wearing thin clothing and the winter was approaching. In the end, it would be cold and it would snow.

After we got over the bad news, we returned to the area of the villages of Korost and Kritashileski. We turned to the non-Jews of the villages, mostly those who lived in isolated houses near the forests. The truth is we never knew to which house to turn to, and how they would receive us, who would help, and who would inform the authorities about us, and who would even turn us in to the Ukrainian police. There were times when they threw us out without shame

[Page 234]

with cursing, and even by inciting their dogs against us. Thus, with no choice, we had to return to the forest, hit, ashamed, hungry, and scared. We developed a method for trying to get food. Two of us would stay in the forest, and one would go to one of the isolated houses near the forest. If he was received in a decent manner, he would give the other two a sign and they would join him. But if he was not received in a decent manner, he would flee as fast as he could, disappointed and desperate.

One time my mother turned to one of the isolated houses for a little food and rags to cover our bodies from the cold fall nights and mornings. In this case, she was received very badly, with cursing and inciting of their dogs. This was how most of the Ukrainian acted toward us. She returned to us crying and exhausted. The three of us cuddled up amongst the thick bushes in the forest for the night's sleep, hungry and despaired.

The Height of Despair

Mother suggested that the next day we turn toward Stepan in order to see if someone of the Jews of Stepan was still alive, and maybe we could get organized there and live there again. We would not turn ourselves into the Ukrainian police, who would do with us as they pleased. My sister and I, who were against mother's suggestion, pleaded quietly, and fell asleep.

Exceptional Individuals among the Non-Jews

When dawn came, we were frozen, hungry, and scared. But along with this, my mother encouraged me by the fact that she changed her mind with regard to turning ourselves over to the Ukrainian police. Then I decided to turn to one of the isolated houses near the forest in my usual manner. I knocked on the door. It was still very early in the morning. The door opened, and a bearded farmer opened the door, and was appalled by my appearance and by my face. I shook from the cold of the morning, and was wearing rags, barefoot, and scared of what was to come. He invited me in and asked what I wanted. He invited me to sit down and gave me warm pancakes, milk, and warm cereal. I thanked him, and asked him if I could have a little food, and a piece of clothing to bring to my mother and sister who were starved and cold from the forest. He asked me about my identity. After being a bit suspicious, I told him all that we had gone through. After hearing my story and seeing the tears in eyes of the farmer and his wife, the farmer said to me: "Run to the forest, bring your sister and mother. But do so carefully and in secret so that neighbors do not see. They may turn you and us in."

[Page 235]

Therefore, I ran quickly, and called for my mother and sister, and we arrived at the house of the farmer. We were received very nicely. He put us in his threshing floor. His wife came with a bowl of hot potatoes, bread, pickles, and onions. After we ate, he told us to go up to the attic of the threshing floor. He told us to cover ourselves with hay and be quiet so that the neighbors would not hear or feel our presence.

Therefore, we settled down, and enjoyed the "king's" food that we were served. After we ate and covered ourselves with hay, we fell asleep. That day passed after a warm sleep in the hay and with full stomachs, and we felt good from the nice treatment we received from the farmer and his wife, amongst the cruel sea of hatred and estrangement. We prayed that this would last for many days.

The next day, at dawn, the farmer awakened us and gave us food. He explained in a frightened and sad voice that we must quickly escape to the thickness of the forest as he heard from his neighbors that tomorrow the Ukrainian police are coming to the area to look for Jews who have escaped. We ran quickly to the forest, as the morning cold bothered us, and we tried to go into the thickness of the forest. But because we did not know the area, instead of going into the forest, we came to another group of houses near the forest.

Meeting Two Survivors from Stepan in the Forest

While we were walking in the forest, we ran into two people under trees. As the beginning, we were startled, but immediately we recognized them. They were two youths from Stepan -- fleeing for their lives. One of them was Yaacov, the son of Rebbi Mendel, the blacksmith, and the other was the son of Bezepsha, the butcher. My mother turned to them and asked them to join us as one group and together we would find a way to exist in the conditions of the forest and the hostile surroundings. The youths turned down her offer. They claimed the opposite, that it was easier to hide and escape if it was a smaller group. Disappointed from their response, we continued on our way in the forest, feeling lonely and lacking all for the future. We lied down in the forest in order to warm ourselves in the sunrays. We fell asleep for a short while. But suddenly we heard shots nearby. We got up quickly, ran to an area of thick trees, sat down, and ate the food the farmer gave us.

Toward evening, a farmer found us, and began inquiring where we were from and what we were doing, and if we have gold or silver. After hearing our story, he was convinced that we were indeed poor and lacking all. He told us that this morning two Jewish youths were caught by the Ukrainian police and were taken to Stepan. They were the two youths we had met.

[Page 236]

He suggested we move away from the area in order that we won't get caught.

Escaping from Murder and Staying
Near the Polish Village of Only

That night we did not sleep well, because of what the farmer told us and because of the cold. At dawn, we continued on our way into the thick forest, and we moved away from the houses. On the way, we ran into forest berries which we collected and ate. After walking the whole day, we realized that we were getting close to a village as we heard dogs barking. We saw an unknown village with houses that were nicer than the ones we had seen up to now. It was dusk and we used our usual method. Mother stayed in the forest, and my sister and I walked carefully toward an isolated house near the forest. We met a non-Jewish woman who gave us a portion of food, as we requested. We thanked her and left her courtyard. As we left, a tall elderly farmer entered the house that we left. A few minutes later, we heard him scream "stop" in German. He continued running after us and said he would turn us over to the Germans. As fast as we could, we fled to the forest to find our mother, and to tell her what happened.

We went deep into the forest, and found for ourselves a hidden place to sleep for the night. We lit a campfire, baked the potatoes, and ate them. Thus one more night passed. The next day, at dawn, we continued on our way, in order to move away from this village because we were afraid of that non-Jew. This village was a Polish village, called Only. Without knowing where we were going, toward evening, we got close to a Polish village, called Peni, which was near the city Sarny. We entered an area of swamps with small islands with bamboo, and we settled ourselves on one of the islands.

Afterwards, I entered one of the houses and asked for food, and they gave me food. This poor farmer told me that we were not far from the city Sarny, and told me we should stay away from the city for our own safety. That night we slept amongst the bamboo and ate our meal. The next morning, at dawn, we left the area after a difficult night of mosquitoes and cold. We went deeper into the forest. The morning was cold, and we had to walk on puddles of frozen water barefoot.

[Page 237]

We continued, not knowing where we were going. That same non-Jew suggested that we go in a certain direction that would lead us to the village, Kerchon, two days away. He said there were Jews hiding there, and only with their help, would we successfully pass the difficult winter in the conditions of the forest.

At dawn, we awakened, and turned toward the forest, toward the direction of the village, Only, where we came from. We knew the general direction, but we were far from knowing the surroundings or the way. We went deeper into the forest looking for berries, but we didn't find even one berry. To our surprise, we did not get near any village. With no choice, we continued on our way, tired, hungry, and scared. We tried to change our direction, and try to listen to the dogs barking or another sign of life. We had no luck that day. We were tired. Therefore, we settled down for the night, and decided that we would try again tomorrow.

A Meeting with a Survivor from Stepan

When we sat down on a pile of leaves that fell from a tree, we suddenly heard the noise of steps coming closer. We stood close to the tree and tried to see who was coming. Even though it was the time of sunset, our mother saw a known village Jew with a boy. We ran toward happily and hoped we would get from them help how to get out of the center of the forest.

It turned out that the Jew was Rabbi Yaacov from Kritshilsk near Stepan and his grandson. They were also refugees that had succeeded in escaping. Rabbi Yaacov, who was a man with a black beard, asked if we had come about food today. We answered negatively, and told him all that had happened to us and where we were headed for. We invited him to join us. First, he answered "Thank G-d" that we kept the fast of Yom Kippur because today is Yom Kippur, and he saw this as the intervention of G-d. He took out bread and onions and divided it amongst all of us, and asked us to eat because this is our meal to end the day of judgment. He continued: "Who will give that we will be redeemed this year so that we will be able to avenge the blood of our relatives who have been destroyed." We ate and drank from a jug of water that Rabbi Yaacov had. Rabbi Yaacov directed us how to get out of the center of the forest and to get to houses and to go in the correct direction leading to the direction of Only-Kerchon. He said good-by to us and said that he was planning to stay in this area and get aid from one of the non-Jews in order to survive the winter. It was very important to save the life of his six year old grandson. Mother thanked him and we began to walk in the direction that he pointed us in.

[Page 238]

The Aid of a non-Jewish Widow with a Good Heart

It started to get dark and we saw light in an isolated house at the entrance to the forest. It turned out that we were very close to a village, but we went around in circles until we finally got out of the forest. According to our method, my mother and sister stayed in the forest and I moved toward the isolated house. The house stood on a hill and near it was a large barn and threshing floor. Nearby there were fields and only several kilometers distance, there were faint lights of houses. I understood that this was an isolated farm. I entered the courtyard and I ran into a dog that did not look dangerous. I came close and knocked on the door. It was answered by a woman who asked: "Who is bothering me from my night time sleep?" I answered: "A poor orphan boy that lost his way in the forest and I ask for your help with a little food and with advise of how to get in the right direction." My moving story with my shaking and winning voice convinced her to open the door and let me in the house. My worn out clothes, my bare feet, and skinny and scared face convinced her even more that I was speaking the truth, and she had compassion for me. She let me in and called to G-d and crossed herself. This was another sign of her fear and her compassion together.

The house was warm, and the woman and her three daughters, ages twelve, ten, and six, were eating dinner by the table. I was invited to sit down with them, and eat with them. But I asked them for a bit of food and matches, in telling them that my mother and my little sister are waiting for me in the forest. The woman pressured me to tell who we were and what we were doing in the forest. In hesitation, but being sure that I could trust this woman, I told her our story. The woman expressed her feelings again by crossing herself. She told me to call my mother and sister from the forest and that we could sleep on the threshing floor tonight, but she said we must leave a dawn as she was afraid what might happen to her. I ran as fast as I could to the forest, by the signs I left myself in order not to loose my way. I met my mother and sister and invited them to come, telling them the story on the way.

We entered the courtyard and knocked on the door. The non-Jewess opened the door and let us in while crying as she saw what a poor situation we were in. She sat us on a bench in the corner of the kitchen and gave us a plate of potatoes, with another plate of milk with bread and onions. She apologized to us that she had no salt. We ate what she gave us, and gained some strength back from the fast day, the cold, and the hardships that we had gone through. Then she gave us warm milk. My mother thanked the non-Jewess and kissed her hands. Then my mother asked her if we could stay in her threshing floor for a couple of days.

[Page 239]

After much hesitation, the woman was convinced by my mother and the woman agreed that we stay there for three days, on the condition that we do not leave the threshing floor during the day, and she will bring us food and drinks. In the evening, we could enter her house to get warm and to drink something warm.

She gave us food and led us to the threshing floor. In one of the corners of the threshing floor, we settled in on a stack of hay, and we fell asleep. We slept well as the threshing floor and the hay was like king's bedding as opposed to what we had gone through the past weeks -- fear, cold, hunger, and sleeping under the stars. Our mother began to thank G-d that had not totally forgotten us and hoped that she would again be able to convince the non-Jewess to let us stay with her for the winter. If we will go through the war and be freed, we could compensate her with our belongings which were with non-Jews.

During the day, we lay in the hay and from time to time we ate from the food the non-Jewess gave us. We were alert all the time to hear voices or if someone was coming near the threshing floor. Our first day passed. When it was dark, the non-Jewess invited us into her house. She gave us warm milk and a warm dinner. She again gave us food for the next day, and mother suggested to her to let us stay on the threshing floor for the whole winter. Mother said she would sew for her and wash clothes for her during the day and evening.

The women was not convinced and explained to mother that this was not possible, because in the end the people from the nearby village would visit her and they would discover us, especially her brother-in-law who lived in the nearby village and was a policeman for the Germans in Sarny. Along with all her good will and understanding for our situation, she was not willing to take the chance and place herself and her daughters in danger. She requested that we leave in five days. But the women promised that she would give us warm clothes for the journey. We thanked her and went out to the threshing floor for the night. This time we didn't fall asleep so quickly as we were afraid that the brother-in -law who was a policeman would discover us. At dawn, we awakened and listened for every noise of voices of men or a cart approaching. We planned how to escape from the side door, if someone would enter through the main entrance. Thus the second day went by. The fact that she had no salt bothered us, and caused us to be have nausea, because during the day we only ate sweet potatoes.

At dark, we entered her house, and she gave us a warm drink and warm food and gave us some clothes, old shoes, and rags to wrap our legs with. We returned to the threshing floor for the night. We got settled in the hay, but mother suggested

[Page 240]

that she go out for a walk to she where the houses were that she saw as lights from the crack in the wall of the threshing floor. She had two reasons for doing this: 1) to get some salt, matches, and some clothes, and 2) to collect some information about the brother-in-law who was a policeman, what he was like, and how dangerous he was. If it turned out that there was indeed a brother-in-law policeman and that he was dangerous and could drop by for a visit, we must escape tonight and turn toward Kerchon.

We were left in the threshing floor. We cuddled up in the hay, and tried to fall asleep. Our mother went on her way. I could not fall asleep because I wanted to see my mother return from her dangerous night trip in a strange area. It seemed a long time until mother returned. She finally returned with salt, matches, bread, onions, and some clothes. My mother learned from the non-Jews in the nearby village that indeed there was a brother-in-law policeman and that he made money from the possessions of the Jews that he robbed in Sarny. They also told her that he came to visit his sister-in-law at least once a week.

When we heard this, we decided to leave the next day. We fell asleep and another night passed. With dawn, we struggled with the idea if we should say good-by to the non-Jewess or leave without saying good-by. We decided to say good-by to her and to thank her for being so good to us. But we were scared that the brother-in-law would appear or someone else.

A Scary and Threatening Character

Suddenly we caught a discussion of a man with the non-Jewess in the courtyard before the threshing floor. This scared us and we felt that we were in danger. The moment that we decided to escape through the back opening of the threshing floor, the door opened and the non-Jew entered and as if by surprise asked us what we are up to and who we are, and afterwards said that we should come with him to the police. My mother began to beg before him and to ask for mercy. The non-Jew asked if we had in our possession gold or money. We said no, and they he commanded us to leave immediately the threshing floor. My mother thanked him. We took our packages quickly, and we turned to leave the threshing floor in the direction of the forest. The non-Jew entered the woman's house and at the same time she walked out of the house and asked us to enter the threshing floor again. In the threshing floor, she talked with us and explained to us that this was her brother-in-law, the policeman, but that we should not worry because nothing bad will happen to us. She will give us more food, and we must leave the threshing floor tomorrow at dawn. It turned out that she asked her brother-in-law to come in order to scare us and cause us to leave earlier.

My mother began to say a thanksgiving prayer that we were saved, and we listened carefully to all that was going on in the courtyard. That day of tribulations passed.

[Page 241]

In the evening, the woman invited us into her house for a warm drink and gave us uncooked potatoes, matches, onions, and bread. We agreed that at dawn we would leave.

We returned to the threshing floor and fell asleep. At dawn, we awakened, took our packages, and turned to the forest in the direction of Only. From there, we had to get to the train tracks that lead from Sarny to Rovno. Our plan was to walk by the train tracks and get to Kerchon. Before we left, the women directed us according to signs so we would not get lost.

The Continuation of Our Wanderings in the Forest in the Direction of Kerchon

The cold air of the morning was strong and even though we had clothes, we trembled from the cold and fear of the future and of the long way ahead of us. We went in the direction of the town of Only according to the calls of the chickens. The fall sun rose, and we sat down to enjoy its warmth. We ate bread and onions, and we began to plan our way to the train tracks. Since we were not sure of our way, we decided to turn to one of the houses in Only and ask for directions. My mother and sister remained in the forest. I turned to the house that was closest to the forest. In the courtyard, I met a farmer. I turned to him in Polish and asked how to get to Kerchon. The farmer asked who I was and what I was doing here. I told him that I got lost in the forest, that I am an orphan from Stepan, and that I am on my way to relatives in Kerchon for the winter. The farmer invited me into his house, and gave me warm milk and cereal, and explained to me that I must go in the direction of the train tracks to Kerchon, and if I don't loose my way, I should get to the Cheftzi-Kerchon district by evening. The farmer continued to ask me what happened to my parents. I began to trust him and I told him the whole truth. The farmer gave me some more food and a warm jug of milk for my mother and sister, and blessed me on my journey.

An Encounter with the Germans

When I got to my mother and sister, I gave them the warm milk. After they drank it, we packed our things and went in the direction explained to me, and I was the leader. After an hour in the forest, as we were told to stay away from any path, but to walk parallel to the paths in order not to loose our way, we arrived at the train tracks. Now we must walk parallel to the train tracks for 20 kilometers until we reach the village of Kerchon.

[Page 242]

We continued walking parallel to the train tracks as we tried not to be seen, but still be close to the tracks in order to not loose our way. After a few kilometers in the forest, we would again get close to the train tracks. We continued in this zig-zag fashion.

It was the afternoon hours and we sat down for a short rest and to eat. We went into the forest to look for forest berries and cranberries. We collected berries and ate them as we were also very thirsty. When we finished resting, we continued on our way in order to find the train tracks. We got closer and closer to it. We suddenly found ourselves by the tracks and saw a sign -- Nimovitz Train Station. As we hurried to get into the forest, we heard a car coming near on the train tracks. We moved even quicker. We turned our heads around. We saw it was a train car with two Germans on it armed with a machinegun. They even shot a few bursts of bullets into the forest. Perhaps they were just shots in order to scare us, or that they saw us fleeing into the forest. The shots scared us, we lied on the floor, and did not move until there was quiet. They we quickly got up, looked around, and continued on our way, looking for a place to sleep for the night. Since we were in a pine grove, we collected dry branches, and lit a small fire to warm ourselves and to bake potatoes. Thus we spent the night in the middle of the way to Kerchon, by the campfire. The next day we woke up at dawn, collected our bundles, and continued on our way along the train tracks, hiding amongst the trees.

Looking for Jews in the Forests of Kerchon

After walking almost the whole day, we came close to a village area in the late afternoon hours. We knew this because of the barking of the dogs. We saw houses and fields. We thought that we had arrived at Kerchon. We sat down to rest and eat what we had left. We meant to go to one of the houses in the evening to ask if we really were in Kerchon and where the Jews were in this area.

Aid and Words of Encouragement from the Leader of the Polish Partisans

As we were sitting and talking, we heard voices of people coming in our direction. We stood on our feet to escape, but suddenly we heard a voice say in Polish, "Stop! Don't flee. We are partisans!" We stopped, and we found ourselves surrounded by three armed men with rifles, and one of them also had a revolver.

[Page 243]

He was the leader. They asked where we came from and where we are going to. We told them all that happened to us up to now and what our plans are for the winter. We added that we hoped to be helped by the Jews hiding in the forest in this area.

The leader of the partisans ordered one of his men to give us sheep furs so we could cover ourselves on the cold nights. He explained that we were near a Ukrainian village and Kerchon is on the other side of the train tracks. In other words, we must cross the train tracks. He said we could only cross the train tracks after dark and then enter the first house, whose owner had a large threshing floor. He would take care of it that the farmer would give us food and let us stay in his threshing floor until he would met us with the Jews of the forest. He even told us the names of the Jews. We also knew their names.

Seeing how poor, scared and lacking hope we were, he encouraged us in saying that the Germans will soon be defeated and we will be freed, and then we could avenge them and the Ukrainians. He said that the partisans were acting very strongly and caused the Germans many problems. He said we should not be scared when we hear a large explosion in a hour, as they would be blowing up a German train on the train tracks ten kilometers from here. Mother thanked him and wished them good luck in the battles against the Germans, and even suggested her help. But they said that the partisans only accept young men and women with private guns. We continued sitting and waited for it to get dark, so we could continue on our way as the partisan leader explained to us. Mother saw the partisans as messengers of G-d and made a thanksgiving prayer.

As was promised, we heard a great explosion, and we understood that the paritsan's act was carried out. That made us very happy. It became dark, and we turned to crossing the train tracks. We crawled to the tracks and crossed the tracks with each of us running separately. Then we turned in the direction of the house of the owner of the large threshing floor. We came close to the courtyard, and there was a large barking dog. Within a few minutes, a young farmer came out, called the dog, and came toward the gate. He asked us what we wanted, and we told him. We mentioned the name of the leader of the partisans. He opened the gate for us, and quickly took us to the threshing floor. He brought us food, and said later in the evening he would met us with a Jew of Kerchon by the name of Avraham with the closed eye, who would take us to the forest and get us settled with the rest of the Jews. We must leave the threshing floor tonight, because the Germans will do searching tomorrow, after the explosion.

[Page 244]

The Meeting in the Kerchon Forests with Jewish Acquaintances

We cuddled up in a pile of hay in the threshing floor after we ate the food that the farmer gave us and we tried to fall asleep. We fell asleep for a few hours. We suddenly woke up when we heard a discussion in Yiddish inside the threshing floor. I jumped from the pile of hay and I recognized Avraham with the closed eye, and another Jew by the name of Avraham who was a metal worker from Sarny. Avraham with the closed eye recognized me, my mother, and my sister. My mother told him our whole story. He told us his whole story and that he and his wife, Bluma, were still alive. But all the others had been killed.

The farmer came and asked them to take care of us. He made sure that they had a sheltered place for us during the coming winter, and a good hiding place for us if the Germans came to search. The two Jews said they have this for us, but they were not very happy because we might become a burden for them. My mother tried to explain that we were relatives through his wife, Bluma, and she asked if he could help us. The farmer added to us some more food and some old clothes. We went on our way with Avraham from Kerchon and Avraham the metal worker toward the forest. On the way, each of them entered the houses of non-Jews to stock up on food. We continued on our way to the forest.

Avraham knew his way in the depths of the forest in the darkness of the night. Finally, we got to a tangled grove, and met the rest of the Jews who were in a special building made of logs, covered with leaves and dirt. Near the building, there was a campfire burning. By the campfire, sat Avraham's wife, Bluma, the metal worker, Fissa, his daugher, Hanna, and his grandaughter, Zelda. After opening greetings, it seemed that we were received in a very cold manner. We sat by the campfire and they gave us baked potatoes that were taken from the ashes now. Avraham, the metal worker, opened by saying that we all had an obligation to take care of the widow and her two orphans. But we must take into account the existing plans for hiding the refugees in the forest, so they won't be discovered when the Germans come to make a thorough search.

Again the Individuals among the Surviving Jews

Avraham, the metal worker, was a strange type. On one hand, he was very kind. On the other hand, he was very nervous and apprehensive about being discovered. He said it was very important to hide our tracks in the winter and in the snow, in order not to be discovered. He said we could not all stay together,

[Page 245]

in order to not mix up the plans for hiding already made for the winter.

All the members sat quietly as a sign that they agreed with him. Avraham Hakerchoni (from Kerchon) had to explain to certain non-Jews the reason that we were staying separate in order to prevent misunderstandings. Thus it was decided that the next morning we would be moved to a different part of the forest. There was a shack there that was used in the fall months. Avraham, the metal worker, explained to us that in the winter months, when the snow began to fall, we were to move around as little as possible from the shack to the houses of the village. We should collect for ourselves a supply of food, and to put it in a hole in the ground and to cover it with leaves and branches, so it won't freeze. This referred to bread, onions, salt, matches, and a supply of dry leaves and branches for heating bonfires. If we had to go out, at any rate, we should leave a minimum of footsteps by covering them with the snow.

Avrham Hakerchoni even promised to explain and help us in preparing the shack for the winter, and would help us dig a hole for water close by.

Mother was very sad about all these talks. She cried. But there was no choice, and we had to accept the decision, and thought about how to survive the difficult winter.

That night we fell asleep by the bonfire. We woke up in the morning and ate baked potatoes and onions. Avraham Hakerchoni led us to our new home. After we said goodbye to everyone, Avraham, the metal worker, said to us that we could not visit them under any circumstances, as it would endanger them. But on the other hand, they would find time to visit us from time to time. Avraham Hakerchoni explained to us, on the way, the short cut to the village. He explained where the houses of the villagers who were willing to help us were located.

The Shack in the Forest

We arrived at our shack, we cleaned the floor, and put our bundles down. In the middle of the shack, there was a pit for making a bonfire. We lit a fire. A small distance from the shack, we dug a pit with the aid of Avrahma Hakerchoni about a meter and a half deep. We reached water that was clean and tasty. This promised us water for drinking and washing.

[Page 246]

After we got settled, Avraham Hakerchoni left us and promised to visit from time to time. The three of us remained, and my sister and I went out to look for forest berries. We returned with berries and we ate the potatoes that had baked in the bonfire and ate the berries for desert. Then I collected branches of pine trees to cover the roof of the shack and with a tin that I found near by, I dug in the soft sand near the shack, and I pored sand on the branches in order to prevent leaking and cold. I also collected tall weeds, half-dry, and brought them to the shack. I spread them under us for bedding. Thus the day went by, and I planned to go to the village in the evening in order to collect food and other supplies for the coming winter. We tried to navigate in the shortest way, according to Avraham Hakerchoni's directions. As we got farther away from the shack, we left ourselves signs so we would know the way back to the shack.

Even though it was dark, we were not afraid of the animals. We were warned about the danger of the wolves in the winter. If we run into a wolf, we should scare him away by lighting a dry tree. The flame scares him away. After a half an hour, we got to the edge of the forest, and we saw the lights from the windows of the houses in the village. In a bent over position, we crossed the field and came close to the first house.

Manka -- the Guardian Angel

I knocked on the door, and a fat, short Polish woman appeared, and asked us to enter. In the house, her husband and her daughter were seated. It was very pleasant and warm in the house, as opposed to the cold and wind outside. The woman told us to sit near the heater, where we could get warm. Even though this was a first visit, we did not totally surprise them, and they knew of our existence in the area. We understood this because the woman asked about our mother, the widow. We told them about how we got settled in the shack, that mother was weak and tired from the tribulations of the traveling until we got to Kerchon. We answered their questions about where we came from, what town, and how we escaped. Tears fell from the woman's eyes, and she did not stop crossing herself, and saying prayers.

She and her husband were disturbed by the fact that Avraham and his people did not let us stay with them, but sent us to a separate place. Wasn't it shameful that an escaped Jew dids not want to help someone who was weak and needed help? They served us warm food -- cereal, borsht, and potatoes. The non-Jewess found some of her daughters' clothes and gave them to my sister. She warmed water in a big pot, and suggested that my sister go in back of the heater and shower and wash her hair. She suggested

[Page 247]

that I let my sister stay with them for the winter, because my sister would not survive the difficult winter in the forest. She insisted that my sister already stay the night, and that I return to the forest and tell my mother. If my mother was against this, we could return her tomorrow. The non-Jew went outside and gave me a sharp axe and said this would help me in the forest -- to cut wood for heating, for building, and for protection from animals, and people.

The woman gave me cooked food -- warm cereal and warm milk, bread, cheese, potatoes, and matches. I thanked her and went on my way back to the forest to the shack. I tried to go back the way I came and according to the signs I left myself. Within a half an hour, I got to the shack, and I found mother napping by the fire. Mother awakened when I entered, and I gave her the warm food that I brought her. She drank a little of the milk. I told her of the warm heart of the non-Jewess, Manka, and that I left my little sister with her for the night, as she suggested. Mother was happy and we decided that tomorrow mother would come with me to visit my sister in the village. I added some more wood to the fire, and I fell asleep with mother in the shack for the night.

Organization in the Forest for the Winter

The next day, I was busy digging a ditch in the corner of the shack for hiding potatoes for supply, so they would not freeze during the winter. Then I collected some tall weeds and covered them. Then I used the axe to cut some dry wood, and I prepared a pile of wood for heating for the winter. Then I collected some berries. During the afternoon, I took advantage of the nice day and the fall sun, and took off my rags and shook out my clothes from the lice. I took a bucket of water and washed myself a bit. Mother did the same. Thus we prepared ourselves for the visit with the nice non-Jewess, where my sister was.

At dark, we went on our way that I already knew, and in a short time, we arrived at the house of Manka. After knocking on the door, and identifying ourselves, she opened the door and received us warmly. My sister jumped and hugged us as if she had not seen us for years. The woman sat us by the oven, and gave us warm and well cooked food. We enjoyed the food. My mother did not stop thanking the woman for her good heart, and thanked her for the suggestion to keep my sister in her house for the winter. The woman said she would teach my sister how to knit while she would sit by the oven during the day. My mother told Manka about her diseases and her suffering. Manka gave us sour milk

[Page 248]

in a big jug and additional food for storage. After two hours in her house, we said goodbye, thanks, and blessings.

Another Righteous Woman

When we went out of the house of Manka, my mother suggested that we try to enter the next house in order to fill our supplies for the winter and the snow. We left our bundles by the door and knocked on the door. A tall and thin non-Jewess opened the door, and asked us to enter. Apparently, see also already knew about us. This woman looked very pleasant, and tried to help us to her best ability. She suggested to us to eat. But we thanked her and told her that we had just eaten in another house. After an hour of talking, she gave us potatoes, bread, onions, pickled cucumbers, and cheese. She also gave us some clothes. We thanked her and went one our way. On our way out, we collected our bundles that we left outside, and continued on our way back to the forest. After a short time, we arrived at the shack. We lit the bonfire again, placed the potatoes in the pit that was set up for them, and placed the rest of the food and clothes aside. Then we got ready for a night's sleep by the bonfire.

Thus we continued our daily lives as the winter came closer. The days got gradually shorter and colder. We tried to go to the village as little as possible, but we needed to collect supplies for the winter--potatoes, matches, salt, and onions, in order that we need not go to the village during the snow.

In our surroundings, it was usually very quiet, except for birds chirping, and voices of animals. Nothing usually bothered us. But at any rate, we always listened, and tried not to make unnecessary noises, in order not to stand out.

Danger of Destruction and Escape

One morning we heard steps of people getting close. I got closer and looked from the shack. I knew it was Avraham, the metal shop worker and his wife. They entered the shack, said hello, and asked how we were getting along. He made a lot of noise and talked a lot. His wife was a lot quieter and smiled from time to time when he talked. He said that he heard for a reliable non-Jew in the village, that there will be an "oblaba" -- searching with tracking dogs of the Germans in the area of the forest of Kerchon. We are quite far from the village, and he did not think that they would get to us. But we must be careful and be very alert.

He and his wife were on their way to a distanced area in another direction from the village, on the other side of the railroad tracks. They planned to stay in hiding for a couple of days, until this searching was done. My mother suggested that they take me with them

[Page 249]

for my safety, and that she stay by herself. This was to lessen the danger for us. Avraham, the metal shop worker, agreed immediately, but I refused to leave my mother by herself. My mother insisted, and convinced me to join the two of them. With tears in my eyes, I left my mother and left her alone.

Avraham, the metal shop worker, was at the head, and he left me and his wife farther back. He went into the depths of the forest, getting farther away from the village. In the end, we stopped, and sat down to rest and eat bread and forest berries that we collected. Avraham opened his mouth and began to plan the future out loud. It seemed that he had not exactly decided where we should hide and where we should go. His wife, Chaya, said her opinion that we had gone far enough and that she was tired, and that we should look for a place in the nearby surroundings, in one of the deep groves. Avraham quieted her in an unpleasant manner, and that she shouldn't give her advice, and that she should totally trust his judgment. His wife, of course, was quiet immediately. He ordered her to continue after him. From time to time, he told us to lie down or stop, and he would listen carefully that he didn't hear any suspicious noise.

Thus the day passed and it began to get dark. It was very windy and the sky was very cloudy. We continued by the same method until we found ourselves by the railroad tracks. Avraham stopped, and told me to cross the tracks by running bent down and to wait for his wife and himself. I did just that. Then his wife crossed the tracks in the same manner and then Avraham. We then continued walking quickly because we were afraid it would start raining. Avraham said nearby there was an isolated house, and about one kilometer from the house, there was a pile of hay under a hay roof. We must steal ourselves to the pile of hay, cover ourselves and stay there for a couple of days. If we were successful doing so without being heard, we could stay there until the searching would be completed. We didn't think that any one would find us.

The Hiding Place in the Hay Stack

Within a half hour, we found ourselves before the hay stack. With the help of Avraham, I climbed on the pile first. Then his wife climbed on the pile with Avraham's help from below and I pulled her up. After joint cooperation, we got on the hay stack, and then Avraham climbed on it. On the top of the pile, we felt the strong wind. We then fell into the hay stack and in that way, we protected ourselves from the cold and the wind.

[Page 250]

Avraham and his wife had food -- bread, onions, cooked potatoes in their peels, cheese, and drinking water. Avraham gave us a rationed portion of food, and I fell asleep for the night. I didn't sleep so well because I worried about my mother and my sister, each of them far away from me.

That night it rained heavily and there were strong winds. By morning, the rain stopped a bit and the winds calmed down, but it was very cold and the sky was very cloudy. Avraham said soon heavy snow would fall. We were at the beginning of the month of January 1943. Very shortly, snow began to fall, and the surroundings were totally white. According to Avraham, the change of weather will affect the accessibility of the Germans to the area. If they haven't done their searching as of yet, they will not do so in the days to come. Therefore, he planned that we get off the pile of hay when it became dark, and that we continue on our way in the forest, to our living quarters. On the way, we shall enter some houses of non-Jews in the village and collect food, and we will know if the Germans did their search.

Our Return to the Forest and to my Lonely Mother

We got down from the hay stack and walked quickly. We had to walk slowly at the beginning, because our feet had fallen asleep because we were under the hay stack all night. Avraham said it was good that we continued because the snow would cover the hay stack tonight, if we continued staying there. We arrived at the railroad tracks, crossed them by running, and got close to the houses of the village of Kerchon. Avraham suggested that he and his wife enter one of the houses, and that I enter another house, and that we meet near the last shack by the forest. He who came first would wait for the others, and that we should not stay more than an hour in the village. Thus it was.

I knocked on a door and after identifying myself as a poor orphan, they let me in. An elderly Polish woman stood at the entrance of the house. When she saw that I was frozen and very poor, she let me in her house quickly, and closed the door. She sat me down by a warm oven. The house was warm and pleasant, and her family sat around the table, four men, women, and their children. The non-Jewess figured out who I was and without asking too many questions, she gave me warm cereal and other warm food. After I finished the large bowl of cereal, someone else offered me warm milk, and I finished it without any trouble. When I finished eating, they were all surprised that I ate so much. I told them for almost two days I hadn't eaten, and before that, I mostly ate baked potatoes. I answered their questions about my mother and my sister, without saying that my sister was staying with a non-Jewess in the village.

[Page 251]

The old woman prepared for me food for the way -- potatoes, cooked meat, and pickled cucumbers. They gave me dry rags for rapping my feet. The others were wet and worn out. I thanked them and continued on my way.

It was very dark outside. I heard dogs barking and wolves whining. The snow continued to fall, and I moved toward the shack we decided to meet at. When I got near the shack, I heard a whistle in another direction, and I moved toward it. Then I ran into Avraham and his wife. We continued into the forest, and Avraham asked me how I was received in the house I went to. He was surprised that they received me so well, because he said this family was not usually so nice, at least to him. As we continued to walk, Avraham continued to tell us what happened to him one night, when he ran into a family of wolves. He got them to leave when he lit a bit of dry wood, which he always kept with him. Of course, the fire acted very well, and caused the wolves to leave immediately. He heard that the wolves preyed on a dog of one of the villagers that night.

He explained the great importance of not walking in the snow in order to prevent leaving tracks. We must be careful and not to eat too much, and not go to the village in any circumstances. If one must go to the village, we should do it during a snow storm, because the tracks get covered. We should cover up our tracks at any rate.

After a half an hour walk, he explained to me the way to my mother's shack, and told me how to go. He said he and his wife will go their way. He reminded me to be careful and hide my tracks. I continued on my way by myself. There was a snow storm, and it was very dark. I ran into a branch here and there, but I continued with all my strength. I was anxious to see my mother and to know how she was. I wanted to be with her. Avraham's stories about the wolves scared me, but I continued on my way.

After walking a half of an hour, I found myself near the shack. I entered inside, and found my mother sleeping with the bonfire almost out. I lit the bonfire again, and then my mother woke up, and I gave a bit of the food I brought. She ate a bit, and I told her my story, and what happened when I was gone. My mother complained of the cold, and how her whole body was aching.

[Page 252]

I put the food supplies in the pit. I warmed some water by melting snow in a can I had, and gave mother something warm to drink. I added wood to the fire, and then I put mother and myself to sleep, wrapped in rags that we had. Our backs were to the fire, and they were warm. But the front part of us was very cold. But we comforted ourselves that another night of tribulations had passed.

The Tribulations of Winter and the Isolation in the Forest

The cold outside became worse. The snow storms would come back, and the piles of snow around the shack would get higher. It was hard work to shovel the snow in front of the shack so we could have a passage. We continued our daily routine, and we made sure that the bonfire was always lit, for heat and for baking potatoes, our major form of food. The supplies of the other food were finished during the days we couldn't go to the village. For drinking water, every morning we broke some ice that was above the water pit. In order to warm ourselves, we would boil the warm water in the can that we had, and drink the warm water. That helped us warm ourselves, because it got colder every day. We rationed ourselves potatoes, so they would last this long period of the winter. We hoped the weather would improve.

Mother was very weak, and the cold was very difficult for her. She suffered from heartburn and constipation, which got worse as the week past. We were worried by the situation. Our supply of matches was running out. We tried our best to keep the fire going all the time, but it burned out sometimes, and we would have to use the matches to light the fire again. Mother warned me that we shouldn't fall asleep at the same time, in order that one could watch that the fire wouldn't go out. She said people fall asleep when it is very cold, and could freeze to death while sleeping. She asked me to awaken her from time to time, and she did the same with me. It happened from time to time that we fell asleep at the same time, because we were weak and exhausted, from lack of healthy food, and because of the intense cold.

One morning we woke up frozen, the fire went down, and we had very few potatoes, and very few matches. After a few tries to light the fire which were not successful, we were half frozen, hungry, and isolated from the outside world because of the snow storm outside. Mother stood with my help, and we tried to move our limbs by walking in the shack in order to relive our frozen limbs. We decided we must find a way to the village to get more food and matches, or we would be "lost".

[Page 253]

Finding a Way Out in Times of Need

Our problem was how to find the way to the village as all the paths and roads to the village were covered with snow, and there were no signs. Also we were weak, hungry, and half frozen. It was very difficult for us to walk in the snow. But at any rate, we took our bundles, my axe, and went on our way. The walking was very difficult, and half of our body was covered with snow. My mother and I felt our feet freezing, especially our foot soles. We moved our feet, as if we were moving logs. We walked as if our feet were artificial. I would have to pick up my mother from time to time. We continued at a very slow pace. We noticed that it began to get dark, and we didn't see any sign of the village. In usual times, it took a half an hour or an hour to get to the village.

On the Verge of Freezing and Death

With our last strength, we got to a pine grove. I recognized the area, and I knew that in this grove there was a shack. I left mother to sit, and I tried to find the shack, trying to push myself through the thick pine grove filled with snow. After many efforts and trial with my axe, I got into the grove, but I didn't find the shack. It got dark, and I returned to my mother, who sat bundled up and asleep amongst the snow storm and the intense cold.

I woke her up, and reminded her of what she had told me -- that it is forbidden to fall asleep in the cold, and that we could die. My mother answered that it didn't really matter, and that she is going to die. I broke out crying, and begged her not to fall asleep. I suggested to her that I would go in the direction of the village, because it seems that we are close to it. My mother remained sitting by herself, and I wrapped her as well as I could with the rags I had. With the last of my strength, I went in the direction of the village. Even though it was dark, I found the correct direction, and I found myself near the houses of the village. I went to the closest house, knocked on the door, and the tall good-hearted woman who was the neighbor of Manka opened the door. When she saw how frozen and poor I was, she crossed herself several times and cried. She took me in and got me close to the fire. I told her that I couldn't feel my feet. She took off the rags that were on my frozen feet, and rubbed them with snow until I began to feel them again. She then rubbed pig fat on them and told me to put them

[Page 254]

Before I began eating, I began to cry and told the woman about my mother's state and where she was situated. I asked her to give me something warm to drink, matches, and some food, so I could go quickly to my mother. The woman convinced me to finish eating, and she would in the meantime prepare what I requested. She prepared for me new rags for my feet with dry hay and I put them on. My feet and the rest of my body were a lot better after the warm meal.

I was very worried about my mother, and I hurried to bring to her what I had. I put my bundles on my back, which included a bottle of warm milk. I ran to my mother. The warmth of the milk bottle bothered me, and I put it on the ground for a short period of time in order to switch hands. But the milk of the bottle spilled when I placed it on the ground. I felt very bad, and I wrestled with myself to go back to the woman and ask for more warm milk, or to hurry to the forest to my mother. I decided to go to my mother as I was already very far from the house.

After a half an hour, I found my mother. I gave her the bread, cheese, and cooked potatoes. But mother barely ate it. I collected some branches, and lit a bonfire. I collected logs that I cut with my axe. The fire got stronger. Mother recovered a bit, and we hoped to last until morning, and then find the shack in the grove.

Shortly it was dawn. I collected some more wood, and increased the fire, without worrying that we would be seen or heard, because if I didn't, we would freeze. I made a huge fire, and placed my mother nearby, once with her back to the fire and once with her face to the fire, in order to warm her. I went in the direction of the grove, and very soon I found the shack. I returned to my mother, and dragged her with all my strength in the direction of the shack. She could not stand on her feet.

My Dying Mother

After a short time, I was able to get mother into the shack. It was as cold inside as it was outside. I took all of our belongings, and with my axe, I collected a pile of dry branches, and made a fire in a special tin in the shack that was made by Avraham, the metal shop worker. It was an old bucket that stood upside down with its opening toward the ground. On its lower part was an opening for placing the wood and lighting the fire. Lower down there was an opening for ventilation. On its upper part, there was a pipe chimney through the roof of the shack to the outside. I was able to light the fire and the tin bucket was very hot.

[Page 255]

Thus we were able to get warm. I quickly melted snow in a tin and boiled water. My mother drank from the hot water, and tasted a bit of the food I brought. I thought she was getting a little better. I took off the rags from her feet, and took care of them the way the non-Jewess took care of my feet. I rubbed her feet with snow, and dried the rags on our hot "heater", and wrapped her feet. My mother said that she didn't feel her feet at all. She asked me to let her fall asleep. I promised her that I would keep the fire going. I went outside to prepare a supply of branches for the fire.

When I came back with the supply of wood, I saw her snoring and making strange distortions, opening and closing her eyes. I ran to her and screamed: "Mother, mother!" I gave her warm water in the tin. She drank a bit, and recovered a bit. She said she almost died, and it was forbidden for me to bother on her deathbed. I began crying and begged her to recover. She promised that she would make all the efforts to recover.

My Mother's Death in My Arms

Thus another day passed in which we had a roof over us. I tried not to fall asleep, as I saw my mother's situation was getting worse from minute to minute. I gave her warm water from time to time. At dawn, my mother began to convulse again, I tried to help her, but I didn't know what to do. My mother mumbled all sorts of names that had no relation to one another. She mentioned my father's name, my brother's name, her father's name, her mother's name, and other names of family members. Then there were no more signs of life and her eyes opened.

I began to cry very strongly, and tried to call "mother, mother, wake up! Don't leave me alone, please, mommy." I kissed her and hugged her with all my strength, and I felt that her body was cold and hard. I placed her head on the ground, and covered her face with rags. I lowered my head, and began to cry about her fate and my fate. An hour later, I uncovered her face to see if there was a miracle and that she was alive, but to no avail. I began to think what I must do now.

A Lonely Orphan

I decided that I must turn to Manka's house and get advice on what to do, as I didn't know where the rest of the Jews were. I left the shack that I had entered with my mother. The snow storm calmed down outside, and the clouds dispersed. But it was very cold outside. But the sun was shinning and it warmed me up a bit. I sighed and thought why my mother couldn't have reached this moment,

[Page 256]

so she could enjoy the sunrays. I continued on my way to the village during the day without thinking of the dangers involved in this.

I arrived at the edge of the forest and I stopped and looked around well ahead and to the sides to see if there were any suspicious people. I didn't see anything exceptional but some farmers near their homes. I ran quickly to Manka'a house, and in the courtyard, I met Manka's husband. He was surprised to see me in the middle of the day. He quickly placed me in the threshing floor and told me to wait and he would go to call for his wife. His wife appeared. Manka, the compassionate and good, comforted me. She asked me not to go in the house and not to tell my sister at this point. She promised that she would find the Jews of the forest as soon as possible and tell them what happened. Then they would bury my mother. She gave me some food and told me to return to the forest and wait for the Jews. I of course did what she requested. Quickly and carefully I went back to the forest, to the shack, where my mother died a few hours earlier. Even though I was sure that my mother was dead, I went up to her body again, took off the covering on her face to see if there were any vital signs of life. But I realized the bitter reality.

The Burial of My Mother in the Forest

I sat and waited for the Jews to come to help me to bury my mother. Suddenly, I heard voices come near. I went outside of the shack, and saw the two Avrahams, two other men, and Rabbi Pesa. Avraham

Hakerchoni hugged me and tried to calm me down. It seems that Manka's husband knew of the hiding place of Avraham Hakerchoni and the rest. He called him to leave the hiding place, and told him that he had something important to tell him. Since Avraham trusted him and knew his voice, he came out of the house and he told him about my mother's death. Avraham told me all of this, and that he would organize the rest, and they would take care of the burial.

We went a bit away from the shack, and in the same grove found an iceberg that was a bit high. One of the men, a relative of Avraham Hakerchoni, by the name of Yosef, had knowledge about the burial laws. He decided on the place of the grave. Then they began to remove the snow. After that, they dug. At the beginning, the progress was slow, as the upper layer of earth was frozen. But later, the earth was sandy, and the digging moved along quickly. They finished digging the hole, they cut poles of wood to cover the body, and they set up a framework in the hole. Then they entered the shack and took the body of my mother who was wrapped in her rags, and lowered it into the grave. The dark, knowledgeable fellow said a prayer and then I said Kaddish. The grave was covered.

[Page 257]

They placed a wide pole on it with its upper part divided and on it my mother's name -- Mrs. Tibel Prishkolnik, the daughter of Rabbi David Tzukerman from Brozna.

Under the Auspices and Guardianship of Avraham and Bluma

Avraham Hakerchoni hugged me and tried to calm me down. He began moving me away from my mother's grave. He moved the rest of the people away. He said from this moment on, my sister and I will be together with him and his wife, and will be under his and his wife, Bluma's, auspices. What happens to him and his wife, also happens to us.

When we got close to their living quarters, which was very close to our shack and to my mother's grave, Avraham, the metal shop worker, gave orders how to make access to the shack. He organized us in single file and commanded us to go after Rabbi Pesa, and to leave a minimum of tracks. He and Avraham Hakerchoni were at the end of the line, and they had in their hands containers with snow for covering up our tracks. Thus in a short time, we arrived at their shack, and here we found Bluma, Chanah -- the daughter of Pesa from Kazimirka and his granddaughter, Zelda, and Chaya, the wife of Avraham, the metal shop worker. All of them pitied me and tried to comfort me. They tried to analyze the reason for my mother's death. Most of them claimed that the main reason was that she was sick from before, and her general weakness didn't allow her to withstand the intense cold. Therefore, she died. Perhaps, maybe it was for the best. Who knows what hardships are before us? Bluma fed me and said that I should lie down to rest on the bed of rags near the fire.

The rest of the Jews that were present at my mother's burial, were close to Avraham Hakerchoni and even they were from Kerchon. There was a mother, a son, a daughter, and brother-in-law, Yosef, who the one who was well versed in the burial laws. He also said to me: please remember today is the first of February, 1943 -- the day of the death of your mother.

The relations between Avraham and especially his wife with his relatives were very bad. Therefore, they hid out in a different part of the forest and had nothing to do with the relatives. Avraham Hakerchoni knew where they lived. Therefore, he invited them to be present during my mother's burial.

During the first week in their shack, they didn't let me do anything. I sat most of the time in front of the hot oven, and they would give me baked potatoes and onions from time to time. Everyone liked me, and Bluma and Chanah especially took care of me.

Thus the grey daily routine continued in the shack, which was warm enough. From time to time, I would go out to collect dry branches for heating, and would put in and take out potatoes from the ashes of the fire,

[Page 258]

at the bottom of the heater. Part of what we would do during the day was to take care of our clothes -- looking for lice and killing them, or shaking our clothes over the bonfire.

The lice were very bad. In addition to the fact that we had very little food, the lice sucked the last of our blood without mercy, and they multiplied, and got fat on our expense. From time to time, arguments would break out between Avraham, the metal shop worker and Rabbi Pesa about Avraham's exaggeration with regard to his strange ideas and his carefulness about camouflaging our tracks. Sometimes the situation would get so "hot", that only Bluma and the wife of Avraham, the metal shop worker, could calm them down. From discussions I heard, I found out that near Milinsk, there was a large group of Jews, amongst them Jews from Stepan and Bronza. They were hiding in the forests of the Ukrainian village of Brono. Pesa said he knew the non-Jews of the village, but didn't trust them too much. He thought that there was danger of destruction of the Jews there, if they didn't escape soon.

About two weeks after I was staying in Avraham Hakerchoni's shack, on a night of a heavy snow storm, he suggested taking me to see my sister. He said we should take extra clothing and some food. We were on our way. We arrived at Manka's house very quickly. We entered the house after knocking on the door, and identifying ourselves. Manka received us warmly and with compassion. She called my sister.

The Fact of My Mother's Death was Told to My Sister

We hugged each other, and I broke out in a bitter cry. I told my sister what happened to our mother. My sister joined the crying. Manka calmed us down, and promised to continue keeping my sister until the intense cold passed. But, if I wanted, I could take her with me to the forest. I agreed to this and thanked her. Manka's husband and she criticized the Jews in the forest again for not helping us, and that they didn't let us join them in the days of intense cold. Avraham Hakerchoni tried to justify their actions because of their fear of tracks and noise of too large of a group. But the Poles were not convinced and continued to claim that this shame would not be forgiven. Avraham was offended, hurried to leave, and promised to meet me at the entrance to the forest in an hour.

Manka hurried to prepare a good warm meal for us, gave me some clothes to switch my worn out and dirty clothes, and gave me a supply of food. I thanked her for everything, and sat with my sister, sad and depressed, by the heater. We brought up to idea that from now on, we were lonely orphans without someone to lean on. We could only lean on each other. I, as the older brother, took on the responsibility for her existence in all conditions and circumstances. I told her that when spring comes, Avraham Hakerchoni and his wife will separate from the rest of the group.

[Page 259]

Avraham will help me build a new shack in a place he would choose. Then she could join me and we could live together. My sister claimed, with tears in her eyes, that she was impatiently waiting for that moment, even though she felt good with Manka and that they were very nice to her.

Then I took my bundles, and separated from my sister with a kiss. I thanked Manka again and turned to meet Avraham. At the edge of the forest, Avraham Hakerchoni waited for me and we continued on our way to our living quarters. The snow continued to fall and covered our tracks. But near the shack, Avraham covered our tracks. I walked first, and he after me, spreading snow from his container in his hand in order to cover up our tracks. We returned to the shack and continued with our grey routine. The days passed and we felt that it was less cold, and that the weather got better. We could get enjoyment from time to time from the sunrays and its warmth -- the end of the winter and the beginning of the spring.

At the beginning of April, we had another occupation, and that was milking the white and erect birch trees. It was enough to make a groove in the bottom of the trunk of the tree. Then sweet sap would drip out of the groove. It was so tasty -- sweet water. Since the dripping was slow in general, we would place near the groove in the trunk of the tree a thin branch, and then the drops would drop into the bucket. This caused us much enjoyment. I was an expert at this, and I would collect the sap for most of the members of the shack. Of course, all the knowledge about this activity I acquired from Avraham Hakerchoni.

The Inner Struggles of the Survivors

The nights were not always so calm. From time to time, I would hear the discussions of Avraham Hakerchoni. and his wife, Bluma, as a slept nearby them. The arguments would get stronger and they would accuse one another for losing their children in the Holocaust. She would accuse him that he didn't return to the ghetto on the day of the escape in order to look for their children who were staying with Bluma's mother. He and she, it appeared to me, worked outside of the ghetto of Brazna. There the two children stayed with Bluma's mother. Avraham would explain that there was no reason to return to the ghetto, because when they heard the rumor of the destruction of the ghetto, the ghetto was already being destroyed. He would have only risked his life, without even saving his children. The argument would always end in heavy sighing and crying by both of them.

This of course caused me to think of all that we had gone through at the time of escaping the ghetto. This caused me horrible nightmares.

[Page 260]

The Appearance of Spring in the Depths of the Forest - the Hiding Place

At the beginning of the spring, the rain caused the snow to melt. There were only, here and there, islands of snow left. The chirping of the birds and the clearing of the sky made it clear to us that spring was beginning. This encouraged us a bit, at least life would be a bit easier without the intense cold, and the terrible problem with the tracks of our feet.

The Building of a Separate Shack

Avraham Hakerchoni and I went to work building a new shack. Avraham was a man of great energy, and of great ability to improvise. I tried to help him to the best of my ability, with carpentry of the wood, and cutting and taking down branches. We worked all day straight through, with short breaks for eating. After one day of hard work, a large shack stood hidden amongst the many trees of the forest.

Thus we continued a whole week and improved the shack, including making a roof covering of branches and earth, and straightening the floor inside and making furniture. Also, there was a double bed in one corner for Avraham and his wife, a second double bed, a dining table, and a hole for water. The beds were not connected by nails as we had none, but by tying soft branches, and straps from the bark of trees. Everything was strong and stable. Close to the shack, we dug a wide hole for storing potatoes and other vegetables. With the help of Avraham, the metal shop worker, we built a heater from old metal that Avraham Hakerchoni once brought from the village. The heater was wide and had a chimney with a shield to prevent sparks from spreading in the night.

After finishing the work, we cleaned the shack, spilled white sand on the floor, and cleaned the courtyard before the shack. Our new house was ready. The next day we moved things over and about noontime we said goodbye to the others. Bluma came to live with us in the new shack. Avraham Hakerchoni was very proud of his work, and he really did a very good job. Bluma was satisfied. Avraham said that if everything went well, they will have a new baby soon, and pointed to the place in the shack where they would place the cradle. The baby should be born in the summer and this would make it easier to take care of him. Bluma said it was too soon to talk about it, and they shouldn't discuss this.

From time to time, we would go to the village to supply ourselves with food, and enjoy a warm meal. My left big toe was frozen and hurt me a lot.

[Page 261]

On one of our visits at the non-Jewess in the village, I complained about the pain on the toe of my foot, and she suggested I take off the rags on my foot. She brought for me a bowl of hot water. I placed my sore foot in the water and it seemed that my foot had begun to rot. The non-Jewess brought a clean and soft cloth and cleaned the toe carefully. She made a bandage with non-salty pig fat. She also suggested that I come to her from time to time so she could take care of the toe, and not to neglect the toe, otherwise it would get worse. I thanked her a lot, and returned with Avraham Hakerchoni to the forest. One time I asked from Bluma and Avraham to bring my sister back to the forest, as I had agreed with Manka. I felt a need for this for several reasons: 1) I felt myself very lonely since my mother died, and 2) even though I knew she was doing fine with Manka, I understood that sitting by the heater for days on was not too comfortable. Since the spring had arrived, she would enjoy being a "free" bird in the underground, along with her brother. I took into account that she would feel good with Avraham and Bluma in the new house.

My Sister Joins Us in the Forest

On one of my visits to the village, I came to Manka, and I told her that I was ready to take my sister to the forest. I thanked her very much for all that they had done for her during the winter. Manka gave me a warm meal as usual, and took care of the sore on my foot. Since the toe didn't look too good, she decided not to put anymore pig fat on it, but a special leaf from the house plants. She cleaned the sore well and made a new bandage. She gave me a supply of leaves to use when I changed the bandage from time to time. Manka gave my sister a lot of used clothes. My sister kissed the family goodbye, and we then turned to the forest. Bluma and Avraham received her with open arms, and Bluma explained to her the way of life in the forest. My sister said she would help in the upkeep of the house.

My sister began to get used to the life in the forest. I think she felt less lonely since she was with me. Bluma taught her to prepare potato soup with onions and garlic. She was busy with the tasks of the house. She would fix her clothes and also my clothes. On the nice days, we would take off our clothes and wash them. We would boil them in boiling water in order to get rid of the lice. Then we would wash them from time to time in warm water. But we never got rid of the lice. We would be more successful sometimes and would prevent the lice from spreading. My sister helped Bluma prepare diapers and the rest of the things for the baby to be born.

Thus we continued our lives. I left my sister in the forest, and at night would go to the village by myself. During the day, we would go out to pick mushrooms, under the supervision of Bluma

[Page 262]

who could distinguish between poisonous and edible ones. We would cook the mushrooms in the potato soup -- which would make our usual potato soup a little different.

The Danger of the Bandrovechim in the Forest and Taking Precautions

Avraham Hakerchoni returned one evening from a visit in the village and told a horrible story of how Bandrovechim, National Ukrainian partisans, assaulted Jews who were in the forest near Milinsk-Broni. The Poles told Avraham that the activity of the Ukrainian Nationalists was increasing. They were rebelling against the German rule and formed an independent government in Stepan. The Poles, who were very worried from this growing activity, began to organize themselves for self defense, and increased the guard duty at night.

All these things concerned us greatly. It was known that the Ukrainian Bandrovechim were even more cruel than the Germans. There was a new danger upon us -- perhaps they were in the forest in our area. We took some precautions -- being more quiet and camouflaging our living quarters even better. One time we went in a different way in order not to form paths or tracks.

One morning Avraham, the metal shop worker, and his wife, Chaya, appeared. This was the first surprise visit in our new shack. Avraham, the metal shop worker, opened with a story of the results of the assault of the Bandrovechim on the Jews near the Milinsk. According to him, the nationalist Ukrainians murdered five Jews, among them children and women. The rest of them, who escaped, got to our forest and some of them are hiding in the houses of good non-Jews in Milinsk. Avraham described the present situation as very serious, and he brought plans how to flee from this area, and to prevent a concentration of too many Jews together. According to him, we were about a hundred people.

Bluma began to argue with him, claiming that there was no logic in changing our place. Actually here, near Kerchon, it seems safer, because the Bandrovechim will not dare to get near here because of their fear of the Polish defense, unless they plan to attack the whole village. If this was the case, we would have heard of this from the Poles. Avraham, the metal shop worker, suggested a plan of observation by sitting on trees in the area, from a certain distance from our living quarters, to observe, and to warn if there was any danger approaching.

It was decided by Avraham Hakerchoni and Avraham, the metal shop worker, to make a meeting with all the men who are now in the forest. Thus, there was such a meeting with the new Jews who escaped

[Page 263]

the area of Milinsk. Amongst them stood out a tall and skinny fellow by the name of Francis. It seemed that he had initiative and was very forceful. There were men from the Katz family, the Brier brothers, Benyamin, Yosele, and Shalom. There were several fellows from Stepan -- Shimon, the red head, the son of the baker, the brothers from Korost -- Yosel, Mania, Aharon, and Avraham. Chana, the daughter of Nahman Shenker from Stepan, was also amongst them. There were also two girls from Sarni, the wife of the doctor with her young daughter from Brazna, along with several other men from Brazna. But I knew very little about them except children stories and knowing the Tzukerman family and that they had known my mother very well.

Francis explained that we must divide into two groups for two reasons: 1) so that we would make less noise and tracks, and 2) in the case of a capturing, we all won't be captured at once. He claimed that he had a rifle and revolver and some more weapons for self protection in the worst case. He explained that in the case of shots, we must lie down on the floor, and it is best in back of a heavy trunk of a tree or in the back of a hill. With regard to the idea of Avraham, the metal shop worker, about observation from the trees, he tended to accept the suggestion partially. He said we should have patrols every couple of hours during the day and at night for checking the situation and for warning. He suggested that we should be as quiet as possible.

In summary, the first suggestion of dividing the camp into two was accepted and to keep good communication between them. It was decided that Francis, his wife Mindel, her old mother, her brother and his wife, who was also Francis's sister, would live nearby us. The Katz family, the father, the oldest brother, Zerech, the young brother, the oldest sister, and the two younger sisters, Faysa Hanah and his granddaugher, Avraham, the metal shop worker, and his wife, and the rest, including, the girls from Sarni, the doctor's wife and her daughter from Brazna, and the other Jews from Brazna and Milinsk would live farther away, in a second area.

I was very jealous of Francis because he had weapons, and I tried to get near his weapons, to touch them, and to learn how to use them.

We continued our lives as our fears of every leaf moving were great and very strenuous on our nerves. Every day we would hear rumors, and new and horrible stories. We continued in the same manner to collect food from the village, as the appearance of the Germans in the village was not very probable. From the stories of the Poles, we learned that the situation of the Germans on the Russian front was worse and they began to retreat. Along with this, there was the activity of the partisans, who supported the Russians on one hand and the Ukrainian Nationalists on the other hand. They told us that the Germans were planning a big revenge action on the Ukrainians in Stepan. There was a rumor that when the Ukrainians rebelled in Stepan recently, they hung several Germans from the government in Stepan on phone poles.

[Page 264]

These stories encouraged us, and especially the rumor of the retreat of the Germans and their fall in Russia, and the possibility of revenge of the Germans against the Ukrainians. All this gave us a little hope, that perhaps we would be redeemed one of these days. This was in spite of the fact that the news was general and not usually based on fact.

Along with all the fears that were caused because of the situation, I had self confidence based on the fact that we had a reinforcement of Jews -- strong men with some weapons that they possessed. We would meet with them often and listen to discussions, arguments, prophesies, and evaluations about our chances of getting through the war and being free soon. We found friends who were orphans, and we would go out together and collect mushrooms and forest berries.

One morning, Avraham Hakerchoni returned from a patrol in the forest, and he announced to us that he met a Jew, a person he knew from Korost, his wife, her sisters, and her brother. It was apparently Rafael, the partisan, who could tell that he was the leader of the partisans, and he has different and strange plans about how to deal with the Germans. According to him, he had a secret connection with the headquarters. I knew the truth from his wife, and from his sisters, and especially from his little sister – Devora (Devorke) who said that he had escaped from a group of Ukrainian partisans who turned into Ukrainian Nationalists. Therefore, he is in our area. Rafael would be by himself for hours, even for days, as he would tell about the meetings with the partisans, and terrorist acts on railroad tracks and German installations. Most of the Jews of the forest belittled these stories and thought they were only in his imagination. Once he pointed to a square package that was placed near him, and said this was terrorist material that would soon be activated, and would blow up another train of the Germans.

Collecting Food for the Winter

The summer was coming to an end and time for the harvest: the grain crops, the fruits, and the field crops were ripe. On one of our visits to the village, it became known to us that the Ukrainian Nationalists raided the Polish villages in the area of Stepan, killed, robbed, and burned. The residents of the village, being surrounded by Ukrainians, were afraid for their future, and decided to evacuate the village as early as possible, and to move to one of the nearby cities. This was according to the recommendation of the Germans, who said that when they are on the front, they could not promise to protect them. And so, after a few days, the Poles began to evacuate their village. We said goodbye to them, and especially to Manka and to the rest of the good people, with tears in our eyes. They tried to give us utensils and clothes, and said everything that was left in the fields, in their houses, and in their barns was ours, and we should use it. And thus it was.

[Page 265]

As soon as the Poles left the village, we began to take care of ourselves with regard to food supplies for the winter. It was the time to collect from the fields. Almost everything was left in the fields and a lot in their houses as they left in a hurry. It was known to us that Ukrainians from the nearby villages would visit. Therefore, we made our visits in the evening or at night.

Avraham Hakerchoni was the expert on finding all sorts of bargains, like household utensils, like a millstone or a barrel of pickled cucumbers, pickled cabbage, cheese, or oils. With the cooperation of Avraham, we collected everything from the fields -- potatoes, grain crops, vegetables, and fruit.

In our hiding places in the forest, we set up huge wooden barrels from the village, and we filled them with wheat and rye grains, after threshing, drying, and cleaning. By the shack, we set up a millstone with great difficulty, which we brought with a small cart that we pulled from the village to the forest. We also brought a mortar and a pestle from wood for grinding the oily grain after drying in the sun or by the fire. On one of our visits, we discovered a barrel with salty preserved cheese and we took it to the forest. We dug two huge holes and filled them with potatoes and carrots, and covered them with hay and sand so they would keep for the winter and would not freeze. When fall arrived, we had collected for ourselves a supply of potatoes, wheat and rye grains, onions, garlic, some preserved cheese, pickled cucumbers and cabbage, oil grains, beans, and some salt. All the others Jewish residents of the forest did the same. At the beginning of the evacuation, we caught a bull that had run off to the forest. Mr. Pessa, the butcher, took care of slaughtering of the bull and dividing the meat to everyone. It was enough for several weeks.

The Birth of Peretz

One day, Bluma had to give birth. With the help of several Jewish women, she gave birth, and they named him Peretz (Perchik). We had a new member to our shack who was happily received with much love. But we were worried that his crying could be heard by the enemy. But we were comforted by the fact that the fall winds got stronger and would make more noise than the baby's cry. The conditions for taking care of the baby were not good, but we tried our best. As far as I remember, there were a few more births in the forest, and the babies grew up in the conditions of the underground.

[Page 266]

The Victims in the Forest

There were two tragedies. A Jew from Brazna was shot while taking potatoes out of the field near the railroad tracks. We did not know if the bullets were from the Germans or from the Ukrainians. In the evening, he was brought to the forest and was buried by my mother. My mother's grave turned into the cemetery.

The other case was Rafael, the partisan, who disappeared or was kidnapped. When he went to the village early in the morning in order to collect fruit, with his wife's little sister, Devorke, she returned to the forest by herself and told how she saw him being taken by two strong unknown men who spoke Ukrainian. She saw how they tied his hands in back of him, how he was blindfolded, and led away. She was told to go back immediately to the forest. She arrived running and out of breath. She told the story of what happened to Rafael, while crying. His wife and the rest of his family were very sad, and this worried the rest of the Jews in the forest. There were several hypotheses: 1) since they were Bandrovechim, they knew there were Jews in the forest and looked for them in order to kill them, and 2) if they were Russian partisans, they would let him go, or they would try him on some crime. This was very difficult for us. We hoped to see him one day. But the days passed and we heard nothing from him. It was clear that he was killed.

The Cruelty of the Bandrovechim towards the Poles

One morning, we heard great explosions from the area of Stepan. We guessed that they were the bombings of the Germans, and we were glad that they were avenging the cruel Ukrainians, blood thirsty, who murdered and robbed the Jews along with the Poles. The houses of the Poles looked like the houses of the Jews when they entered the ghetto. They were destroyed, looted, destroyed doors and windows, and even houses. That is what they did in the village of Kerchon.

Along with all the worries and difficulties, we continued to supply ourselves with food and wood for heating in the winter that was approaching. In the evening, by the bonfire, we would ground the grain on the millstone, and store it in bags. We cleaned and sifted the beans, the onions, and the garlic. After drying it, we would store it.

[Page 267]

The High Holidays in the Forest

The High Holidays of 1943 arrived. The services were held near Mr. Katz's shack. I remember very well the services of Yom Kippur. We were the whole day outside by the shack, we prayed, and listened to the adult prayers. But we also listened to any noise, being afraid that someone was coming near us. Our situation got worse because of the many Bandrovechim. But on the other hand, we had a feeling that the Germans were falling and that our redemption was near. There was a great desire to pass this and remain alive -- to avenge what was done to us. Yom Kippur passed and everyone went back to their shacks.

The Persecution by the Gang of the Ukrainian Murderers

A very sad and worrisome case took place. From the direction of the other concentration of Jews in the forest, we heard shooting. After a short while, several fellows came to us after escaping. They told us of the story of the attack of the Bandrovechim and how they captured the Jews. This caused great panic, and it was decided to leave everything and move over to the grove near the railroad tracks of Sarny-Rovno. We thought that the Bandrovechim would not dare get close to the railroad tracks because of their fear of the Germans and that the Germans, being worried with their defeat and afraid of getting involved with the partisans, would not enter the forest to search.

That same night we fled to the railroad tracks, and we assembled, everyone with their bundles in their hands. We were very careful to be quiet, and not to make a bonfire during the day and the night. When we did light a fire, we made sure that no sparks were in the air by using fitting wood. It was decided that the real solution was to start digging large living quarters, deep in the ground, which would be covered by logs, branches, and earth. In this large shack, all the Jews who remained were to live.

Therefore, a collective building effort began, organized and managed by Avraham Hakerchoni and Avraham, the metal shop worker. In the meantime, the rest of the Jews were found and nothing bad had happened to them. There were those who the Bandovechim caught. But they only wanted to know where the rest of the Jews were and if they had a connection with the partisans. In the end, they let them go and said that they were invited to live in Stepan, along with the rest of the Jews of the forest. They claimed that they needed craftsmen, and there must be some amongst the Jews. They claimed that the Jews of Stepan had lives of their own with all the rights and that Stepan has been under independent Ukrainian rule for some time. They suggested that we decide within a week to come of our own freewill, and that would be best. If not, they would bring us to Stepan against our will, as it is for the best.

[Page 268]

This seemed to us very strange, and there were arguments amongst us. There were a few who tended to believe the Ukrainians, but most didn't believe them, and understood that this was a trap in order to kill the remaining Jews in a total manner. But we picked several fellows to go to Stepan and to see the reality there.

We, seventy people -- men, women, and some babies -- crowded ourselves in the huge underground shack. We didn't light the fire during the day, only at night. During the day, it was freezing, as the winter arrived. At night we warmed ourselves by the heater and baked potatoes. The crowding was horrible and made life very difficult. But it seemed that the suffering was on the way to redemption.

After a day after the men left for Stepan, they returned very frightened, as they met a non-Jew from one of the villages who asked them where they were going. After they told him their story, he asked to come with them to the forest. Later he told them that the story of the Bandrovechim taking care of the Jews was a lie, and that they shouldn't go to Stepan. He also told them that the front was getting closer, and it seems that within a month the Russians will be here. If we had lasted this long, we should hold on a little longer and hide, because the day of freedom is near. He said that we shouldn't worry about the Bandrovechim because they are busy hiding from the Russians who are getting closer.

He was really the messenger of G-d, one of the righteous men of the nations of the world. The fellows returned to us and told us what "the guardian angel" told them. Then we decided that we should get organized where we were, and that we should get as much food as possible, without moving when the snow began in order to prevent tracks in the snow.

None of Your Honey and None of Your Sting

One day, after we succeeded to organize most of the supply of food and even to grind flour, Avraham Hakerchoni decided to go out with me to the other side of the railroad tracks. There were a few abandoned houses of Poles. These houses were not far from a village of Ukrainians who were known for their cruelty. Bluma tried to convince us not to go, but Avraham said he would carry this out, because of his stubbornness.

[Page 269]

We left at dawn. Outside it was still dark, and by the early morning hours, we reached the houses. It looked very abandoned and it seemed that the Ukrainian neighbors had stolen most of the things, including doors and windows that were taken down from the houses. Avraham found by one of the houses a beehive. He decided that he wanted the honey. He knew that he had to take precautions against possible bee stings. He knew from experience the use of smoke, and the possibility of flooding with water. Since smoke would reveal us, Avraham decided to equip ourselves with many different rags, and cover our bodies including our faces, so that we had air to breath, and try to overcome the bees by flooding with water. Thus we did, but we were attacked by the bees, and I felt that that were penetrating past the rags and that they were stinging my whole body. Avraham felt the same thing. After we poured buckets of water into the first beehive, Avraham suggested that we retreat and clean ourselves from the bees. We cleaned ourselves from the bees and saw that we had been stung on our whole bodies. But Avraham was stubborn to get the honey. After a short rest, we moved toward the hive that we had flooded again, and began to take pieces of wax that were full of honey. We filled our buckets, and we were stung again, but continued with our work. We placed the honey in back of the trees. We looked for large containers to carry it back. We found two large milk jugs, we cleaned them with water, and began to fill them with honey, as we separated the honey from the wax in order to save room. After we tasted the honey, it gave us the desire to get additional amounts of honey.

Very carefully, while looking out to see that the Ukrainians from the neighboring village did not see us, we continued with our work, as we did the first time. We were successful in filling two jugs with honey, which only needed to be strained and purified. We got stung again, but we were already immune. We moved away from the houses and from the hives in the direction of the grove in the forest, and we planned to rest until the sun set, and then to pass the railroad tracks in the direction of the shack. We lied down to rest and licked the honey, but the pain from the bee stings increased, and I saw how Avraham looked and how I felt. We were swelling up from minute to minute. My eyes swelled up, and I barely could see anything.

In the meantime, the sun set. Avraham found a strong branch and we placed the two jugs on our shoulders and continued on our way to the shack. We passed over the railroad tracks by running. We got to the shack late that night, because the jugs were heavy and because of the bee stings. We walked slowly and heavily.

Bluma and my sister were happy to see us alive, knowing that we took a big risk. We showed them what we had brought back and began the work of straining and purifying the honey on white pieces of cloth. In the end, there was left a large amount of honey,

[Page 270]

which added to our food supply greatly. Avraham and I suffered from the bee stings for more than a week. I even had a high temperature. Bluma took care of me and Avraham with all sorts of leaves and moist clothes with water and honey. After a week, we felt better and the swelling began to go down.

Organization for the Winter Days -- a Collective Framework

As long as it didn't start snowning, all seventy residents of the shack tried to help in organizing for the coming winter. Avraham and I, like the others, carried on our backs sacks of potatoes and hid them near the shack. My sister and Bluma baked supplies of bread, and we dried it so it would last the winter. We brought supplies of honey, onions, garlic, and anything else we could carry. We dug a well nearby with the cooperation from everybody. The preparations continued as long as it didn't begin to snow. We organized our daily life and found a place for everybody in the shack. We set up metal heaters, made by Avraham, the metal shop worker, and the chimneys were slanted sideways and downwards so the sparks wouldn't fly at night. Nearby the shack, we collected dry trees for the heaters.

Even though it was very difficult not to heat during the day and only at night, the majority received this decision without reservation. Everyone had in their hearts the feeling that was sometimes expressed in discussions that we had gone through the worst, and that we were near to being freed, and that we should suffer the maximum for this short time, so not to fail.

The Bells of Redemption and Freedom on the Horizon

When all the preparations were finished, December, 1943 arrived and the snow storms began along with intense cold. We heard from far away bombings and the sounds of artillery, mostly at night. An airplane that we heard every morning and evening along the railroad tracks of Rovno-Sarny, stopped flying. The tension of what was to happen was in the air.

Every night we would set up a number of guards outside of the shack in order that they could search, guard, and listen, and if necessary warn of a danger approaching.

[Page 271]

The Beginning of Liberation from the Forests - the Departure for Freedom

One night two fellows entered and told that they heard voices in Russian from the direction of the railroad tracks nearby. Immediately the two Avrahams, Francis, and some other Jews joined them, and got close to the tracks and tried to listen. They clearly heard voices in Russian, and footsteps in the direction of Sarny to Rovno.

After we returned to the shack, there was a strong argument. Many of the residents tended to believe that according to all the signs and rumors up to now, the Russians had arrived and that we would be soon free. But a small part of the residents, including Avraham, the metal shop worker, said this was not possible and at most this was a group of partisans that was passing by, and that we should not show ourselves because then the Germans would follow.

The Meeting with the Liberating Russian Army

Thus the discussions continued and the listening and surveillance continued at night. Finally there were compromisers amongst the residents that suggested sending a group to Hutor, the nearby Ukrainian village, there lived a reliable non-Jew who Francis knew. Francis was the head of the group. We were all very tense, and in inhumane conditions, we awaited impatiently for the group to return. The wives of the men who were sent were very scared.

One night four men went out in the direction of Hutor, taking advantage of the snow storm which covered their tracks. The next day, before noon, the weather improved and we were expecting them to return that night. But during the day, they came happy, approaching the shack, singing in Russian. Avraham, the metal shop worker, who was always suspicious, began to go crazy and swear to them how they could endanger us in the middle of the day, and why they weren't careful to cover their tracks.. They made fun of him and began saying: "Jews, we are liberated! We met Russian soldiers and at their head a Jewish commander. We got an exact report from him about the situation on the front. The Russians are making progress on all the fronts. There now are battles in the area of Kobel and they are making progress in the direction of Lavov, to the center of Warsaw. The Germans are fleeing and are very scared." They suggested that we take the necessities and go in the direction of Milinsk. Avraham, the metal shop worker, claimed that he did not believe them, and that it is at the most partisans. He refused to leave the forest until formal Russian representatives would arrive and invite us to be liberated.

The majority made fun of him and were quick to leave the forest. We walked on the railroad tracks toward Milinsk. It was the liberation march of the starved, full of lice, fear, with rags on our feet, partially barefoot, marching in the cold and snow, happy, knowing that we were free.

[Page 272]

As we marched, the Russian Army passed by us, proud and self confident. When they saw our sad case, they threw us canned goods and clothes.

Organization of Life after Leaving the Underground

By evening, we arrived at Milinsk. Avraham Hakerchoni led the convoy. We all stood by the village council building. Avraham and the rest of the Jews of Milinsk entered the building to the head of the village council, and requested that they be given their homes back. And each family received a room in houses that belonged to the Jews before the war. In a large house in the center of the village, Avraham Hakerchoni, Bluma, Pertzik got organized in one room, next to them Pessa, his daughter, and his granddaughter, next to them the Briyerim, and next to them my sister and me. The rest of the Jews were in houses that belonged to some of them in the past, others in houses they were given and that were owned by Jews in the past. Milinsk was a railroad station between Sarny and Kostopol. The non-Jewish neighbors and the Russian army helped us get organized for the night, by giving us hay mattresses and food. It was the first time I had slept in a house after seventeen months in the forest. We felt free and felt we had rights like all citizens at the time of war.

The next day, we walked amongst the Red Army, and very soon we met Jewish commanders and soldiers. The stations were full of soldiers, in cars, on horses, or by foot that fought against the retreating German army. Trains passed by all the time filled with army, weapons, heavy tanks, artillery, and bombs that were covered in order not to be discovered. On the roofs of all the cars of the trains, there was artillery against airplanes, machine guns against airplanes, with brave soldiers situated on them.

We talked with the Jewish soldiers and commanders and we heard from them that the Nazis had murdered most of their families. They helped us the best they could by giving us canned goods and some clothing. We turned to the village council and they gave us potatoes and flour. With the aid of the non-Jewish neighbors, we began organizing ourselves at home, including wood for heating the oven that was used for heating and cooking. One of the activities that we placed must effort on was destroying the lice. We sorted all of our bundles and burned the extra clothing. My sister washed the clothes, first in lukewarm water and then boiled them in hot water. We washed our bodies in hot water from buckets and bowls. We washed our cut hair in hot water and with kerosene -- according to our neighbors' suggestions. This activity wasn't completed after one time, but we did this a number of times, until we felt free of the burden of the Nazi persecution and the lice.

[Page 273]

After a short time, I got sick and felt a strong pain in my knees. I couldn't stand on my feet. The non-Jewish neighbors helped my sister take care of me. Bluma and Chanah took care of me with family remedies. An army doctor, who was brought by one of the non-Jewish neighbors, took care of me. Within a couple of weeks, I felt better and began to walk again.

In the meantime, several orphans from Stepan came to Milinsk, and they told us that there were several fellows in Stepan who were still alive. I began to plan a visit to Stepan, in order to 1) to see how much the town had been destroyed; 2) to hear who was still alive; and 3) to collect some of our belongings and our relatives' belongings that had been left with non-Jews at the beginning of the war.

At the beginning, the plan was postponed because we were afraid of attacks from the Bandrovechim. We had to take care of our daily existence. Therefore, the men who were of army age, were drafted to the army. Bluma organized a cart with horses, with the help of the Red Army. One morning I traveled with them to the forest, to the place where we hid, and by the shack, we took out potatoes and some grain from the grain that was leftover from our time in the forest. This involved great danger from the Bandrovechim. But along with the accompaniment of some Russian soldiers, the task was completed as planned. This promised us food for a certain period of time.

[Page 274]

Destruction of Stepan's Jewish Community

by Y. Koifman (told by Avraham Tachor [Musik])

Translated by Yona Landau

Edited by Mira Eckhaus and Daniel Shimshak

The Retreat of the Soviets and the Entrance of the Germans

I was fourteen in June 1941, when the Soviet army retreated from Stepan, and the Germans came in their place. To our surprise, even though there was great fear of the Germans, there was not a massive fleeing of Jews from Stepan. Only a few fled with the Russians, and most of the people of the town stayed. They hoped that they could "live" under the German rule. The first few days that the Germans were in town, they did not physically hurt the Jews. They began taking Jews to forced labor to fix the bridge on the Horyn River, that was destroyed at the time of the battles. They asked for all the gold and silver, but did not murder people. From the beginning they asked the Jews to wear the Star of David on their sleeves. After a month, it was obligatory to wear a yellow patch on one's back and on the lapel of one's clothing.

Transfer to the Ghetto

The situation totally changed in September of that year. Suddenly they began to make fences around the alleys that went out of the street of the synagogue. The next day they assembled all the Jews of the town at the market square and announced to them from this day on they were to live in the ghetto. It took a day and a night to move into the ghetto. They did not allow the Jews to take any belongings, except personal belongings. The Ukrainians raided the town, and stole all the Jews' possessions from their houses.

Men over age fourteen were placed in the area from the street of the synagogue to the area of the bridge; and women and children up to age fourteen were placed in the other part of the ghetto.

The crowdedness in the ghetto was unbearable. A number of families lived in one room. Despite the horrible conditions, they tried to maintain cleanliness and stay human. Food was very sparse: 150 grams of bread per person, a little soup, and a little bit of potatoes. Sometimes they would steal some food into the ghetto, but it was dangerous.

The Seder Night in the Ghetto

I will never forget the seder night in the our apartment. We all gathered together -- father, mother, my brother Yitzhak, grandfather Rabbi Zoniya Koifman, Moshe Koifman and his wife Hudal, Moshe Bebchuk,

[Page 275]

Shlomo Neiman and Yerachmiel Koza. The mood was very low. The food was very sparse, a little potatoes, and a thing of pitah, to remind us of matzah. Grandfather Zoniya began reading the haggadah in a very depressing manner. After "the meal", Shlomo Neiman began to defy G-d and asked grandfather: "You are thought to be a righteous man, tell me, why do we deserve this, why did G-d choose us to be trampled and viciously attacked? Maybe He doesn't see how they are mistreating us?" Suddenly grandfather got up from his seat, his face got pale, and he raised his hands upward and screamed in a voice not like his: "G-d of the universe, I do not question your actions, I have no doubt in your existence, I receive with love and understanding all the suffering that is upon us, because You are One, Your Name is One, and there is no one like You. I didn't comprehend these words of blasphemy that were heard here. I believe in You with great faith…".

Everyone was totally silent and the atmosphere was heavy. In order to honor grandfather, the argument was not continued. Till this day, I remember grandfather from that night.

The Picking of the "Judenratt"

In August, the Germans requested that the "Judenratt" be chosen, that its task was to keep order in the ghetto, to pick the Jewish police, and to mediate between the German government and the Jews. There was an argument as to who should be the head of the Judenratt, and in the end Yosef Wachs was chosen, a Jew who knew how to speak German and they thought he would "get along" with the government some how. Wachs was not the nicest of Jews and many times he was more harsh than the Germans required.

There were Ukrainian and Jewish guards on the gates of the ghetto. It was possible to steal out of the ghetto sometimes, and I did it many times, but it was very dangerous. There began the cutting of hair and the shaving of beards of the Jews. I remember that my grandfather begged that he would not have to do this. But when this did not help, he wrapped his beard in an envelope and asked his son, Moshe to bury his beard with him when the time came.

Suddenly they began to request from the Judenratt to send Jews to forced labor camps in Kostopol. The conditions in the camps were horrible. Jews tried to get out of this, but Yosef Wachs always sent the amount of Jews required in the quota.

The Destruction of the Ghetto

In Elul 1942, rumors started in the town that something was going to happen in the next few days. We didn't really know what was going on in the world, it was all from rumors. The people of Stepan didn't know what was going on in the neighboring village, and the opposite.

[Page 276]

My father, Mechal Tachor, worked in the forests and in a German grain warehouse in the village of Botiki. I fled from the ghetto and joined him in his work. One day the manager of the warehouse came to me and told me that we can't continue working there and must return to Stepan. Our hearts told us something horrible was going to happen. We had no choice and the next day we started walking to the town. On the way, we met a Ukrainian farmer, who knew father, and he said to us: "Where are you going, yesterday they took all the Jews of Stepan to be killed." We were very stunned and didn't know what to do. We went to the forest, and it was father's intention to go to the village Sadliski, a Polish village. Many of father's acquaintances were from this village.

We came to the village and we entered the house of a farmer by the name of Lutzian Onichovski. He was a righteous man of the nations of the world. In his house, we found Yoel Baruch Becker, who worked at that time for the farmer in fixing his roof. It is clear that when we met him, it was very dramatic. Yoel Baruch was stunned to hear the horrible news of what happened to the Jews of Stepan.

Lutzian couldn't keep us for a long time and we went out to the groves in the area of the village and we hid there. One farmer saw we were there and informed about us. A policeman by the name of Grishchenko along with the informant farmer began to lead us to a cart back to Stepan. My father begged before the farmer and reminded him that he was once his friend. The farmer answered him wickedly: "New times have come, and we no longer have a friendship…".

On the way, we jumped from the cart and began to flee. I ran first, then my father, and then Yoel Baruch. They shot at us, but we continued to run. I turned my head back and I saw my father on the ground, and the rifle of the farmer was pointed at him. I continued running with all my strength, a long time past, and in the end I fell with no more strength. When I awakened, I found myself lying in a swamp. I didn't know where to turn. In the end, I decided to return to Sadliski to Lutzian.

I didn't see my father again.

Lutzian Onichovski, after hearing our story, took me in, and hid me in a pile of hay. In the evening, he would take me into his house so I could get warm by the heater, fed me, and give me to drink. Lutzian had a cousin, his name Michko, and he wanted to turn me in to the Germans. But Lutzian threatened him with his axe and said to him, if he would turn me in, he would kill him and his family. As time went by, Batya (Becker) Sheinboim arrived from the forests to Lutzian. He took her in, and treated both of us with love and affection.

Later it became known to me about the extent of the destruction of the Jews of Stepan. The Germans and the Ukrainians put all the Jews of the town on carts and led them to Kostopol. There were prepared pits, everyone was shot with machine guns, and buried there. One a few escaped as they jumped from the carts.

[Page 277]

My Way to Israel

The Ukrainians took over the Polish villages and destroyed them. I fled along with the rest of the Poles that were left in the area that was in the German's control. I crossed the railroad tracks by Antonobaka and from there I fled to the forests near Finsk, there the partisans were in control. I stayed there until the Red Army liberated the whole area. Since I was saved from death, it was clear to me that I couldn't stay on the cursed land of Poland, where all my loved and dear ones had been killed and I must some how get to the land of Israel. There was the only remaining member of my family, my uncle Yisrael Koifman. But before I left Poland, I wanted to see my hometown. I decided to return to Stepan.

On the way, I met a Ukrainian farmer and I asked him about the Jews of the town. He looked at me in a wicked manner and said: "They are there, even too many…".

I arrived at the town, to a valley of death. I found a horrible destruction. The city was empty of Jews. I came to the house of Yoel Baruch, that was somehow not destroyed, and I found some youths and a few adults. This was all that was left of a town in which there had been thousands of Jews, full of life and Jewish culture.

A Jewish Soviet army officer wanted to turn me over to Deniprofetrobsk so I could learn a trade, but it didn't work out and I traveled to Sarny. There we found some Jews, and when the repatriation of the Jews of Poland began, I traveled to Bitom. From there, I got to Czechoslovakia, from there through Austria to Italy. From Italy, they placed us on the "Antzo-Sirni" boat and we came to Israel.

[Page 278]

Memories of 1939-1946

by Benzion Bebchuk

Translated by Yona Landau
Edited by Mira Eckhaus and Daniel Shimshak

Drafting into the Red Army

In September 1939, about the week of Yom Kippur, the Soviets arrived to Stepan. On the market square before the entrance to the river, the tanks and artillery were placed. We, the sons of the town, got close to the soldiers and commanders of the Red Army and talked with them. We found out that there were many Jews in the army. During Yom Kippur, many Jewish soldiers and commanders came to the synagogue for all the service and fasted along with us.

The economic situation of most of the Jews of the town became worse when the Soviets ruled the town. Small businesses, with which was what most of the residents of the town were involved, stopped. People didn't come to buy, and merchandise was not available. In order to get bread, one had to wake up early, to stand in line, and sometimes you would come home empty handed.

The real troubles began when Soviet identification cards were given, especially for those who dealt with commerce. They didn't have enough work and there were rumors that they were to be sent to the coal mines in Dunbas, in Russia.

In this situation, a group of men went to work in Milinsk, which was 18 kilometers from Stepan (a small railroad station between Rovno and Sarny). The type of work was cutting wood boards. We would work there during the week, and for Shabbat and the holidays we would return by foot. Along with me were fellows like Chaim Gershon, Pinchas Began, Pinchas Magid, and others. The situation continued like that until June 1941, when the Germans attacked Russia. On that day, there was a huge draft. I was drafted along with many fellows my age.

The Draft Day

When I was on my way to work in Milinsk, on Monday morning, I was surprised by a messenger of the town council with a draft order. It said that I was to report to the city square before the post office at 12 noon. My mother prepared for me a package of food and things for the way, along with a prayer book and teffilin. I reported to the place, and there were five hundred draftees. We were led from the bridge to Milinsk and from there by foot to Sarny.

[Page 279]

I remember that many of the town accompanied us to the bridge. The draftees and those who accompanied us knew that this was not good news. Everyone was sad, with heart aches, and tears. For a few moments, I got away from the line and met with my parents; I worried about what would be. Would I see this poor town again, my parents, my sister, and the people of the town? (I didn't see them again, they were all annihilated.).

When we got to Sarny, we ran into German bombings. We were hungry and tired. We were put on a train to Kiev along with other draftees from the area and from there by foot, through the forests, in very bad conditions, including sleeping outside. Then they drove us to the Oral area. There we were organized into a work battalion, "the Satroy Battalion", whose purpose was to supply supplies to the front. We lived in shacks. Later we were moved to metallurgy factories in Sabredelovsk. Up to this time, most of the Jews of Stepan were together, but now they separated us. A small group and I stayed in this area until the end of the war. From here I left Russia, through Poland, to Israel.

The Jews of Stepan who were with me in Russia were: Yaacov Harojnir, Zeleg Tenyes, Yonah Tenyes-Weitznodel, Shmuel Sheinboim, Ben-Tzion Sheinboim, Pinchas Magid, Hershel Sanders, and Bryer from Milinsk.

Here is a list of the Jews of Stepan whom I met when I was wandering around in Russia: Nahum Leib, the shoemaker (today in the U.S.A.), Pialkov, Shrale the Gevetes, Chaim Dov from Tchertrisk, the two boys of Hershel from Korost, Yachniok from Korost, Vava, the son of the hatmaker, the Kerzner, Avraham and Label Morik (today in the U.S.A.).

[Page 280]

German Bombings and the Beginning of the Ghetto

by J. Pery

Translated by Yona Landau

Edited by Mira Eckhaus and Daniel Shimshak

The Jews of Stepan were depressed those days, the time of the retreat of the Russian Army and the rumors about the coming of the Germans to the town were greater.

A few of the youth who were active in the "Komsomol" left the town and retreated with the Russians to Russia. Most of them remained alive. The clerks of the Russian authority tried to convince the Jews to flee to Russia. But it didn't work and the Jews didn't want to do this. It was difficult to break away from a home, to wander, and to be a refugee.

Amongst the Jews of Stepan, there were a number of refugees who came before from a German controlled area of Poland. Most of them were of the opinion that life was not easy under the German regime, but annihilation was not to be expected. Therefore, they told us not to go with the Russians into Russia. This was the excepted opinion. But along with this, many had their doubts and they felt that a heavy cloud was approaching, and the Jews would become abandoned.

A few days before the Germans entered, the retreating Soviet lines were bombed and several Jewish homes were hit. Most of the Jews left on time from their homes to the suburbs of the town and were therefore saved. At that time the house of Altar Bass was hit. He, his wife Esther, his son Shabtai, and his daughter Freidel were killed. In the same house, Asal, the mute, Motel Koifman, the shoemaker, and his daughter Asal were killed. His son, Yaacov was saved at that time, but was killed during the annihilation. His oldest son, Shmuel, a smart boy, was taken prisoner by the Germans while he was serving in the Polish Army in 1939, and it was unknown what happened to him after that.

Another house was hit, that of David Bram. His two children were killed, his son Baba, and his daughter, Roza. Bram was hurt badly in his spinal cord, and was invalid until he was killed along with the rest of his family when the ghetto was destroyed.

Several days later, the Germans entered the town. The Ukrainians were happy, and helped to hurt the Red Army, they made ambushes and killed Russian soldiers. The Ukrainian villagers from the area of Stepan broke into the Jewish houses and destroyed and stole things of value. In some cases, the German Army guarded the Jews' houses so they wouldn't be broken into.

[Page 281]

After three weeks since the entrance of the Germans, there was a decree that all Jews had to wear a Jewish star on their sleeve. Jews were attacked on the street -- hit and humiliated. On the evening of Yom Kippur, there was another decree, to put on a yellow patch. There were Jews who had to cut their beards.

On the day before Succot, Ukrainian authorities were picked by the Germans to measure the area of the Jews' houses on Shkoolna Street and the alleys nearby. The Jews were placed with minimum belongings in the market square, and were placed in the ghetto in very crowded conditions. There were two or three families in a room. The ghetto was divided into three areas: a camp for women and children up to age thirteen, and elder people above the age of 65. A third of Shkoolna Street turned into the men's camp, from the house of Yukel, the Shamash, to the end of the ghetto in the direction of the bridge. The houses of the craftsmen who were allowed to live outside of the ghetto, were in the alleys near the ghetto, from the house of Moshe Yosel by the bridge and to the house of Itzik Meir Kogot.

A few days after the Germans entered the town, several Russian parachutists were caught. The Ukrainian nationalists caught them. At this time, they said that three Jewish farmers near Stepan helped them and hid the Soviet parachutists. These Jews were taken to the German authorities, and along with the Ukrainians, the Germans tortured them.

[Page 282]

How Could It Happen to My Town Stepan
"Eicha" to My Town Stepan

by Yitzhak Nunik z"l,
the son of Rabbi Ben-Tzion Hamelamed,
who made aliyah in the year 1934 and died in the year 1968

Translated by Yona Landau

Stepan, my town, a beautiful landscape, surrounded by wheat fields, forests, and plains for pasture.
Looks on to the Horyn River, that is the natural border from the east -
How do you continue to exist when my people were cut off from you with cruelty?

Generations of Jews were raised in you and in your surroundings to Torah and work,
They contributed from their capabilities and their knowledge to all the residents of the area,
With no difference to religion or race, --
How did you loose my brothers, my sisters, my people, their elderly, their youth, and their children?

How did you not hid them in hidden spots of your thick forests
and prevent the loss of my people?

How did you, the Horyn River, not wash in your great stream
the hatred of the thirsty for blood -- the predators?

Your roades are full of mourning and your houses are abandoned,
The synagogues are silent, defiled by the impure.

Is it possible that only the wind whistles the Orphan's Kaddish through the willow

[Page 283]

Amongst the Gentiles

by Aaron Grossman, a Survivor of the Town

Translated by Yona Landau

Edited by Mira Eckhaus and Daniel Shimshak

Aaron was a shepherd to one of the non-Jews of the area. It was in those days that youth went out of the ghetto in secret to be shepherds to non-Jews. The youth were fed and worked and even brought food to their starving families in the ghetto sometimes.

Aaron's mother with her children succeeded to escape from the ghetto when the Jews of the town were lead to the pits of death near Kostopol. The mother succeeded in getting to Aaron, and together they escaped to the forests near the village of Kaminka.

According to Aaron's estimation about 500 Jews fled from the ghetto and from the carts that lead them to Kostopol and fled to the forests. The Ukrainians lead by the Germans began searching and pursuing, and they were successful in catching most of the Jews who fled. Many of the escapees were turned over to the police or were killed by the non-Jews of the area, who were interested in gold, jewelry, and even uprooting gold teeth from the mouths of the dead. About 300 of the Jews of the town were caught within two days, who were in hiding in the ghetto, in basements and attics. Some were returned to the town council by the village and local non-Jews. This group was organized and killed by shooting near the forest of Hakolnia on the other side of the Horyn River. They were buried in a communal grave on one of the sand hills.

From the stories of the non-Jews after the liberation, several stories were known of sick, elderly, heavy, or those who refused to move from their houses, who were shot in their homes, some even in their beds.

In one case, a Jewish child was caught, the son of Minikal, Yosile Woschina. The child who was subject to pressure of threats and scared revealed the hiding place in the forest of the rest of the Jews of the area. Many of them were indeed captured at that time.

At the same time that Aaron's mother and her children escaped, but later they were captured and killed. Aaron, his sister Malka, and his little brother Avraham were successful in escaping at this opportunity. While they were wandering and hiding in the forest, they met their uncle, Yona Grossman, his son Yosele, and his young daughter. The uncle gave Aaron gold, and advised the children to separate from one and another in the hope that this way at least someone would stay alive. Thus Aaron, his sister, and his little brother separated from the uncle and his children. Another time Aaron, his brother, and his sister separated from one and another. His little brother was caught and killed.

[Page 284]

Aaron and his sister escaped from the fingernails of the murderers, because policemen were interested in their gold.

After several days, the non-Jews of the area told him that his uncle, Yona, gave all of his gold to one of the non-Jews, in order that they could hide and live together. The non-Jew shot Yona and killed him, and the little girl was wounded and died after three days of being seriously wounded. They buried her with her father in the same grave. Yona's son escaped, and after many tribulations, was saved.

There were only a few Jews left in the forests and in hiding, and when it became known to the Bandrovechim, the Ukrainian Nationalists, they tried in 1943, with all their force, to spread rumors that they are willing to take care of the Jews who were left and to give them a free and proper existence in Stepan, since they had rebelled against the German rule. The truth was different -- their real intention was to uproot and destroy in order that there would not remain any living evidence to the atrocities that they committed on purpose and with intention.

Aaron, his sister, and some other Jews, being desperate and suffering in the forests, even tended to believe the promises of the nationalists for a minute and began to move in the direction of Stepan. But by luck, they met a righteous non-Jew, who warned them that they mustn't go to the Bandrovechim, because their end would be bitter. Therefore, Aaron, his sister, and the other Jews listened to him, and stayed away from Stepan, and continued with their everyday tribulations in the forests.

One of the most terrible parts of everyday life was the lice. There were even some who suffered so much from the lice that they died. Hershel Magid was one of the victims. Shaul, the son of Shmuel Zilberman, also died from lice and from decay of his toes that froze.

Three fellows: Yaacov Rekes, Aaron Shenker, and a boy by the name Grover tried to get to the partisans, but on the way ran into the Ukrainians who tore them to pieces and killed them.

[Page 285]

Sea of Hate

by Y. Pery

Translated by Yona Landau

The hostility of the non-Jews of the area for the Jews of Volyn, Stepan, and the area was known, and the background for this hostility is well explained in "The Ways of the Days of the World", Volume 7, of Dubnov, Chapter 1, Pages 6-7 -- "The Tribulation in Poland and the Messianic Movement Between the Jews".

What stands out and is even painful is that it was not necessarily the simple people, but the intelligent Ukrainians in the town, those who were thought to be enlightened and noble, those who acted as educators and friends to the Jews, who turned their skin overnight and became haters of Israel. They had not patience and wanted to immediately see the town "purified" from Jews.

A personal example of this phenomenon was a senior educator, the principal of the elementary school in the town for tens of years, who raised and educated generations -- Harihu Damidiuk. He was one of the first and outstanding who signed the petition to the Germans, in which the Ukrainians, residents of Stepan, requested to get rid of, as soon as possible, the Jews in the ghetto in the town. Amongst those who signed the petitions were mostly the Ukrainian intelligentsia of the town.

It was known of additional Ukrainian intelligentsia who turned their skin, and sadistically enjoyed becoming the ruling authorities under the Germans. Sasha Karomaff, the head of the Ukrainian police and his helper, Kola Karomaff, the son of Tzatzik, who was on the police force, stood out in their sadistic actions toward the Jews of the town when he killed them with a machine gun with his own hands, and he was even in charge of this activity. There were many others.

[Page 286]

Between Life and Death

by Yitzhak Wachs

Translated by Yona Landau
Edited by Mira Eckhaus and Daniel Shimshak

Yitzhak, born in1918, in the small village of Vervecha, near Stepan, who grew up in a family of eight people, including five brothers and a sister. Yitzhak's father was a farmer in the village, and also had a factory of lime. We helped with running the farm in addition to our studies. We lived in peace and in good neighborly relations with the Ukrainian villagers in our area. There were three additional Jewish families in the village.

When the Germans entered our area, they stole from us cows and horses. Hooligans from the villagers began to hassle us and persecute us. At the beginning, there was a decree that we must wear a yellow patch on the front and the back of our clothes. In the beginning of 1942, we were moved to the ghetto of Stepan, which had 2,500 Jews in it. The conditions of the ghetto were very difficult: very crowded, rations of food, filth, and work for men from age 16 to55.

Since we were experts in making lime, they transferred me, my father, my uncle, Chaim Wachs, to work in the small village of Vervecha. We were there until August 1942. One day the Germans appeared in a car and took us to the ghetto. From the discussion amongst the Germans, I understood that the Germans intended to annihilate all the Jews of the ghetto. My uncle escaped to the forest, but was caught by the Ukrainian nationalists and killed.

When we arrived to the ghetto, I heard from everyone that the Germans intended to annihilate the Jews in the ghetto, and I began to plan possibilities of escaping with my family from the ghetto. My brothers, Chaim and Sheptel, were in forced labor camps in Kostopol. My mother and little brother Motel escaped from the ghetto and got to the area of the village of Vervecha by themselves. My mother and sister were caught by the Ukrainians, and hit to death. My brother Motel escaped to one of the friendly non-Jews, who was one of the few who still helped Jews with compassion and caring.

On the day of the annihilation, at dawn, I along with my brother Yaacov were put on one of the carts that led the Jews of the town to their death near the village Karchovila, ten kilometers from Kostopol. There the Ukrainians and the Germans had prepared huge pits, and the Jews were shot by the pits, and were buried in a huge brothers' grave, some only wounded and buried alive.

When the cart got near the place, Yaacov, my brother, and I decided to escape, and indeed we fled to the trees of the forest. Even though the Germans opened fire on us, we succeeded to escape. After wandering, we got near the village of Vervecha. We ran into an old non-Jew, Nalowyaika Vasil,

[Page 287]

who said that he was willing to help us. He hid us in his threshing floor, even though it was dangerous for him. After that, we found our little brother, Motel, and our other brothers, Chaim and Sheptel, who also succeeded escaping from the Germans.

The situation in the village got worse. The Germans along with their partners, the Ukrainians, increased the searching from house to house, from threshing floor to threshing floor, and we were forced to wander and hide all the time in inhumane conditions. My brother Sheptel was caught by the Ukrainians and the Germans, and was tortured in order that he would reveal our hiding place. But he withstood the inhumane torturing for four days, and didn't reveal to them anything, and in the end he died.

I got sick of life, and at midnight I turned to the head of the Ukrainian nationalist gang in the village by the name of Helkon Zinka, who had studied with me in school in the past, and I said to him: "I have come so you can kill me." He responded: "No, I don't want to kill you. But I command you and your brothers hiding in the village to leave today, because in the end you will be caught by my friends and they will kill you." At this period of time, the nationalist Ukrainians began to attack Polish towns, and thus most of the Poles were centralized in the area of the village, Hota-Stepanseka, and they organized themselves for defense. We fled from Vervecha to Hota-Stepanseka. Here we were taken in willingly by the Poles as an additional work force and for defending ourselves together.

After several successful Ukrainian attacks in which they burned houses and fields, the Poles had to leave their last fortress in Hota-Stepanseka and to wander to Rechavlobaka, a railroad station town, and to live under the German rule. We joined them with several other Jewish youths from Stepan and the area. Since it was clear that the Poles would be sent to work in other areas of Poland or Germany, my brothers and I decided to move over to the area of Minsk. After wandering, we joined the partisans. My brother, Yaacov z"l, my brother, Motel, and I were in the battalion of the commander Kerokov. My brother, Chaim z"l was in the battalion of the commander Tankov. Thus we acted until we were freed by the Red Army, and returned to Stepan and the village, Vervecha. My two brothers, Yaacov and Chaim, fell in their fight against the nationalist Ukrainians in their desire to avenge the Jewish blood spilled.

I reported to the Soviet authorities about all the collaborators amongst the Ukrainians murderers. Some of them were caught and punished.

After that, I left the area and moved to Israel. I live with my family in Ashdod. My brother, Motel, moved to Canada, and lives there with his family.

[Page 288]

Forced Work Camp

by Yonah Rassis

Translated by Yona Landau

Edited by Mira Eckhaus and Daniel Shimshak

The Germans set up by the railroad track in Kostopol, on the way to Ferminka, a closed forced labor camp. They made a barbed-wire fenced area around the buildings of the clerks built by the Poles.

Yona Rassis, a son of the town of Stepan, was one of seven hundred young people who were centralized in this camp, and he tells this:.

In the summer of 1942, the Judenratt in Stepan was commanded to draft 200 youths to the work camp in Kostopol. The Shotz Plolitzi Ukrainians filled this task and at their head Comisar Ginter. The youths walked by foot to Kostopol and were surrounded by Ukrainian horsemen. The policemen hit cruely anyone who stopped walking or walked too slowly. Some fell on the road because of lack of strength. In the end, we reached Kostopol. We were housed in a courtyard or in some buildings that were surrounded by a barbed-wire fence. There were seven hundred youths from Stepan, Lodvipol, Brizna, Osoba, Derojna, and Selishitz Zoota.

The discipline in the work camp was like in an army camp. Every morning they would wake everybody and after a quick washing, they would take us out for the roll-call. If we didn't get in order quickly and in the right order, we would be hit and we had to do hard exercises, and running.

Ben-Tzion Lipshitz, a man of Derojna, who was amongst the seven hundred men in the forced labor camp told that the people lived on the top floors of the clerk houses, and below lived the people of the Shotz Politzi. This arrangement prevented the people who lived on the second floor any possibility of going down to the rooms without seeing the Ukrainian policemen on the bottom floor. The major work place was the government track (the saw mill) that was run by the Ukrainians. The place was filled with policemen from the Shotz Politzi. The work was hard. The management saved money by not using machinery since hand labor was cheaper. They took apart and loaded boards and beams, brought wood to the sawmill machines, pushed empty and full cars of trains, and moved cars from track to track. They didn't have set work hours. They worked according to the orders of the heads of the factory, and sometimes even continued working into the night time.

Amongst the prisoners of the camp were Poles and amongst them stood out a Catholic priest on whose back the Germans placed a red patch, like they did with the rest of the Poles. Before the end of the summer, when the time to annihilate the Jews approached, the Poles were let out of the camp. When there was no need to employ all the seven hundred prisoners at the saw mill, they were sent to work in other areas.

[Page 289]

Yonah Rassis worked a couple of days by Ginter and was sent a couple of times to work in the ghetto. When the prisoners of the camp worked in the city, they were brought to and from work in army order, marching in rows of eight. The food given to them was very little, twice a day thin soup and two hundred grams of bread. Sometimes their relatives succeeded in bringing into the camp a cart of food that all the prisoners divided amongst themselves.

From the stories of Yonah Rassis, it seems that guarding in this camp was not as severe as in the ghetto. When there was a fear of smallpox, he fled from the camp and returned to Stepan for two weeks until he was cured. The Judenratt of Stepan sent someone else in his place to work. After he healed, Rassis went back to work in Kostopol.

Ben-Tzion Lipshitz moved at the beginning of the German occupation from Derojna to Selishitz Zoota, the town his wife was born in, and was sent from there by the Judenratt to the work camp in Kostopol. He told that the Judenratt of Selishitz exchanged every couple of weeks its men in the work camp with other men. Near the time of the annihilation, the switching was stopped, according to German orders. The work quotas that were sent to Kostopol from the towns of the area were increased from week to week. Selishitz Zoota was required to send 25 men and later the quota grew. At the beginning, refugees were sent from Selishitz by free will, because in Selishitz they lived in very crowded conditions. When they finished sending the refugees, the senior members of Selishitz were sent.

Ben-Tzion Lipshitz had a head of the Ukrainian camp named Shvechinko. He was a kind of engineer who developed in the area of the camp workshops for metal shop work, carpentry, and other professions. Shvechinko was a moderate man and treated the people of the camp fairly. Ben-Tzion saw him only once go crazy. It was after the massacre of the Jews of Rovno. The Germans divided spirits to the Ukrainians after the killing. Shvechinko was drunk after the massacre, and when Ben-Tzion entered his area, he threw on him a bucket of coals, and it struck Ben-Tzion's head. But when he saw Ben-Tzion full of blood, he became sober and helped to put bandages on him.

Yonah Rassis told much about the abuse of the Germans and of the Ukrainians in the camp. Not only did they work very hard, but they were commanded, when they were exhausted, to dance in front of them in the market square, a sadistic hobby of Ginter, that the Ukrainians took upon themselves, and exaggerated even more so.

[Page 290]

Escape from the Beast's Claws

by Yonah Rassis

Translated by Yona Landau
Edited by Mira Eckhaus and Daniel Shimshak

The forced labor camp was annihilated on Monday night and the next day the Germans and the Ukrainians destroyed several other concentrations of Jews in the area. A few days before the annihilation, we felt that something was going to happen. A reinforcement of the Ukrainian Shotz Politzi arrived. They had everyday intensive training sessions, the guard duty in the camp was reinforced, and our movement around the camp was reduced. The guards would torture us for the smallest offense, and they would hit us very cruelly.

We were young and even though the living conditions in the camp were difficult, we were still healthy. We would ask each other: "Will we make the work of murder of the Germans and the Ukrainians easier and be like sheep led to be slaughtered?" The answer was clear: We have nothing to loose. It is better that we try to save ourselves than give our necks to be killed. We didn't have weapons, and the policemen had weapons of all sorts. We decided to flee. There were thick forests in the area. If we would just get to the forest, we would be saved. We heard that lately groups of Russian partisans appeared in the forest, and we hoped that we would fall into their hands, and would be able to join them. But it was difficult to find the right time in the days we had left.

On Monday, we went out to work as usual to the government sawmill. The guard duty was increased, and our movement was reduced. Work was finished earlier that day, and we returned to the camp. That afternoon, additional Ukrainian policemen arrived, and immediately joined the other guards. In the late afternoon and the early evening, they were busy with training and order exercises. We decided to do all we could to get away from the murderers.

The man who initiated and planned the massive escape was Gedalia. I don't remember what town he was from, but there is no doubt in my mind that he was a man of great courage. It began around ten o'clock that evening. The courtyard of the camp was lit with projectors, and around the area, armed guards stood with their weapons cocked.

One unit of the Shotz Politzi entered the houses and began to take us downstairs to the courtyard. They did this with the anger of murderers, with hits and blows. We went downstairs, and according to command, we got in rows of eight. Another unit of the Shotz Politzi began to get near us, and surround us. We felt this was our only and last chance.

[Page 291]

I was sure all seven hundred prisoners felt the same. Suddenly Gedalia, our leader, screamed: "Hura! Hura!" We all joined him in calling "Hura!" All the pain and suffering that had accumulated in our hearts, came out in this cry.

The Ukrainians and their German commanders were shocked from this cry of seven hundred prisoners, which expressed terror. We took advantage of their shock, and we jumped from the rows, and we fell on the enemy, pushed them, kicked them, and ran forward toward the gates. Our enemies recovered quickly, and began shooting. But we were able to get out of the courtyard and spread out. According to Gedalia's orders, each man was alone to save himself.

I never ran so fast in my life. We jumped over fences, pits, and barriers, until we reached the forest. It was very scary; the shooting was everywhere and whistled over us. Men ran, fell. There were those who remained where they fell, and there were those who got up when they fell and continued running as fast as they could. We met farmers who were on their way to the ghetto at Kostopol to steal what they could. Many of them stopped us and killed some of us.

That night we ran around the forest and from time to time we changed direction in order to mix the enemy up. In the end, many succeeded to get out of the shooting and danger area. After we got away from the shooting, we organized ourselves in groups and after a short rest, we continued walking the rest of the night. At dawn, we arrived at the village Pankov. It was difficult to estimate how many succeeded to escape. I think many escaped, but after that the Germans began the big hunt in the forest. The Germans promised the residents of the villages that for every living or dead Jew brought to their headquarters, they would receive a "prize", a kilogram of salt. The farmers were tempted, and many of us paid our lives for a kilogram of salt.

We were a small group of Jews. We met in the Chadnik forest Lazar Salfoi from Kostopol, his wife, his daughter, and his little son. We put up two booths that nights and slept there that night. After a couple of days, the Salfoi family and I were trapped in the forest by a gang of Ukrainians from Andra. They ordered us to raise our hands and they searched us. I was used to this from the saw mill. I lay down on the floor, jumped away from them, and began running. They shot in my direction and wounded my hand, but didn't catch me. I was saved from death. I saw how they murdered the whole Salfoi family one after the other. The little boy who remained asked for mercy, but they hardened their hearts and killed him.

When we were in the forest, it became known to us that on the night of our escape, the ghetto of Kostopol was annihilated.

[Page 292]

Stories of Escapees

by Y. Pery

Translated by Yona Landau
Edited by Mira Eckhaus and Daniel Shimshak

There are survivors of Stepan who fled from the pits or the carts of death, and succeeded after many tribulations and hiding, to go through the war and be liberated by the Russians in the beginning of 1944. Most of them were youths or children that succeeded in escaping with or without their parents, to slip into the forests or to far off villages.

One group escaped instinctively to the direction of Korost, a Ukrainian village area, as they fled along the Horyn River. Everyone tried to stay away and flee, and there was no kind of communication between one and another. Many times one would try to stay away from another from fear of being discovered, if they were in a big group.

Many of the escapees were caught by the Ukrainian villagers and were turned over to the Germans, because of their hatred for the Jews, or because they wanted to steal golden teeth, and gold of those murdered.

Part of this group met about the time of the Soviet liberation at the beginning of 1944 in the forest, by the Polish town of Kerchon, by Milinsk. They were: Yona Rassis, the son of Shmuel Rassis, the grandson of Rabbi Yukel, the Shamash; Shimon Bongart, the son of the baker (After the Soviet liberation, he volunteered to avenge the Ukrainians who cooperated with the Germans. During his army service, he was lost track of.); Chana Shenker, the daughter of Rebbi Nahman, the glazier; Yeshayahu and his sister, Sosel (Sara) Prishkolnik from the Gotas family; Leah, Sonia, Devora, and Moshe Woschina from Korost near Stepan, who are today in Canada though Devora stayed in Russia; the brothers Mania and Avraham Yabniok from Korost and their brother Yosel who fell to the hands of the Ukrainian nationalists though after freedom by the Soviets, and their brother Aaron who fell while serving in the Red Army; Nehemia Weinstein who stayed in Russia, his brother Chaim z"l who was shot by mistake by the Polish partisans in the forest; Shoshana- Rezel, Rachel Sara, and Avraham Chait, and Avraham Binyamin who was killed by the Ukrainian murderers while volunteering to catch the collaborators of the Nazis, the Ukrainian nationalists.

Another group of survivors of Stepan who escaped from the pits of death or on the way to the pits of death were mostly youths and children who fled to the direction of the "Hota" of Stepan, in a Polish rural area. There many were caught by the Ukrainian police and by locals. A few survived, youths who were separated from their parents.

[Page 293]

There were those who from the beginning hid on farms that were far off from well populated areas, by friendly non-Jews, and paid them. There were those who betrayed the Jews for money or because they hated Jews.

Amongst the stories of the survivors, it is known of these cases of those who were caught and killed: the wife of Ben-Tzion Sheinboim and her children z"l; the father of Michael Patshnik, Yaacov z"l; the father of Avraham Tachor, Michael z"l; the father of Yitzhak Woschina, Dodla z"l; the father of Hershel Magid, Yosef z"l, who hid amongst the non-Jews almost up to the liberation and in the end was killed by the Bandrovechim, as his wife Freidel and her sons Hershel and Eliyahu were saved; Yonah Grossman; and many others for whom facts about them are unknown.

Those who remained living in this group were close to Polish villages in this area until they were attacked by the Ukrainian nationalists. They helped the Poles to defend themselves at the beginning, and in the end they wandered along with the Poles. Some of them, mainly girls: Batya Becker, Feril Bebchuk, and Henia who passed the war with Arian papers in work camps in Germany, and the rest of the youths were near the areas of the partisans in the area of the swamps of Finsk. Thus they went through the war until the Soviet liberation at the beginning of 1944, and went back to Stepan. From Stepan they continued to Israel via Poland. Some moved to the United States and to Canada.

The survivors of this group were: Rezel Kagan, Michael Patshnik, Shendel Bass, Avraham Tachor, Aaron Grossman, Malcha Grossman, Luzar Vasrashtrom, Shika Becker, Shlomo Greenstein, Yaacov Greenstein, Batya Becker, Ferel Bebchuk, Motel Weismann, Heiyna Helnakas, the butcher, Sonia Winer, Beila Bebchuk, Shmuel, the tailor (Korzak), who was killed when he volunteered to avenge the Ukrainian nationalists, Yitzhak Veshchina, the son of Dodel, Yoski Grossman, the son of Yonah, Shlomo Ronkas, the grandson of the Melamed Menibel (who remained in Poland), and Freidel Magid with his sons, Hershel and Eli.

[Page 294]

Escape from the Murderers

by Batya Sheinboim (from the Becker family)

Translated by Yona Landau
Edited by Mira Eckhaus and Daniel Shimshak

Batya, with her mother and her little sister Brendala, Bronia Sheinboim with her children, Henia Tachor, Batya Tachor, Sonia from the Tachor family with her baby, all escaped the carts that went to Karchovla, ten kilometers from Kostopol, the place of killing of the Jews of Stepan and the area.

Most of them jumped from the carts and tried to flee to the forests, knowing that death was near. They were caught in the shooting of the Ukrainian policemen and some were caught and returned to the carts that led them to their deaths. Henia Tachor and her grandchild were caught and killed. The rest escaped to the forests and got to the area of Kamionka. There they met Jews of other towns. The tribulations of the forest were many -- hunger, lice, fear of every leaf that moved, wandering from place to place because of searches by the Ukrainians in the German command who were accompanied by dogs, the danger of being murdered, or being turned over to the police by the same non-Jews who we turned to for help, for bread or for hiding.

It happened that a non-Jew turned against us because of his hate for Jews or because of the desire for money, gold, or jewelry of the refugees.

The feeling of being chased was very strong and people were very scared. In one case, Aaron and Brendala Becker hid in back of a pile of hay, and on the other side of the same pile, another Jew hid. When they heard a noise on the other side of the pile, both sides became very scared, until they found out about each other and they learned their real identities.

Aaron Grossman tells that the strong people had the ability to survive in the conditions of the forest and the hostile surroundings. For example, it is told of Brendala Becker, a thin girl with curly hair, that she was very brave and carried her burden in those crazy times. She would go to the houses of the non-Jews, even though it was very dangerous, and would return with a lot of food to the forest to the hiding place of her sister, her mother, and the rest of the people of the town. After a while, she was caught along with Sonia Tachor. They were taken to the town, tortured, and killed. The mother of Batya, Bonya Tachor, couldn't take the tribulations of the forest and died in the forest. Bronya Shenboim and her children were caught and killed.

After additional searches and living together with eighteen Jews from her area in the depths of the forest in inhumane conditions, with fear and terror always, Batya was left alone. She finally got to a righteous non-Jew,

[Page 295]

a Pole by the name of Lutzian Onochobaski, from the Polish village of Sadlisko. He hid her. The woman being very religious asked the priest from Virka, a near by Polish village, and he suggested to her to help the Jews even though it was dangerous. Within a short time, Avraham Tachor came to the same town and stayed with the same non-Jew, Mosik, along with Batya. One of the relatives of Lutzian who hated Jews and was very violent, tried to turn Mosik in to the authorities. But the non-Jew who was hiding the Jews threatened to kill the family of the violent relative. Thus the danger passed.

In 1943, when the Ukrainian uprising began in Stepan and the area against the German authorities and attacks on Polish villages began in order to annihilate the Polish residents, Batya and Mosik wandered together along with other Poles to nearby towns and cities. There Batya met two Jewish girls from Stodin, by the names of Fayeh and Etta. Together along with five Poles from the area of Recholovka (a railroad station) turned to the direction of the forests, in order to join the partisans. On the way, they ran into shooting by the Ukrainian nationalists and most of the group was killed.

Batya returned to Recholovka, and with the girl from Stodin by the name of Ita Shinis, they traveled as Poles to Germany by Sarny and Rovno. They fixed their papers and were on their way. They were scared that they would meet a non-Jew who knew them and would identify them as Jews. Thus they went through the war with double identities, and survived. In one case, Batya met a Jewish girl, Henia, the daughter of Helenka, the butcher. But each one didn't pay attention to each other because they were afraid that they would reveal that they were Jews.

[Page 296]

The Story of Sonia Weiner -- Escapee
Testimonies from the Death Pits

By Sonia Weiner

Translated by Yona Landau

From one of the survivors, Sonia Weiner, it became known that she had succeeded to escape naked from the death pits, while she was placed there by the Ukrainian police under the German command. After many tribulations and wanderings, hiding in the forest and by non-Jews, she survived. She is in Canada today.

A similar story was heard from one of the survivors, a village Jew from Vorvachia, who escaped after he was thrown into the pit with the rest of the Jews. When it got dark, he awakened, being totally covered with blood, and escaped to the forest.

[Page 297]

The Struggle for Life

By Fredel Magid (from the Weingarten family)

Translated by Yona Landau
Edited by Mira Eckhaus and Daniel Shimshak

My husband, Yosel Magid, worked as a professional miller outside the ghetto and outside of the town, and didn't return to live in the ghetto.

On the night of the massacre of the Jews of the ghetto, I succeeded with my little son, Eliyahu, to escape from the Ukrainian policemen who directed the Jewish convoy to get onto the carts. I lost my son Hershel when I escaped. I ran in the direction of the cemetery, in order to hide amongst the graves and bushes. Here I met a friendly non-Jew who suggested to me to get away from the cemetery because they would easily find me there and kill me. I continued fleeing along with my little son, and we got to a farm area named Polinka, isolated and far from the town. Here we hid in the threshing floor without the permission of the farmer. When the farmer found us out, he gave us food and asked us to leave the place because he was afraid something would happen to him.

We continued to flee at night, and we got to the village Komrivka, through the forest. On the way, we saw dead bodies floating on the Horyn River. They were the bodies of Jews who jumped from the carts to the river at the time the carts were lead to the death pits. There were those who jumped to the river in order to escape what was to happen and there were those who committed suicide.

When I arrived at Komrivka, I turned to one of the non-Jews. He was a religious non-Jew. He was compassionate to us and hid us in a pile of hay in his threshing floor. With the aid of this non-Jew, I made contact with my husband, and it became known to me that my son Hershel survived and was with my husband. After a couple of days, my husband, Yosef, joined me, and we spent a couple more days in the threshing floor of that righteous non-Jew who helped us when we were in danger.

One night, when the farmer brought us our daily portion of food, he told us that we must leave that night because the Bandrovechim arrived at the village and were searching for surviving Jews in order to kill them.

That night, we carefully left the threshing floor to the forest, and we arrived, after a night of wandering, to the nearby village Valoshin. Here we convinced a non-Jew to hide us and for gold that we had, he agreed to hide us in a pit in his threshing floor. The conditions in the pit were horrible. Water and food were given to us very sparingly. We mostly lacked drinking water. We developed a method of melting ice in our hands. These pieces of ice froze on the damp walls of the pit at night, and thus we had the addition of water for our use.

[Page 298]

We were hidden by this farmer for a couple of months, and when we had no more money, he told us to leave. We went to another non-Jew in the area, who was a very religious Christian and feared G-d. He thought that he would convince us to convert to Christianity. But along with this, he helped us with food and hiding. Every night, he would visit us in the threshing floor, and try to convert us to Christianity.

At the end of 1943, the Ukrainian nationalists threw out the last few Germans authorities from the town, and proclaimed an independent Ukrainian rule. They said that every Jew who would leave his hiding place would be given good treatment and would be allowed to work in his profession in order to make a living. My husband, Yosel, being needed in his profession as a miller of flour, believed, in all innocence, the Ukrainian promise. He left his hiding and came before the Ukrainians in rule at that time in the town. They indeed employed him for a period of time as the main miller of the heads of the town. We changed our hiding place closer to the suburb of the town, "the colony", on the other side of the bridge. Here we were hid by a non-Jew we knew.

One morning the non-Jew announced to us that the Bandrovechim killed my husband along with some other Jews who were under their care. That was six weeks before the Soviets entered the town. The non-Jew suggested to us to flee immediately because the Bandrovechim will also look for us in order to kill us. Therefore, I took my two children and fled to the village, Voloshin. There we were hid by the compassionate non-Jew again. One day my little son noticed in a crack in the door of the threshing floor the uniform of a Russian soldier. Thus it became known to us the fall of the Germans and the Bandrovechim.

In the beginning of 1944, we moved back to Stepan, which was empty of Jews. We were amongst the few who survived. Within a couple of days, some girls and fellows joined us as they left their hiding places and were left refugees. Within a short time, we left our town, and traveled to Poland, and from there to Germany, and we immigrated to America, where I live with my two sons, each of whom raised a family of his own.

[Page 299]

The End of Stepan

By Meir Grinshpan

Translated by Yona Landau

During the first part of July 1941, the Red Army began to leave Galilot, Volyn , and Polisia. During the middle of the month, they left Stepan, which was twenty kilometers from the train station Mokbin, and forty kilometers from Darajna. The hearts of the Jews trembled, when rumors spread that the Germans were getting near the town from the side of Lootzak and the village Tzoman. On the eighteenth of July 1941, the town was conquered by the Germans.

On the first days of the new rule, there was barely felt a bad relation by the Germans toward the Jews. If something happened, they said it was because of the transition of the authorities. But when the Ukrainians got close to the Germans and began to help them, we began to feel the cruelty and insolence of the Germans. The Germans and their helpers began to cut the beards of the Jews, to steal their possessions, to ruin synagogues and holy articles, and to hit Jews on the street. Within a short time, the Jews were forced to wear a yellow patch on their clothes, they were limited in their movements, and were forced to do forced labor in difficult conditions.

For half a year the situation continued the same way. But horrible news arrived about the acts of the Nazis toward Jews in other places. The panic and the bewilderment grew in the town. Life got more difficult from day to day. At the beginning of 1942, the Germans set up a ghetto in Stepan for the Jews and ordered the Jews of Stepan and the village Jews from the area to move into the ghetto. They were not allowed to take their possessions with them, except hand luggage. One cannot imagine the situation of those taken from their homes, leaving their possessions to be stolen, and locked up in the ghetto under strict control. There were those who tried to escape, hide, and not enter the ghetto, or even flee from the ghetto in the middle of the night. But many were caught, hit, and returned to the ghetto.

The ghetto was in existence until August 1942. Many got sick and died in the ghetto, and the rest -- were sick of living. On that day, Jews were taken out, group by group, and led, some in carts, some by foot, twenty five kilometers away, near Kostopol. There were already prepared pits, and the end came to the Jews of Stepan. Only a hundred Jews escaped on the way and from the place of annihilation. The rest -- elderly and children -- 3,000-3,500 souls -- fell to the impure swords of the wicked and were destroyed from earth. Amongst those destroyed were people of the town and their businessmen: Pinchas Goldenstein (from the committee of the community of Kostopol), Avraham Noz (a dedicated Zionist), Moshe Yosef Dargoff (the head of the committee for craftsmen and the charity of the community), teachers, and others.

That was the end of Stepan.

[Page 300]

The Image of the Judenratt Chairman – Yosef Wachs

by the Editors

Translated by Yona Landau
Edited by Mira Eckhaus and Daniel Shimshak

Opening Words

It was a difficult task to describe the character of Yosef Wachs, the head of the Judenratt in Stepan. We had doubts about how to relate to his behavior and to the type of his rule over the Jews in the ghetto in the period of humiliation and depression.

The little that was written on this subject was sorted out after continual consultation and discussions amongst the members of the editorial board and some additional Holocaust survivor friends who felt the events of this bitter period.

In the end, Yosef Wachs was described by those who knew him well before the wicked rule of the Germans, and by those, who perhaps didn't know him so well, when he was in the powerful position of the head of the Judenratt.

The Description of Yosef Wachs

When the Jews entered the ghetto, the Germans through their collaborators, the local Ukrainians, made the representatives of the Jews choose amongst themselves who would represent them toward the Germans and the Ukrainians.

Therefore, the Jews of town congregated in the big synagogue and Avraham Goz was chosen to be the head of the Judenratt, and Yosef Wachs was chosen as his deputy. Yosef Wachs got up and proclaimed that he is not willing to be the deputy, but only the head. Avraham Goz, being a gentle and humble man, gave into Yosef Wachs immediately. The community accepted Yosef Wachs as the head.

Yosef was known to the Jews of Stepan as extraordinary, conceited, walked on the street with his head in the air, tried to stay away from relations with the Jews of the town, and was attracted to the groups of the Polish authorities and Polish intelligensia. It was known that he wasn't very sensible, even though he was intelligent.

When the Soviets entered and ruled the town, he tried to get a position, but was not accepted because he had property at the time of the Polish regime until 1939.

[Page 301]

When he was chosen as the head of the Judenratt, it was as if he was satisfied, his personal ambition was filled. He had an absolute regime. He organized the Jewish police around him. Most of them did as he said (except a few, who kept humane). Baruch Kreizer, Sheptel Yokelson, Avraham Weitznodel, the son of Korzek, were remembered for their humane behavior.

Yosef established as his holy goal to fulfill exactly, or even more than required, the requests and decrees of the Germans in all areas of life in the ghetto in that period, if it was turning over furs of individuals, fulfilling work quotas, or sending men to work camps. With this attitude, he made sure that there was a normal level of hygiene in the horrible crowding conditions that were in the ghetto, but made the living conditions in the ghetto very difficult because he went exactly according to the orders of the Germans. He punished those who dared to smuggle in food through the ghetto fence by hitting them and putting them in a jail hole. He also punished very severely those who dared to sneak food on their bodies when they returned from work outside of the ghetto.

From what some of the survivors said, he really believed that if his actions were acceptable in the eyes of the Germans, they would not destroy the Jews. But in the difficult conditions of life, decrees, and burdens too heavy to take, it seemed that Yosef's regime was not right. There were many cases where he played favorites. The Jews of the ghetto complained about Yosef's behavior, and viewed him as a collaborator of the Germans with regard to the decrees, the living conditions, and annihilation.

On the day of the annihilation, there were rumors that Yosef traveled to Kostopol to a representative of the Germans in order to try to prevent the annihilation, but he had no luck. When he returned that night to the town, he was shot in the back when leaving the building of the Ukrainian police.

He was the first victim that night of the destruction of the total Jewish community of Stepan.

The few who succeeded in escaping from the carts on the way to destruction were Mitak, his son, and the second wife of Yosef Wachs and a few other youths, among them Dotzia Goverman, who lost their lives when they jumped from the bridge to the river, as they guessed what was to happen to them by the pits.

[Page 302]

The Ruins of My Town

A Visit to Destroyed Stepan

by Y. Pery

Translated by Yona Landau
Edited by Mira Eckhaus and Daniel Shimshak

One day, I decided to travel to my town, Stepan, even though I knew that none of my family remained alive. I stuck close to a convoy of the Red Army, and with their protection, I arrived safely. Firstly, I turned to our street, the street of the synagogues.

The synagogues remained in their positions, but were empty. The doors and the windows were broken open and uprooted. The main synagogue was used for a warehouse for grains that were collected as tax for the government. Our house and the big barn by it were no longer in existence. I found an empty lot, and I could barely imagine where our house stood. Several other houses were dismantled, and there were some other empty lots.

Ukrainians lived in the several houses that remained. They were our neighbors in the past, and they acted as if this was their property always.

The feeling was as if life stopped in the town, and bereavement and orphanhood was everywhere.

I tried to talk to the Ukrainian neighbors, and other acquaintances from the town, and to try to get them to talk about the way things happened that the Jews of the town were taken in carts from Stepan to pits to be killed near the village of Karchovela, about ten kilometers from Kostopol.

Most of the Ukrainians that I turned to evaded the subject and didn't answer my questions. Most of them claimed that they were closed in their houses at the time, and they didn't know details except that the ghettos and the town were emptied of Jews, and that they were killed by the Germans.

In one case, I ran into a Ukrainian who was known as a friend of the Jews in the period even before the war. He was liberally minded, and was always willing to help. He described the following to me -- which he said he partially saw himself and partially heard from others:

The Germans with the aid of their Ukrainian collaborators organized three hundred carts harnessed to horses. The convoy was organized into a single file along the 3rd of May Street,

[Page 303]

in which they were turned in the direction of Kostopol. On that same day -- the eleventh of Elul, August 1942 -- the Jews were put on the carts at dawn, and led to a forest near the village Karchovela, near Kostopol. Thus two thousand Jews were led on their last way, surrounded by a large chain of Ukrainian policemen under the German command: girls, boys, mothers with babies in their arms, old men, old women, and cripples. During the trip, girls, boys, and men tried to escape from the carts. Many were shot with no mercy, some succeeded in slipping away to the forest, but most of them were discovered later on by the Ukrainian police.

Most were cuddled in the carts, some crying, some praying aloud, some silent, but their faces showed fear and terror with no bounds. These people did not try to escape as they saw the wild reactions of the Germans and the Ukrainian policemen, who killed with no restrictions when someone as much as tried to get off the cart.

A number of pits were dug and prepared ahead of time that turned to brothers' graves for the innocent victims.

The heavens, the earth, and the trees of the forest were mute to the total destruction of the Jews of Stepan and its surroundings by several brutal soldiers of Hitler and the Ukrainian collaborators.

According to stories of eye witnesses who escaped from the pits themselves, the Jews were made to run naked to the pits, being hit and pushed constantly, and forced to lie down with their heads in the ground. The murderers shot them in the pits. Many were buried alive.

It happened that about two months after this huge killing, their blood bubbled from the earth that covered these pits. Workers from among the Ukrainian farmers were drafted and forced to open these pits in order to spill extinguishing lime on those murdered, in order to prevent the spreading of plagues from the bad smell that came from the pits. Those farmers saw something too horrible to describe: babies, little children, elderly men and women, men, women, youths at a time of development and blossoming -- all lying on each other. The bodies were whole, and one could still identify each person. There was no sign of being shot by bullets on most of the bodies. This proved that most were buried alive.

A few days after the big killing, three hundred Jews of the town were caught, those who hid in basements, attics, or suburbs of the town. They were all shot dead. They were buried in a pit in a brothers' grave in the forest.

[Page 304]

Thus the Ukrainian summarized his sad story: "When I walked about the town after the murder, I relived that horrible act. It seemed to me that life had stopped in the town, the silence of death prevailed over everything."

The question is asked: how did this horrible event take place and people were destroyed alive after working and living their lives in their poor and modest homes? Will a day come when the Creator will bring before Him all those who murdered in cold blood innocent people, and tried to cover their bodies with sand in order to quiet and cover up the tracks of their malicious crime that will never be forgotten?

A mass grave in the forest near the village of Karchovela, 10 km from Kostopol - here the Germans and their Ukrainian partners massacred the Jews of Stepan and the surrounding area, who were buried in mass graves, most of them still alive

In the period of time that I was in my destroyed town, I met several youths who had a story that was similar to mine. There was also Frieda Magid and her two children, and also the sisters from Korost, Leah, Sonia, and Devorke, and their brother Moshe. I stayed with them. Sonia was active, and she helped me get police accompaniment, and to go to a non-Jewish acquaintance in order to look in her belongings that she was given to hold. The non-Jewish woman claimed that she didn't have anything belonging to us, and she barely opened the door of her house. Of course, after the threats from the police officer, she came around, and took out a suitcase of objects and clothes that were familiar to me. I received some of them and the police took the rest.

[Page 305]

I did this again, and I even got something. It became known to me that a non-Jewish acquaintance had some of our valuable articles, like my mother's expensive fur. I went to this man's house, but I met there only an old grandmother who told me that the non-Jew, his wife, and their son died of typhus. She didn't know what happened to the oldest son or what happened to the daughter.

I turned to a non-Jewish acquaintance who worked with the police, and he inquired and found where the daughter was. He knew that the oldest son was hiding in the forest with the Bandrovechim. That non-Jew took me to the house of the aunt of the daughter, Nadia.

As I approached the house, I put myself in danger, despite the non-Jew's warnings who claimed that he could not deviate from his way and be held up. I entered the house and I recognized Nadia's aunt. She gave me a warm meal, but she claimed that she didn't have any of our belongings, and that she didn't know where Nadia was. I began to threaten her that I would blow up her house, holding my hand in my pocket as if I was holding a grenade. In reality, it was a shoe brush. In the end, she softened up and took Nadia out of a closet. Nadia began to cry and claimed that she had nothing. After some additional threats, and after I claimed that the area was surrounded by army, she softened up and took me to her hiding place. From there, she took out my mother's fur, two expensive bed covers, and some clothes. I barely was able to take it all on my back. I hurried to catch up with the police convoy, but looked back all the time to be sure that the Bandrovechim were not chasing after me. There was such danger as they were in this area.

Again I organized the group of clothes and other items and joined a Red Army convoy on its way to Milinsk. In the meantime, there were several attacks of the Bandrovechim on Red Army units, and they also attacked several Jewish youths who served as volunteer policemen trying to search for the Bandrovechim. The heart ached for these victims amongst us after all they had gone through and for what they tried to do -- to avenge the non-Jews who abused and butchered their relatives.

I arrived in Milinsk and my sister was happy to see me alive and along with me a collection of clothes and valuable articles. It was possible for us to sell them and raise our standard of living, and to dress in a more human manner.

My sister started to go to an elementary school. In the morning, she studied with her Jewish friends, and in the afternoon, she took care of the home. Youths would come to us and we would host them as family members. My sister would even wash their clothes.

[Page 306]

One day, four non-Jews from Stepan entered our apartment. It seemed that they were on their way to join the draft of the army. Of course, I recognized all of them. They requested to stay with us that night. I agreed, but amongst the four, I recognized immediately one who hit me very hard when I was a shepherd when we were in the ghetto. At first, I thought to avenge him, but quickly I changed my mind. I settled for reminding the rest of the non-Jews about this situation, and I quoted the well known verse from Jesus: "You throw on me, and I give you bread." The non-Jew blushed and began to explain that he hit me not because I was a Jew, but because I was a shepherd who didn't watch over his sheep and my cows went on his cultivated field. Along with this, he apologized and was very sorry, and admitted that his actions were very stupid. Thus this case ended.

Since we weren't far from the front, at night we had to flee from our houses to the outside in order to find cover from the night air attacks of the Germans on the railroad tracks and on the railroad convoys that led equipment and draftees to the front.

On one of my visits to Sarny, I wasn't successful in getting a ride on the train to Milinsk. I had to look for a place to sleep for the night. The city near the railroad station was destroyed, bombed firstly by the Russians and now by the Germans, because it was the most major train intersection close to the front. I went farther away from the railroad station to the suburbs of the city, and I found a place to sleep for the night in one of the houses. It was a scary night. From the early hours of the evening until the morning, the bombings and the anti-aircraft artillery didn't stop. We found a communal shelter -- a large basement of a destroyed house. Around us, bombs fell very close by. By morning, the bombing had stopped. I went quickly to the train station that also had been hit by bombs and its tracks were hit. But the Red Army along with large groups of railroad workers improvised and fixed the major track which allowed the flow of trains to the front. I succeeded to get on one of the trains and to get to Milinsk safely.

This was another time in which I was saved from death.

One of the high ranking Jewish officers of the Red Army arranged for a group of youths from Stepan and Milinsk to study in a technical school in Russia, I think in Kiev or even farther away. They organized themselves, each with his belongings in his hands. After saying their goodbyes, they were on their way with letters of recommendation. After a little while, the youths returned. They ran into all kinds of criminals who stole their belongings, and in some cases, took off their shoes while they were asleep. When they finally got to the school in Kiev, they were accepted and given standard clothing, but the conditions of the school were very bad. Most of the students of the school were professional criminals. As most of the youths were orphans and were lacking experience in life, they became victims of theft, abuse, and threats to be hit. When they saw the situation that they were in, they organized and one night they caught a train back to Milinsk and returned home.

[Page 307]

The Yearning for Zion and its Fulfilment

When we were still in Milinsk, I heard that there were a few Jewish survivors in Brazna. One day I decided to travel to Brazna. I got to the train station in Mokion, on the way to Kostopol, and from there, I got on a very slow train to Brazna, and I arrived at Brazna. Here I met the Tzukermans that were still alive, Eliezar z"l, his wife, and their one son. Another son served in the Red Army, and also Zalman Tzukerman, his son, and a woman who ran the house, called Moshka. They received me nicely, and here it became clear to us that nobody from our close relatives remained alive. They reminded us that we have an uncle by the name of Efraim in America.

One day Zalman took me for a visit to one of the non-Jews in order to look for money and articles that my Uncle Yankel z"l, my mother's brother, entrusted with him. But the trip was in vain. The non-Jew claimed that he didn't have anything, and we returned empty handed.

Immediately when the youths from Kiev came, we began to organize to make Aliyah to Israel. We heard from Jews who we met in our trips to Rovno, Sarny, and Kostopol that there was a way to flee through Hungary and Rumania. Several youths got on a train that led them to Lemberg. From rumors, we knew that they indeed were successful in getting to Israel, but in a very difficult manner with many dangers. There were signs of an easier way.

Since we were Polish citizens until September 1939, we had the right to sign up to travel to Poland in the framework of the trading of populations between the Ukraine and Poland. We signed up in Rovno with the right of going over to Poland. But we had to wait our turn.

In the meanwhile, we were busy making arrangements for our trip with the clear hope that we might get to Poland. We heard there was in Poland an organization of immigration towards Palestine. We knew that we had a cousin in Tel Aviv by the name of Genia, who had been in Israel since before the war. We prepared a supply of food for the road, toast, and we packed our bundles that were with us, and we said goodbye to Bluma, our neighbor, who remained the only Jewess in Milinsk. She was waiting for her husband, Avraham Hakerchoni, who served in Russia in the Red Army. Even though he was an invalid, he did not get out of the army. Bluma and her little son, Perchik, waited with expectation and with impatience. Now she had to stay and wait.

One clear morning, we got on a train, and we arrived in Kostopol. Here there was organized a long train including Jews and Poles from Brazna, Kostopol, and the nearby area. The convoy was moved by a locomotive that led us in the direction of Lvov--Lemberg.

[Page 308]

It took a couple of days because the track line was full of army convoys that moved to the front and from it, and we were of secondary priority. It became known to us at one of the stations on the way from soldiers and residents that the war with the Germans was over. The Russians conquered Berlin, and the Germans signed a surrender pact. This made us very happy, but we were also very sad because all of our relatives and friends didn't reach this moment of the fall of the German murderers.

We continued to move forward, and after a superficial border check, the train passed the Poland-Russia border near the city of Feshmishel. We continued to move forward on the land of Poland. Here representatives of the Red Cross and the Polish Repatriation Committee received us. They gave us food and some monetary aid, and we finally arrived at our final station -- the city of Bitom in Shelazia. The city was rather destroyed, the residents were German. Many of the residents left the city when it came under Polish control. We were given a place to live.

A Visit to Defeated Germany

Amongst the Jews there was a rumor that it was possible to acquire used clothing in good shape at a good price from the Germans. Therefore, we went out to do business. We would buy clothing in the bargain market in Bitom, and when we wore clothes of the Red Army, we would get on the trains to Karkov. Here we would sell our merchandise in the market and make money. In Karkov, we would stay with groups of Jews in a house on Strodom Street. We continued doing this business activity. It kept us busy, but I began to worry about the future of my sister and me.

I heard from the senior clerks on the Jewish committee in Karkov that there was a possibility that my sister could be in a children's institution in Zakopna, where she would receive education, clothing, and good living conditions. I was very happy and I traveled to Bitom. I took my sister with me. Several other orphan girls from the tailor's family and other families joined her, and I brought them to Zakopna. Here I saw a wonderful institution run by Helena Kichler. My sister fit in quickly and felt very good there. I, wearing my Red Army uniform, would visit her from time to time.

One time a group of friends got organized and decided to travel to conquered Germany for business. There was a widespread rumor that one could acquire expensive articles in exchange for pig oil. We bought an amount of pig oil and got on the train to Lodge. Here I met my cousin, Moshe Frishkolnik and his friends who joined us on our way to Gadansk on the Baltic Sea. We were able to move freely in Gadansk as we were dressed in Red Army uniforms. We were able to equip ourselves with expensive clothes in exchange for pig oil. After this adventure, when we could see the Germans humiliated and poor, we had a feeling of revenge. We returned to Karkov, sold the merchandise, and continued with our usual business: Karkov-Katovitz-Bitom.

[Page 309]

Waves of Anti-Semitism in Poland after the War

In the meantime, anti-Semitism increased in Poland, and there was danger to the Jewish children in Zakopna. Therefore, we moved them to Karkov. My sister was put in a group of youths -- the Union of Zionist Youth -- with the purpose of preparing them for Aliyah to Israel.

Once we were caught by the Russians -- N.K.W.D. -- when we had large amounts of money and clothes that we acquired in Katovitz-Bitom. They arrested my friends and me, and held us in custody for several days. After interrogation and threats, they confiscated a large amount of the money and clothes, and threatened to send us to Siberia if we continue to travel on the trains. We saw that our business activity had come to an end. I decided to join my sister's group along with my friend Michael Fetshnik.

The anti-Semitic tension increased, and one night, there were rumors that a pogrom would break out against the few Jews left in Karkov -- refugees of the German sword. Several youths were placed on guard duty near Jewish concentrations in the city and organized self-defense. My friends and I, wearing Red Army uniforms, thought we could help in defending the community when there would be the need. When we heard the next day that the pogrom began, we went out to the streets to see if we could defend the Jews who were attacked. We ran into several efforts to attack Jews on the street. We got involved while speaking Russian. We threatened that we would immediately bring the Russian commander, and thus we were successful in the driving away the rioters.

Joining the Zionist Youth Group of "L'matara"

We were received to the kibbutz with open arms. The counselor, Yanka, interviewed me, and when she heard that I studied in the "Tarbut" School before the war, and she began to speak to me in Hebrew. I understood every word, but I couldn't speak. When she saw that I was embarrassed, she explained to me that it will come back. She was confident that after a few days of reading, hearing, and study, I will be able to speak well. And thus it was. After a week, I was among the few who spoke fluent Hebrew, and I was able to teach beginners.

The group of the kibbutz was very pleasant. We all were orphans about the same age. The counselor, Yanka, even though she was a bit tough, tried to educate us and make up for everything we were lacking, basic manners, elementary knowledge with regard to manners and general education. We took care of the house, cooking, washing clothes, and other services. We received aid from the Jewish Committee and the political party. Some of us worked for Jews and made money for all of us. The atmosphere was very pleasant.

[Page 310]

A group of graduates who finished the training before us left Karkov on their way to Eretz Yisrael. We were next. We trained ourselves for what was to come. We prepared appropriate clothing, back-packs, learned Hebrew, Zionism, and general knowledge. I was active in teaching Hebrew to those my age who were beginners. There was good cooperation among everyone. My sister was very well liked. It was our turn to make Aliyah.

The Beginning of Immigration to Israel

After traveling on the train, we arrived at the border point between Poland and Czechoslovakia. We passed the border as Greeks returning from the camps in Germany, but that only seemed likely, perhaps, to the simple policemen, because their commanders knew who we really were. In Czechoslovakia, we stayed in Prague. We visited in the city, and visited the Jewish archeology. We also visited the modern washing house -- there they washed clothes and dried them at the same time that we showered. This was very important and necessary for us. That reminded me of the taste of Paradise when I bathed in a warm bath in the bathhouse in Karkov, shortly after arriving there. This was my first bath since I took a bath in my home before the destruction.

After staying in a transition camp in Prague, we crossed the border within the framework of Aliyah Bet, and we took the train to Lifheim in Western Germany. There the people of the Jewish Agency, the Brigade, the representatives of UNRA, and the Joint received us. We received better food and were able to go the school.

The Agricultural Training in Germany

After a short time, we were moved as a group to Rithofen, nearby Ording. This was an agricultural farm of an SS German, and we stayed there for training. The son of the German, Stanger, and his workers were with us on the farm. They were excellent agricultural counselors, and they taught us how to carry out every stage of the work done on the farm. The work on the farm included cultivating the fields of vegetables and fruit, working in the big barn, running motorized equipment, and working in the chicken coop and the pig pen. The young Stanger was meticulous about work with himself and his workers. They guided us and watched over us to see that we carry out the work well and in an orderly manner. He personally gave us all sorts of jobs in the thorough manner that was characteristic of Germans.

In general, it can be said that we took the training seriously and learned a lot. I think it educated me to love work and to do it in a good manner. We learned how to run the farm, to prevent waste, and to appreciate order and cleanliness.

[Page 311]

My sister squinted as a result of a childhood disease. After she went through several tests, it was decided to operate. She underwent the eye operation in Ontaburg. She was in the hospital for several weeks after the operation and felt very lonely, especially because her eyes were covered after the operation. I tried to visit her often with friends from the group. After a month, she returned healthy to the group, and she was encouraged when she looked in the mirror and saw her eyes were like those of all girls.

After a period of nine months, we received a thorough agricultural education and learned to love work. We also learned general subjects, Hebrew, and Zionism, and we felt trained to make Aliyah. I think our good education was as a result of the efforts of our counselor Olek, who took the place of Yanka. Most listened to Olek and he affected us in a positive way.

The Illegal Immigration

After preparing our back-packs and clothing, we were on our way. We arrived by train to Lipheim and from there to a hall. In the hall, there was a convoy of illegal olim, mostly youth, under the auspices of the emissaries of the illegal immigration. They were dressed in U.S. Army and U.N.R.A. uniforms, and put us on American army trucks covered with canvas. Thus we traveled toward the German-Italian border, in the disguise of an army supply truck.

Passing Over the Snowy Alps -- Stealing Over the Italian Border

We were taken off the trucks and explained that we must pass over the snowy Alps and cross over the Italian border by foot. We were divided into groups of mixed boys and girls. At the head of every group was an activist of the Aliyah Bet, who was familiar and knew well which passageways in the Alps were good for crossing by foot and with the possibility of infiltrating the border without being caught by the border guards.

When we got off the trucks, it became dark. The goal was to cross the border at night, and by dawn to be on the other side of the border, then get on a train to Milano, where a meeting was set with the representatives at the train station. The marching and climbing on the mountains with each person with his back-pack on his back, was not easy. The weak amongst us, especially the girls, had difficulty and some even stumbled. But everyone helped each other, extended hands to help and took the back-packs of the weak. Thus we continued slowly during the night until we found ourselves on the other side of the border at dawn.

[Page 312]

Living in Italy

At the meeting point, it became clear that one group had been caught by the police and returned after a short interrogation. Of course the group did not despair and the next night, they crossed the border at a different point and this time they were successful. After two days, we all met again in Milano in Scola-Kadorna. There we were given a basement for living and learning quarters. We were there for several weeks. We got our food from the cooperative kitchen of the Joint. We spent our free time with the group learning Hebrew, hearing lectures, taking walks in the city, visiting the zoo and the opera. I was a Hebrew teacher for the beginners. I learned English with the help of one of the girls.

Later we moved to a fancy house near Rome. We were there for several weeks in much better living and food conditions. We continued doing the same thing, and after a few weeks, we were moved to Bari, which was an illegal immigration camp near the beach. The local Italians thought it was an asylum for those who survived the German quarantine camps. We continued our preparations and at night got onto the illegal immigration boats with the help of rubber boats.

Sailing to Israel

We, the boys, helped to get the people on the rubber boats as people were placed in the water up to their waists and held a tight rope. The boat was relatively far away from the shore. After several days, it was our turn, and we got on the illegal immigration boat, "Moledet".

The Aliyah and Being Expelled to Cyprus

After tribulations and the forceful resistance to the English, we arrived in Haifa. There we were taken off of the boat by force and taken to the expulsion boat to Cyprus. We were nine months in a closed and guarded camp in Cyprus. We developed activities, studies, exercise, training in self-defense, sport, etc.

[Page 313]

The Aliyah

In December 1947, we made Aliyah with the youth Aliyah within the framework of the monthly quota of the English. We were several days in Atlit, a closed camp guarded by the Arab Legion.

In Palestine, the riots began, and we were moved to Kibbutz Tel Yitzhak. Here we worked half a day in different agricultural and service work, and half a day we completed our school studies. At night, we guarded the kibbutz, and even guarded on towers in the area of Tel Mond, on the border of the Arab Triangle.

Within the framework of the Haganah, we secretly underwent training in the use of weapons, placing grenades, night ambushes, and Morse code. One of the boys by the name of Mordecai Kam z"l fell when he acted as a signaler in the defense positions in the area of Tel Mond, and he was buried in the cemetery on the hill of Tel Yitzhak.

The War of Independence continued. I was drafted in the I.D.F. in August 1948. My sister traveled to Jerusalem and took part in a course for children's care by WIZO. She lived in Beit Wizo in Jerusalem and I would visit her often.

In 1950, my sister, Sara (Sosel) married and raised a family. Her family name today is Kaplan, and she lives in Rishon L'tzion.

In 1951, I married my wife, Helina (the daughter of Shlomo and Rachel Reichman), from the city Seminovitz near Katovitz in Poland. I raised a family and lived in Ramat Gan. My wife, Helina z"l, who was also a survivor of the Holocaust, and made Aliyah illegally with me within the framework of the Zionist youth movement.

[Page 314]

On the 29th of Nisan 5736 (29.4.1976), fate was cruel to us, and my wife died suddenly and she was only forty-six years old.

May her memory be blessed! We will never forget her; she will remain in our hearts forever!

The late Helina Pery (née Reichman)

[Page 315]

The Avengers among the Survivors of Stepan

by Yeshayahu Pery

Translated by Mira Eckhaus
Edited by Daniel Shimshak

As soon as Stepan and its surroundings were liberated by the Red Army, at the beginning of 1944, the survivors of the town, who were boys between the ages of fourteen and twenty-one, gathered together and came to Stepan. The encounter with the ruin was extremely shocking. In the former Jewish alleys, everything was deserted and silent.

The fact that you met Ukrainian acquaintances and neighbors from the town, boys and girls your age, as well as old people the age of your parents and relatives, hit you harder and hurt you very much. Can it be possible; can it be possible – that they are alive, while the rest of our family members and relatives were exterminated completely, as if they have never been alive? The ache was great when we saw the people around us living a normal life and most of them using furniture and clothes that were looted from the Jews. A significant part of them lived in Jewish houses, as if the houses were their property since long ago.

This gave no rest either day or night. Horrific dreams were the result of the meeting with the bitter reality. We, the boys, concentrated in a number of abandoned Jewish houses and we had a commune life. Some of us tried to reclaim objects that were handed over to the gentiles during the German regime, but only a few succeeded in their mission and that was due to the intervention of the Soviet secret police, which in any case demanded its share.

Among the older boys were those who volunteered for the local special police to fight Ukrainian nationalists and search for Ukrainian collaborators. And there was no lack of such oppressors. We will not forget the young men who decided to take revenge and fell victim in the conduct of this war. The late Shmuel Korzek Hayat - a strong young man who remained the only one of his family, was committed to this task. He persistently and tirelessly set out on dangerous missions to look for the Ukrainian nationalists in the forests of Stepan and capture them. Like him, were two young men from Vebratze, Chaim and the late Avraham Wachs. The three men mentioned above died the death of heroes while on duty in their desire to avenge the pure blood of their people that was spilled like water.

A brave young man named Shimon Bongart, who was saved because he hid in the forests, also took part in the combat operations against the Ukrainians nationalists and collaborators with the Nazis. In one of the operations, he returned crowned with victory when he succeeded in defeating and killing one of the greatest oppressors named Daratz. After that, he enlisted, along with other survivors of his age, and went to fight the Nazis as part of the Red Army. Shimon's traces have not been known to this day and no one knows what happened to him.

[Page 316]

One of the girls named Sonya Woschina, from Korost, a village near Stepan, was very active and cooperated with the secret police to discover war criminals and bring them to justice. She spared no effort. More than once, she joined in the capture of the criminals, being armed with a firearm, and went on searches in remote neighborhoods. She encouraged us, the boys, to tell the police everything we knew about the activities of those Ukrainians, their look and their acts. She even assisted in repatriating property that was in the hands of the Ukrainians that they refused to return.

A Meeting in Stepan with the Town's Jews who Served in the Red Army

by Yeshayahu Pery

Translated by Mira Eckhaus
Edited by Daniel Shimshak

When I was in Stepan, I learned from those Ukrainians that a number of Stepan Jews, who were enlisted to the Red Army, passed through the town, heading west towards the front. The names that were mentioned were: the son of Itzik Meir Kogot, the late Gershon and the son of the late Yushtein – the late Ponka. All of them received a vacation of few days to visit the town in order to find out about the fate of their families. The gentiles told them in their own version about the fate of the town's Jews and their bitter end.

From the mouths of the Ukrainians who talked to the lads it became known that the lads were very upset and the expression on their faces testified that they were committed to take revenge on the Nazi enemy. After a very short period of time, the town council received a message from the Red Army, that Gershon Kogot had fallen on the Kovel front and had received the highest excellence award of the Soviet Union - "Hero of the Soviet Union". We also learned about the heroic fall of Ponka Yushtein, who also fell not far from Stepan in his war against the Nazi enemy.

It seems that other residents of Stepan, who served in the Red Army, fought the Nazis and had not returned`54 from the battlefields, they acted like the above two friends and sacrificed their lives to take revenge on the cruel enemy. These are their names: the late Aharon Yachniuk, the son of Rabbi Yaakov Yachniuk from the village of Korost, the late Herschel Prishkolnik, the son of Rabbi Yaakov Prishkolnik, the chazan of Stepan, the late Shimon Bongart and many others whose traces have not been known.

[Page 317]

In Memorium

A candle in memory of the people of our town and the surrounding area

    A candle in memory of the people of our town and the surrounding area, who immigrated to Israel, lived there and passed away.

May their memory be blessed forever!

The editorial staff

1. The late Gitel Bichonski (née Galperin), immigrated to Israel after the Holocaust, passed away on 30th of Av 5719, September 1959.

2. The late Tzipa Kolodny, immigrated to Israel after the Holocaust.

3. The late Raizel Kushnir, immigrated to Israel in 1935.

4. The late Yankel Gutman, immigrated to Israel with the outbreak of the Polish - German war in 1939.

5. The late Nuniya Hochman, may god avenge him, the son of Rabbi Herschel the shochet, immigrated to Israel with the outbreak of the Polish - German war in 1939. He served in the Hebrew Brigade, fought against the Nazi Germans on Italian soil, and fell in the line of duty there.

6. The late Rachel Jacobs (née Waldman), immigrated to Israel in 1936.

7. The late Gonik Yitzchak, the son of Rabbi Ben-Zion the melamed, immigrated to Israel in 1934, passed away on 18th of Kislev 5728, 1968.

8. Tanchum Bebchuk and his wife, from Yablinke, a village near Stepan. They immigrated to Israel after the Holocaust.

9. The late Tanchum Sheinboim, immigrated to Israel in 1935, passed away in 1936.

10. The late Berta Krokover, immigrated to Israel in 1934, was a member of kibbutz Negba, passed away in 1935.

[Page 318]

11. The late Yitzhak Weismann, immigrated to Israel after the Holocaust, passed away in October 1972.

12. The late Yechiel (Chilke) Bastos, immigrated to Israel after the Holocaust, passed away in July, 1973.

13. The late Moshe Bebchuk, from Yablinke, a village near Stepan, immigrated to Israel in the thirties of the twentieth century.

14. The late Moshe Avraham Zilberman, immigrated to Israel in the thirties of the twentieth century.

15. The late Adina (Idel) Perlmutter (née Bebchuk) late, immigrated to Israel after the Holocaust, passed away in 1972.

16. The late Yeshayahu, the son of Yaakov Prishkolnik, immigrated to Israel in 1930, passed away in 1935.

17. The late Chasiya Gorinstein, the daughter of the dayan Rabbi Pinchas Gorinstein of blessed memory, immigrated to Israel from Canada after the Holocaust and passed away in Netanya in 1974.

[Page 319]

In the Memory
of the Late Yitzhak Weismann

by Dvora Weismann

Translated by Mira Eckhaus
Edited by Daniel Shimshak

Yitzhak was one of the young men who, during his youth in Stepan, worked and activated the Zionist youth in the town.

At first, he was a member of Hashomer Hatzair and later moved to the ranks of Beitar and became one of the prominent Beitar commanders in the town.

Yitzhak was active, together with his friends, in introducing the Hebrew language and the Zionist consciousness into the hearts of the youth in the town.

Yitzchak grew up in a special family, a family of hardworking people, who were devoted to each other. The special thing about this family was that several uncles and aunts, along with their families, lived together in the same house, worked and placed their income in a common fund, in order to ensure dignified lives of all the members of the house - and all this peacefully and without quarrels and disputes.

His vigorous Zionist activity stopped when the Soviets entered the town in 1939. With the outbreak of the Russian-German war, in 1941, Yitzhak was recruited into the Red Army and sent to the depths of Russia. In Russia, he married Dvora, the cousin of Dr. Gorin, the famous dentist from Stepan. Even when he was in the depth of Russia, under difficult living conditions, Yitzchak did his best to help his acquaintances and the people of his town whom he met in Russia. The incident that is well remembered is when one of the townspeople, the late Chaim Salvotski, passed away, and Yitzchak sold his pair of shoes in order to burry Chaim in a Jewish funeral.

At the end of the war, it was only natural that Yitzchak and his wife would immigrate to Israel. And indeed, they immigrated to Israel in 1949. After their preliminary difficulties with the absorption as well financial difficulties, he managed to be accepted for a role in the Executive Committee of the Histadrut. Here he stood out for his talent and dedication to work and was well liked and accepted by his co-workers.

Yitzchak and his wife Dvora raised and educated their son Yeshayahu, the late. Yeshayahu graduated the Technion with a degree in structural engineering. He fell in defense of the homeland next to the Suez Canal, in the War of Attrition in 5730.

Their daughter, may she live a long life, is a lawyer by profession, started a family.

The fall of the talented and beloved son took a heavy toll on Yitzchak and after an illness he passed away from sorrow and great grief.

[Page 320]

Yitzchak was among those who encouraged and supported the idea of publishing Stepan's book. He described with great talent several characters of the town's Jews and made a considerable contribution to this book.

Yeshayahu (Shai) Weismann, may God avenge him

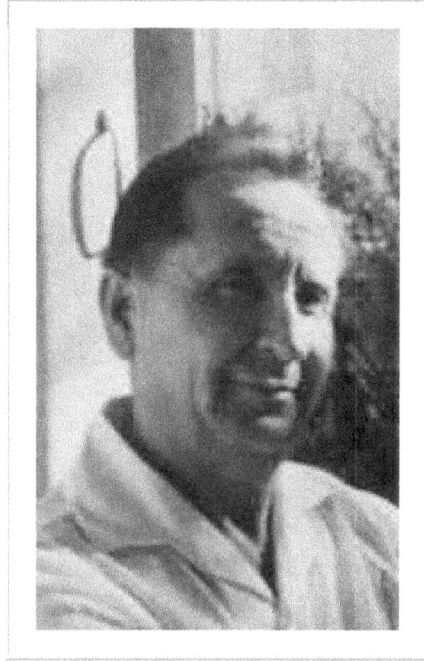

The late Yitzchak Weismann

[Page 321]

Epilogue

Concentration and Compilation of the Material for Stepan's Book

by Yeshayahu Pery

Translated by Mira Eckhaus

Edited by Daniel Shimshak

With awe and duty at the same time, I bore the burden of collecting the material, recording testimonies and memories from my townspeople, collecting photos and bringing up memories that were kept in my heart and that cried out to be written for us and for generations to come.

Most of the time I spent on this sacred goal was spent in my spare time after working hours. And so, I am very thankful for being privileged to reach the desired goal and to be an active partner in the establishment of a memorial in the pages of this book to my town of Stepan which was destroyed, and for everything that was in it and no longer exists.

While I was doing this sacred work, I must have been a nuisance to my family and took quite a bit of time from my late wife Helina and my children, may they live long lives.

How heartbreaking it is that my wife didn't get to see Stepan's book, being an active partner of mine in advice and even in action, and especially for the patience and understanding she showed for my extensive and prolonged involvement in this book.

I hope that my active part in this book will serve as a memorial for the holy community of Stepan, for all the members of my extended family who were murdered, and in memory of my wife, the late Helina Pery (née Reichman).

[Page 322]

With the Editing of Stepan's Book

by Yitzhak Ganuz

Translated by Mira Eckhaus

Edited by Daniel Shimshak

With the editing of the material that the remnants of the town of Stepan wrote and collected for the book, we became aware of the town itself, its history, its people and its scenery. And it seems that we were born in Stepan, we walked in its streets, we prayed in its synagogues, we washed ourselves in the Horyn River and in its forests we sought concealment and protection from the gentile soldiers that wanted to destroy us.

This book, which is only one link in the large-scale enterprise of the memoir books that appeared and will appear, and which were intended to serve as tombstones for the Israeli communities that were destroyed, and for the vibrant Jewish life in these communities, makes its contribution in the description of the life of the town before the Holocaust, and in the description of the tragic period of the Holocaust itself. A tombstone of feelings of love and longing, whose content is full of fire and tears.

Thirty years after the destruction of the town Stepan, the remnants of the townspeople recreated in writing a list of all the families in the town according to their dwelling place. This is unequivocal evidence that the town and its residents still live in their hearts, and that the memory of those whose lives were cut short by the Nazi beast and its assistants, is not forgotten in the souls and lives of the remnants. Despite the time that has passed and the long distance, their memory is not forgotten.

Fragments of evidence about shreds of life, atmosphere, struggle for life between the straits of doom and bereavement, in the ghetto, in the forest near the killing pits, after all, they are like a source of inexhaustible material for the historian, the researcher, the writer who is talented, has an understanding heart and a discerning eye, that they have the duty to create works that have impact and meaning for generations.

The chapters of Yeshayahu Pery's story about his wanderings and hiding in the forest with his mother, about his sister who stayed in the village among the gentiles, the description of the forced labor camp and their destruction as been told by Yona Rassis, excerpts from the testimonies of Yitzhak Wachs, Aharon Grossman, Batya Sheinboim and Avraham Tachor - they are memorial stones that we must pass on from a father to son, which must be bound in the bundle of eternal memories of the nation.

There was only one Jewish family, the family of Yankel der Kosmichover, among about a hundred Ukrainian families who hate Israel, in a small, remote and poor village on the main road between Stepan and Kostopol, and despite that, this Jewish family kept its image and character. We all should pass on its image to our children.

[Page 323]

In the book, in a thoughtful and careful way, the expats of Stepan expressed their reflections and their perception of the figure of the chairman of the Judenrat in the ghetto, a controversial figure, a subject for in-depth historical and psychological research regarding his role and his fate in the worst Jewish tragedy of all.

It was impossible to include in the book every piece that was written and I hereby apologize to their authors. These were things that seem to us to be of secondary importance against the background of the ongoing town life between the two world wars. These fragments of life and episodes found and will continue to find expression in the Israeli literature that was written and will be written about the life of the town at that time.

Among the chapters that indicate the depth of our brokenness and the intensity of the evilness of our murderers and haters, this memory will also be mentioned in this book, which serves as a monument for the crowned community of Stepan.

[Page 324]

Explanations of Words and Terms that Appear in the Book

1. **Odpost** - a fair bigger than usual - following the influx of masses of Christians as pilgrims to the churches in the town.
2. **Otlichenik** - an excellent student.
3. **Olyarnia** - olive press.
4. **Onotzes** - linen cloths for wrapping the feet before wearing them (instead of socks).
5. **Bodke** - a residential structure in the forest, made of tree branches covered with leaves and soil, covered with branches on top for camouflage.
6. **Brusnitzes** - juicy and sour berries.
7. **Ze Nesha Veshe Wallnostz** - the slogan of the Poles at the beginning of their independent rule in 1920, meaning "for our independence - your independence", and its intention is - we should all make efforts to fulfill our common goal.

8. **Zemlanka** - a well-disguised underground structure in the forest. It was used as a residence for those fleeing from the persecution of the Nazis and their assistants.

9. **Luchina** - a wood chip with a high content of flammable resin material (pine tree), it was used to light the houses of the villagers who could not afford to light their houses with candles or kerosene lanterns.

10. **Suchoi** - dry - very thin, low in fleish.

11. **Sinitzes** - wild strawberries.

12. **Pasteles** - a substitute for shoes self-produced by local villagers, braided from tree barks.

13. **Puchvalnaya Germute** - certificate for an outstanding student at the Soviet primary school.

14. **Felsher** - a practical healer, without any formal certification.

15. **Kolbesnik** - someone who prepares sausages.

16. **Cloister** - Prevoslavic or Catholic Church.

17. **Karchun** - the name of a Polish village - near the railway line Malynsk-Sarny.

18. **Koochma** - a round hat made of sheep's fur.

19. **Koromislov** - a yoke for carrying buckets of water from the river or the well.

20. **Kanchik** - a stick with leather strips on the end - used by the Rabbi in the cheder to punish his students.

[Page 325]

21. **Karbunchik** - a money note from the time of the tsar.

22. **Tzirolnik** - a book.

23. **Rosel Fleisch** - bean stew with garlic and meat – it is more acceptable on Friday's afternoon with a fresh challah for Shabbat.

24. **Repatriatzia** - at the end of World War II in May 1945, those who were citizens of Poland until 1939 were given the opportunity to emigrate from the Soviet Union to Poland within the borders after the end of World War II.

25. **Shul-Gas** - the street of the synagogues - the center of Jewish life in the town.

26. **Shteit-Of** - wake up - the call of the shamash at dawn to get up for the work of the Creator.

27. **Latkes** - potatoes fritter.

28. **Ladishka** - a specially shaped clay basin used as a container for milk and its products.

29. **Zoyere Milch** - soured milk - equivalent to leben nowadays.

30. **Kishke** - an intestine filled with grit flour and fat - a traditional meal on Shabbats together with the cholent.

31. **Zibeles Mit Ayer Un Schmaltz** - egg salad with onions and chicken or goose fat.

32. **Griven** - crusts of goose or chicken fat.

33. **Zlotovka** - from the word "zloty", the name of a golden Polish coin.

34. **Baz Trees** - ornamental trees with fragrant blue-lilac blossoms in early spring.

35. **The Vaal** - an artificial hill in Stepan, a kind of park surrounded by artificial hills with grass and trees - formerly an ancient Polish fortress.

[Page 326]

Family Photos

Translated by Mira Eckhaus

[Page 327]

The Adelstein family

Shaul Weitznodel family

[Page 328]

The Mendel (Toykch) Bastos family

**Yechial Bastos
– passed away in 1937 in Haifa**

**Moshe Aharon Tekes
- immigrated to Israel in 1934
– passed away in 1977**

[Page 329]

Pesel and Mottel Becker

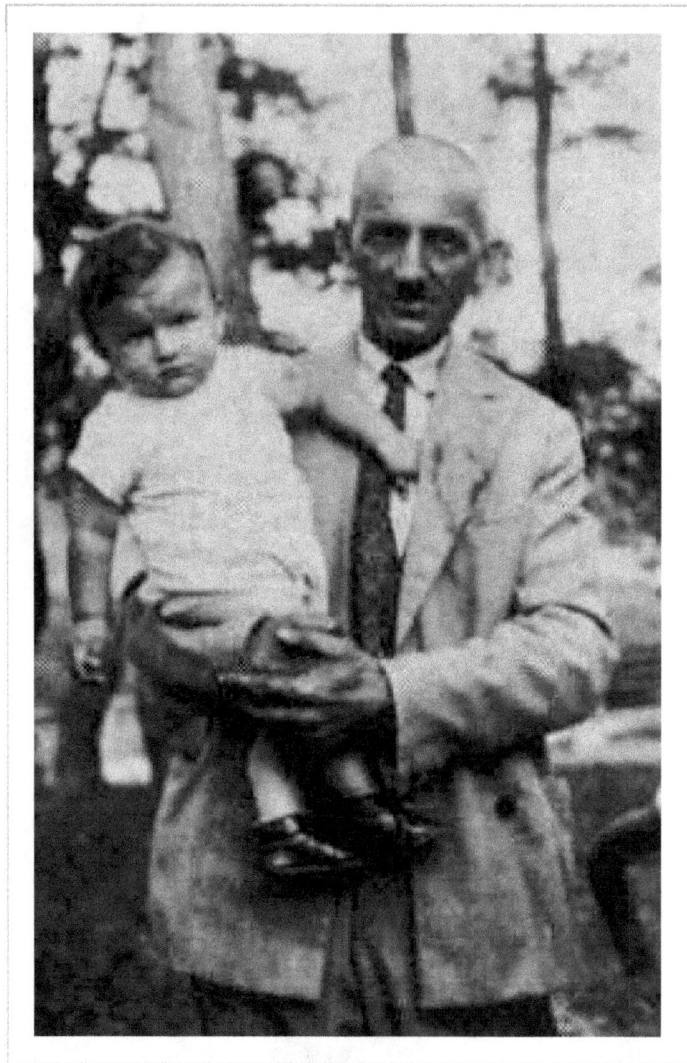

Meir Tachor with his grandson Moshe'le Sheinboim, the son of Brunia and Ben Zion Sheinboim, may they live a long life

[Page 330]

Members of the Woschina family

The children of Moshe (Minikel) Woschina: Yosa'le, Mirka and Ziskind

Yitzhak (Mirkes) Woschina, his wife Malia and their daughter Susel

[Page 331]

The Family Members of the Late Ben Zion Weitznodel

Ben Zion, his wife Malka, the sons Yona and David, the daughter Slova Mann, may she live a long life

Avraham (Meide) Mann, the husband of Slova. Slova, may she live a long life

**Hana, Slova's mother, who died of typhus in
Stepan in 1920**

**Slova's brother, who died of typhus in
Stepan in 1920**

[Page 332]

Some Members of the Weismann Family (the Motelikes)

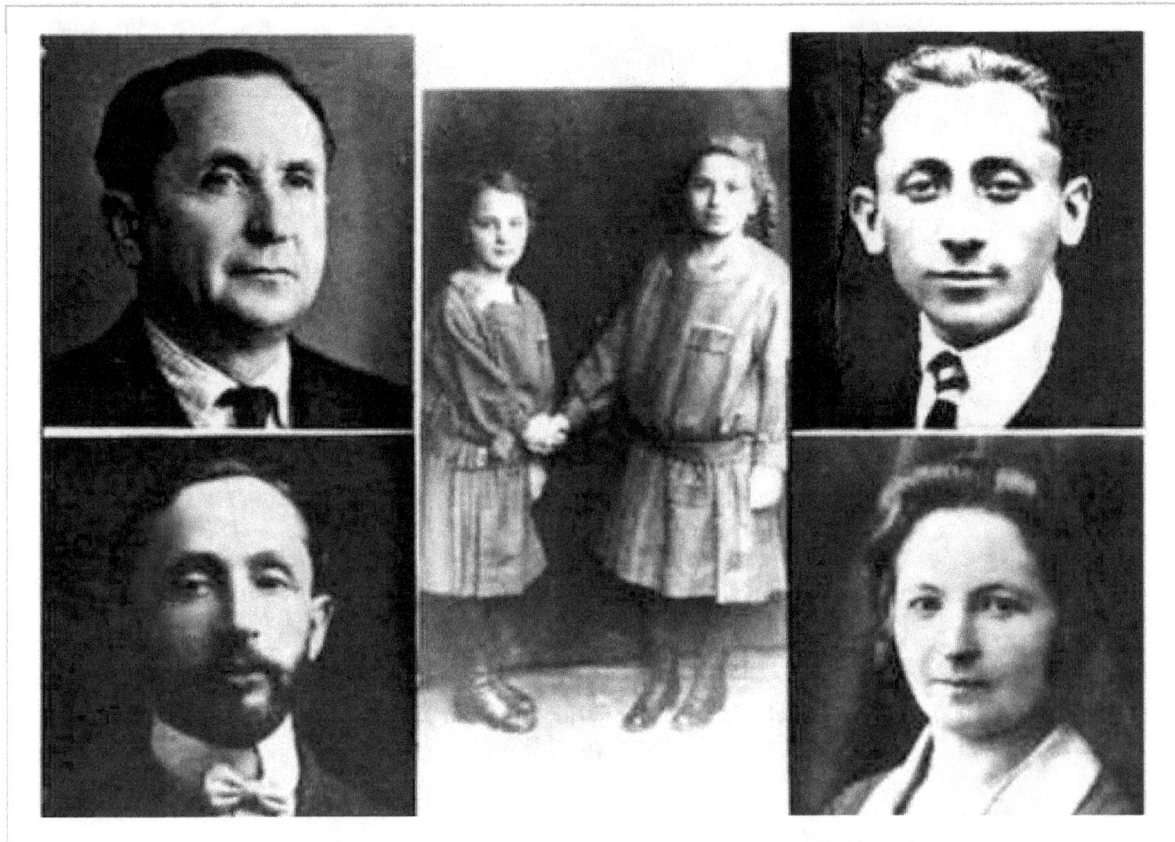

The family of Yitzchak Weismann (the Motelikes), Mordechai, Yitzchak, Gitel, Michla, and Gitel, the daughter of Simka Levin - Yitzchak's

[Page 333]

The Zelishnik family: Israel, his wife Hana, grandmother Zalta Kotler, the four children of Israel, and Hana

The Sheinboim family:
Yitzhak, Abba, Rachel, Golda and Yaakov.
Isaac, father and Yaakov, may they live a long life

[Page 334]

Members of the Yachniuk Family from Korost near Stepan

Sarah Yachniuk

**Shalom Woschina
and his daughter**

Beila Woschina (née Yachniuk), Rosa
Gendler (née Yachniuk) and Zvi Gendler,
may they live a long life

Yosef (Yosel) Yachniuk

[Page 335]

Members of the Magid Family

Leibel Magid

Banka Magid

Dochia Magid

Herschel Magid

Yosel Magid

[Page 336]

Members of the Malamud Family

Yechiel Malamud, his wife Rivka and their son Yehoshua

**Mother - grandmother Michalia,
the brothers Yaakov, Asher and David.
The brother Yehoshua — may he live a long life**

[Page 337]

Petchnik family: Yaakov, his wife Odel, the daughter Sima, the son Sander, grandparents and relatives. The son Michael (today Ronen) – may he live a long life

**Slova Mann (née Weitznodel), may she live a long life,
her sister Reiche Gordon and her sister Raizel, may she live a long life**

[Page 338]

Label Packhauz family

**The family of Avraham Bebchuk, the son Ben Zion,
may he live a long life**

[Page 339]

The Krokover Family

Grandmother Rivka and her son Yosef, Yosef's first wife, Golda, passed away in 1925, and Yosef's daughter, Berta, passed away in Kibbutz Negba in 1936

[Page 340]

Members of the Yaakov Rudnik Family from Kosmachov

Grandma Sheindel, the father of the family Yaakov (Yankel), the mother Freidel, the sons Leibush, his child and wife, Moshe, Avraham. The daughters Sonia, Fania and Leah. Fania and Leah, may they live a long life

[Page 341]

The Family Members of Mottel Rassis

The mother of Mottel Rassis - Dova, her daughter Sosel and her husband Gabriel Feldman and relatives

Mottel Rassis, his wife Esther, his daughter Sheindel, his son Aba'le and a relative with her child. Mottel Rassis, may he live a long life, lives in Israel

[Page 342]

The Family Members of the late Tanchum Sheinboim

The Sheinboim family: the elder brother Chaim, his wife Shifra and their son, the mother of the family Ita, the sister Bracha (Boziah), Bracha's husband, Shmuel Echtenbaum, the brother Ben Zion, his wife Brunia (née Tachor), the brother Shmuel, the aunt Necha Blay and the uncle David Baram. Those of them who survived the Holocaust: Shmuel Echtenbaum, Ben Zion and Shmuel Sheinboim, may he live a long life

Rosa Mopas (née Neiman)

[Page 343]

General Public Photos

Translated by Mira Eckhaus

Among the first activists in the Zionist movement in Stepan, the brothers: Avraham and Yitzhak Goz, Slavotsky and his wife, Moshe Bebchuk and his wife Leah (née Tachor), Rachel (Hoka) Goz, Rivka Tachor (née Koifman), Raizel Kushnir, the multifarious at the "Tarbut" school in the town, Moshe Koifman

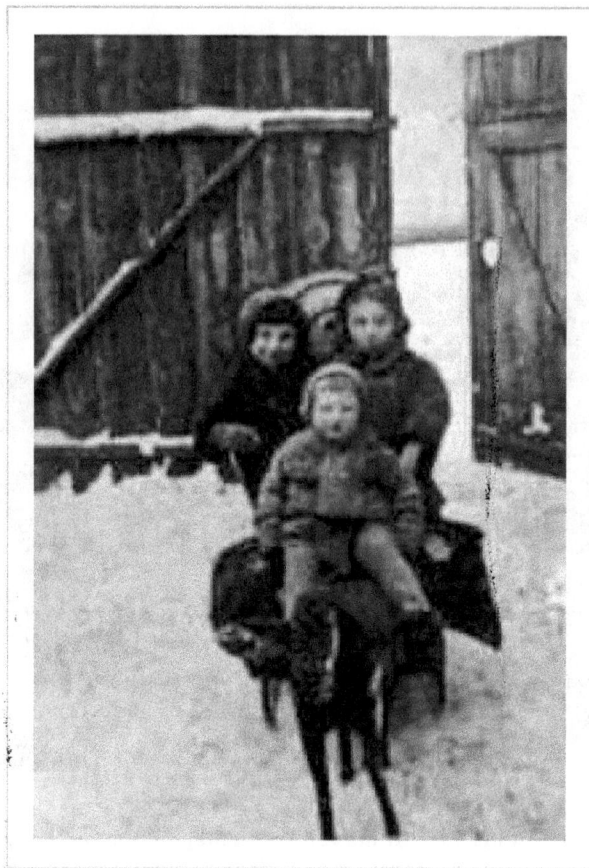

**Breidele Becker and her cousins Yehudit and Sonia,
the daughters of Leah and Moshe Bebchuk**

[Page 344]

ישיבת ראשי הכתות של דרגא א
סטיפן תרצ"ב

A meeting of the class heads of Level 1, Stepan, 5692

Hashomer Hatzair activist group in Stepan

[Page 345]

Histadrut Beitar in Stepan, Level 1, 5693,
in the center - the head of Beitar, the teacher Yeshayahu Neiman

A journey to the great outdoors, the view of the entrance to the town from the direction of the bridge. Shalom Woschina, his wife and daughter, the wife of the dentist Dr. Gorin and Aharon Woschina - may he live a long life.

[Page 346]

Hashomer Hatzair operators in the great outdoors in Stepan

The Hashomer Hatzair activists' group in Stepan

[Page 347]

Some of the Hashomer Hatzair activists in the town

Some of the activists of the Zionist movement in the town

[Page 348]

Finia Rosenfeld, Yitzhak Chodler and the girls of the town

[Page 349]

**Shlomo Trachter, Yitzhak Chodler and Finia Rosenfeld
Beitar Activists in Stepan**

**Leah Rosenfeld her friend
Dova and their friend**

The Beitar camp on Lag Ba'Omer 5694 in the Stepan Forest

Company of Level 2` girls in Stepan, 5693

[Page 350]

**Mordechai Rassis, who lives in Israel, may he live a long life,
and his friend from youth, the dynamic and educated Mordechai Goz,
before he was murdered by the Nazi beast**

Zvika Gorinstein, one of the
Betar activists in the town

Part of the Hashomer Hatzair activists in Stepan
before the Holocaust: Rosa Kogot, Rosa Rex, Zelda
Gelman, Ronia Arkin, the daughter of Alenke the butcher

[Page 351]

Jewish youth against the background of typical houses in Stepan

**Jewish youth - students of the public Polish school with their teachers.
Among the teachers - Moshe Kelt and Kamerman**

[Page 352]

Some of the Town's Girls of Whom Most Were Murdered by the Nazi Oppressor

**Bella Geller, Raizel Shienes, Raizel Bebchuk
and Slova (Weitznodel) Mann, may she live a long life**

Rebecca Feldman, Rivka Gelbort

[Page 353]

Mania Slavotsky, a member of the Plotnick family, Odel (Prishkolnik) Weitznodel, Rosa (Bebchuk) Shpritz and Genia (Prishkolnik) Kramarski – may she live a long life

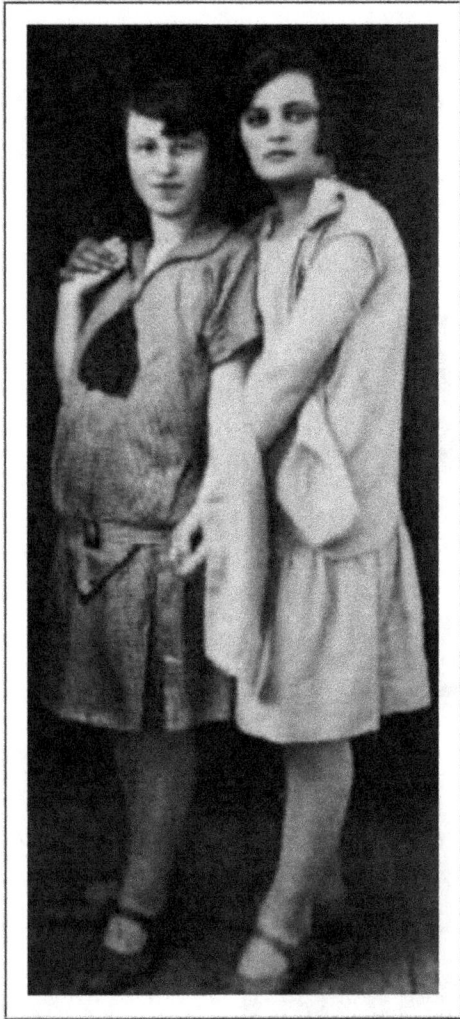

Mania Slavotsky & Sosel (Rassis) Feldman   **The sisters: Odel, Genia and Miriam Prishkolnik**

[Page 354]

Mania Slavotsky, a member of the Plotnick family, Odel (Prishkolnik) Weitznodel, Rosa (Bebchuk) Shpritz and Genia (Prishkolnik) Kramarski – may she live a long life

[Page 355]

Sheva Bebchuk, Friedel Gorinstein and Sheindel Eidelstein

Sonia Tachor and Rebecca Feldman

[Page 356]

The remnants - Stepan's survivors in the displaced persons camps in Germany at the end of World War II

Some of the girls of the town who were murdered by the Nazi oppressor

[Page 357]

The officials' houses - a forced labor camp for men from Stepan Jews in Kostopol

Next to the mass grave of the Jews of Stepan in the Karchobela forest, near Kostopol

[Page 362]

English Section

Editors' Notes

With the editing of the writings of the survivors of Stepan we became so well acquainted with the town, its inhabitants and surroundings and it seems to us that we too walked in those streets, prayed in their synagogue, bathed in the Horin River and in the forests sought places to hide from our enemies.

This book is one of many that have been published about Jewish communities partly of totally destroyed during the Holocaust. This book will make its contribution by describing life in the town before and during the Holocaust. This will serve as a monument for generations.

[Page 361]

The recollection of the survivors were recorded in great detail some 30 years after the destruction of their town. This shows that to this day the memories of the people and homes of their town are still in their hearts and the passing of so much time has not dimmed their memories.

When sometime in the future, historians will write a complete work about the Jewish communities of Eastern Europe before and during the Holocaust, this book will provide a valuable source of information.

The stories of Yeshayahu Pery, wherein he writes of hiding in the forests with his mother and sister, and their stories about the survivors such as Yona Rassis, Yitzhak Wachs, Aaron Grossman, Batia Scheinboim, Avraham Tachor who describe their escape from t he death trenches and the problems of day-to-day living in the underground. All therse experiences, form part of the sad story of the Jews that it is incumbent upon all of us to pass from generation to generation, father to son so that we will remember to the end of time. We should also never forget the story of the isolated Jewish family Yankel Kosmotchov who lived amongst a hundred hostile Ukranians. Even so he succeeded in guarding his and his family's identity as real Jews.

The book has attempted to describe as objectively as possible the image of leaders of the Judenratt, Yosef Wachs. Only history and the passing of time will be the final judges of his activities during this most terrible time of the Jews of Stepan.

I apologise to everyone that all the proferred material does not appear in this book. We tried to include the more important facts but because of lack of space were not able to use material which in our opinion was less important. We trust that this book will serve as a m onument to the suffering of all Jews including those of STEPAN.

[Page 363]

Preface

This book was written under great emotional stress about the town of STEPAN in Volyn, eastern Poland. It serves as a monument to the memory of the majority of the Jewish inhabitants who were mercilessly murdered by the Nazi invaders with the help of the local Ukrainian inhabitants.

We compiled the history of those horrible days from writings, photographs and recollections of the few survivors in order to present a picture of the STEPAN Jewish community which was, but no longer exists.

Despite the passing of tens of years, time has not healed the pain and horror of the truly awful period. The editors, to the best of their ability with information in hand, have attempted to present a true picture in the greatest details - especially in those instances of families of whom no one survived.

We feel obliged to mention at this point the late Yizhak Weismann. He was one of the first to begin recording the stories describing the various family images. He was not able to finish this work. He died of grief at the loss of his son Shai Yeshayahu who fell in the defense of his country during the War of Attrition. Yitzhak's efforts served as a guide to the continuation of this work.

We would like to emphasize at this point our gratitude for the advice and guidance which contributed greatly to the contents of this book by our friend Yisrael Koifman.

It is quite possible that this book may not have seen the light of day without the concentrated efforts of Yeshayahu Pery (Prishkolnik). Mr. Pery, now living in Israel, was born and raised in Stepan. At the age of 13 he fled from the Nazis and Ukrainians and spent the next 17 months living of the land in the forest - up to the liberation by the Russians. Even at the time, during his travel to camps in Germany and Cyprus and on the way to Israel he began making notes and collecting information which in fact formed the nucleus of this book. On his arrival in Israel he convinced others to join him in his efforts to publish the sad history of the Jews of Stepan.

Not many people of STEPAN were writers as such. However, many of those who remained to the best of their ability contributed stories of their recollections, including photographs. In particular we wish to thank Leah Hashavia, Batia Sheinboim, Shlomo Sheinboim, Ze'ev Gorinstein, Mordechai Rassis, and Yeshayahu Pery, for the efforts of reconstruction of the town as it was home by home.

We know this book is not a work of great literary value. It was not intended as such. Its purpose was to record the story of Stepan and its Jewish inhabitants in the times of the Nazi terror. To the best of our ability we have recorded the recollections and memories of all the contributors. However, we do apologize in advance for duplications, which have crept into these pages. We have done this purposely in order to permit everyone to tell his story. The result? A book to serve as a permanent record in memory of STEPAN.

Some Facts About Stepan

Germans invade the Soviet Union on June 22, 1941.
Stepan Ghetto was erected on Chol Hamoed Sukkot, October 5, 1941.
Stepan Jews were exterminated and ghetto liquidated on 11th of Elul, 5702 or August 24, 1942.
Stepan was liberated by the Russians on January 12, 1944.
Number of Jewish survivors from Stepan – 44 (as reported by Shmuel Spector, see below).

References to the Holocaust in Volhynia

The Holocaust of Volhynian Jews, 1941-1944, by Shmuel Spector, Yad Vashem, The Federation of Volhynian Jews, P.O. Box 3477, Jerusalem 91043, 1990.
The Moses of Rovno, by Douglas K. Huneke and Herman F. Graebe, Compassion House, 240 Tiburon Blvd., Tiburon, CA 94920, 1985.
The Stepan Yizkor Book, edited by I. Ganuz, collected by J. Pery, 1977, 364 pages.

NAME INDEX

www.ingramcontent.com/pod-product-compliance
Lightning Source LLC
Chambersburg PA
CBHW082004150426

42814CB00005BA/220